THE SELEUKID RO

The Seleukid empire, the principal successor-state of the empire of Alexander the Great, endured for over two hundred years and stretched, at its peak, from the Mediterranean to the borders of India. This book provides a wide-ranging study of the empire's economy and the methods used by the Seleukid kings to monetize and manage it so as to extract tribute, rent and taxes as efficiently as possible. It uses a variety of Greek literary sources and inscriptions, cuneiform texts and archaeological and numismatic and comparative evidence to explore in detail the manner of exploitation of their lands and subjects by the Seleukid kings, their city-building activity, the financing of their armies and administration, the use they made of coinage and their methods of financial management. The book adopts a highly original numerical approach throughout, which leads to a quantified model of the economy of an ancient state.

MAKIS APERGHIS originally studied engineering at the University of Cambridge. He returned to the study of ancient history and was awarded a doctorate from University College London (2000).

THE SELEUKID ROYAL ECONOMY

The Finances and Financial Administration
of the Seleukid Empire

G. G. APERGHIS

CAMBRIDGE
UNIVERSITY PRESS

CAMBRIDGE UNIVERSITY PRESS
Cambridge, New York, Melbourne, Madrid, Cape Town, Singapore, São Paulo, Delhi

Cambridge University Press
The Edinburgh Building, Cambridge CB2 8RU, UK

Published in the United States of America by Cambridge University Press, New York

www.cambridge.org
Information on this title: www.cambridge.org/9780521117760

First published 2004
This digitally printed version 2009

A catalogue record for this publication is available from the British Library

ISBN 978-0-521-83707-1 hardback
ISBN 978-0-521-11776-0 paperback

Contents

v

Figures

Tables

Preface

This book is likely to be controversial. It reflects a view on how ancient economic history could be written that is probably not shared by the majority of scholars. It also ventures across a number of disciplines, where those more knowledgeable than I am may well find fault with my methods.

The book is influenced by several factors. It reflects an original training in engineering, where I was taught two things well: mathematics and how to go about analysing a problem from first principles. A career followed in the computer-software business, where I learned that the logical approach of systems analysis can also be put to good use in the field of ancient history. A side benefit is that the ability to actually program a computer certainly gives one greater freedom in exploring problems.

The study of ancient history had occupied me for many years, and when I received formal training, it was at the hands of excellent teachers at University College London. This resulted in a Ph.D. in February 2000 and the dissertation on which this book is based. Amélie Kuhrt, my main supervisor, first interested me in the Seleukids, but it was, more importantly, the influence of her teaching of the history of the ancient Near East that decided me to embark upon a study of the Seleukid empire as, in many ways, a continuation of its predecessors in the region. Amélie painstakingly read and corrected my work and continuously added to my knowledge as I progressed. Michael Crawford, my second supervisor, encouraged me to break away from the trodden path and develop original ideas, but he also controlled my excesses in the many areas of his expertise, whether an incorrect translation of a Greek text or a shaky interpretation of a source or a dubious calculation. I owe a great deal to both of my supervisors and a particular debt to Robert van der Spek for his detailed criticism and many useful suggestions as the book matured into its final form. I would also like to thank several other scholars for having gone to the trouble to read the entire text at various stages in its development and for their comments, advice and encouragement: Dominic Rathbone, John Davies, Andrew Meadows, Joe Manning and Miltos Hatzopoulos.

Finally, this book has, no doubt, been influenced by the fact that I am Greek, but it is, I hope, an honest attempt to view the Seleukid empire from a distinctly non-Hellenocentric standpoint. Accordingly, I have placed myself very firmly in Asia, in Mesopotamia mostly, where the Greek heartland of the Aegean was as peripheral as Baktria. From such a stance, it is clear how considerable the debt owed by the Seleukid empire was to those that preceded it in the Near East.

On a personal note, I could never have attempted and completed this very enjoyable study of the ancient world without the consideration and support of my wife, Myrto, and children, Dimitris and Atalandi, to whom I dedicate it.

Abbreviations

BE	*Bulletin Epigraphique*, in *Revue des études grecques*, cited by year and entry number.
C. Ord. Ptol.	M.-Th. Lenger (1980) *Corpus des ordonnances des Ptolémées*, 2nd edn. Brussels.
ESM	E. T. Newell (1978) *The Coinage of the Eastern Seleucid Mints*. New York.
IG	*Inscriptiones Graecae.*
IGCH	M. Thompson, O. Mørkholm and C. M. Kraay (eds.) (1973) *An Inventory of Greek Coin Hoards*. New York.
IGRR	R. Cagnat, J. Toutain and P. Jouguet (eds.) (1927) *Inscriptiones Graecae ad res Romanas pertinentes*. Paris.
I. Cos	M. Segre (1993) *Iscrizioni di Cos*, 2 vols. Rome.
I. Labraunda	J. Crampa (1969) *The Greek Inscriptions*, in *Labraunda*, vol. III/1. Lund.
I. Priene	F. Hiller von Gaertringen (1906) *Die Inschriften von Priene*. Berlin.
Loeb	Loeb Classical Library (1988) *Oeconomica*, included in *Aristotle*, vol. XVIII. Harvard.
LSJ	H. G. Liddell and R. Scott (1996) *A Greek–English Lexicon*, 9th edn with a revised supplement. Oxford.
OGIS	W. Dittenberger (1903–5) *Orientis Graeci Inscriptiones Selectae*, 2 vols. Leipzig.
RC	C. B. Welles (1934) *Royal Correspondence in the Hellenistic Period: a Study in Greek Epigraphy*. New Haven, Conn.
SEG	*Supplementum epigraphicum Graecum* (1923–). Leiden.
*Syll.*³	W. Dittenberger (1915–24) *Sylloge Inscriptionum Graecarum*, 4 vols., 3rd edn. Leipzig.
WSM	Newell, E. T. (1977) *The Coinage of the Western Seleucid Mints*. New York.

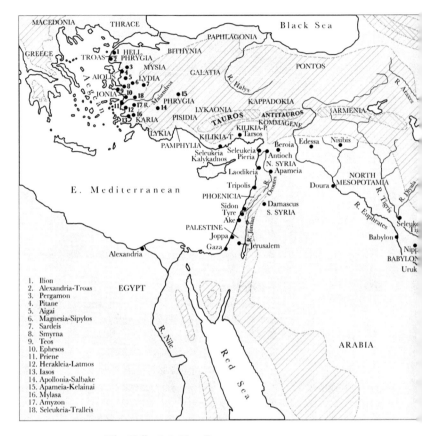

1. Ilion
2. Alexandria-Troas
3. Pergamon
4. Pitane
5. Aigai
6. Magnesia-Sipylos
7. Sardeis
8. Smyrna
9. Teos
10. Ephesos
11. Priene
12. Herakleia-Latmos
13. Iasos
14. Apollonia-Salbake
15. Apameia-Kelainai
16. Mylasa
17. Amyzon
18. Seleukeia-Tralleis

The Hellenistic Near East

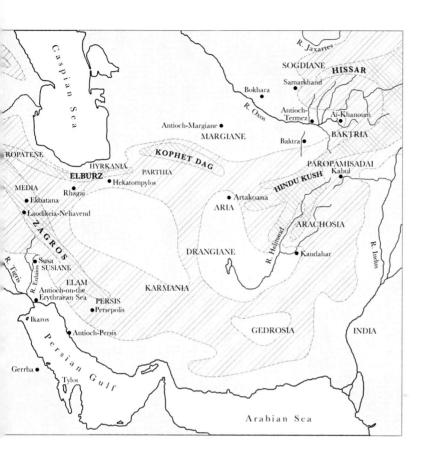

Caspian Sea

ROPATENE

HYRKANIA

ELBURZ

KOPHET DAG

SOGDIANE

HISSAR

Bokhara

Samarkhand

R. Jaxartes

R. Oxos

Antioch-Margiane ●

MARGIANE

Antioch-
Termez

Aï-Khanoum

Baktra

BAKTRIA

PARTHIA

PAROPAMISADAI

Kabul

MEDIA

Rhagai

Hekatompylos

Artakoana

HINDU KUSH

Ekbatana

ARIA

Laodikeia-Nehavend

ARACHOSIA

ZAGROS

DRANGIANE

R. Helmand

Kandahar

R. Indus

R. Tigris

R. Eulaios

Susa

SUSIANE

ELAM

Antioch-on-the
Erythraean Sea

KARMANIA

PERSIS

Persepolis

Ikaros

Antioch-Persis

GEDROSIA

INDIA

Gerrha ●

Persian Gulf

Tylos

Arabian Sea

Introduction

The finances and financial administration of the Seleukid empire have usually been considered only briefly in general surveys of the Seleukids or the Hellenistic world.[1] Some attention has, however, been given to the subject in more specialized works dealing with Seleukid institutions, society and economy.[2]

There is a great deal that is unclear. How did the Seleukid kings derive their revenue? On what subject populations and activities were tribute and taxes assessed and what forms did these take? Was the system generalized or was it adapted to the specific conditions of each region? How large was the resulting income for the kings? What other incomes accrued to them? In what way did the kings exploit the land and the natural resources of their empire? What role was played by the new city foundations and the temples? Why were land grants made? What expenses were incurred by the Seleukids to run their empire? What was the purpose of coinage in the economy and what considerations determined the denominations minted and the levels of production at different mints? What was the organization that managed the finances of the empire and of the kings personally? And what was the bottom line? Was this a wealthy empire or did it live a hand-to-mouth existence, which developed into an acute financial crisis following its defeat by Rome at Magnesia (190 BC)? Finally, how did the Seleukid state compare, in the way it ran its economy, with a modern one?

This book is an attempt to answer these and other questions and to present as complete a picture of the finances and financial administration of the Seleukid empire as possible from the available source material. In time, it deals mainly with that period when one can justifiably speak of

---

[1] For example, the works of Tarn 1927; Rostovtzeff 1941; Préaux 1978; Will 1979 and 1982; Walbank 1981; Grant 1982; Gruen 1984; Musti 1984; Green 1990; Sherwin-White and Kuhrt 1993 and Shipley 2000.

[2] For example, the monographs by Bikerman 1938; Bengtson 1944; Musti 1965; Cohen 1978; Kreissig 1978 and Ma 1997 and 1999.

an empire, from 311 BC, when Seleukos Nikator retook Babylon, up to the loss of Mesopotamia in 129 BC, but it also discusses briefly the situation down to the final extinction in 64 BC. In geographical range, it covers all the territories that at one time or another, if not concurrently, were ruled by the Seleukids: from the Aegean and the border with Egypt to Baktria and Sogdiane and the north-western frontier of India.

In Part I the available sources are discussed briefly. The existing classical literary and epigraphic material has been extended by much valuable cuneiform documentation, which throws new light on the Seleukid empire. A number of scholars have already pointed to continuity between Seleukid administrative practice and that of the Achaemenid empire,[3] but this is looked into more closely, with the result that some older evidence can confidently be applied to the Seleukid period. To these sources are added the results of archaeological excavations and, particularly, settlement surveys. Furthermore, die studies of Seleukid coin issues and hoard analyses provide useful information on the output of mints and the circulation patterns of coinage.

Part I continues with a brief historical summary, which concentrates on the extent of the empire at different times and the problems it faced. This is essential for Seleukid finances and financial administration to be seen from the proper perspective. Finally, the cardinal problem faced by the early Seleukid kings is presented, as a hypothesis, and the measures they took to solve it are outlined; the remainder of the book addresses these measures in detail.

Part II is a brief overview of the underlying economy of the empire. In order to understand the system of taxation, one needs to know what forms economic activity took and the possibilities open to a governing power to extract a surplus for its own needs. The physical characteristics of different regions are described, along with the results of settlement surveys, which give some idea of population levels and trends, and a very rough estimate of population by wider region is attempted. Agriculture and animal husbandry, natural resources, trade and industry are all considered in order to establish their potential for generating taxation revenue for the administration. Of particular interest is the establishment of prices for different commodities, which are useful in linking production estimates to taxation revenue levels. The exploitation of land comes up in this part, in connection with the founding of new cities and the granting of land to individuals and temples, while the status of the peasants working the land is also briefly considered.

---

[3] For example, Briant 1979, 1982c and 1990; Kuhrt and Sherwin-White 1994b.

Part III deals with the surplus that was extracted by the Seleukid kings from the economy as tribute and taxation and with its expenditure. Here ps.-Aristotle's *Oikonomika* is used as the starting point, and each aspect of the royal and satrapal economies described there is examined. This work turns out to be very helpful, as it establishes the framework for a detailed discussion dealing with the different sources of imperial revenue, 'incomings' and 'outgoings' to and from royal lands and treasuries and the major expenses of army, provincial administration and court. The purpose and usage of coinage is also examined at some length. The information derived is put together in a very approximate quantitative model of the Seleukid royal economy, which links the main parameters: population, production, royal revenue and expenditure, and coinage. Finally, the system of financial administration is investigated, based mainly on epigraphic evidence, and this is found to owe much to Achaemenid prototypes.

The theme repeated throughout is that the Seleukid kings paid particular attention to developing the economic resources of their empire. These they tapped in an efficient manner in order to generate the funds required to retain their hold on power, which they were successfully able to do for more than two centuries. Many of their methods, perhaps surprisingly, were not totally unlike those of a modern state.

The title of this book is obviously borrowed from Claire Préaux's study of Ptolemaic Egypt, *L'économie royale des Lagides*. I too have tried to identify the different forms of revenue and expense of a Hellenistic king (the royal economy) and the system of financial administration. Préaux's *dirigiste* view of the Ptolemies – their active involvement in and direction of the economic life of Egypt – is to some extent valid for the Seleukids also, but the methods used by the latter were quite different. As can be seen from the outline given above, I have attempted to go further than Préaux. Starting with an overview of the major elements of the economy, quantified to some extent, I have constructed a more detailed model of its most important part, the royal economy.

In my view, any consideration of economic matters cannot really be useful unless it involves numbers, since it is no good discussing taxation revenue, for instance, unless one can say what the total amount may roughly have been. With regard to the Seleukid empire, this is a labour that historians have tended to shy away from, perhaps because, as Rostovtzeff put it, 'the information is miserably inadequate'.[4] However, despite the uncertainty associated with numbers derived from the rather limited evidence, an attempt is made to quantify at every stage. This is obviously a risky

---

[4] Rostovtzeff 1941: 422.

procedure and will leave me open to much criticism. Indeed, as I cross many areas of specialization in search of useful data, experts in these fields will undoubtedly find fault with some of my choices and conclusions. But it might be helpful to wait until all the evidence has been presented, including that from totally different areas. To begin with, some figures, such as a population estimate, may appear very shaky indeed, but, in the course of the discussion, these are tested against new estimates derived from independent data, and the more the results converge, the more confidence there will be that the important numbers are roughly correct. When the final model is presented, it will be seen that its various parameters fit together reasonably well, which cannot solely be the result of chance. This will, it is hoped, provide support for the main ideas and conclusions of this book and might also prove useful to scholars assessing other ancient economies.

PART I

Preliminaries

CHAPTER I

Sources and methods

I. CLASSICAL LITERATURE

The classical authors usually employed as sources for Seleukid history have been exhaustively discussed by others[1] and so will not be treated here yet again, but only referred to where appropriate. However, the source net has been spread to include those writers reporting on the Achaemenid empire (e.g. Herodotos, Xenophon, the Alexander historians), and particularly on its administrative practices, because of the considerable degree of continuity that seems to have existed in this area between it and its Seleukid successors, as will hopefully be demonstrated.

2. PS.-ARISTOTLE'S *OIKONOMIKA*, BOOK 2

This economic treatise has been attributed to the school of Aristotle and is fundamental in any study of the economy of the Hellenistic world, despite its brevity and difficulty of detailed comprehension. A short theoretical section deals with the four types of financial administrations ('economies') that could be observed at the time, in decreasing order of importance: those of a kingdom, a satrapy, a city and a household. This is followed by a presentation of stratagems by which rulers or administrators solved specific financial problems.

In chapter 7 the theoretical section is translated and discussed at some length, including the question of its date. In chapters 8–11 the evidence from the Seleukid period for the different aspects of the royal and satrapal economies, as referred to by ps.-Aristotle, is presented and analysed in detail.

---

[1] For example: Rostovtzeff 1941; Préaux 1978; Will 1979; 1982; Davies 1984; Sherwin-White and Kuhrt 1993; Shipley 2000.

3. GREEK INSCRIPTIONS, PAPYRI, PARCHMENT AND *OSTRAKA*

Much of the evidence concerning the different forms of taxation and aspects of financial administration in the Seleukid empire comes from the **inscriptions** of Greek cities. Nowhere is the information direct, of course, as the intention of an inscription was not to provide a manual of current administrative practice, but to record something of particular interest to the city, for example a royal order or concession affecting it, the correspondence of officials called upon to implement the order, a decree honouring a citizen or Seleukid official.

The epigraphic evidence is heavily weighted towards the cities of Asia Minor, because these have been, on the whole, more thoroughly excavated than elsewhere and also simply because of the 'epigraphic habit' of the Greeks. However, one does have sufficient data from other areas, such as the important Ptolemaios dossier from Skythopolis in Palestine, the Baitokaike land grant from northern Syria, the Ikadion letter from Failaka in the Persian Gulf, the royal order for the appointment of a high priestess from Laodikeia-Nehavend in Media – which will all be referred to in due course – to be able to perceive similarities between the methods of administration in different parts of the empire.

Papyri are an extremely rare source for the Seleukid economy, the most important one being a papyrus from Doura-Europos.[2] However, papyri relating to Ptolemaic Palestine and Phoenicia or Ptolemaic possessions in Asia Minor can sometimes indicate financial structures that were left in place by later Seleukid administrations in these regions.

Parchment is also rare, of considerable interest being the early second-century BC administrative text on leather from Baktria, which records details of a transaction that probably has to do with taxation.[3] There is also an interesting parchment from Avroman in Kurdistan.[4]

A neglected pottery sherd (*ostrakon*) from Babylon may well provide the key to pay in the Seleukid army,[5] while other *ostraka* from Baktria are probably elements in a tax-collection procedure.[6]

One problem with all Greek documents is that translations can vary considerably. The Greek language possesses much variety in its use of words, whose meaning ultimately depends on the context. This may be relatively unclear to the translator, often a philologist, called upon to deal with a difficult military or economic text, and it can have misleading results. For this reason, I have provided my own translation of all Greek texts used.

---

[2] Welles, Fink and Gilliam 1959: no. 15; Saliou 1992.
[3] Bernard and Rapin 1994; Rea, Senior and Hollis 1994; Rapin 1996.   [4] Minns 1915.
[5] Sherwin-White 1982.   [6] Rapin 1983.

As objective a translation has been given as could be managed, without ascribing preconceived ideas to the interpretation. Sometimes, a less specific expression has been adopted than that used by other translators, which may give an impression of somewhat imperfect English, but serves the purpose of leaving open the precise meaning until the analysis has been completed. A good example is the use of the terms ἐξαγώγιμα (*exagōgima*) and εἰσαγώγιμα (*eisagōgima*) in the *Oikonomika*, which have been crudely, but more generally, rendered by me as 'goods that may be sent out' and 'goods that may be brought in', rather than the more elegant, but incorrect in my view, 'exports' and 'imports' that have typically appeared in translations of this text.

4. LOCAL LANGUAGE SOURCES

Previous studies of the administration and economy of the Seleukid empire[7] have relied almost exclusively on classical sources, both literary and epigraphic. Increasingly, however, cuneiform texts from the core of the empire, Mesopotamia, are being transcribed and translated and help to throw light on administrative practices in this region in the Seleukid period.[8] Of these texts, particularly important are the *Babylonian Astronomical Diaries*, for a study of commodity prices, and the two collections of tablets known as the *Persepolis Texts*. Other cuneiform documents from Mesopotamia parallel the Greek inscriptions found elsewhere or provide what is almost totally lacking in classical sources, namely details of specific legal and administrative transactions.

a. The Babylonian Astronomical Diaries

These important cuneiform texts, written in Akkadian, are precisely dated records of meteorological and astronomical observations compiled in the temples of Babylon between 652 BC and 61 BC.[9] They frequently contain market prices for five agricultural commodities and wool, and they sometimes note political, social or economic events. There is a heavy concentration of data in the Seleukid period, with some price(s) being quoted in 245 separate months of ninety regnal years.

But first, there is the question of the purpose of the *Diaries*. The astronomers who recorded their observations were primarily interested in

---

[7] Bikerman 1938; Rostovtzeff 1941; Bengtson 1944; Musti 1965; 1966; 1984; Kreissig 1978; Ma 1997; 1999.
[8] Kuhrt 1996. [9] Sachs and Hunger 1988; 1989; 1996; Del Monte 1997.

establishing over generations a set of data from which astronomical predictions could be made and probably also forecasts of good or bad harvests. They were not interested in political or economic matters as such, except in their possible dependence upon natural phenomena. If something did not occur in Babylon itself, it was carefully recorded with the phrase 'It was heard.' The Babylonian astronomers, with no political axe to grind, come through as completely dispassionate writers, having absolutely no reason to falsify the record, in particular with regard to what is of most interest here: commodity prices.[10]

In chapter 5.6a commodity prices from the *Diaries* are plotted graphically and trends observed during the Seleukid period. Changes are noted that may have been due to political events or administrative decisions, which are dealt with in chapter 13.10.

b. The Persepolis Texts

During the excavations of Persepolis in the 1930s, two collections of cuneiform tablets, written in the Elamite language, were discovered. They are a product of Achaemenid administration in the Persian homeland, the later Hellenistic satrapy of Persis.

The larger of the two archives, the *Persepolis Fortification Texts* (*PFT*), consists of 2,120 published texts[11] and at least as many unpublished ones, and deals mostly with the collection, storage and distribution as rations of various commodities at storehouses in an administrative area centred on Persepolis, between regnal years thirteen and twenty-eight of Darius I, that is, 509–494 BC. The recipients of these rations were the king, members of the royal family, officials, travellers, animals and, principally, workers engaged in many activities, not least the construction of the royal palaces at Persepolis. Included are 96 larger tablets, which contain either lists of the individual commodity issues of particular storehouses in a given year (journals) or summaries of movements in and out of the storehouse and balances remaining (accounts) or, occasionally, both types of information.

The smaller archive, the *Persepolis Treasury Texts* (*PTT*), contains 129 texts dating from between regnal year thirty of Darius I and year seven of Artaxerxes I, that is, 492–458 BC.[12] Each text details payments made in silver to officials or workers in place of part of their barley, wine or meat rations.

---

[10] Spek 1993a.   [11] Hallock 1969; 1978.   [12] Cameron 1948.

One may justifiably ask what these two sources, nearly two centuries older than the start of the Hellenistic period, have to do with Seleukid financial administration. It will hopefully be demonstrated in chapters 9 and 13 that the *PFT* especially, but also the *PTT*, show continuity between Achaemenid and Hellenistic administrative practice and help to throw more light on what, in their absence, would have been rather uncertain interpretations of a number of Greek documents.

c. *Legal and administrative cuneiform tablets from Babylonia*

A number of such tablets, written in Akkadian, have been found in official or clandestine excavations in Babylonia, but by no means the larger number has been translated and published. There is a reasonably comprehensive review of these sources up to December 1986.[13]

Most of this material comes from two centres, Babylon and Uruk, but other Babylonian cities also provide some evidence. The essential difference between Babylon and Uruk is that the former has produced mainly administrative documents and the latter mainly legal texts. This is quite a serious shortcoming, as one does not thus possess a comprehensive picture of what went on at each centre and it is quite possible that administrative and legal procedures may have differed somewhat in different cities. What interests one, however, is whether they were applied under a common Seleukid administrative 'umbrella'.

A few cuneiform texts from Babylonia play exactly the same role as inscriptions do in Greek cities: they constitute a public record of privileges or commitments granted to a city or temple (which in Babylonia were inextricably linked).

d. *Other documents*

An interesting indirect source for the Seleukid empire is a Sanskrit work, the *Artašastra*, a treatise on administration by, reputedly, Kautilya, the prime minister of Chandragupta, the Mauryan emperor.[14] Taken in conjunction with fragments of Megasthenes appearing in Strabo, Diodoros and Arrian's *Indika*, it can throw light on how similar problems were managed in a contemporary neighbouring imperial state, with which the Seleukids were in contact.

---

[13] Oelsner 1986.   [14] Stein 1922; Sharma 1988: 4.

An early source is the *Murašu Archive* from Nippur, which describes the activities of a family of agricultural contractors of the late fifth century BC, who leased land from absentee Persian landlords, fief-holders and other property owners, together with water rights from the administration, and subleased them to farmers along with the necessary seed and equipment.[15] The Murašu also undertook to pay taxes on the land to the royal exchequer in silver. The archive gives us some idea of the economy of Mesopotamia at this time and the relative costs of agricultural production, which may be applicable to the Seleukid period.

5. ARCHAEOLOGY

a. Settlement surveys

A settlement survey in a particular region attempts to locate areas of habitation and cultivation and to define periods of occupation and use in these areas. Its tools range from the study of ceramics found on the surface, as a result of controlled traverses of the area on foot, to stereoscopic air photography and satellite imagery.

The method is, by definition, approximate. Pottery types may not be known sufficiently well for precise dating. Lower occupation levels may not show up in surface remains, in particular from rural sites covered by an expanding urban centre, while smaller sites may be missed altogether if the survey traverses are spaced too far apart. The time period is necessarily a long one, typically a few hundred years, and the problem arises that not all sites discovered are likely to have been occupied simultaneously. Since ceramic remains are typically found over the entire area of the survey, because of the scatter of human and animal waste used as fertilizing material, a threshold intensity has to be set somewhat arbitrarily, above which one may define a settlement. For this reason, the area occupied in a surveyed site, or cultivated around it, is rather approximate. Finally, even assuming settlement areas may have been determined with some accuracy, it is difficult to convert these into population figures. Despite all these faults, settlement surveys are a valuable tool for observing general population and economic trends, particularly in the countryside, which is an area that archaeological excavation deals with less and historiography rarely touches upon.[16]

In chapter 4.1–5, the results of some settlement surveys in the regions and period of interest have been noted. Here it might be well to establish three

[15] Stolper 1974; 1985.   [16] Cherry 1983.

general points, the first two concerning the area and density of habitation of settlements and the third the population that could be supported by a given area of cultivable land.

For the reasons noted earlier, the settlement area measured in a survey probably represents a *minimum*, although a detailed survey will miss only the smallest sites, which may not anyway have contributed much to the total population. However, there is still the problem that all the sites in the surveyed area may not have been occupied at the same time. In that sense their number represents a *maximum*, although the shorter the time period covered by the survey, the more chance of simultaneous habitation at its sites. To some extent these two opposing factors cancel each other out, but it is generally safer to round population figures upwards.

Regarding density of occupation, one has two lines of approach. In the first, modern settlements can be studied in the region concerned. For example, an analysis of fifty-four rural sites in the Susan plain[17] has shown that population density at the village level *decreased* slightly with size of settlement, as presumably more land was set aside for communal needs, ranging from 267 persons per hectare in the smallest eighteen villages of average size 0.4 hectares to 159 persons per hectare in the largest eighteen villages of average size 2.5 hectares. A figure of about 200 inhabitants per hectare seems to have been the mean or, in other words, a family of four inhabited an area of some 200 square metres, which would cover a small house, a vegetable garden and space for a few domestic animals. One can probably use this as a rough figure for antiquity up to the level of a small town, which conventionally occupies not less than 10 hectares and so has a population of about 2,000 inhabitants.

Beyond this, one enters the sphere of urban centres, where different and complex relationships hold and another approach becomes necessary. The need for defence becomes more important and encircling walls cut off the town from the surrounding region, while a larger proportion of the town's inhabitants is not involved with the production of food and has to rely on the countryside for its sustenance. Fewer gardens can be afforded and some multistorey housing makes its appearance. Despite the increase in area of administrative and public buildings and open spaces, it is probable that some established ancient cities were more densely occupied than villages. For example, Tyre is reported to have had a circumference of 2.75 Roman miles (Pliny, *HN* 5.15.77), or an area of about 100 hectares, and Alexander is said to have slain 8,000 of its inhabitants after his successful siege of the city

---

[17] Wenke 1975/6: 90.

and enslaved 30,000 (Arr. *Anab.* 2.24.4–5). If one accepts these figures, the population density works out at about 380 persons per hectare, although it may have been inflated because of the siege.

An ancient city's population was not totally determined by the circumference of its walls, as settlements would tend to cling to the outside, particularly along its approaches. But this might also work in a reverse manner, since, although walls existed, areas devoted to cultivation might be included within their perimeter. Furthermore, a city might find itself in a phase of population and economic decline and be more sparsely inhabited than it had been in the past. There is no indication, for example, that Babylon was nearly as densely populated in the Seleukid period as earlier, particularly since some of its inhabitants may have moved, or been moved, to Seleukeia-Tigris after that city was founded about 305 BC, as the centre of gravity of Mesopotamian administration and economy shifted eastwards to the Tigris (ch. 6.2e).

In some cases, one does have population estimates by ancient authors as well as indications of areas of cities. The shape of Alexandria has been described as an outstretched Macedonian *chlamys* ('robe') between the sea and Lake Moeris, with a length of 30 to 40 *stadia*, a width of 7 to 10 *stadia* (at its narrowest) and a perimeter of 110 *stadia* to 15 Roman miles (Diod. 17.52.3; Strabo 17.1.8; Pliny, *HN* 5.11.62; Jos. *BJ* 2.386; Stephanus, s.v. Ἀλεξάνδρεια), which would give an area of about 1,500 hectares. Diodoros also informs us that in his time, *c.* 60 BC, the city had more than 300,000 free inhabitants (17.52.6) which, when a certain number of slaves are added, should correspond to a population density of not less than 200 persons per hectare.[18] Although I have presented a somewhat simplistic analysis, it gives a useful order of magnitude.

For the purposes of this book, the average population density of a town or city will be taken at 200 persons per hectare, the same as for a village, recognizing that it may, in some cases, have been appreciably higher or lower.[19]

[18] Fraser estimates the population of Alexandria at one million, and he tries, unconvincingly, to reconcile this figure with Diodoros' 300,000 free residents by assuming these to have been males only and adding in 400,000 slaves (1972: 57, n. 358). Beloch opts for half a million inhabitants in the Hellenistic period (1886: 259).

[19] Adams and Nissen consider 200 persons per hectare as the norm both at different times and for settlements of widely varying gross size in Mesopotamia (1972: 28). Doxiades and Papaioannou use 200 as a global average in antiquity for village built-up areas (1974: 52). Sumner estimates 40 in urban areas and 100 in rural for the Persepolis plain (1986: 12), but this is probably too low, in my view. Alcock implies 125–300 for rural Bahrain (1994: 183). Marchese takes 125 for urban centres in the Maiandros flood plain, but concedes that the figure may have been higher (1986: 307–21). Marfoe uses 100–200 for south-eastern Anatolia (1986: 43). Kramer adopts 100–150 for settlements in

Regarding the area of cultivated land required to support a person in an ancient agricultural economy, there seems to be a consensus at between a half and one hectare,[20] with irrigation farming, because of its greater productivity, tending to the lower figure and dry farming to the higher. If, for example, a settlement survey uncovers an ancient irrigation system and comes up with a certain area of irrigated land, a population will be estimated based on half a hectare per person.

b. Site excavations

Archaeological reports of Seleukid-period cities are particularly helpful when they provide outlines of fortifications, which allow one to make estimates of city surface areas and populations (ch. 6.2b). The material remains of a city may also be useful in establishing likely industries operating there and patterns of trade (ch. 5.4–5), although it is not the purpose of this work to deal with the underlying economy in other than outline form.[21]

c. Clay sealings from Mesopotamia

The practice of attaching to a papyrus or parchment roll one or more clay sealings of the shape of a medallion or enclosing the roll in a *bulla*, a sort of clay 'napkin-ring', is well attested in Seleukid Babylonia.[22] The documents have all perished, but the seal impressions left on the medallions and *bullae* provide some insights regarding Seleukid financial administration.

A number of collections of such sealings have appeared from excavations in Uruk and Seleukeia-Tigris and have been published.[23] The most impressive, however, numbering about 30,000 sealings from the so-called Archives Building of Seleukeia-Tigris, has not yet been studied extensively from the point of view of administrative practice, but mainly with regard to the iconography of the private and official seals used.[24]

central Iran, but more in the Mesopotamian alluvial plain, although he recognizes that city densities could be appreciably higher (1982: 168). Pastor assumes a surprisingly high 450 for settlements in Israel (1997: 9). Adams, finally, gives some population densities for Middle Eastern cities in the early twentieth century: Baghdad 102.2 persons per hectare, Damascus 400, Aleppo 400, Erbil 526 (1965: 24, 122).

[20] Doxiades and Papaioannou 1974: 49; Kramer 1982: 181–3; Osborne 1987: 46; Hodkinson 1988: 39; Garnsey 1988: 46; Gallant 1991: 82; Burford 1993: 67; Pastor 1997: 9. Préaux estimates 2.5 irrigated hectares were required to sustain a family of four in Ptolemaic Egypt (1969: 67).

[21] See Rostovtzeff for a fuller discussion of trade and industry in the Hellenistic world (1941: 1200–301).

[22] McDowell 1935: 1–10.

[23] Rostovtzeff 1932; McDowell 1935. See also Wallenfels 1994 for a study of cuneiform tablets at Uruk and their sharing of seals with *bullae*.

[24] Invernizzi 1994.

6. NUMISMATICS

Because of the paucity of literary sources for the Seleukid empire, the
evidence from coinage has often proved invaluable in recreating political
history and studying royal ideology. The manner and date of the secession
of the satrapy of Baktria and Sogdiane, for instance, have usually been
linked to the gradual change of iconography and legends in the coinages
of Antiochos II and Diodotos from the Baktrian mint(s) (ch. 2).

Here I am only interested in the use of coinage as a factor in the Seleukid
economy and, specifically, what role it played in Seleukid economic policy.

a. Coin catalogues

The starting point is a determination of which Seleukid mints operated,
what coinage issues they produced and when. The pioneering works of
Newell (*WSM*; *ESM*), which provide this information, have been extended
and corrected, where necessary, by other scholars (mainly Mørkholm, Le
Rider and Houghton).

A new comprehensive catalogue of all Seleukid mints, denominations,
coin types and control marks is clearly required and the first part has now
been published.[25] This is potentially a very useful source for any future
discussion of the Seleukid economy.

b. Die studies

The focus of Seleukid numismatics in recent years has been the area of
die studies. Although far from complete, a picture is gradually emerging
of the obverse and reverse dies used in coinage issues at different mints.
From the number of specimens of a particular issue that have been found, in
relation to the number of obverse dies used for it, the so-called index figure,
statistical methods[26] allow one to predict the total number of fully used
obverse dies in the issue, including those that have not been discovered as
yet. The greater the index figure, the greater the accuracy of the prediction
and, at around five or six, there is a 95 per cent chance that all fully used
obverse dies will have been accounted for.[27] But the proviso in using any
statistical approach is that the sample be fairly random, for example not

---

[25] Houghton and Lorber 2002. The authors were kind enough to provide me with a draft of the first
volume, dealing with the coinage of the Seleukid kings to Antiochos III, for which I thank them.

[26] McGovern 1980; Carter 1983; Esty 1986.

[27] Mørkholm 1991: 17.

influenced by one major hoard, in which coins struck from a particular die predominate.

The method adopted here is the one proposed by Esty,[28] which takes into account variability in die life, with a pattern that has some short-lived dies (presumably faulty ones), most dies in a relatively narrow range of usage and a few lasting longer than expected. The result is a best estimate of the total number of dies, plus a low and a high estimate between which there is a 95 per cent statistical chance that the real solution will lie.[29] All the figures within this range do not, however, have an equal chance of being the true one, since, as one approaches the best estimate, the probability of a correct answer increases. Although some scholars avoid using these methods for die prediction when the index figure is less than three,[30] it is permissible to do so, as long as one recognizes that the answer is a range of figures, with a certain degree of uncertainty, and not a single exact result.

Once the number of obverse dies in a coinage issue has been determined, the next question is 'What was the average number of coins produced per die?' Clearly this will have depended upon the material and denomination of the coins, the quality of the dies and the skill of the mint workers.[31] The surviving gold is all of excellent quality, probably minted partly for prestige reasons, and may have required die replacement sooner. For bronze issues, on the other hand, there is generally very much less concern about appearance and it is possible that a die may have been used for much higher levels of production. Regarding silver, most Seleukid tetradrachms are of a high standard, while the difficulties of engraving and striking smaller denominations show up in the comparatively lower quality, but whether this means more or fewer coins per die is not clear. As will be seen in chapter 11.3c, the striking of small silver was mostly discontinued after the first Seleukids, so it is mainly the tetradrachms that are of interest and that constituted the bulk of the currency in circulation.

The only firm evidence for average production from an obverse die gives between 23,333 and 47,250 for silver staters from Delphi *c.* 335 BC[32] and 30,000 for a particular issue of Roman *denarii.*[33] Obverse die output of

---

[28] Esty 1986: 204–7.

[29] An unequal distribution of die lifetimes is assumed, negative-binomial with parameter two, coinciding with the gamma distribution of Carter 1983. The expected total number of obverse dies (k2′) is calculated using the formula given by Esty (H1). Next the corresponding number of equal-lifetime dies (k′) that would give the same total output is determined (H6) and the 95 per cent confidence limits for this (C2), which are then translated into corresponding 95 per cent confidence limits for the unequal-lifetime case (H5).

[30] For example, Callataÿ 1995: 295.   [31] Howgego 1995: 32; Callataÿ 1995: 296.

[32] Kinns 1983: 18.   [33] M. H. Crawford 1974: 694.

between 20,000 and 30,000 coins is what several scholars consider likely for a Hellenistic coinage, with 30,000 as the favoured number.[34]

An average figure of 30,000 coins from an obverse tetradrachm die, equivalent to 20 talents in value, will be used here and this will be shown to be fairly consistent with what the sources indicate expenditure may have been at times when tetradrachm issues were required (ch. 11.5c). Indeed, this figure is possibly slightly on the low side for Seleukid issues.

For gold coins, information is lacking. Gold is a softer metal than silver, so die-wear was probably less. Despite this, however, it is likely that considerably less was produced from a stater die,[35] not only because of the higher quality of coin desired, but mainly because gold, being in shorter supply, was more likely to run out before the die had reached the end of its useful life. So, somewhat arbitrarily, only half of the average production of a tetradrachm die is considered here for a gold stater die, or 15,000 coins, equivalent to 50 talents of silver, based on a gold to silver ratio of one to ten.

c. Coin hoards

In addition to die studies, important numismatic sources that can throw light on the Seleukid economy and financial administration are the *Inventory of Greek Coin Hoards* (*IGCH*), the *Coin Hoards* updates (vols. 1 to 1x) and numismatic publications with the details of the hoards contained in these summaries, as well as those that are more recent.[36] A computerized system has been developed to store and analyse information concerning the location, date of burial and content of coin hoards within Seleukid territory, whose key results are given in Appendix 1 as Coin hoards lists 1–3. With these, it is possible to go some way towards analysing patterns of coinage circulation in both space and time.

---

[34] Hopkins 1980: 107; Mørkholm 1991: 16; Price 1992: 66; Callataÿ 1995: 299–300. T. V. Buttrey rejects the idea that a meaningful average can be calculated at all, but not the statistical approach for estimating the total number of dies, provided the sample is large enough (1993; 1994; Buttrey and Buttrey 1997).

[35] Also Callataÿ 1995: 298.

[36] I am indebted to Andrew Meadows, Curator of Greek coins at the British Museum, for a pre-publication version of *Coin Hoards* vol. 1x.

CHAPTER 2

Historical summary

The finances and financial administration of the Seleukid kings can be best understood against a historical background of the major events of their reigns, particularly those affecting the extent of their territory (and revenue), or requiring considerable military effort (and expenditure).[1]

a. Seleukos I (311–281 BC)

The Seleukid empire is considered to have been founded with the return to Babylon, between 13 May and 3 June 311 BC, of Seleukos Nikator. That is how Seleukos' son, Antiochos (I), saw it when he inaugurated dating by the Seleukid era.[2]

In 311 BC, Seleukos controlled hardly more than Babylonia, that is, southern Mesopotamia, and almost immediately faced a threat from Antigonos Monophthalmos, who had just concluded a peace treaty (311 BC) with his major rivals, Ptolemy, Kassandros and Lysimachos, and was now free to turn his attention eastwards. The subsequent war between the two Successors is not described in classical sources, but cuneiform documents attest to its ferocity, as Antigonos invaded Babylonia (310 BC) and ravaged the land.[3] In 308 BC, in a critical battle, Seleukos was victorious and probably extended his rule into northern Mesopotamia at this time.

In the next few years, free from problems in the West, Seleukos marched east and took over, one by one, the satrapies of Alexander's empire that, in the turmoil of the clashes of the Successors, had been left free to fend for themselves. Most of the Indian territories had, however, already been lost to

---

[1] See Sherwin-White and Kuhrt 1993 for the history and institutions of the Seleukid empire. Also Will 1979 and 1982 for a political and military history, with full references.

[2] Austin 1981: no. 138 for a Babylonian king list giving dates of reigns according to the Seleukid era, which started on 1 Nissan (April) 311 BC in the Babylonian calendar and 1 Dios (October) 312 BC in the Macedonian. Spek discusses the date of Seleukos' return to Babylon (1992: 244–6). See also Boiy 2000: 119, n. 19.

[3] Grayson 1975: no. 10.

Chandragupta, the founder of the Mauryan empire, a few years earlier and the attempt to recover these by Seleukos was unsuccessful. In a peace treaty (303 BC), the Indian satrapies, as well as Paropamisadai (the Kabul valley) and at least parts of Arachosia and Gedrosia (south-eastern Afghanistan and Baluchistan), were ceded to Chandragupta, while Seleukos is reputed to have received 500 war-elephants in exchange.

Strengthened by the resources of his new possessions in the East and the elephants, Seleukos moved westwards to join the coalition against Antigonos. The fruits of victory at Ipsos (301 BC) may have proved somewhat disappointing, since only northern Syria fell to his lot. Koile Syria, that is, southern Syria, Palestine and Phoenicia, should also have gone to him, but Ptolemy had made a pre-emptive occupation of this province and Seleukos was reluctant to take up the issue then. The problem remained, however, a festering wound in Seleukid–Ptolemaic relationships.

In Asia Minor, Seleukos now faced his erstwhile ally at Ipsos, Lysimachos, with Pleistarchos' buffer-state of Kilikia in between. Kilikia was occupied in about 294 BC, while most of Asia Minor and parts of Thrace were added to the empire in 281 BC after the victory of Korupedion. At this time, the Seleukid empire had reached its greatest geographical extent, and the southern parts of Kappadokia and Armenia were also subject to its rule.

Meanwhile, Seleukos had inaugurated his great building projects. Of his major cities, Seleukeia-Tigris is likely to have been founded as a capital in about 305 BC,[4] at the time when Seleukos took the title of king. The Syrian tetrapolis of Antioch, Seleukeia-Pieria, Laodikeia and Apameia was created in about 300 BC and numerous smaller foundations began to appear all over the empire (ch. 6.2).

b. Antiochos I (281–261 BC)

The assassination of Seleukos in Thrace, far from his main centres of power, created a period of turmoil, until his son, Antiochos, was able to consolidate his position, although he had been co-ruler with his father, with responsibility for the East, since c. 291/0.[5] Taking advantage of Antiochos' problems,

---

[4] Sherwin-White 1983a: 270.
[5] In the *Astronomical Diaries*, Seleukos is shown by the dating formula to have been sole ruler at least until August–September 292 BC (Sachs and Hunger 1988: no. -291). The first appearance of Antiochos as co-ruler with his father is in September–October 289 BC (Sachs and Hunger 1988: no. -288), but, even before this, as crown prince, Antiochos played an active administrative role in the East. A Babylonian text (Grayson 1975: 26–7, no. 11) shows him dealing with the Erišnugalu temple at Ur, the construction of Seleukeia-Tigris (possibly), certain undetermined affairs of Babylon and a treaty of some kind.

Ptolemy II managed to acquire a foothold in Asia Minor and effectively controlled the southern coast and parts of the western one with a string of naval bases. While conceding these losses, and perhaps those parts of Kappadokia and Armenia that had been gained by his father, Antiochos kept the Ptolemaic forces at bay where it really mattered, on the borders of northern Syria, in the first Syrian War (274–271 BC). An able ruler, Antiochos continued the city-building activity of Seleukos with even greater intensity and should probably be given credit for the measures that had the greatest impact on Seleukid finances and financial administration, which provided the basis for the strength and longevity of the empire (ch. 13.10).

c. Antiochos II (261–246 BC)

Another able ruler, Antiochos II faced a Ptolemaic threat immediately upon his accession to the throne, but was able to counter it successfully in the second Syrian War (261–256 BC). Indeed, it is probable that he recovered for the empire parts of Ionia, Pamphylia and Kilikia Tracheia.[6]

In the East, however, the situation may not have been so rosy and it is possible that the secessionary tendencies of Diodotos, satrap of Baktria, began to be displayed in this reign. The date of the loss of Baktria is highly controversial. A 'high' date, as early as 255 BC, has been proposed[7] based on the sequence of Baktrian coinage issues that first depict the head of Antiochos II on the obverse and the 'Thundering Zeus' type of Diodotos on the reverse, then the legend ΒΑΣΙΛΕΩΣ ΔΙΟΔΟΤΟΥ replacing ΒΑΣΙΛΕΩΣ ΑΝΤΙΟΧΟΥ and, finally, the portrait of Diodotos himself on the obverse. Since no coins of Seleukos II were ever issued in Baktria, it is suggested that he cannot have reigned there.

It is difficult, however, to find a suitable political background for these changes, such as a serious weakening of the central power that could have induced a satrap to revolt. The only such opportunity may have been the period of the second Syrian War, when Antiochos was otherwise engaged, but it is difficult to see why he would have made no attempt to reassert himself in Baktria once his hands were free again. In any case, a rebellious satrap would be unlikely to show that he still maintained ties with his erstwhile, but still living, sovereign by using the latter's portrait on his coinage. And if this were not a revolt, but a concession of joint kingship by Antiochos to Diodotos, it would be totally against the practice of Seleukid kings, as long as adult sons were available to them for this role in the East.

[6] Will 1979: 239.   [7] Bopearachchi 1994: 516–17; Holt 1999: 19.

Thus a 'high' date for Baktrian secession is most unlikely. On the other hand, a 'low' date, as late as 239 BC, does represent the end of a period in which a gradual loosening of ties could have taken place and is to be preferred.[8] This will be discussed further below.

d. *Seleukos II (246–225 BC)*

Upon succeeding his father, Seleukos II faced the immediate and serious threat of a rival claimant to the throne, the infant son of his father's second wife, Berenike, daughter of Ptolemy III. The third Syrian War (246–241 BC) was initiated with a Ptolemaic invasion of Kilikia Pedias and northern Syria, which reached as far as Mesopotamia. From his base in western Asia Minor, Seleukos was able to launch a counteroffensive and eventually recover the lost provinces, except for the coastal area around Seleukeia-Pieria in northern Syria. He had to pay a price, however, for support received from his brother, Antiochos Hierax, who was appointed viceroy in the West, but soon asserted his independence and took control of Seleukid territories in western Asia Minor. An attempt by Seleukos to curb his brother met with defeat at the battle of Ankyra (239 BC). At the same time, an expanding Attalid kingdom began encroaching on Seleukid possessions in Asia Minor, eventually ousting Antiochos Hierax.

From the eastern satrapies, the situation must have appeared confused at this time, with rival claimants to the Seleukid throne engaged in constant warfare far away, too preoccupied to pay attention to local affairs. We are told that Andragoras, the satrap of Parthia, was the first to revolt, but later succumbed to the Parthians. Diodotos of Baktria apparently followed soon after and this set off a general secession of other provinces.[9] The sequence of Diodotos' numismatic issues referred to earlier may be interpreted as a kind of fence-sitting, with the satrap waiting to see which way the balance would tip in the clash between Seleukos and Ptolemy III. By retaining the portrait of the dead Antiochos II on issues of the Baktrian mint(s), Diodotos was apparently playing safe with his loyalties.

When Seleukos continued to be preoccupied with his brother, a tentative claim of kingship was not unduly risky, if made under the protective umbrella of the portrait of the last recognized Seleukid king, Antiochos II. The inhabitants of Baktria would, no doubt, have come around to the idea

---

[8] Sherwin-White and Kuhrt 1993: 107–11. In Wolski's view, secession starts with Antiochos II and ends with Seleukos II (1982: 142).

[9] See Holt for a discussion of the texts relating to Baktrian secession and the numismatic evidence (1999: 58–60).

in due course, but once Seleukos II had been decisively defeated at Ankyra (239 BC), there was no longer any need for pretence and Diodotos' portrait, type and legend on his coins could make his kingship claim solid. Thus, although Baktria may have formally seceded from the empire in 239 BC, the Seleukid hold on the province had probably been effectively lost at the very start of the reign of Seleukos II in 246 BC and this probably means the loss of revenue too.[10] No wonder then that Seleukos, once he had made peace with his brother after Ankyra, set out to recover the lost eastern provinces of Parthia and Baktria, but, as we know, his expedition proved unsuccessful.

With the Parthians now controlling the exit from the Caspian Gates and the principal route to the East,[11] Margiane is likely to have gone the way of Baktria. Perhaps northern Aria also did at this time, if not slightly later, since Euthydemos, the Graeco-Baktrian king, is found putting up resistance there in 208 BC against Antiochos III during the latter's Anabasis of reconquest. Southern Aria could, however, be accessed from Mesopotamia by way of Persis, Karmania and Drangiane and it is likely that this southern group of satrapies remained Seleukid, since the evidence suggests that Antiochos traversed the region peacefully on his return from the Anabasis.

The status of Persis does, however, present a problem. As in the case of Baktria, there is a dispute about when it acquired its independence from the Seleukids, if it ever did. A local dynasty, centred on Persepolis, is evidenced by the coins it issued. The number of rulers who minted these coins is sufficiently large to support those who see an early date for the founding of the dynasty, perhaps just after the death of Seleukos I (281 BC). On the other hand, there is evidence in the sources for Persis as a Seleukid satrapy in the reign of Antiochos III (Polyb. 5.40.7). Furthermore, in describing Persis, Strabo refers to its history as one in which Parthian rule succeeded Macedonian (15.3.24), which would have taken place in the 140s BC. It is possible to reconcile these views by considering that the Seleukids exercised suzerainty over local dynasts in central Persis throughout this period,[12] much as they did with other such dynasts in Asia Minor and elsewhere, as part of the satrapal administration. There is no way of knowing the precise relationship, but one can assume that some tribute was levied and Persian

[10] Also Lerner 1995/6: 103; 1999: 29–30.

[11] Also Bernard 1994: 506; Will 1994: 440; *contra* Sherwin-White and Kuhrt 1993: 84–90.

[12] Also Koch 1988: 95; Sherwin-White and Kuhrt 1993: 76–7. Wiesehöfer places gradual independence from the reign of Antiochos IV (1994: 138), while Grainger considers abandonment of the Persepolis area to a local dynasty, with Seleukid approval, *c.* 300 BC (1990b: 149).

troops were called upon when required, as, for example, at the battle of Raphia in 217 BC (Polyb. 5.79.6).

In the reign of Seleukos II, then, the Seleukid empire suffered its first serious territorial amputations at its two extremities: Asia Minor in the West and Parthia, Baktria and other regions in the East. The southern coast of Asia Minor, as far as Kilikia Tracheia, remained firmly in the hands of the Ptolemies.

e. Seleukos III (225–223 BC)

An attempt to retake western Asia Minor was initiated by Seleukos III in his very short reign, but without tangible results.

f. Antiochos III (223–187 BC)

At this low point of its territorial extent, the Seleukid empire was fortunate in acquiring a young ruler with considerable administrative and military capabilities, whose long reign, after a difficult start, constituted a series of important conquests and reconquests in all directions, that mostly came to naught after one crushing defeat.

Many of the original Seleukid territories of western Asia Minor were retaken early in Antiochos' reign by an army sent out under Achaios, only to be lost again when Achaios decided to take the royal diadem for himself. The revolt of Molon in Media and parts of Mesopotamia (222–220 BC) was crushed after a few false starts. A first expedition of conquest against Ptolemy IV in Koile Syria, the fourth Syrian War, ground to a halt after the defeat at Raphia (217 BC), but its one tangible gain was the Ptolemaic enclave of Seleukeia-Pieria. After this, Antiochos turned his attention to western Asia Minor, where he defeated Achaios and retook Sardeis (216–213 BC).

Antiochos next embarked upon his great Anabasis to the East, with Armenia as his first objective (212–211 BC). Then it was the turn of Baktria, but the long and unsuccessful siege of Baktra (208–206 BC) must have been somewhat of a setback. Euthydemos of Baktria recognized Seleukid suzerainty in the end, but this was probably short-lived,[13] while it is possible that the Graeco-Baktrian kings may also have controlled Aria and Arachosia at this time. Sophagasenos of Paropamisadai also submitted peacefully and the return journey by way of Drangiane, Karmania and Persis went without incident, suggesting that these territories had been controlled by the

---

[13] Sherwin-White and Kuhrt 1993: 198–9; Bernard 1994: 478.

Seleukids all along. In 205 BC Antiochos is to be found on an expedition in the Persian Gulf asserting Seleukid power with the foremost Arabian city there, Gerrha, receiving tribute and, more importantly, probably ensuring that, in future, more of the lucrative Arabian and Indian trade was to be channelled through Seleukid territory.

With the East apparently under control, Antiochos could now set his sights on the West again, with a preliminary expedition to western Asia Minor to see how matters stood there. The time was not yet ripe, however, for any major action in this area.

In the South, such an opportunity had arisen with the death of Ptolemy IV and the accession of a minor, Ptolemy V, to the throne. In a sense, the Ptolemies were now to be repaid in the same coin for the trouble that they had caused at the start of the reigns of earlier Seleukid kings. The fifth Syrian War (202–198 BC), highlighted by the victory at Panion (200 BC), brought all of Koile Syria, a rich and populous province, into the Seleukid empire for the first time.

The Ptolemies were given no respite and a combined land and naval force moved along the southern and western coasts of Asia Minor, taking one Ptolemaic possession after another and bringing most Greek cities under Seleukid sway. This operation was paralleled in the interior until, by about 192 BC, apart from a small Attalid enclave, virtually all of southern and western Asia Minor was Seleukid, and Antiochos had also acquired a foothold in Thrace. The Seleukid empire had again reached a huge extent, not far short of what it had been under Seleukos I.

After the thirty-year struggle to achieve this position of dominance, Antiochos' fall was sudden and steep. The ill-fated expedition to Greece and the crushing defeat suffered at the hands of Rome at Magnesia (190 BC) put paid to Seleukid rule in western and much of southern Asia Minor. Those territories east of Media and Persis that had been loosely held before were probably lost irrevocably after the death of the king,[14] and Armenia too must have asserted its independence again. But these losses were not as catastrophic as has sometimes been made out[15] and were offset, to some extent, by the gain of Koile Syria.

g. *Seleukos IV (187–175 BC)*

There was no change to the political position under Seleukos IV and this was one of the rare, mostly peaceful periods of Seleukid history.

---

[14] Also Will 1994: 445–6.   [15] Also Briant 1994a: 459.

h. Antiochos IV (175–164 BC)

The situation changed drastically under Antiochos IV, after a quiet start.
The sixth Syrian War was launched against the Ptolemies, perhaps as a
response to the loss of Asia Minor.[16] After a victorious first invasion of
Egypt (169 BC), Antiochos was checked in his second attempt by the ulti-
matum delivered to him by the Roman legate Popilius Laenas at Eleusis
(168 BC). Frustrated in the West, Antiochos turned his attention eastwards,
where the Parthians were now beginning to make dangerous incursions into
Media and the tribes of the Zagros seem to have thrown off the Seleukid
yoke. The procession (*pompē*) at Daphne (166 BC) has been presented as
a megalomaniac's attempt to reassert his authority after the humiliation
suffered at Eleusis, but it is more likely that it was part of the preparations for the eastern expedition, which Antiochos perhaps saw as another
Anabasis. The Maccabean revolt, which broke out at about this time,
became a thorn in Seleukid flesh and was only dealt with successfully
when the bulk of the army had returned from the East after Antiochos'
death.

i. The later kings (164–64 BC)

The century after Antiochos IV is characterized by internecine warfare
between rival houses laying claim to the Seleukid throne, destabilizing
interventions by Rome and the Ptolemies in favour of one or another
claimant and constantly increasing pressure from Parthia on the eastern
borders. The resources of the empire were fatally weakened and the critical moment arrived when first Media, *c.* 150 BC, and then Babylonia, the
economic heartland, *c.* 140 BC, were overrun by the Parthians.[17] A valiant
attempt by Antiochos VII to recover the lost territories was initially successful, but finally foundered in defeat in the mountains of Media (129 BC)
and Mesopotamia was irretrievably lost.

   In the West, the Jews had essentially asserted their independence by
129 BC and were embarking upon a period of expansion of the Hasmonean
kingdom, while, one by one, the links subjecting the Phoenician and Pales-
tinian coastal cities to the Seleukids were being cut, as issues of independent
silver coinage show: Tyre in 126/5 BC, Sidon in 112/11 BC, Askelon in 104/3
BC and Tripolis *c.* 100 BC.[18]

---

[16] Austin 1986: 461.   [17] Also Sherwin-White and Kuhrt 1993: 217–25.   [18] Mørkholm 1984: 103.

From 129 BC onwards, one can no longer speak of a 'Seleukid empire', but only of a kingdom centred on northern Syria and Kilikia and then of rival principalities contending with one another for land and power. This internal turmoil left the field open for a foreign takeover, first by Tigranes of Armenia (89–69 BC) and finally by Rome in 64 BC.

CHAPTER 3

The posing of a problem

In 311 BC, Seleukos Nikator returned to Babylon with the aim of carving out a territory for himself, much as the other Successors were doing at this time. As one can deduce from his subsequent actions, his first priority seems to have been to defend himself against Antigonos Monophthalmos and consolidate his position in Babylonia, his second to increase his power by adding the Iranian satrapies to his realm and his third to join the coalition against Antigonos, which yielded him northern Syria in 301 BC (ch. 2).

At this point the resources available to Seleukos were a huge territory, with a large population and productive resources (chs. 4, 5), but essentially forming an economy where, with the exception of Babylonia, commodity-based exchange was the norm and where the Achaemenid king's revenue and expenses had been primarily in kind. Seleukos was now in contact with a Mediterranean world where a political game was being played, which relied on gold and silver in coin for the payment of the armies employed by a contender, as he sought to promote himself against his rivals and safeguard his own gains. Seleukos' problem was that he probably had insufficient silver revenues and reserves with which to play this game.

Alexander's capture and coining of most of the stored bullion of the Achaemenid empire, reputedly valued at 180,000 or more talents-worth of gold and silver (Strabo 15.3.9), may not have materially changed the picture in the Asian territories, except for the Mediterranean fringe. Coined mainly at Babylon and Mediterranean mints towards the end of his reign and immediately afterwards[1] and issued mostly as settlement payments to disbanded soldiers and pay to mercenaries, it is questionable how much could actually have been expended in Asia. The Achaemenid system of taxation (mainly) in kind was still in place and there would have been more than enough from this to feed the army. Even the 50,000

---

[1] Price 1992: 72–3.

talents-worth of bullion, said to have remained at Alexander's death (Justin
13.1.9), must have been rapidly coined for the military needs of the Successors in the next decade or so. We know, for example, that Antipatros
sent Antigenes to collect the remaining treasure from Susa (Arr. *Ta meta
Alexandron* 1.38).

The evidence of the *Astronomical Diaries* suggests that underlying commodity prices in Babylon remained remarkably stable for nearly two hundred years from the end of Achaemenid rule, influenced temporarily only
by dire shortages caused by political events and war, by good or bad harvests and by the time of the year in relation to the harvest (ch. 5.6a). No
general increase in prices of an inflationary nature is observed, such as
could have been caused by a large influx of gold and silver and, even had
there been the possibility of one, the markets of the East may not have
been able to respond immediately with the necessary products or services
required by the Greeks. Thus it is likely that the coins that found their way
into soldiers' pockets remained there, to some extent, or were expended
mostly in the Aegean world. That some of the precious metal in circulation
ended up in the Ptolemaic treasury as a result of the grain export drive and
import restrictions of the Ptolemies is well known. And that some of it
remained in treasuries under Seleukos' control is also likely, but how much
is questionable.

The situation, as Seleukos Nikator may have viewed it towards the end
of the fourth century BC, was hardly encouraging. Some royal revenue was
certainly collected in silver, but most was probably still received in kind.
On the other hand, the military and other payments envisaged for the
future were likely to be overwhelmingly in silver. Consequently, a significant
imbalance existed, or would shortly exist, regarding precious metal, which
would impose a serious drain on the treasury. Some gold and silver was,
of course, available from mines in Baktria and Karmania (ch. 5.3a), but it
is unlikely that this could have made up the difference, while the mineral
resources of Asia Minor were at this time in the hands of Lysimachos.
Therefore, it was necessary to devise some method for permanently halting
the drain of silver and ensuring that the treasury always had an adequate
supply for its needs.

The Ptolemies had a similar problem and the solution they adopted is
well known: a grain export drive to earn the silver they lacked and import
restrictions to keep it in the country and, ultimately, in their possession.[2]
There is no record in the sources of the measures that Seleukos actually

---

[2] Préaux 1939 is still the best overview of the Ptolemaic royal economy.

took, but one can observe their impact and so postulate their existence in six complementary areas. These measures seem to have been followed up and extended by Seleukos' son and successor, Antiochos (I), and maintained by other Seleukid kings well into the second century BC, although some may have already been initiated by Seleukos' predecessors in Asia, Alexander and Antigonos Monophthalmos. This is not to suggest that there was anything like a detailed long-range plan, or even any systematic thinking on how to administer a newly acquired empire. What emerged were probably commonsense solutions to a crucial problem that was quite evident: how to increase silver revenue and survive in the post-Alexander world. In subsequent chapters, each measure that the Seleukid kings apparently took will be discussed at length.

The first measure – although not in any chronological sense, since all are likely to have been applied at about the same time – seems to have been to increasingly require tax payments, especially from the agricultural sector, to be made in coin. For the peasant, this meant converting his commodity surplus into silver, as can be seen from the tribute assessment of villages in western Asia Minor (ch. 8.1a–f) or the sale of grain from royal land (ch. 9.2).

This measure could not work well unless the peasant had a market in which to sell his produce, an urban market. The old towns and cities of the empire, for example those along the coasts of Asia Minor and Phoenicia, or in Babylonia, or the satrapal capitals, already provided such markets, but there were huge areas in northern Syria and Mesopotamia and the Upper Satrapies with scant urban development (ch. 4.1–3). This is where the second measure, the founding of new cities in little-urbanized regions with rich agricultural potential may have come in (ch. 6.2), markets thereby being provided which could deal in coin. It is possible that the kings' grants of land to cities, temples and individuals were conditioned largely by the desire to find, in each case, the most efficient means of generating precious-metal revenue (ch. 6.2–4). Any commodity surpluses from royal land could also be disposed of in urban markets (ch. 9.2).

The third measure was to maintain an adequate supply of coinage and this was apparently achieved by locating mints in almost all the satrapies to serve the needs of their respective populations. On Alexander's death, only one mint operated in the East, at Babylon, and perhaps a second at Susa, but, under Seleukos and Antiochos, mints were opened up in several major cities. Seleukid coinage will be discussed at length (ch. 11), including the relationship between the output of a mint and the population and production of the region it served (ch. 12.5).

The fourth measure was to switch increasingly to coins as the medium in which the administration made its payments. This was necessary for the Greek soldiers and western mercenaries who made up the bulk of the Seleukid armies and probably constituted the most important area of expenditure (ch. 10.1). The pay the soldiers now received in coin could be expended in town and city marketplaces and would eventually find its way back to the royal treasury as rents and taxes.

The fifth measure was to search out systematically every area of activity where tax or rent could be imposed, at as high a level as was feasible, commensurate with considerations of policy. The basic objective was to maximize royal revenue, particularly in silver, one aspect of this being the sale of natural resources monopolized by the king (ch. 8.2).

The sixth and final measure was to create an efficient financial administration to collect revenue and control expenditure in a systematic way, answerable directly to the king (ch. 13).

It remains to be seen in what follows whether Seleukos and his successors did solve the problem they faced: how to increase silver revenue and survive.

PART II

The underlying economy

CHAPTER 4

Geography and population

At its peak, the Seleukid empire stretched from the Aegean to the borders of India. In this vast area existed regions with quite different physical characteristics and climates, which naturally had a bearing on the sizes of populations that could be supported and their economic activities.

For the purposes of this study, five major regions are considered (see map), which not only had a certain uniformity within themselves, but also some continuity in their association with the Seleukids. The original core of the empire was Mesopotamia, to which were soon added the Upper Satrapies – the eastern regions as far as India – followed by northern Syria and Kilikia. Asia Minor did not have a continuous history of Seleukid rule and the last major region to be acquired was Koile Syria, that is, southern Syria, Phoenicia and Palestine.

Because of the scarcity of evidence, the analysis that follows is rather sketchy, but aims nevertheless at rough regional estimates of population, which were obviously one of the determining factors in the Seleukid economy.

Since population figures are clearly going to be the subject of much disagreement, it should be emphasized that great accuracy is not a requirement here. What is presented, based on the available evidence, is simply a best estimate of a range of figures. While there is a certain probability that any other figure outside the range may be true, this probability becomes increasingly smaller the further one diverges from the best estimate.[1] So, for example, if Mesopotamia is calculated to have possessed four to five million inhabitants, it is rather unlikely that the true figure would be less than three or more than six million. When the populations of several regions are added together, the practical range of probability of the total is not the sum of the individual ranges, but narrower. For a total of five 'Mesopotamias', for example, the best estimate would still be sixteen to twenty million, but

---

[1] In statistical terms, one is dealing with something like a Gaussian distribution of estimates.

anything outside these limits much less likely.[2] In other words, although the estimate for an individual region might be somewhat off the mark, that for the entire Seleukid empire, using this method of estimating different regions independently and then totalling, would not be.

I. MESOPOTAMIA

Most of central and southern Mesopotamia lies below the 200 millimetre annual-rainfall line, which is considered the minimum required for dry farming. Thus economic life in antiquity was almost totally dependent on the great rivers, the Euphrates, the Tigris and their tributaries. Only a relatively narrow region in the North between the Euphrates and the Tigris, the Jazira plain, and another east of the Tigris in the foothills of the Zagros were not dependent on irrigation.

Peaceful conditions in the Achaemenid and, especially, Seleukid periods brought about a revival from the significant decline in settled area and level of urbanization that had taken place earlier in the first millennium BC.[3] In southern Mesopotamia (Babylonia), many of the great urban centres along or near the Euphrates continued to flourish, for example Babylon, Uruk, Sippar, Nippur, Borsippa, Cutha, Larsa, Kish and others,[4] if not at the level of their previous glory. Of all the major cities, a decline is noticeable mainly in Ur, affected by a shift in the course of the Euphrates.[5] But, starting at the end of the fourth century BC, there seems to have been a definite movement of economic activity eastwards to the lower Tigris and its tributary, the Diyala, almost certainly due to the establishment of the capital at Seleukeia-Tigris and of other cities further east and the corresponding extension of the irrigation networks fed by these rivers (ch. 6.2a).

A detailed survey of the central Euphrates flood plain, the area centred on Babylon,[6] showed an increase in number of settlements, from 221 in the Achaemenid period, with a total area of 1769 hectares, to 415 in the Seleukid-Parthian period and 3201 hectares. The 55 'urban' sites – defined conventionally as having a size of at least 10 hectares – occupied 55 per cent

---

[2] If the chance of one extremely low or high figure is small, the chance of two or more lows or highs occurring at the same time becomes much smaller and 'pushes' the balance of probability nearer to the middle. A good example is the roll of a die. The chance of the smallest or highest number, a '1' or a '6', occurring is one in six in each case. If two dice are rolled, the chance of two '1's or two '6's is now dramatically reduced, to one in thirty-six in each case. Even a total of '3' has only a one in eighteen chance of being realized, as does a total of '11'. With five dice, the practical range of probability will narrow considerably more.

[3] Brinkman 1984: 172–3.   [4] Oelsner 1978: 102–6; Spek 1992: 235.

[5] Oelsner 1986: 73–7; Kuhrt 1990: 187.   [6] R. McC. Adams 1981: 177–9.

of the total area.[7] At 200 persons per hectare (ch. 1.5a), the best estimate for total population approaches three-quarters of a million.

In southern Babylonia, the survey of an area of roughly 2,800 square kilometres centred on Uruk showed a severalfold increase of population from the low reached in the Middle Babylonian period. Neo-Assyrian and Neo-Babylonian documents attest to a region comprising 80 towns and 700 hamlets,[8] not too different from that centred on Babylon. There is a flowering of Uruk in the Seleukid period, with the city probably occupying about 300 hectares at this time,[9] and with a population of about 60,000, but there are indications that the population was still low in relation to the potentially arable area.[10] Assuming cultivation of 0.5 hectares of irrigated land per person for subsistence (ch. 1.5), the population of southern Babylonia is likely to have been not far short of half a million.

Between these two survey areas lay Nippur. The sources refer to 189 settlements here, mostly next to canals, but there could have been more.[11] Indeed there is no reason why this well-irrigated region of some 6,000 square kilometres (although there is some overlap with the surveyed areas), situated as it was on the roads from Babylon to Susa and from Uruk to Seleukeia-Tigris, should have been any less densely populated than that of Uruk further south. There is evidence of extensive occupation in the Seleukid period and the city of Nippur itself covered some 80 hectares.[12] A population for this region of just under half a million is indicated.

For Strabo (15.3.5), the entire stretch along the Euphrates, from Babylon to its mouth, was 'well populated'.

A third detailed survey, along the Diyala tributary of the Tigris east of Baghdad,[13] showed an 'immense expansion' in the Seleukid period from the previous Achaemenid levels, in settlement area (fifteenfold), extent of irrigation and degree of urbanization. This was almost certainly fuelled by the presence of the capital at Seleukeia-Tigris (immediately to the west of the survey area) and Greek foundations such as Artemita and Antioch in this region, named Sittakene initially and Apolloniatis later,[14] which Strabo calls 'extensive and fertile' (16.1.17). The total settlement area of 1,507 hectares given by the survey suggests a population approaching half a million.

The excavations at Seleukeia-Tigris indicate a walled area of at least 550 hectares,[15] enough to have supported a population of about 100,000

---

[7] This is not surprising, as urbanization was a common phenomenon in large parts of the ancient Near East, in contrast with the Mediterranean world (Spek 1994: 7–11).

[8] Oelsner 1986: 77–97.   [9] Potts 1997: 287.   [10] Adams and Nissen 1972: 55–7.

[11] Zadok 1978: 326.   [12] Oelsner 1986: 100–9; Gibson 1992: 50–1; Spek 1992: 239.

[13] R. McC. Adams 1965: 63.   [14] Tscherikover 1973: 97.   [15] Invernizzi 1993: 235.

initially, although probably more later.[16] As in the case of other major urban centres, the city would have attracted to it the many rural settlements and small towns needed to feed it.[17] The region of Seleukeia-Tigris may thus have supported a population of up to half a million, or even more eventually.

In the south-eastern corner of the Mesopotamian plain lies Susiane, modern Khuzestan. After the devastation caused by the Assyrian king, Ashurbanipal, in 648 BC, the region showed a period of economic growth with the establishment of an Achaemenid capital at Susa, refounded by the Seleukids as Seleukeia-Eulaios. A survey of the major part of the Susan plain has produced an Achaemenid settlement area of only 141 hectares, apart from the city itself, with no indication of any increase in the Seleukid period, which is surprising in view of the extremely high productivity that Strabo (15.3.11) attributes to the region.[18] But the Mesopotamian plain itself extended much further to the south, as far as the Persian Gulf, with Greek foundations, such as Seleukeia-Hedyphon and Alexandria/Antioch-on-the-Erythraean Sea, noted in this area. To the east, Elymaïs or Elam, astride the Royal Road to Persepolis, may have been administratively linked to Susiane and the *Persepolis Fortification Texts* show how relatively populous and economically active this region of successive fertile valleys was.[19] A number of Seleukid foundations are also attested in this general area, pointing to further growth.[20] Thus, the total population of Susiane in the Seleukid period is likely to have been of the order of half a million.

Moving up to the middle reaches of the Euphrates in northern Mesopotamia, there is no extensive settlement survey and one has to rely on the evidence of Xenophon, which suggests a rather sparsely populated region, with few towns and large semi-desert stretches along the river (*Anab.* 1.5),[21] but where a number of small cities were founded by the Seleukids (ch. 6.2a).

On the other hand, the eastern bank of the Tigris, which Xenophon followed on his return march, appeared to him to be more fertile and populous, with rich villages and a large Achaemenid estate (*Anab.* 3.4.24, 31),

---

[16] The figure of 600,000 by Pliny (*HN* 6.122) in his time, the first century AD, appears far too high.

[17] A similar pattern is noted at Susa (Wenke 1975/6: 110) and Aï Khanoum, whose plain has shown at least 500 rural sites, with a gravitation of population towards the city (Gardin and Lyonnet 1978/9: 137–8).

[18] Wenke 1975/6: 94, 102–12. Boucharlat suggests that Hellenistic Susa was not significant until the end of the third century BC, when there was strong commercial activity (1985: 79). This can be associated with the opening up of the Gulf trade by Antiochos III.

[19] The number of commodity storehouses in Elam in the *PFT* is comparable to that in the Persepolis plain (Koch 1990: 247–62, 297–307). See also Aperghis 1996 for the Royal Road and the boundary between Elam and Persis.

[20] Tscherikover 1973: 98–9.   [21] Also Joannès 1995: 174.

and he also noted a considerable city on the western bank (*Anab.* 2.4.28). At this point, the Tigris traverses the heartland of Assyria, with Hellenistic Adiabene to the east. The earlier-held image of total devastation of this region, following the collapse of the Neo-Assyrian empire in 612 BC, is certainly false and some of the old urban centres continued to be inhabited, if not at earlier levels.[22] Arbela, for example, is mentioned as an Achaemenid regional capital[23] and possible treasury,[24] as a city by Arrian (*Anab.* 6.11.6) and as the later administrative centre of Arbelitis.[25] The region saw the establishment of a number of Hellenistic settlements: Alexandria-Adiabene, Demetrias-by-Arbela and others, in the regions of Adiabene and, further south, Khalonitis.[26]

In northernmost Mesopotamia, between the Euphrates and the Tigris, the Jazira plain is 'quite fertile', according to Strabo (16.1.23), and rainfall agriculture is possible, but the conditions are generally more suitable for pastoral activity.[27] A survey in a relatively small area of 475 square kilometres produced seventy-six small Seleukid-period settlements, none urban,[28] although this may have been an accident of the particular area investigated. The region had suffered a population decline earlier, with the Assyrian collapse, and the establishment or refounding of Greek cities, for example Edessa/Antioch-Kallirhoe, Karrhai, Nisibis/Antioch-Mygdonia and others,[29] is an indication of policy-determined growth in an underpopulated region (ch. 11.5c on the mint at Nisibis).[30]

Finally, along the shores of the Persian Gulf, a Seleukid garrison is attested archaeologically on Ikaros (Failaka) and there is a possible presence on Tylos (Bahrain), perhaps a naval base.[31] The foundations attributed to Seleukos I – Arethousa, Chalkis and Larissa (Pliny, *HN* 6.159) – may have lain somewhere along the western shore of the Gulf, but could have been nothing more substantial than bases for the Seleukid fleet safeguarding the Indian/Arabian trade route. The Oman peninsula is once referred to in a combined land and sea battle involving Seleukid forces at the straits of Hormuz (Pliny, *HN* 6.152), but this incident may indicate no more than a temporary military presence. The creation of the satrapy of the Erythraean Sea is certainly evidence of the heightened interest of the Seleukids in this region, because of the exotic trade goods passing through, from the time

[22] Kuhrt 1995b; Wilkinson and Tucker 1995: 63. [23] Driver [1957] 1965: no. 6.
[24] Kuhrt 1995b: 246. [25] Kuhrt 1990: 185–6.
[26] Tscherikover 1973: 96–7; Chaumont 1982. [27] Smith and Cuyler Young 1972: 23.
[28] Wilkinson and Tucker 1995: 65. [29] Tscherikover 1973: 84–90.
[30] A survey near Urfa, ancient Edessa, by Marfoe, showed a steady increase of settlements in the Hellenistic period (1986: 44–5).
[31] Also Alcock 1994: 183–4.

of Antiochos III's expedition to Tylos and Gerrha in 205 BC (Polyb. 13.9), but, overall, the picture in the Gulf is one of smallish military establishments rather than colonization on any scale.[32] The Arabs of the desert fringe remained independent, but may have had an obligation of military service.[33]

The settlement surveys and Greek foundations considered above constitute a partial picture of Seleukid Mesopotamia. Some regions seem to have benefited at the expense of others, the Seleukeia-Tigris and Diyala areas certainly and probably also the Jazira plain in northern Mesopotamia, the Tigris valley and districts to the east, while the traditional Babylonian heartland may have come out a relative loser. A total population of Mesopotamia during the Seleukid period (311–129 BC) of between four and five million does not appear unlikely.

For comparison, the total population of Iraq in the 1947 census amounted to 4.8 million, plus about a quarter of a million nomads, although probably slightly underestimated.[34]

2. THE UPPER SATRAPIES

All the Iranian territories, from the Zagros eastwards to the borders of India, are included in this region. The provinces of Persis, Karmania and Drangiane comprised a southern band and Media, Hyrkania, Parthia, Margiane, Aria, Baktria and Sogdiane a northern one. Further east, Alexander's Indian provinces and the Kabul valley (Paropamisadai) were lost early on (303 BC), in the settlement with the Maurya Chandragupta, and certainly most, if not all, of Arachosia and Gedrosia.[35]

The 200 kilometre-wide Zagros constitutes the western border of the Upper Satrapies, extending some 1,000 kilometres in a south-easterly direction from the junction of the Armenian mountains with the Elburz range through Media to Persis. It is a land of alternating mountains and valleys parallel to the range axis, with one major transverse valley penetrating the chain, that of the Diyala river, along which ran the important route linking Seleukeia-Tigris to Ekbatana, the capital of Media.

Classical sources depict the relationship of the Achaemenid empire with the peoples of the Zagros as one in which the former paid tribute in order

---

[32] See Salles 1987, Le Rider 1989 and Potts 1990 for an overview of the Persian Gulf in the Seleukid period.
[33] Sherwin-White and Kuhrt 1993: 17–18. [34] D. G. Adams 1958: 40–1.
[35] See Sherwin-White and Kuhrt (1993: 72–90) for a summary of political developments in the Upper Satrapies in the third century BC.

to be allowed to use the through routes, but this is a misunderstanding of the voluntary annual gift-giving practice of the Persian kings in return for a state of peace and the provision of troops.[36] Alexander had tried to make the Ouxioi submit to a condition of tribute (Arr. *Anab.* 3.17.6) and had attempted also to reduce the Kossaioi (Arr. *Anab.* 3.15.2–3), but probably with only temporary success, since Antigonos Monophthalmos was soon compelled to fight his way through against the Kossaioi (Diod. 19.19.2–8). It is questionable whether the Seleukids ever exercised full control over the area, or even wished to do so, given its relative economic unimportance, as long as the roads remained open and contingents of tribesmen could be called upon to serve in the royal army when required.[37]

In **Persis** the Achaemenid settlement pattern in the Persepolis plain has been the subject of a detailed survey,[38] which identified sites with a total area of 675 hectares. It estimated that the population was only 43,600 on the basis of densities of 40 persons per hectare (urban) and 100 persons per hectare (rural), but this appears far too low and, with 200 persons per hectare, the population should be nearer 150,000. In any case, this area represented only the central core of Persis. The evidence of the *Persepolis Fortification Texts* points to numerous storehouses and settlements in the south-eastern part towards Neyriz, the Pasargadai area to the north-east and, especially, the western regions bordering on Elam, as it is referred to in the *PFT*. Elam, a region of hills and valleys, extending as far as the Mesopotamian plain, also seems to have been quite densely populated.[39] This entire region Strabo (15.3.1) characterized as 'all-productive and plain, excellent for the rearing of cattle and abounding in rivers and lakes', contrasting it to the mountainous area to the north and the hot, unproductive seaboard to the south. The 20,000 Persian soldiers recruited by Peukestas from his satrapy for Alexander (Arr. *Anab.* 7.23.1) also point to a substantial population.

In the other regions of the Upper Satrapies, until one reaches Baktria and Sogdiane, there are no extensive site surveys to rely on.

Taking the southern band first, Strabo (15.2.14) described **Karmania** as a large and 'all-productive' country. **Gedrosia**, on the other hand, differed little from the barren coast of the Ichthyophagi. **Drangiane** constituted the fertile region surrounding lake Hamun, well watered by the river Helmand and on the main route from Media through Aria to the Kabul valley and India beyond. This route continued up the Helmand and its

---

[36] Briant 1982a: 81–94.
[37] Sherwin-White and Kuhrt suggest that the arrangement under the Achaemenids was probably confirmed by the Seleukid kings (1993: 17).
[38] Sumner 1986.   [39] Koch 1990: 247–310; Aperghis 1996.

tributary, the Arghandab, into **Arachosia**, a region of hills and fertile river valleys between the Hindu-Kush to the north and the Registan desert to the south.[40] Although population density in these regions may have been generally low, the total area is substantial and the population supported should not be underestimated.

Along the northern band of provinces, only the southern part of **Media** was ever Seleukid, since Media Atropatene had acquired its independence shortly after the death of Alexander. Strabo (11.13.7) wrote that the country was mostly mountainous, but that towards the east it was low-lying and fertile, in which part, Rhagiane, there existed numerous cities and 2,000 villages (11.9.1). Greek cities were established here too, mostly along the main route to the East (11.13.6), and Ekbatana was in the Seleukid period an important administrative centre.

East of the Caspian Gates there is the problem of when the provinces of **Parthia** and **Hyrkania** were lost to the nomadic Parnoi, the later Parthians (ch. 2). **Parthia** was, according to Strabo (11.9.1), not large and, in addition, mountainous and poverty-stricken, but he is here referring only to the northernmost parts. The southern districts of Khorene and Komisene, with the capital Hekatompylos, were clearly different, a string of fertile oases between the mountains and the Dasht i-Kavir desert further south, astride the main route to Baktria and India. **Hyrkania** was a totally different world in the south-eastern corner of the Caspian, 'exceedingly fertile, extensive and in general level, distinguished by notable cities' (Strabo 11.7.2).

Further east lay **Margiane**, centred on its huge oasis and the valley of the Murghab, whose political fate may probably be linked with that of Baktria. The fertility of the oasis was noted by Strabo (11.10.2) and Antiochos I enclosed part of it with a wall 1,500 *stadia* long (roughly 270 kilometres), which works out at some 300,000 hectares of enclosed area.[41] With half a hectare of irrigated area required to support a person (ch. 11.5a), this would indicate a population of about half a million. Antioch-Margiane (Merv), an Alexandria refounded by Antiochos I in the oasis, had an outer fortification enclosing an area of roughly 340 hectares,[42] a huge city of possibly as many as 70,000 inhabitants. A large population for Margiane is thus not unreasonable, as Strabo (11.10.1) calls this province and Aria 'the most powerful districts in this part of Asia'.

---

[40] Bernard considers that Paropamisadai, Gedrosia and Arachosia were lost to the Mauryas before the settlement of 303 BC (1985: ch. 3).

[41] Masson estimates an area of 6000 square kilometres for the Merv oasis, twice as much (1982: 141).

[42] G. Herrmann *et al.* 1993: 41.

South of Margiane was the region of **Aria** on the route to Drangiane and India. The northern districts may have been lost early on to the Graeco-Baktrian kings, but the southern part probably remained Seleukid until the end of the reign of Antiochos III. There is nothing in the way of surveys that could help one estimate its population, but there is Strabo's view above (11.10.1) of its importance.

Furthest east lay **Baktria** and **Sogdiane**, for which a 'low' *effective* date of secession *c.* 246 BC has been considered (ch. 2). The northern border of **Baktria** was traditionally set at the Oxos in ancient sources (Strabo 11.11.2), with Sogdiane extending beyond this river to the Jaxartes. In practice, the area north of the Oxos as far as the Hissar range was, from an economic/cultural point of view, identical to Baktria.[43] Settlement in this wider region was conditioned primarily by the Oxos and its tributaries flowing down from the Hindu Kush, the Pamirs and the Hissar range, and the extensive irrigation networks that relied on these. In some cases the smaller rivers did not have enough flow to reach the Oxos channel and ended up forming oases, as at Baktra (Balkh), while, in between, the semi-arid steppe and mountain piedmonts could support only limited pastoralism.

That Baktria was quite densely populated in the Hellenistic period emerges from classical sources,[44] from archaeological excavation of some major cities, for example Baktra, Aï Khanoum, Termez, Samarkhand and others, and from settlement surveys that have covered much of the Oxos basin.[45]

The foundation of a major Hellenistic city, such as Aï Khanoum, stimulated settlement, irrigation and cultivation nearby, there being nearly 500 rural sites in the Aï Khanoum plain.[46] There appears also to have been a marked increase in settlements in other areas of Baktria, with about 300 sites showing Hellenistic remains, whereas Achaemenid cultural traces are practically non-existent.[47]

The survey information dates mainly to the Khushan period (first century BC onwards), but is useful in quantifying what must have been to a considerable extent earlier developments. Urban sites in the Oxos basin number four large cities of over 100 hectares each, twelve smaller cities of

---

[43] Leriche 1994: 534.

[44] Strabo 11.11.4 for Alexander's reputed foundation of eight cities in Baktria and Sogdiane; Justin 41.4.5 for the '1,000 cities of Baktria'; Strabo 15.1.3 for the '1,000 cities' of the Graeco-Baktrian king, Eukratides (although the term 'settlements' would be more appropriate); Diod. 18.7.1–2 for the Greek colonists who revolted after the death of Alexander and were so many that they could raise 20,000 foot soldiers and 3,000 cavalrymen, but Holt discounts the idea that these settlers were massacred by the Macedonians (1993: 91).

[45] Staviskij 1986.   [46] Gardin and Lyonnet 1978/9: 137.   [47] Lyonnet 1990: 86.

15–80 hectares each and twenty-one towns of 5–14 hectares each, therefore a total urban area of probably not less than 1,000 hectares. The irrigated area centred on these cities and towns is estimated at about 320,000 hectares and contained numerous rural establishments.[48] A more detailed survey of a small part of this region, the Aï Khanoum plain, for the period after Baktrian independence (*c.* 246 BC) yielded an irrigated area of about 100,000 hectares.[49] With approximately half a hectare of irrigated land needed to feed a person, the Oxos basin alone could have supported a population approaching one million.

Further north, there were significant population centres in a number of oases, such as those of Bokhara and Samarkhand, as well as along the left bank of the Jaxartes (e.g. Alexandria-Eschate). The Hellenistic fortifications of Samarkhand (modern Afrasiab) enclose an area of some 220 hectares,[50] suggesting 40,000 inhabitants or more for this city.

A total population can be estimated for Hellenistic Baktria and Sogdiane, together with Margiane, of between one and a half and two million.[51]

It is difficult to arrive at a figure for the remaining Upper Satrapies, since there are no settlement surveys to rely on, but, given the huge area involved, the population was probably several times larger than that of Baktria. For comparison, estimates of Iran's population in the period 1850–1900 range from four to ten million inhabitants, which includes Susiane (Khuzestan), Atropatene (Azerbayejan) and some regions across the Oxos, but not Baktria.[52] Furthermore, a census of 1956 shows a distribution of population, which may be indicative also of that in antiquity, whereby the eastern part of Iran was by no means sparsely inhabited when compared to the western part.[53]

3. NORTHERN SYRIA AND KILIKIA

Northern Syria is situated in a strategic position between the Mediterranean and the Euphrates, west to east, and between Asia Minor/Kilikia

---

[48] Staviskij 1986: 58–9, 101–2. Masson estimates 120 hectares for the fortified area of Baktra (1982: 67).
[49] Lyonnet 1994: 544.   [50] Rapin and Isamiddinov 1994: 548.
[51] Bernard suggests a population for Baktria alone of more than one million in the second century BC (1973: 111).
[52] Momeni 1970: 28.
[53] Momeni (1970: 50, 57) gives populations for different regions of Iran in 1956. Kermanshah, Kordestan, Gilan, Central and Esfahan-Yazd (which roughly correspond to Media less Atropatene): 7.8 million inhabitants (but Teheran is included). Fars-Banader (Persis): 1.3 million, although part of Khuzestan-Lorestan's 2.1 million should be added. Kerman and Baluchistan-Sistan (Karmania and Drangiane): 1.2 million. Mazandaran-Gorgan and Khorasan (Parthia, Aria and Hyrkania): 3.7 million.

and Palestine/Egypt, north to south. It was acquired by Seleukos I after Ipsos (301 BC) and immediately became the focus of his colonizing activities. The establishment of the four major cities of the Seleukis and of other foundations in a region which was hardly urbanized under the Achaemenids undoubtedly gave impetus to rural districts as well, since more area was needed under cultivation to feed the new cities.[54] This remained the heartland of the dynasty until its fall in 64 BC.

Several settlement surveys have been conducted, none very detailed, which concentrate mainly on the northern and central areas, whereas the mountains, coast and south are omitted altogether. The surveys clearly show an increase in the number of settlements and population and an expansion of the settled area eastwards at the expense of the Syrian desert.[55]

The sizes of the Syrian cities are of interest and are discussed in detail in chapter 6.2b. Antioch, Seleukeia-Pieria, Apameia and Laodikeia were all in the 200–300 hectare range, followed by Kyrrhos, Chalkis, Beroia and Seleukeia-Zeugma in the 65–100 hectare range and several smaller foundations.[56] At 200 persons per hectare, these cities would have been planned for more than a quarter of a million inhabitants in total and would have required several times that number in the surrounding rural districts to support them. A Roman census of AD 6 of the *civitas Apamenorum* recorded a population of 117,000 for Apameia, but is unlikely to have reached every inhabitant,[57] whereas the 205–250 hectares of the city itself may have been initially designed for only 40,000–50,000 people. Antioch was the only Seleukid foundation seemingly to have exceeded its planned bounds repeatedly during the Hellenistic period and Strabo (16.2.5) placed it nearly on a par with Alexandria and Seleukeia-Tigris, which could well mean a population of 100,000–200,000 inhabitants by his time (end of the first century BC), or even more. From Antiochos III onwards, northern Syria had very much become the focus of the empire at the expense of Mesopotamia, and population growth, simply because of this, is likely to have continued, albeit at a slower rate.

In the north, **Kommagene** follows the line of the Euphrates. A populous enough region to have later been able to sustain a kingdom of its own, Kommagene may have begun asserting its independence from the Seleukids as early as about 162 BC.[58]

---

[54] Seyrig 1970: 292; Leriche 1987: 57; Grainger 1990a: 27–8.
[55] Matthers *et al.* 1978: 119–23; Grainger 1990a: 15–21, 204–10; Alcock 1994: 181.
[56] Downey 1961; Millar 1987; Grainger 1990a.
[57] Millar discusses the evidence and concludes that the actual population of the territory of Apameia may have been 'several hundred thousand' (1993: 250).
[58] Mørkholm 1966: 107.

In northern Syria, rather than observing shifts of population, as may have been the case with Mesopotamia (to the Tigris-Diyala area) or Baktria (to Aï Khanoum), there are indications of genuine growth from outside and rapid urbanization fuelled by Greek colonization. A significant increase in population is likely, from perhaps as little as half a million in the Achaemenid period to between one and one and a half million by the mid third century BC and perhaps even two million by the mid second century BC, before the loss of Kommagene.[59]

To the northwest, the large, well-watered and fertile plain of **Kilikia Pedias**, washed by the sea and protected by the semi-circle of the Tauros, Anti-Tauros and Amanos ranges, could support a large population in antiquity. A considerable number of Hellenistic cities are referred to in the sources[60] and known by their coins,[61] while a settlement survey has shown dense occupation in the Hellenistic period.[62] In **Kilikia Tracheia** to the west, the larger Hellenistic foundations were restricted to the narrow coastal plains formed by the rivers flowing down from the Tauros, the best-known city being Seleukeia-Kalykadnos.

A population estimate for Kilikia can perhaps be made by analogy with northern Syria, which was substantially inferior in both agricultural area and density of settlements initially, but probably surpassed Kilikia later. A figure of between a half and one million is likely.

4. ASIA MINOR

Seleukid Asia Minor varied in extent from the time of its conquest by Seleukos I after Korupedion (281 BC) to its irrevocable loss following Magnesia (190 BC). At its maximum extent, c. 281 BC, it comprised most parts of the Troad, Hellespontine Phrygia, Mysia, Aiolis, Ionia, Lydia, Karia, Lykia, Pamphylia, Phrygia, Lykaonia and Pisidia. Western and southern districts and major Greek coastal cities were lost to and gained from the Attalids, Ptolemies or usurpers with the fortunes of war, until Antiochos III briefly recovered nearly the entire territory. Southern Kappadokia probably

---

[59] Grainger estimates that nearly half a million new inhabitants moved into northern Syria (1990a: 100). Davies also regards the movement as substantial, but one which should not be exaggerated (1984: 265). Millar goes further, suggesting that a transformation of the map took place (1987: 113).

[60] Cohen 1995: 353–72.

[61] The principal royal mint was that at Tarsos, but mints also operated in some periods at Soloi, Mallos, Alexandria-Issos and Magarsos, as well as at Seleukeia-Kalykadnos in Kilikia Tracheia. Such a scale of coining activity can, in part, be associated with the needs of a large population.

[62] Seton-Williams 1954: 139; Alcock 1994: 181.

acknowledged direct Seleukid rule only to the mid third century BC,[63] while parts of Armenia were subject to Seleukos I, and again later to Antiochos III until Magnesia, and, finally, for a few years to Antiochos IV.[64]

From the mountainous regions surrounding the central Anatolian plateau, major rivers, such as the Kaïkos, Hermos, Kaïstros and Maiandros, flowed west to the Aegean. Smaller rivers exited into the Propontis and the southern Mediterranean coast. These rivers constituted the chief factor in the economic development of the region, with the urban centres concentrated along their valleys and trade routes following their courses to central Anatolia, the Euphrates and beyond.[65]

A survey of the Troad indicates that, immediately after Alexander, the region may have contained about twenty smallish Hellenistic towns with a total population of about 100,000.[66] The reorganization initiated by Antigonos Monophthalmos with the founding of Antigoneia, renamed Alexandria-Troas by Lysimachos, eventually resulted, through synoikisms, in only five or six cities.

A survey of the lower Maiandros flood plain[67] points to rapid urbanization in the interior regions of the Maiandros and its tributaries, which continued through the third and second centuries BC, particularly as the trade route up this valley became the most important. Greek cities were well established by the fourth century BC nearer the coast, but several new foundations were added inland during the Hellenistic period and a number of Karian centres developed *polis* structures. This does not necessarily indicate overall population increase, as many smaller communities seem to have simply been absorbed by their larger neighbours.

The cities in this region numbered at least sixteen in the Hellenistic period and increased to twenty-seven by the Roman, by which time virtually all the land had become part of some city's territory.[68] Only two cities seem to have had a sizable walled area, Tralleis with 140 hectares and Magnesia-Maiandros with 100. The area of each city's territory in the Roman Imperial period has been estimated, as well as the corresponding population, urban and rural, using densities of 125 persons per hectare for urban areas and 30 and 10 persons per square kilometre for arable and non-arable rural areas respectively. The resulting population figures are about 30,000 for Tralleis, 20,000–23,000 each for Magnesia-Maiandros and Tabai, 10,000–20,000

[63] Sherwin-White and Kuhrt 1993: 45.
[64] See Schottky 1989 for Greater Armenia and Media Atropatene to its east.
[65] Magie 1950: 34–52; Cohen 1995. [66] Cook 1973: 363–8. [67] Marchese 1986: 246–51.
[68] See discussion and tables in Marchese 1986: 307–20. The total population figure is derived by taking Marchese's upper estimate for urban population density.

for seven other sites, and smaller populations for the remainder, yielding a total of 180,000. The total population of the survey region in the Roman Imperial period was estimated at 339,000 of which 113,000 was urban; the Hellenistic *poleis* represented about 53 per cent of the total, and native communities that were to acquire *polis* status later, the remainder.

However, if the figure adopted of 200 persons per hectare is used for urban areas (ch. 1.5a), and rural population density is increased to the maximum allowed by the survey – 36 persons per square kilometre – the total population of the region would approach 450,000 inhabitants, Tralleis would reach 43,000, Magnesia-Maiandros 32,000 and Tabai 29,000, while the average population of a city's territory would exceed 15,000.[69]

These population figures are all for the Roman Imperial period. For individual *poleis* they may have differed in the Hellenistic period, as cities expanded or contracted according to their political or economic fortunes. However, it is possible that the total population was not significantly lower.

The two surveys summarized above cover areas of Asia Minor that come up quite frequently in the sources, but constitute only a small part of a very large region. The number of Hellenistic cities in all of western and southern Asia Minor is considerable, numbering at least 100.[70] If the average population of 15,000 for a city and its territory from the Maiandros region is taken as representative, the total population of the area controlled by Greek cities could have been as high as one and a half million. The lower Maiandros basin was apparently heavily urbanized, with Hellenistic cities and their territories containing just over half the population (see above). Other regions, particularly Lykia, Pamphylia, Pisidia, Lykaonia and parts of Phrygia show relatively fewer Hellenistic foundations,[71] so probably had a greater proportion of native populations unattached to cities. Thus, the best estimate for the total population of western and southern Asia Minor in the Hellenistic period lies between three and four million inhabitants.

For comparison, in 1912, this region had an estimated population of not more than six million. Furthermore, 3.2 million Muslims were recorded in a census of 1878, which, with the addition of Christians, would give a total population at the time of the order of four million or slightly more.[72]

---

[69] By way of comparison, Cavaignac estimates populations of the older Ionian cities at 30,000–50,000, based on fleet sizes (1923: 35).

[70] See Cohen for the Hellenistic settlements of the region (1995: 145–351). Older Greek or native cities that were not refounded in the Hellenistic period are not included.

[71] Cohen 1995: 277–351.

[72] McCarthy includes in his estimate the vilayets of Aydin, Hüdavendigar and Konya, and the sanjak of Biga, which extend somewhat more into central Asia Minor than did the Seleukid territories, thus making the estimate somewhat on the high side (1983: 112).

5. KOILE SYRIA

Three parallel bands of territory running north to south constitute this region: (1) a narrow coastal strip widening into small plains, each supporting a Phoenician or Canaanite city, (2) the valley between the Lebanon and Anti-Lebanon ranges changing to the south into alternating hill country and small plains as far as the Negev desert and (3) the Damascus oasis, the Hauran and the less fertile districts across the Jordan shading off into semi-arid steppe.

Starting at the northern end of the coastal strip, each major Phoenician city, Tripolis, Byblos, Sidon and Tyre, controlled a number of subordinate towns and villages and a territory that sometimes extended quite far inland.[73] Further south a similar pattern held for the Canaanite cities: Ake-Ptolemaïs, Dor, Joppa, Askelon and Gaza. Of what was probably the largest city, Tyre, there is mention in Arrian (*Anab.* 2.24.4–5) of the population besieged by Alexander amounting to not less than 38,000, but this is probably indicative of only the city and perhaps its immediate environs, not of all Tyrian territory.[74] Sidon rivalled Tyre in size and Ake-Ptolemaïs was also considered a large city (Strabo 16.2.22, 25). The territory of Joppa could supposedly muster 40,000 men in time of need (Strabo 16.2.28), but this is probably an exaggeration. All told, a population approaching half a million for the coastal strip seems reasonable.

Progressing north in Palestine, new settlements appeared in Idumaia in the Hellenistic period, influenced by the development of trade through Gaza, while Marisa grew into an important centre.[75]

For the hill country of Judaea, centred on Jerusalem, a population estimate can be made based on the recruitment capability of the Jews at times of emergency during the later phases of the Maccabean revolt (152–143 BC), which was about 30,000–40,000 (1 Macc. 10.36, 12.41). Allowing for some male adult non-combatants, the total population of Judaea has been estimated at not less than 200,000[76] in an area of some 2,400 square kilometres, of which only about two-thirds is cultivable, which would indicate a relatively high population density and explain the Diaspora and the Hasmonean expansion as some form of release. Jerusalem itself, despite its prominence in literary sources, must have been rather small and poor, located off the main coastal and inland trade routes.[77]

---

[73] Grainger 1991: 5–12.
[74] Avi-Yonah estimates 40,000 inhabitants for Hellenistic Tyre (1978: 223).
[75] Berlin 1997: 6–8.   [76] Bar-Kochva 1977: 167–70.   [77] Berlin 1997: 8–9.

The Seleukid general Nikanor is said to have estimated that he could raise the 2,000 talents still owed to the Romans after Magnesia by enslaving the Jews of Judaea and selling them at ninety persons to the talent (2 Macc. 8.10–11). This would require 180,000 prisoners. Presumably Nikanor had a fair idea of the total population (head taxes having been applied in Judaea in this period) and could make allowances for those who would be killed or would escape. So a maximum figure of a quarter of a million for Judaea does not appear unreasonable.

Samaria shows evidence of colonization and some population growth in the early Hellenistic period, as witnessed by the establishment of the Macedonian colony of Samaria. In the western part, the 1,200 or more field towers of the Seleukid period identified in site surveys have been associated mainly with wine production, but also storage generally, perhaps one tower to a military settler family. These field towers, the numerous oil-press installations and the well-developed rural road system have been taken as indications of a flourishing market economy for wine and olives down to Hasmonean times, when there is some evidence of abandonment of settlements.[78]

In inland Galilee, archaeological survey shows a complete absence of early Hellenistic sites, perhaps because much of Galilee may have belonged to the king himself as royal land.[79] A sudden expansion of settlements dates to the second century BC.[80] On the borders of Galilee and in the Golan, the establishment of Greek cities such as Skythopolis, Philoteria, an Antioch and a Seleukeia point to some economic development of this area, whose natural outlet to the sea was at Ake-Ptolemaïs, the capital of the province of Koile Syria-Phoenicia, but population probably still remained low.[81]

East of the Jordan, the establishment of a chain of Macedonian military colonies, as a breakwater against nomadic incursions from the desert, probably led to some population increase in this sparsely inhabited region, but this is not noticeable in a number of surveys from this area.[82]

The overall picture for inland Palestine from surveys and literary evidence points to a population of not more than half a million.[83]

---

[78] Applebaum 1986: 258; Dar 1986: 248–53; Berlin 1997: 10–11.   [79] Applebaum 1986: 259.
[80] Meyers, Strange and Groh 1976: 8; Alcock 1994: 182.
[81] Freyne 1980: 104–38; Berlin 1997: 12–4.   [82] Alcock 1994: 183.
[83] Arav records only somewhat more than 200 Hellenistic sites that have been surveyed in this area, with cities tending to be small, as measured by fortification perimeters, e.g. Samaria 2.5 kilometres (30–40 hectares), Philoteria 2.75 kilometres (35–45 hectares), Jerusalem 1.7 kilometres (about 20 hectares) (1986: 190, n. 250). Broshi considers that a peak population of about one million was reached in Palestine only by c. AD 600 (1979: 7).

For comparison, an Ottoman census of 1877–8 for Palestine showed 441,000 inhabitants, including the coastal districts, but excluding those east of the Jordan. This had risen to 772,000 by 1914–15.[84]

Further north, in southern Syria, the valley between the Lebanon and Anti-Lebanon ranges (Beka'a) was described by Strabo (16.2.16) as 'fertile and all-productive'. To its east lay the Hauran, a fertile district, and the oasis of Damascus, 'accorded exceptional praise' (Strabo 16.2.20). This ancient city had probably served as the Achaemenid satrapal centre, but in the third century BC lay too near the contested border dividing Ptolemaic Koile Syria from Seleukid northern Syria and its economic importance may have been somewhat reduced. For southern Syria, a population not exceeding half a million seems reasonable, which would give a total of one to one and a half million for all of Koile Syria.

6. A DIFFERENT APPROACH TO POPULATION

Any estimate of ancient populations is likely to be a hazardous one. What has been attempted above using settlement surveys and some literary sources is probably open to much disagreement. However, when assessing an economy, a population estimate is a necessary step and an approximate figure better than none. If population can now be approached in an independent way and the results turn out to be similar, there will be more confidence in them.

a. Achaemenid tribute

A possible source for comparative populations in the Seleukid empire is the tribute list for the Achaemenid empire given by Herodotos (3.89–95). The tribute assessment no doubt took into account, in a general way, the productivity of the land, its natural resources and the extent of industry and trade, but all these factors lead in the end to a certain size of population that could be supported.[85] True, we do know that Artaphernes measured the

---

[84] McCarthy gives the following population figures in 1877–8: 232,645 for the sanjak of Jerusalem, i.e. mainly Judaea, 128,530 for the sanjak of Balga-Nablus, i.e. mainly Samaria, and 79,675 for the sanjak of Ake, i.e. mainly Galilee (1990: 7–10).

[85] When discussing Media, Strabo compares it with Kappadokia and notes that the tribute paid to the Persians seemed to be in proportion to the 'size and productivity of each region' (τῷ δὲ μεγέθει καὶ τῇ δυνάμει τῆς χώρας) (11.13.8). Population is also essentially proportional to the area and supporting capacity of the land. Thus, Strabo can be taken to imply that tribute is proportional to population.

land in Ionia in 493 BC and levied taxes on this basis (Hdt. 6.42), and the
Murašu Archive from fifth-century BC Nippur also points to an Achaemenid
cadastral survey in a part of Babylonia about 500 BC.[86] Yet land area, by
itself, cannot have been the dominant factor, as on that basis Egypt would
have paid a tribute of roughly 270 drachms per square kilometre, Lydia 75
and Ionia 65.[87] Clearly Egypt was agriculturally far more productive and
so supported a denser population, which justified the much higher tribute
assessment.

I will assume then that the Achaemenid tribute was *roughly proportional*
to population and use the tribute given by Herodotos for each of the twenty
nomes (3.89–95). When a nome cannot be identified geographically by its
peoples, their association with others serving in the same contingent in
Xerxes' army (Hdt. 7.62–80) may help to locate them in adjacent regions.[88]

The Asia Minor nomes I, II and III paid respectively 400, 500 and
360 Babylonian talents, but included Thracians of Asia (= Bithynians),
Paphlagonians, Mariandynians (around Herakleia) and Syrians (= Kap-
padokians),[89] peoples who lay outside the limits of the Seleukid empire. If
these are excluded, the total tribute from western and southern Asia Minor
probably amounted to about 1,000 talents.

Nome IV contained only Kilikia and was assessed for 500 talents, of
which Darius received only 360 as tribute. Kilikia has a considerable area
and this nome may also have comprised Kommagene.[90]

Northern Syria, Koile Syria and, probably, Cyprus were included in
nome V and paid 350 talents, or perhaps 300 talents, or even less, without
Cyprus. In the Achaemenid period northern Syria was apparently little
developed in comparison to what it later became when the major Seleukid
cities were founded there (section 3 above). For this reason, the greater part
of the tribute from this nome is assumed to have come from the Phoenician
cities, Damascus and Palestine, so perhaps 250 talents from Koile Syria and
only 50 from northern Syria.

Egypt and Kyrene comprised nome VI, and were assessed for 700 talents, with the lion's share undoubtedly coming from Egypt, so perhaps 650
talents. The problem is how to deal with the other item of royal revenue
mentioned by Herodotos (2.149), namely the proceeds from the fisheries
of Lake Moeris, amounting to 240 talents annually (or 360 talents in Diod.
1.52). No doubt the Persian king acquired revenue from his properties in
all satrapies in addition to tribute, as will be seen for the Seleukids in

<hr>

[86] Stolper 1974: 52–3.   [87] Andreades 1933: 92.   [88] Burn 1984: 120–6.
[89] How and Wells 1989: 282.   [90] How and Wells 1989: 282.

chapter 8.1–2, and therefore the revenue from Lake Moeris should be discounted in any comparisons of tribute between satrapies.

Nome VII is associated with the Gandarians and other tribes in north-western India, outside Seleukid territory.[91]

Nome VIII, covering Susiane and the territory of the Kossaians to the east, referred to as Elam in the *Persepolis Fortification Texts*, contributed 300 talents, or perhaps 150 talents for Susiane alone, bearing in mind the significant population indicated for Elam in the *PFT* (section 2 above).

Mesopotamia, excluding Susiane, is represented by nome IX and yielded 1,000 talents.

Nome X, containing Media, was subject to 450 talents, but this included Media Atropatene, an important region, which was never Seleukid, so perhaps 300 talents for the remainder.

Nome XI is associated with the Kaspians and other tribes and contributed 200 talents in tribute. Perhaps this region covered the southern shores of the Caspian Sea and may have included Hyrkania, although it is curious that the Hyrkanians are not specifically mentioned here by Herodotos, but nor are they mentioned anywhere else in the tribute list.[92]

Baktria in nome XII was assessed for 360 talents, but perhaps extended north of the Oxos to the Hissar range.[93]

Nome XIII covers the region between the Black Sea and the Caspian, outside Seleukid territory.

Nome XIV mentions the Sagartians, the Sarangians and the inhabitants of the Erythraean Sea, amongst others. With a rather large assessment of 600 talents, this nome may have comprised most of Persis (probably apart from a tribute-free core), Karmania and Drangiane along with parts of Oman and the islands of the Gulf, which, if excluded, could bring the tribute down to perhaps 500 talents.

Nome XV is associated with the Sakai of the extreme north-east, outside Seleukid territory.[94]

Nome XVI mentions the Parthians, Sogdians, Arians and Chorasmians and 300 talents of tribute. If the Chorasmians are excluded, the tribute may come down to perhaps 250 talents.

Nome XVII includes the Parikanians and the Ethiopians of Asia and a rather large tribute of 400 talents. The latter people are associated with the contingent from India in Xerxes' army (Hdt. 7.70) and this nome may

---

[91] How and Wells 1989: 283. [92] How and Wells 1989: 284.
[93] How and Wells 1989: 284. [94] How and Wells 1989: 285.

have covered Arachosia[95] and Gedrosia, as well the much more populous lower Indus, all outside Seleukid territory after 303 BC.

The Matienoi in nome XVIII are associated in Xerxes' army with the Paphlagones (Hdt. 7.72), and the Mares in nome XIX with the Kolchoi (Hdt. 7.79). Both nomes may thus be located in northern Asia Minor, outside Seleukid territory.

Finally, nome XX is clearly the upper and middle Indus region, outside Seleukid territory.

It will be assumed that relative amounts of Achaemenid tribute between regions are *approximate* indicators of relative populations. Even allowing this to be true, it would apply, strictly speaking, to about 500 BC, and the situation in the Hellenistic period might not have been the same if the rate of change of population had differed significantly from region to region. Except for northern Syria, however, no other region provides any indication that such may have been the case, although shifts of population within regions are indeed noted, for example to the Tigris and Diyala in Mesopotamia or to Aï Khanoum in Baktria.

To move from relative to actual populations, it is possible to use Egypt as a point of reference, since the number of its inhabitants at different times has been recorded in a variety of sources.

b. The population of Egypt

Diodoros (1.31.6–9) mentions that 'in times past' the population of Egypt was seven million inhabitants (ἑπτακοσίας μυριάδας) and in his own time (mid first century BC) not less than three million (καθ᾽ ἡμᾶς δε οὐκ ἐλάττους εἶναι τριακοσίων), while Josephus (*BJ* 2.385) provides a figure of seven and a half million, excluding Alexandria, for the second half of the first century AD. Since it has been difficult to reconcile these two wildly different figures, and one manuscript omits the τριακοσίων, most editors have emended it to τούτων somewhat arbitrarily and translated Diodoros as 'in our times not less than this (i.e. the figure in times past)'.

However, it has been plausibly argued that a population of seven million or so for Egypt is completely wrong for the Hellenistic period and that it probably grew from about three to three and a half or three and three quarter millions in the first hundred years of Ptolemaic rule.[96] The main arguments are as follows:

---

[95] Vogelsgang 1985: 79–80.

[96] The argument has been developed by Rathbone, who also estimates a maximum of five million inhabitants in the Roman period (1990: 104–13). He is supported by Bagnall and Frier 1994: 54–6.

(1) Since all the Diodoros manuscripts, apart from M (a secondary codex), give the population in his time as not less than 300 myriads, one cannot ignore them.[97]

(2) Early nineteenth-century figures include an estimate of two and a half million by one of Napoleon's officers in 1808 and four and a half million from the census of 1847–8.[98]

(3) Estimates in the 1880s put the total land in cultivation then at about 25,000 square kilometres. If this figure is also taken as a maximum for antiquity, it would provide a carrying capacity of, at the very most, five million inhabitants (on the basis of half a hectare of irrigated land per person).[99]

If Egypt (without Kyrene) paid 650 talents in tribute and Mesopotamia (with Susiane) 1,150 talents, the population of Mesopotamia should have been, in the same proportion, five to six million compared to Egypt's three to three and a half.[100] Similarly, populations of other regions should have been as shown in table 4.1 below, in column 3.[101]

But Scheidel considers five to seven million for the Roman period more likely (1999: 322) and Lo Cascio would accept even a figure of eight million then as feasible (1999: 163). Other scholars also seem to discount the high figures of Diodoros and Josephus, e.g. Cavaignac, with five or six million inhabitants for Egypt under Darius I (1923: 2) and Beloch, with not more than five million under Tiberius (1886: 258). Préaux, however, adopts a high estimate and calculates revenue on the basis of a population of six or seven million in the Ptolemaic period (1969: 48).

[97] This is accepted by Lo Cascio, who then goes on to argue that, since Diodoros' figures must have been based on official information, a *laographia* (census) of adult males only is implied for the three million. Thus the total population should be more in line with Josephus' figure (1999: 158–60). In my view, this argument will not stand. In the text, Diodoros is clearly referring to total population in both the earlier period and his own and essentially comparing the two figures, as he does the number of villages in the two periods. It is not impossible, however, that Diodoros may have based the estimate for his own time on a census of adult males and then extrapolated from it.

[98] Scheidel 1999: 315–16 and Lo Cascio 1999: 163 consider that these early nineteenth-century figures are underestimated, but will not venture beyond five and a half and four and three-quarter million respectively by 1850.

[99] Scheidel quotes an inscription of Ptolemy V, which gives a total of 24,800 hectares of cultivated land in Egypt, thus essentially supporting Rathbone (1999: 319). Lo Cascio argues that Rathbone has underestimated both the cultivated area and the wheat yield, which would result in higher carrying capacity (1999: 164–71). However, to reach his estimated population of eight million for Roman Egypt, rather than Rathbone's five million, a somewhat unlikely 60 per cent increase is required in a combination of these two parameters.

[100] A final argument against a population of seven million for Egypt is that, by comparing Achaemenid tributes of the two regions, Mesopotamia should have had a population exceeding twelve million, which is totally at odds with the results of site surveys.

[101] Cavaignac estimates populations under Darius I: six to eight million for the three Asia Minor nomes (1923: 34), three to four million for northern Syria and Koile Syria (1923: 17), five million for Babylonia and 600,000 for Assyria (1923: 24). Beloch estimates four to four and a half million for western Asia Minor, two million for Asia Minor south of the Tauros, i.e. Kilikia, two to two and a half million for Bithynia and Phrygia in the second century BC (1886: 242), seven million for northern Syria and Koile Syria in the first century BC (1886: 252), six to eight million for

Table 4.1 *Estimated population of the Seleukid empire by region (in millions)*

Region	Achaemenid tribute	Population from tribute	Population from surveys
Egypt	650	(3–3.5)	3–3.5
Mesopotamia, with Susiane, but not Elam	1,150	5–6	4–5
Baktria, Sogdiane, Margiane	360	1.5–1.75	1.5–2
Media	300	1.25–1.5	(1–1.25)
Persis, Karmania, Drangiane and Elam	650	3–3.5	(2.25–2.75)
Parthia, Hyrkania, Aria	250	1–1.25	(0.75–1)
Northern Syria	50	0.25–0.5	1–1.5–2
Kilikia	360	1.5–1.75	0.5–1
W. and S. Asia Minor	1,000	4–5	3–4
Koile Syria	250	1–1.25	1–1.5
Total of Seleukid territories	4,370	18.5–22.5	15–20

7. TOTAL POPULATION

The population figures derived from Achaemenid tribute match the results of site surveys and literary sources reasonably well, with the exception of northern Syria, which must have experienced a huge increase in population in the Seleukid period due to the establishment there of a capital and other major cities and the associated emigration of Greeks and others to this area. The difference for Kilikia may be due to a lack of territorial correspondence between the Persian and Seleukid satrapies. In column 4 of table 4.1 final population estimates are provided by region, where brackets represent figures obtained by using Mesopotamia's population from surveys scaled down in proportion to the tribute of the two regions. A maximum population of between fifteen and twenty million inhabitants is indicated for the whole area that was at some time part of the Seleukid empire.

Taking into account the political fate of different territories (ch. 2), figure 4.1 shows the range within which the total population of the Seleukid empire is likely to have varied over time.[102]

Mesopotamia and Susiane at the end of the Persian period (1886: 250–1) and a sparse population on the Iranian plateau (1886: 252). These seem to me to be unwarrantedly high estimates.

[102] Given the historical background (ch. 2), reasonable assumptions about levels of Seleukid control are:
  Mesopotamia, incl. Susiane: 100% 311–140 BC; 50% 140–129 BC (partial loss to Parthians).
  Baktria, Sogdiane, Margiane: 100% 306–246 BC (then loss to Graeco-Baktrian kings).
  Media: 100% 306–150 BC (then loss to Parthians).

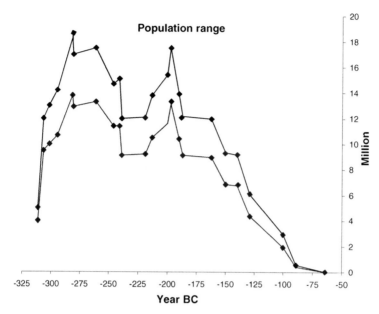

Figure 4.1 Estimated population of the Seleukid empire over time

A peak of fourteen to eighteen million inhabitants was probably achieved *c.* 281 BC, immediately after Korupedion, and another just short of this immediately before Magnesia (190 BC), with the conquest of Koile Syria, the temporary reconquest of the eastern provinces and much of western and southern Asia Minor by Antiochos III and the growth of population that had meanwhile occurred in northern Syria. The critical moment for the empire, with regard to population, was not Magnesia and the loss of Asia Minor, but the far more serious loss of Mesopotamia and the East

Persis, Karmania, Drangiane, Elam: 100% 306–187 BC; 50% 187–150 BC (partially held until loss to Parthians).

Parthia, Hyrkania, Aria: 100% 306–246 BC; 30% 246–187 BC (partially held until loss to Parthians).

Northern Syria: 100% 301–246 BC; 90% 246–219 BC (temporary loss of Seleukeia-Pieria); 100% 219–162 BC; 90% 162–89 BC (loss of Kommagene); 20% 89–64 BC (loss to Tigranes and then Rome).

Kilikia: 100% 294–280 BC; 90% 280–246 BC; 0% 246–241 BC (full Ptolemaic control); 90% 241–197 BC; 100% 197–89 BC.

Western and southern Asia Minor: 100% 281–280 BC (conquest of Seleukos I); 70% 281–261 BC; 80% 261–239 BC; 0% 239–213 BC (loss to Antiochos Hierax, Attalids and Achaios); 40% 213–197 BC; 90% 197–190 BC (reconquest of Antiochos III); 0% after 190 BC (loss after Magnesia).

Koile Syria: 100% 200–140 BC; 90% 140–129 BC; 50% 129–100 BC (loss of Judaea and most Phoenician cities); 10% 100–64 BC (retained mostly Damascus area).

to the Parthians by 129 BC. For comparison, Alexander's empire included, in addition, Egypt and Kyrene, north-western India and the satrapies bordering on it, parts of northern and central Asia Minor, Media Atropatene, southern Armenia and, finally, Macedonia and Thrace, with a population probably totalling twenty-five to thirty million inhabitants.[103]

These population figures will be useful in assessing such matters as the level of income of the Seleukid administration and will be correlated with other evidence in chapter 12.

[103] Avi-Yonah (1978: 219) and Green (1990: 371) estimate a rather high 30 million inhabitants for the Seleukid empire. For comparison, Andreades, quoting Meyer, gives 50 million for the Persian empire (1933: 91), Hammond 1,650,000 for the kingdom of Philip II (1992: 167) and Hopkins 54 million for the Roman empire at the beginning of the reign of Augustus (1980: 118).

CHAPTER 5

Production and exchange

In order to understand how the Seleukid kings derived their revenue, it is necessary to describe briefly the more important elements of the underlying economy of the empire: agriculture, animal husbandry, the exploitation of natural resources, industry and trade. There is room here for no more than a superficial treatment.[1]

I. AGRICULTURE

a. Types of farming

Subsistence farming seems to have been the basis of the economies of most regions of the Near East in antiquity. Except for the Mediterranean seaboard, where trade may also have played a not insignificant role, it is likely that agriculture was the dominant productive activity in the Seleukid empire.[2] In ps.-Aristotle's *Oikonomika*, revenue accruing to the satrapal economy from agriculture is described as 'the first and most important' (ch. 7.1e).

Essentially two types of agriculture were practised: irrigation-based and dry-farming. The former was the norm in areas with insufficient rainfall but traversed by large rivers. The Euphrates and Tigris and their tributaries, and the canals that branched off these, could bring water to most parts of the Mesopotamian plain, while Seleukid-period irrigation networks in

---

[1] Useful for agriculture in the Near East are several articles that have appeared in the *Bulletin of Sumerian Agriculture*, e.g. Charles on irrigation (1988), cereals (1984), legumes and oil plants (1985), onions, cucumbers and the date palm (1987) and traditional Iraqi crop husbandry (1990); Gallant 1985 on sesame and linseed, Halstead 1995 on the use of the ox-drawn plough; Hepper 1987 on gums and resins; Willcox 1987 on trees and shrubs. See also Postgate for the agricultural resources of Mesopotamia (1992: 157–72) and Mieroop on 'feeding the citizens' of the Mesopotamian city (1997: 142–75).

[2] Davies considers that at least 80 per cent of the population in the Hellenistic world was employed in agriculture (1984: 271), while Spek estimates 80–90 per cent for the ancient Near East (2000b: 28).

Baktria, drawing from the Oxos and its tributaries, extended pre-existing systems.[3] The oases scattered throughout the East could be provided for in this way, but sometimes water was obtained by tapping distant sources and conducting it underground to the area to be irrigated, so as to minimize evaporation, for example the *qanat* systems of north-eastern Iran (section 3e below). Characteristic of the eastern parts of the Seleukid empire were, however, vast areas with insufficient rainfall for agriculture on any scale.

Along the Mediterranean seaboard and for some distance into the interior, depending upon the morphology of the terrain, rainfall was sufficient to permit dry-farming to be practised. This was also possible in the hilly areas skirting the main mountain ranges: the Tauros and Anti-Tauros, the mountains of southern Armenia, the Zagros, the Elburz and the Hindu-Kush, and also in the mountain plateaus and valleys. Persis, for example, was described by Strabo as 'very fertile' (15.3.1).

No doubt, in some dry-farming areas, irrigation supplemented the water supply, for example from the Maiandros river in western Asia Minor, the Orontes in northern Syria or the Kur in the Persepolis plain.

b. Produce

Cereals were the staple of the ancient Near Eastern and Mediterranean diets, and in the Seleukid empire the main crop, as in mainland Greece at this time, seems to have been barley rather than wheat. Under dry-farming conditions, barley can grow wherever the minimum annual rainfall is more than about 20 centimetres, whereas wheat requires not less than 30 centimetres, which is seldom exceeded in the Near East.[4] Irrigation can, of course, provide an adequate water supply most of the time, but in Mesopotamia, for example, the dissolved salts carried down for centuries by the great rivers from the surrounding mountains had increased salinity in the soil to such an extent that wheat could only grow with difficulty, whereas barley had no such problem and was also able to withstand disease better. There is no direct evidence for other irrigated areas, but increased soil salinity is likely to have been a general problem wherever there were elevated temperatures and consequent high rates of evaporation, as in much of the Middle East.

---

[3] Lyonnet 1994: 543–4.

[4] Braun refers to wheat-growing in the alluvial valleys of western Asia Minor, lowland Kilikia and upland Lykia (1995: 32–3). Inscriptions from Asia Minor sometimes provide evidence for home-grown wheat, e.g. Document no. 6, the Laodike letter, but, more often, are simply indicative of a dietary preference of the Greeks, which was often satisfied by importing wheat from outside the region.

Characteristic of irrigated cereal cultivation is its much higher productivity. This is principally due to the water supply, which is not only more plentiful but can also be directed to the crops at the right time. The potential this offers of a greater yield (ratio of harvest to seed) can then be realized through more labour-intensive cultivation practices, which involve direct sowing in narrowly spaced furrows, for example by means of a seed-drill, and careful weeding, while the greater density of planting also inhibits weed growth. Whereas barley yields in the Mediterranean dry-farming world were normally around five or six to one,[5] those in irrigated Mesopotamia were much higher. In late sixth-century BC Uruk, yields of as much as thirty to one are noted,[6] while thirteen or fifteen to one, or even more, can be deduced at Nippur from the *Murašu Archive*.[7] Even in the first century BC, Strabo could declare that the crops of barley in Mesopotamia were larger than in any other country, 'three hundredfold, they say' (16.1.14), although he clearly did not believe such a high figure. Still, it might not be too rash to suggest that Mesopotamian barley yields were roughly twice as high as those of the Mediterranean, apart from Egypt.[8]

The importance of high barley yields in Mesopotamia, and those other areas of the Seleukid empire where large-scale irrigation agriculture could be practised, was considerable from the point of view of the governing power. Since cereals probably provided as much as 65–75 per cent of a person's nutritional requirements,[9] less cultivated land was required to support a person where the yield was higher. Compared to the approximately 1 hectare per person of Mediterranean dry-farming conditions, probably 0.5 hectares would suffice in, say, Mesopotamia or along the Oxos or in the Merv oasis (ch. 1.5a). But since the additional labour to cultivate a given plot of land was only somewhat greater than that required for dry farming, it was possible not only to feed more people, but also to generate a larger surplus, if the available labour was utilized to the full. Taxation by a governing power could provide the motivation to cultivate more intensely and, since the potential surplus was large, the level of taxation could be correspondingly so. As will be seen in ch. 8.1f, the level of taxation on grain in Seleukid Mesopotamia may have been as high as 50 per cent. Conversely, one would expect that in the Mediterranean provinces, where the potential surplus from dry farming was smaller, taxation on grain would have been correspondingly lower.

What applied to barley also applied to other cereals, of which a variety was grown, but none had the economic importance of barley. Conditions

---

[5] Garnsey 1988: 95; 1992: 148.   [6] Cocquerillat 1968: 29.   [7] Stolper 1985: 138.
[8] See Potts on land and agriculture in Mesopotamia (1997: 6–86).
[9] Foxhall and Forbes 1982: 71; Gallant 1991: 68, 72; Reger 1994: 87; Garnsey 1998: 230.

in western Asia Minor allowed more wheat to be cultivated, and this was the preferred staple for the citizens of Greek cities, barley being 'poor man's food'. But most wheat was obtained through imports, mainly from Egypt and the Black Sea region, and poor local harvests or difficulties in the supply of imported wheat frequently produced shortages.

In the Mediterranean provinces of the empire, the other major products of agriculture were the olive and the grape. Olive oil served as the main element for the preparation of food and for lighting and was also used extensively for body care and in the manufacture of perfumes and ointments. In the interior, these roles were played by sesame. Wine was, of course, dear to the Greeks, and attempts were made to introduce viticulture in regions where they had established themselves, for example in Susiane and Babylonia (Strabo 15.3.11). Vine growing was also more profitable than cereals, yielding up to five times the revenue on the same land.[10] In the Near East, the date provided an alternative food staple, which could be consumed both fresh and dry and which could be called upon at times of barley shortage,[11] but the date also served to produce an alcoholic drink, as Xenophon noted (*Anab.* 2.3.15). Finally fruit, in great variety, was a product equally of the Mediterranean and of the interior,[12] although no single kind had anything like the importance of the products that have been mentioned above.

From the point of view of the Seleukid administration all these fruit-like products of agriculture, typically referred to in the sources as *xulinos karpos* (literally 'woody produce'), were of interest, as they could be taxed. Given that their production was less labour-intensive than for grain, it was possible to extract a greater part of the crop as tax and still leave sufficient to the producer to satisfy his own needs (ch. 8.1f).

Naturally, additional revenue could be generated if the area of cultivation were increased or more valuable products grown, and there is evidence that the Seleukids attempted to do both. Seleukid-period irrigation systems have been identified in Baktria,[13] while the *qanat* system of Iran was, at least, maintained.[14] But, what is more important, the new city foundations, scattered across the empire, undoubtedly intensified agricultural activity in

---

[10] Pastor 1997: 27, for Egypt.
[11] Vargyas 1997: 339–41. Poyck notes that in a survey of villages in modern Iraq in 1960, 25.6 per cent of the calorie intake was provided by dates and only 40.8 per cent by cereals (1962: 68, table 4.22).
[12] Several types of fruit, some of which cannot be identified, are noted in the *Persepolis Fortification Texts* as being produced, stored and distributed in the region of Persis (Hallock 1969).
[13] Lyonnet 1994: 543–4.
[14] Sherwin-White and Kuhrt 1993: 70. See also Briant 2001 for the *qanat* system, as well as a more general discussion of irrigation and drainage in antiquity.

their vicinity (ch. 6.2e). Regarding agricultural innovation, one may note the reputed attempt by Seleukos I to introduce exotic products, *amomum* and *nardum*, and perhaps cinnamon, from India (Pliny, *HN* 16.135).[15]

2. ANIMAL HUSBANDRY

The conditions for large-scale animal husbandry do not seem to have been favourable in much of the territory of the Seleukid empire, since the raising of animals in numbers requires extensive natural pastures, such as existed in only a few areas, of which the best known are the uplands of Media, where the famous Nissaean horses were reared. The Jazira plain in the shadow of the Anti-Tauros and the mountains of southern Armenia also provided suitable conditions, as did a few areas of inland Asia Minor or northern Syria. In the Zagros, the Elburz, the Hindu-Kush and their foothills, on the other hand, local transhumance may have been an important activity to set beside small-scale farming in the upland valleys, but it was extremely difficult for an imperial power to control these areas and lay its hands on their production, as Antigonos had found to his cost when simply attempting to traverse the region (Diod. 19.19.2–8).[16]

In the Near East, apart from the mountain ranges and their foothills and the land dedicated to agriculture, the remainder, which is probably the greater part, is classified as semi-arid steppe. It is suitable for small flocks of sheep and goats that could provide a subsistence living for nomadic or semi-nomadic populations. To any imperial administration these resources may not have seemed significant enough to have been worth the cost and trouble of exploiting energetically for taxation purposes.

In agricultural areas, the use of animals was probably common. Oxen were required for cultivation, but it is likely that a yoke covered the needs of several cultivators, since the expense of maintaining it with feed-grain must have been prohibitively expensive for the small farmer. The *Murašu Archive* gives us the information that plough animals and equipment were rented in Babylonia for as much as 30 per cent, or more, of the grain crop.[17] In other areas, the horse might be used for ploughing, a cheaper, but far less effective solution. The pack-animal *par excellence* in the ancient Near East was the ass, but camels were also reared for long-distance trade and service as baggage-animals in the army.

Most farmers probably possessed a few sheep and goats for their basic needs in milk products and wool, as is common practice today in the

---

[15] Rostovtzeff 1941: 1164–5.   [16] Briant 1982a: 94–112.   [17] Stolper 1985: 128–30.

region, but larger flocks could probably survive in the vicinity of settled communities, living on natural vegetation and the stubble of grain fields in the right season. In Mesopotamia, in particular, the periodic flooding of the rivers produced stagnant pools of water in low-lying areas, whose surroundings, although not suitable for the growing of crops, could provide enough greenery to support small animals and, rarely, cattle. For the Seleukid tax-collector these flocks and herds, attached as they were to settled communities and therefore more easily accessible, may have constituted a worthwhile target for the application of a tax. But, if the order of satrapal revenues in ps.-Aristotle's *Oikonomika* is significant (ch. 7.1e), that from animals was fifth in importance, which would fit in well, for the Seleukid empire, with what has been considered above as the *relative* unimportance of animal husbandry compared to agriculture and the difficulty of assessment and collection of any tax.

3. NATURAL RESOURCES

In the *Oikonomika* (2.1.4), revenue from natural resources belonging to the king is given second place in the satrapal economy, probably attesting to its importance. The items mentioned there, as examples, are gold, silver and copper and then 'whatever is available in any particular place'. Clearly, precious metals ranked foremost, followed closely by copper, with its dual function of a utility metal and an ingredient of coinage. One is left to deduce from the sources what other natural resources may have been of interest to the Seleukid kings.

a. Precious metals

The evidence for gold and silver deposits in Seleukid territory is slight, and one has only a vague and incomplete picture of the metal resources of the empire.[18] Every ingredient required for producing coinage was present, however, and it may be that the quantities of gold and silver were sufficient to maintain a 'replacement coinage', as the initial 'Alexanders' wore out or were lost from circulation (ch. 11.4).[19]

Gold is mentioned by Strabo in Karmania (15.2.14) and southern Armenia (11.14.9), while the gold dust brought down by the Paktolos near Sardeis had run out by his time (13.4.5) and little remained in the mines

---

[18] Forbes 1950: 150–2, 188–98; Treister 1996: 290, 293.
[19] Bogaert 1977: 380; Sherwin-White and Kuhrt 1993: 63.

of the Troad (13.1.23). On the north-eastern border of the empire, the land of the Massagetai apparently possessed 'gold in abundance' (11.8.6). Indeed, the mint of Baktra produced more series of gold coins than any other (ch. 11.3a), suggesting a link with this source or perhaps with Siberia.[20]

There were probably important silver mines in Baktria and Sogdiane, but the evidence comes from the seventh century AD and later. However, it is difficult to imagine that the important Seleukid mints at Baktra and Aï Khanoum and those of the Graeco-Baktrian kingdom produced their fine and extensive silver coinages without a local source of precious metal.[21] Silver mines are mentioned by Strabo in Karmania (15.2.14), but there were deposits elsewhere in Iran in antiquity, although whether any were mined in the Seleukid period is unknown. Asia Minor seems to have been quite rich in silver ore, and accessible to the Seleukids at some time would have been the mines of the Tauros in northern Kilikia, probably mentioned in Hittite and Neo-Assyrian sources and still operational today, and those in the Troad and on Mount Tmolos in Karia.[22]

b. Other metals

Copper is present throughout the Near East. Syria and Palestine certainly possessed deposits, as did Oman, and there is reference to copper mining in antiquity, although none specifically in the Seleukid period.[23] Further east, Strabo mentions Karmanian copper mines (15.2.14), and Afghanistan as a whole may have been a rich source, but the evidence is all later. The land of the Massagetai bordering on the north-eastern provinces is noted by Strabo (11.8.6) as possessing 'copper in abundance', while in Asia Minor important copper deposits, that may have attracted the attention of the Seleukids, are concentrated in Armenia and the Tauros region.[24]

Tin, necessary to produce bronze, seems to have been mined in Drangiane (Strabo 15.2.10), but whether this was sufficient for the needs of coinage cannot be determined. Imports from Spain and Cornwall, serving the Mediterranean basin, are likely to have found their way to the mints of Syria or Kilikia just as easily as imports from the East.[25]

What seems to emerge from this review of probable sources of currency-producing metals is that there may have been very few in the heartland of the Seleukid empire, that is, Mesopotamia and northern Syria. As long as the outlying provinces could be controlled, a limited supply was available,

---

[20] Mørkholm 1991: 4.   [21] Bopearachchi 1991.   [22] Jesus 1978: 100–1.
[23] Forbes 1950: 300–3; Treister 1996: 290.   [24] Jesus 1978: 98–9.
[25] Forbes 1950: 241–4, 254–5; Treister 1996: 355–6.

but probably only to 'top-up' the existing quantities, essentially the Persian bullion captured by Alexander.[26] Once these 'mining' provinces had been lost, recourse was necessary to an uncertain favourable balance of trade, but more so to stored bullion in both the royal treasury and 'private' possession, hence possibly the spate of 'temple-raiding' by the later Seleukid kings (ch. 8.8b).

Iron seems to have been the one metal of which there may have been no shortage. Iron ore was present in several parts of Asia Minor (the Troad, Lydia, Karia, Lykia and Phrygia) and especially in the Tauros range. Syria and Palestine were also provided with a number of deposits and so was the East (Media, Persis, Karmania, Aria and Baktria).[27] Of the other major metals, lead was essentially to be found in the galena ore from which most silver was extracted.

As to the control of these metal sources, there is no direct evidence that proves royal ownership, but this must be highly likely, at least for the precious metals. Using his position of absolute power, it would be natural for the Seleukid king to exploit the mines for his own benefit, as Philip II had done in Macedonia with Pangaion earlier or as the Romans were to repeat later in Spain.

c.   Wood

The sources indicate that the Seleukids controlled valuable stands of timber in Asia Minor and elsewhere. For the rebuilding of Sardeis, after the damage sustained during the siege and retaking of the city by Antiochos III (213 BC), the king authorized that timber be cut from the forests of Taranza, presumably on Mount Tmolos (Document 9). Shortly afterwards, the Jews were authorized to acquire tax-free timber from the royal forests of the Lebanon and other places for the rebuilding of the Temple of Jerusalem, in order to repair the damage that it had suffered during the fifth Syrian War (Document 12). One reason for Ptolemaic interest in southern Asia Minor was clearly the timber available there for shipbuilding, while, much later, Antony granted the forests of Kilikia Tracheia to Kleopatra (Strabo 14.5.3), suggesting that they may always have been royal property. Similar motivation probably attracted the Attalids to the region of Mount Ida in north-western Asia Minor, although the precious metal mines there also undoubtedly played a role.

Good construction wood was in short supply in the populous Mesopotamian heartland of the empire, where the date-palm had to serve

[26] Golenko 1993: 77.   [27] Forbes 1950: 385–7.

as the ubiquitous building material for beams and lintels, bridges and quays, and, hollowed out, to channel water, but was unsuitable for making planks.[28] However, an adequate supply of timber was available in the Zagros 'in the countries of the Kossaioi and other tribes' (Strabo 16.1.11) and it is likely that the Seleukid kings controlled, if not the supply, at least the import of this wood to Mesopotamia.

And one should not forget the trees grown in the *paradeisoi* of the Achaemenid kings, scattered throughout the empire, which were, no doubt, inherited by Alexander and, after him, the Seleukid kings.[29]

d. Salt

Salt was a vital commodity in antiquity for the preservation of food and for human consumption.[30] One might switch in need from one staple to another, for example from wheat to barley or barley to dates, but water and salt were irreplaceable. Salt was produced from brine, seawater, rock salt and the ashes of certain plants.

Not all areas possessed salt. Along the coasts, there was normally no problem, as salt pans could easily produce whatever was necessary, but it was difficult for an administration to monitor this production. When Lysimachos had tried to impose a salt tax in the Troad, the demand for salt in the region mysteriously disappeared (Athenaios 3.73d), suggesting that the inhabitants, with the sea nearby, had easy recourse to small-scale salt-making operations, which were difficult to detect.

Inland, the situation was different. Mesopotamia was fortunate in that it possessed huge salt resources. Rock salt was present in the 'salt hills' mentioned in ancient texts,[31] but, what is more important, the Euphrates and Tigris and their tributaries carried with them dissolved salt in high concentration. When they overflowed, briny lakes and salines formed in low-lying areas where, because of the compacted fine-grained silt and high water table, the water could drain away only very slowly and evaporation in the hot Mesopotamian sun produced crystalline salt. Palmyra, towards the end of the Seleukid period, began building its commercial prosperity on a trade in salt, while, much later, in Ottoman Iraq, *c.* 1890, twenty state-owned salines yielded many thousands of tonnes annually.[32]

Elsewhere, there was almost certainly salt production from the Dead Sea, but one may reasonably hypothesize that wherever in the eastern regions of

---

[28] Cocquerillat 1968: 31.   [29] Briant 1996: 456–8.
[30] Potts notes a (modern) requirement of about 6 grams of salt per person daily, when living on a mainly vegetable diet in a temperate climate (1984: 229).
[31] Potts 1984: 235.   [32] Potts 1984: 236–43.

the empire there existed a combination of river, oasis or lake together with a hot climate, evaporation would leave behind residual crystalline salt, to be collected and used, although, of course, rock salt may also have been present.

Salt, because of its vital importance to the human diet, was a likely candidate for control by the Seleukid state.

e. Water

The main natural resource in Mesopotamia was water. The Persian king is known to have owned important canals and leased water from these to farmers through a distinct branch of the administration, the evidence coming from the *Murašu Archive* (ch. 1.4d). It is not unreasonable to suppose that Alexander, and after him the Seleukid kings, inherited this key factor of Mesopotamian agriculture, which might explain Alexander's concern to repair the Babylonian canal noted by Arrian (*Anab.* 7.21).[33]

Much of Iran relied on *qanats*, underground tunnels to save on evaporation, leading from aquifers to the land to be irrigated.[34] The Persian king had controlled many of these, if not all, and charged a price for their use (Hdt. 3.117; Polyb. 10.28).

From elsewhere, there is no specific information, but it is likely that large irrigation networks, expanded and maintained by the royal administration in Baktria or Margiane or any other arid region that possessed a vital source of water, would be treated as a royal monopoly.[35]

f. Special products

Wherever a special product existed of some commercial or strategic value, it is possible that the Seleukid kings would wish to exploit it directly. For example, dry asphalt, used for construction and boat-building, was present in Mesopotamia and Susiane (Strabo 16.1.15) and also in the Dead Sea, where its gathering at certain times of the year had been entrusted by Antigonos Monophthalmos to Hieronymos of Kardia (Diod. 19.100.1–2), suggesting royal control at the time. Balsam was only to be found on 'paradises' (*paradeisoi*) near Jericho associated with a palace (*basileion*) (Theophrastos, *Hist. pl.* 9.6; Strabo 16.2.41).[36] A *porphurikon* tax on the

---

[33] Spek gives references in cuneiform sources to the Seleukid interest in the Babylonian irrigation system (2000b: 29).

[34] Beaumont, Blake and Wagstaff 1976: 88–92.   [35] Briant 1980: 93.

[36] Rappaport, Pastor and Rimon regard this as pointing to Achaemenid royal estates initially, which were probably taken over by succeeding rulers (1994: 76–7).

valuable purple dye produced from murex shells suggests particular royal interest (ch. 8.2e).

4. INDUSTRY

a. Production for basic needs

Every city and town certainly had its craftsmen, catering for the daily needs of the urban population and, to some extent, the surrounding countryside. This was a normal part of the symbiotic relationship between an urban centre and its dependent rural areas. Even in large villages, basic crafts must have been practised, such as pottery, masonry, carpentry, textile working, metalworking, although much work would be done by individual householders.[37] Fundamentally, however, the urban economy was founded on a transformation of agricultural products, for example the production of amphorae for oil or wine, the manufacture of ploughs and harnesses.[38]

Given the high level of urbanization in many parts of the empire, by which I mean the large proportion of dwellers in cities and towns of over 2,000 inhabitants – for example the 55 per cent or more in Mesopotamia, as indicated by settlement surveys,[39] or the possibly comparable figure in northern Syria in the later Seleukid period – it is likely that the number of craftsmen working for the local market was large and their output significant. Given the very small scale of most operations, however, and their execution on an almost daily basis, it must have been almost impossible for the administration to monitor them closely enough so as to impose a tax on production, unlike agriculture, where the harvest could be measured fairly reliably once a year, which explains why there is no evidence of a tax on artisan production. Rather, it may have been simpler to impose a head tax on producers, the *cheironaxion* referred to in ps.-Aristotle's *Oikonomika* (chs. 7.1c; 8.6).

b. Production for export

In a few cities there is evidence of production of specialized goods that reached a wider regional or international market. The Babylonian cities were famous for their textile industry, mainly furnishings and woollen clothing; the latter may appear surprising, but temperatures drop considerably in winter in Mesopotamia and frost is not uncommon. Borsippa also manufactured linen in large quantities (Strabo 16.1.7).

---

[37] Sartre 1995: 72.   [38] Sartre 1995: 74.   [39] R. McC. Adams 1965: 63; 1981: 178.

The initial spate of pottery imports from the old Greek world soon died out as production became decentralized.[40] Seleukeia-Tigris, for example, developed workshops that, to begin with, imitated western prototypes, but then developed in original directions, modifying western shapes and functions and combining them with a traditional Mesopotamian stock of commonware, glazed ware and high-quality egg-shell ceramics. After a while, western imports became rare.[41]

A number of cities or regions had become well known for certain products in the Roman period, for example purple stuffs and dyes from Tyre, glass from Sidon, linen from Kilikia, Syria and Phoenicia and textiles from Asia Minor[42] and it is possible that much of this reputation was earned earlier, in the Seleukid period.

There is no evidence in any of these cases that the Seleukid kings attempted to exercise control over industry. Whether they possessed their own royal workshops, as the Ptolemies and Attalids did, is unknown. Certainly, the Achaemenids before them operated royal workshops, as the *Persepolis Fortification Texts* amply demonstrate,[43] and it is not unlikely that the Seleukid kings did also, at least for the basic needs of their courts.

5. TRADE

a. Local trade

Much trade was probably local, with a triangular pattern linking three participants: an urban centre, its rural hinterland and the representatives of the administration in the area, such as provincial or district governors, financial officials, garrisons. Figure 5.1 below illustrates a rather simple model of the flows of foodstuffs, urban products, services, money and taxes in one part of the economy, that based on exchange using silver, where the thicker lines indicate the more important flows.

In this economy, the rural areas sold food to urban centres and the administration and only spent a relatively small part of their silver earnings on the purchase of urban products and services or in rents to urban dwellers.[44] Most, if not all, of the silver they had received was soon returned to the administration in rents and taxes. The urban centres probably earned more

---

[40] Davies 1984: 275.   [41] Valtz 1993: 169–74, 180.
[42] Jones 1974: 145; Sartre 1995: 74.   [43] Briant 1996: 440–2.
[44] As a parallel, Hopkins considers that in Roman Italy only a very small proportion of a peasant's income was used to purchase manufactured goods in towns (1978: 18).

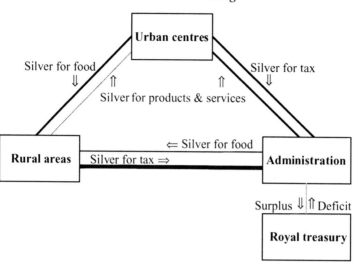

Figure 5.1 A simple model of local trade using silver as its medium of exchange

by supplying the administration with products and services than they did by supplying the rural areas, and these earnings served to pay for their food and taxes. The administration, finally, paid for food, products and services with taxation receipts, and any silver surplus was accumulated in royal treasuries, to be used on occasions when expenditure was higher than normal, for example in order to finance a major military campaign (ch. 11.5). Naturally, both urban centres and rural areas also conducted some trade using silver internally.

The direct evidence for the pattern of local trade described above is slight, but, nevertheless, revealing. In Mesopotamia, for example, a Seleukid garrison in Babylon was paid in silver (ch. 10.1e). In the city's markets, where the garrison might reasonably have been expected to spend its pay, six commodity prices were regularly quoted in silver (section 6a below). Groupings of agricultural fiefs (*hatrus*), which were presumably among those that supplied the city's markets, were required to make tax payments in silver already in the Persian period (*Murašu Archive*, ch. 1.4d) and so why not peasants in the Seleukid? The cycle is complete: administration to garrison in the urban centre to peasant and back again to the administration. The question, of course, is how prevalent this pattern was in the Seleukid empire. There is, unfortunately, no answer that can be based on sufficient source evidence. However, one may reasonably suppose that what went on in Babylon *could* have occurred anywhere else. But see also chapter 6.2, on Seleukid city-building, and chapter 11, on coinage, for a continuation of the discussion.

A parallel commodity-based economy undoubtedly existed, in which town- and city-dwellers and the king and members of the administration, who were owners of rural land, received food from land they managed themselves or leased to tenants for rents in kind. The temples of Babylonia were, for example, probably the largest landowners after the king in Mesopotamia and fed their numerous personnel partly with produce from their agricultural estates. Likewise, a substantial part of the agricultural production of royal land may have gone towards feeding members of the administration and army. In this economy, the outflow of food from rural areas was not balanced by anything tangible, but rather the 'service' of providing a living, peace and security.

It has been suggested in chapter 3 that the Seleukid kings made strenuous efforts to shift rapidly from a commodity-based economy to a silver-based one, for the reasons given there, but one must recognize that, throughout the Seleukid period, both economies operated in parallel. In some regions, notably the Mediterranean coastal provinces and Mesopotamia, the silver-based economy may have come to predominate (chs. 11.4–5; 12.5).

There is no evidence in the sources for the volume of local trade. If the triangular model described above is correct, it must have been more substantial in highly urbanized regions, such as Mesopotamia, northern Syria, Kilikia and coastal Asia Minor, where cities and towns required their food supplies. If, say, the degree of urbanization was about 50 per cent, as in Mesopotamia (ch. 4.1) – which means that half the population lived in cities and towns with over 2,000 inhabitants – then half the agricultural produce of the countryside needed to be transferred to some town or city to be consumed there. This does not mean, of course, that this produce was sold in its entirety in urban marketplaces, since some urban dwellers certainly cultivated their own land and consumed or bartered their produce.[45] Naturally, the larger the urban centre, the greater the trade to be expected with the countryside, and also internally and with the administration, since, presumably, a large city could generate greater flows of goods and services than a small town, particularly as it is likely to have been serving as an administrative centre as well.

[45] Hopkins considers that in much less urbanized Roman Italy at least four families in the countryside fed a fifth in a town (1978: 15). Reger argues that Hellenistic cities strove to live on the production of their hinterlands (1994: 4). Indeed, in the view of Davies, most agricultural produce was consumed locally, within a radius of 30 kilometres (1984: 270–1).

Local trade was the perfect vehicle for silver to be collected by the governing power. As will be seen (ch. 8.1, 7), tax rates on agriculture were probably high, as much as 50 per cent of the value of the crop, which means that the peasant was compelled to sell a great deal of his produce in order to collect the necessary silver to pay his taxes. This put pressure on him both to create a large surplus and then to dispose of it in city and town marketplaces.

b. Intra-regional trade

Intra-regional trade includes, in theory, all exchange within a particular region, but here only that part will be considered that cannot be covered by the definition of local trade given above, thus essentially the trade between urban centres within the region.

The existence, to any significant extent, of this form of intra-regional trade depends mainly on three factors: low transport cost, a certain diversity of products and a relative instability of supply across the region. High transport costs definitely inhibit trade, although they do not prevent it, but, even when transport costs are low, one of the other two factors must normally be present.

Mesopotamia is a good test case. Trade within Babylonia and Susiane relied almost entirely on the network of rivers and canals, which facilitated the transport of bulk agricultural goods. Because of the low gradient of the major rivers and slow current, sailing or rowing upstream would not have presented a serious problem, especially on the Euphrates, except at times of flood or very low water levels. So transport costs were probably low and local agricultural produce could easily be brought to towns and cities. Yet neither of the other two factors was present, as there was almost complete uniformity of agriculture and industry across the region and, since Mesopotamia depended on the water of the great rivers for irrigation, a high or low flow affected all areas more or less equally. Thus a good or bad harvest was likely to be region-wide rather than local, which is not to say that all areas would be equally affected when the harvest was poor, since some might possess adequate reserves and others not. In such cases, this could lead to a certain amount of intra-regional transport of commodities. But, overall, one cannot consider Mesopotamia a good candidate for intra-regional trade[46] and the situation in the Oxos basin in Baktria might be considered similar.

---

[46] Le Rider suggests that commerce was not so active between Seleukeia-Tigris and Susa until the reign of Antiochos III, when the increase noted is probably due to long-distance trade by way of the Gulf (1965: 299). McEwan notes that there is no evidence that the Babylonian temples, for all their wealth,

A different situation held in the Mediterranean coastal area that was at any time Seleukid, stretching from the Hellespont to the borders of Egypt. Here too there was no great diversity of agricultural produce (mainly cereals, olive oil and wine) or manufactured goods, with those exceptions already noted, but transport by sea was relatively cheap and there was a certain instability of supply. Since this was a dry-farming region, the amount of rainfall and its timing during the growing season dramatically affected the quality of the harvest. Thus one area might experience a glut in a particular crop, while its immediate neighbours suffered a dearth, so the right conditions were present for some intra-regional trade.

In the inland areas of the empire, where there were no river systems to facilitate transport, the movement of bulk commodities would have been expensive and was probably quite restricted. Whatever intra-regional trade existed is likely to have involved more specialized products and operated on a relatively small scale.

The overall conclusion is that, apart from a very significant local trade between urban centres and their rural hinterlands, trade within regions may have been restricted to a few specialized products, if they existed, and the satisfying of temporary local shortages, particularly in coastal cities.[47]

c. Inter-regional trade

The same factors that have been discussed above for intra-regional trade apply equally to trade between regions. Again, high cost of land transport was the main inhibiting factor for the movement of bulk commodities, although it did not prevent essential goods from being carried, whereas for relatively lightweight, luxury articles, transport costs would present no obstacle.

For example, Mesopotamia had no metals or good timber. Traditionally, metals had been imported from the Tauros, Oman and the mountains of Armenia, while timber was available relatively close at hand in the Zagros. To balance these imports, Mesopotamia had always exported textiles and the products of metalworking.[48] No sources inform us that these exports

were engaged in commercial enterprises (1981a: 199). Only one text (Beaulieu 1989: no. 3) mentions allocation of silver by the Bit Reš temple at Uruk to merchants, but this could just as easily have been for the purchase of goods needed by the temple.

[47] M. H. Crawford argues that, when the surplus needed for taxation is large, relatively small volumes of goods move from one area to another if unconnected with the needs of the state (1987: 41). Berlin points out that, although Phoenician semi-fine ware was distributed inland, the demand probably came from Phoenicians settled in these areas (1977: 84–5).

[48] Potts 1997.

continued in the Seleukid period, but one may reasonably suppose that
they did, for how else would Mesopotamia have obtained its vital supplies
of metal and wood, since it is unlikely to have been able to export agricultural products in bulk (ch. 12.3a)? There is also some evidence for fine
Mesopotamian pottery exports to adjacent regions, such as the island of
Failaka in the Persian Gulf.[49]

Another possible item of inter-regional trade for Mesopotamia was wool.
Given the very large sedentary population, its need for woollen clothing
and the difficulty of maintaining flocks in the cultivated areas, it is very
likely that trade was conducted with nomadic herders in the semi-desert
fringes and also with the populations of the Zagros, who practised animal
husbandry on a large scale and obviously needed a suitable market for their
produce.

What applied to Mesopotamia must have been to some extent true of
other populous agricultural areas bordering on mountainous regions or
semi-arid steppe, in both of which types of terrain animal husbandry could
be practised and a symbiotic relationship set up with the agriculturalists.
Since much of the Seleukid empire exhibited this alternation of plains and
oases with mountains and deserts, it is likely that such a relationship was
common and provided for trade between adjacent regions, for example
Kilikia Pedias and the Tauros, northern Syria and the Syro-Mesopotamian
desert to the east, Rhagiane in eastern Media and the Elburz to the north,
the Dasht-i-Kavir desert to the south. In all these cases there is likely to
have been some inter-regional trade, but mostly between adjacent symbiotic
regions and so relatively short-distance.

Turning now to the old Greek world, its manufactured products initially found their way to the East, but most were soon replaced from local
workshops (section 4b above), although some speciality items continued
to filter through.[50] Neither is a trade in consumables much in evidence,
to judge from the very few stamped amphora handles that have been
found.[51]

There is only one area where inter-regional trade may have had both
greater importance and a longer carry and that is in the Mediterranean
coastal regions. This has already been discussed for intra-regional trade,
influenced by low transport costs and the variability of supply and demand.
The movement of ships along the coast, with all types of goods for sale,

---

[49] Hannestad 1984: 75.   [50] Rostovtzeff 1941: 1206.
[51] Börker notes that only forty stamped amphora handles have been found in all of Mesopotamia,
compared to hundreds at Mediterranean centres (1974: 46).

including bulk commodities,[52] has been described as a kind of 'Brownian movement' in which traders constantly sought out the latest areas of high supply and demand, so as to transport the desired goods between the two.[53]

d. Long-distance trade

When dealing with long-distance trade, one must first consider the major trade routes that crossed the empire, bringing high-price products from the East to the markets of the Mediterranean, with some naturally being dropped off for sale along the way.[54]

The principal land route from India and the one from Baktria and Central Asia (later to become the Silk Road) came together at Artakoana in Aria (near Herat), skirted the Dasht-i-Kavir desert on the north, crossed the Zagros by way of Ekbatana and arrived at Seleukeia-Tigris. A secondary land route from India, but more difficult, reached Susa after traversing Arachosia, Drangiane, Karmania and Persis, and continued on to Seleukeia-Tigris.[55]

The sea route from India along the coast of Baluchistan and into the Persian Gulf had already been in use for centuries by the Seleukid period and was in the hands of Arab traders, the port of the city of Gerrha (perhaps Thaj) seemingly its main terminus.

From southern Arabia, two caravan routes brought frankincense and myrrh to market, as well as products that originated from East Africa, principally ivory. The first route ran up the western side of the Arabian peninsula to the Phoenician ports and Gaza and, until the conquest of Palestine in about 200 BC, was well beyond the reach of the Seleukids and only served Egypt and the Mediterranean. The second caravan route cut across the Arabian desert to Gerrha, which thus became a nodal point for both Indian and Arabian trade.[56]

From Gerrha and its port there were two main possibilities: a caravan route across the Arabian/Syrian desert to the Phoenician ports or a sea route to the upper reaches of the Persian Gulf where a Seleukid port,

---

[52] See Casson on the grain trade (1984: 70–86) and Bogaert for wine, oil, salted fish, salt, honey, dried fruit, nuts, wood, pitch, firewood, works of art, slaves and metals (1977: 377–81). Davies considers that the slave trade of some Hellenistic cities was not marginal, even before the 160s BC, while trade in the eastern Mediterranean generally showed an increase in the Hellenistic period (1984: 282–3). Sartre notes the wine exports from Asia Minor to Egypt (1995: 77).

[53] Salles 1991: 213.

[54] See Rostovtzeff (1941: 1243–8) and Bogaert (1977: 385–7) regarding routes and products of the eastern trade; also Jones for the Roman period (1974: 143). Indian products included spices, indigo and precious woods and stones.

[55] Le Rider 1965: 306.   [56] Potts 1990: 85–98.

Alexandria, later Antioch-on-the-Erythraean Sea, had been established. A sea-going vessel could continue up the Euphrates, Tigris or Eulaios as far as Babylon, Seleukeia or Susa respectively (Strabo 16.1.9)[57] or unload onto river transports, which could reach Thapsakos on the Euphrates (Strabo 16.1.11), but it is likely that the bulk of the goods were transported by caravan to Seleukeia-Tigris, which almost certainly became the greatest trading centre (*emporion*) in the East. A less used route was by caravan up the coast from Gerrha to the Euphrates and then onwards. It seems that the Gerrhans must have preferred the caravan route to Gaza that bypassed Seleukid territory and, presumably, customs duties and tolls. Perhaps it took the naval expedition of Antiochos III in the Gulf in 205 BC to compel them to redirect part of their lucrative luxury trade to the Seleukid empire (Polyb. 13.9).

From Seleukeia-Tigris the goods collected from Arabia and India travelled west to Antioch and thence to Laodikeia and Seleukeia-Pieria for Mediterranean destinations[58] or traversed Asia Minor to arrive at the Aegean ports, principally Ephesos and Smyrna.

The volume of this eastern trade through the Seleukid empire has possibly tended to be exaggerated, certainly before Antiochos III captured more of it.[59] There is perhaps a tendency to confuse the large-scale operation of the Roman period, especially after the sea route to India came into regular use in the first century AD, with what went on before.

An indication of the magnitude of the eastern trade may be given by the output of the mint created at Antioch-on-the-Erythraean Sea in the reign of Antiochos IV, which was probably intended to serve it. The volume of coinage, as measured by the total number of obverse tetradrachm dies that may have been used there over about thirty-five years, was relatively small, averaging slightly less than one and a half dies per year, or just under 30 talents-worth (ch. 1.6b).[60] Naturally, coins from other mints, Seleukeia-Tigris, Antioch, Susa, would also have been utilized for eastern purchases, and, of course, one does not know how many. However, one wonders

---

[57] Le Rider notes that the Seleukids linked Susa to the sea and attributes the city's prosperity mainly to eastern commerce (1965: 267); also Boucharlat 1985: 76.

[58] Seyrig believes that the prosperity of northern Syria was based on the enormous profits of this trade (1970: 292), which I question.

[59] Shipley accepts that long-distance trade was probably increasing in this period, but only accentuating existing trends. Commerce was not the main concern of the Seleukid kings (1993: 283).

[60] Mørkholm records 23 obverse dies from 37 tetradrachm specimens from Antiochos IV to the first reign of Demetrios II (1970: 31). Using the method described in chapter 1.6b and discussed more extensively in chapter 11.5, the best estimate for the total number of obverse dies used is 48.0, with 95 per cent confidence limits of 23.7 to 87.2. With the best estimate, the total value of coinage produced in thirty-five years at Antioch-on-the-Erythraean Sea was only worth about 960 talents.

how much all this might have amounted to for the royal economy, despite customs duties and tolls all the way to the Mediterranean (ch. 8.3, 4), compared with the 4,000 or more talents annually that the king probably earned from agriculture in Mesopotamia alone (ch. 12.3e). It is perhaps significant that the mint at Antioch-on-the-Erythraean Sea was opened to help to promote trade with the East at a time when traditional Seleukid revenues had taken a dip after Magnesia and the loss of Asia Minor and because of difficulties in the remaining eastern provinces (ch. 2).

Another indicator is provided by an analysis of bronze-coin finds at Susa, which showed no more than 10 from Seleukeia-Tigris for each of the earlier reigns, followed by a sudden increase to 314 under Antiochos III, dropping to 109 under Seleukos IV, 49 under Antiochos IV and rapidly thereafter. Since bronze probably shows the movement of merchants, not merchandise,[61] this pattern fits the hypothesis of the coercion of the Gerrhans by Antiochos III for more of the eastern trade and also points to its relative unimportance earlier.

Of course, by the time that any eastern luxury goods had reached the Mediterranean, apart from those dropped off on the way, the prices had become significantly inflated by the administration's various exactions (ch. 8.3, 4) and the profits of all the carriers and middlemen. Local economies on the way undoubtedly profited, particularly those of clearing-house cities and ports, but most areas were probably left quite untouched.

From a global point of view, considerably more silver probably entered the Seleukid empire in receipts as a result of its exports of eastern trade goods, than was expended in their purchase. A positive balance of trade overall is indicated by the fact that very little Seleukid coinage has been found in other regions, whereas much foreign currency apparently circulated inside the empire, as evidenced by coin hoards (ch. 11.4).[62]

6. PRICES

Commodity prices in the Seleukid empire are of interest because they enable one to determine the value in silver of many different types of transactions, such as a grant of grain to a city, a soldier's rations or even the total agricultural production of a satrapy, as the basis for tax assessment. At the same time, a comparison of prices with those of the Mediterranean region can show to what extent the Seleukid economy was integrated or not with the rest of the Hellenistic world.

---

[61] Le Rider 1965: 446–7.   [62] Mørkholm 1984: 105.

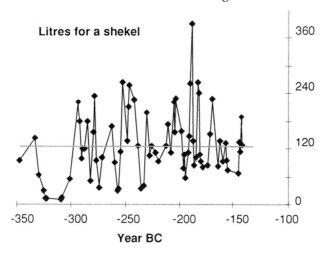

Figure 5.2 Barley prices

a. The evidence of the Babylonian Astronomical Diaries

These valuable texts have already been discussed in ch. 1.4a. Prices at Babylon for five agricultural commodities and wool were recorded for much of the Seleukid period as so many *sut* (= approximately 6 litres) or, in the case of wool, as so many *mina* (= approximately 0.5 kilograms) that one could buy for 1 shekel of silver. There is frequent mention of a market, suggesting that these were indeed market prices.[63]

A good way to look at prices is with a series of graphs, covering about 200 years, from *c*. 350 BC to *c*. 140 BC, that is, from the late Achaemenid period down to the end of the Seleukid in Mesopotamia. To facilitate matters, *sut* have been converted into litres and *mina* into kilograms.

Each graph does not represent price but the *inverse* of price, that is, how many litres or, in the case of wool, how many kilograms one could buy for 1 shekel of silver. When the graph goes up, prices come down. Though this may be inconvenient for the general reader, it is in fact the way in which prices are usually expressed in documents from the ancient Near East. Note that one Babylonian shekel weighed 8.3–8.4 grams, or almost exactly two Attic drachms. Since there is a range of prices in some years, the graph is

[63] Slotsky 1992; 1997; Vargyas 1997: 34; Spek 2000a: 295–7; also Grainger 1999. Temin 2002 has subjected the price data to a sophisticated statistical analysis and concludes that the 'random walk' pattern of prices reflected in the *Astronomical Diaries* cannot be explained other than by the workings of a market.

considered to pass through the mid-point of this range. Although this is an approximation to the average, it is good enough for present purposes, since any tendency to be above the average one year will be counterbalanced by being below it another year and, over the ninety years in the Seleukid period for which there are data, this should even out. In any case, one is not interested in individual figures, but the overall trend. Finally, the continuous price line is only intended as a visual aid, since, obviously, one does not know the prices in years for which there are no data.

What strikes one immediately are the very high prices for **barley** in figure 5.2 (lows on the graph) recorded in five years between 325/4 BC and 307/6 BC. But if one investigates the years in question, one finds that in each there is likely to have been a serious disturbance in Babylon at the time. In many cases the *Diaries* themselves confirm this.

Thus, in May 325 BC (*Astronomical Diary* -324) prices shot up and the market was actually closed for a time. This may be connected with the doings of Harpalos, Alexander's boyhood friend and treasurer in Babylon, who became notorious for his extravagances and later fled in early 324 BC, with whatever he could lay his hands on (Diod. 17.108.4–6). After Alexander's death in Babylon in 323 BC, the Macedonian cavalry blockaded the city in order to impose its will on the infantry, thereby creating a food shortage. Once the succession issue had been resolved, troops and supplies were collected at Babylon to suppress the revolt of the Greek settlers in Baktria and then one enters upon the continuous warfare of the early period of the Successors. Between spring 310 BC and late 308 BC Seleukos fought for his survival in Babylonia against Antigonos Monophthalmos. The so-called *Diadochi Chronicle*[64] tells us of the devastation suffered by the region, which Antigonos ravaged as enemy country.

So between 325/4 BC and 307/6 BC there exist data for five years, with barley prices seriously distorted by political events. There is no knowing what the prices may have been in the intervening years, but they are also likely to have been high, in the climate of war and uncertainty. If one ignores the affected years, however, one is left with an underlying price trend for barley which is surprisingly flat for 200 years, at about 120 litres for a shekel of silver, equivalent to 60 litres for an Attic drachm, which means that the price of an Attic *medimnos* of 51.8 litres would have been nearly 0.9 Attic drachms.[65] Anything below or above this probably reflects the impact of a

---

[64] Grayson 1975: no. 10.

[65] The long-term stability of prices is also noted by Aymard (1938: 25). Slotsky 1997 has performed a computer analysis on the price data using regression analysis, which has resulted in two conclusions: (a) that there was a long-term downward trend in prices in the Seleukid period and (b) that there was little evidence for price seasonality during the year. Both conclusions are, in my view, incorrect.

good or bad harvest, with prices generally tending to drop after the harvest (about the first month of the Babylonian year or, roughly, April), but the short-term fluctuations are enormous. The reason for this is probably the general shallowness of the Babylonian market, which made it more volatile to supply and demand. If much of the grain crop was reserved in a bad year by the great landowners (the king and temples, principally) for their retainers, this could leave very little for the market, with the result that prices would tend to rise sharply. A spate of such bad years could produce a dramatic effect on price. Indeed, figure 5.2 seems to show mid-point prices rising in steps from one level to a higher one as the shortage apparently becomes acuter, before a succession of good harvests allows the price to drop again. It is interesting that the very low prices in certain years are often noted in months seven and eight, which may coincide with a possible second barley harvest in Babylonia, when a sharp drop in price is to be expected.[66]

Note that the average price of barley was the same both immediately before and a short time after the conquest of Alexander. It has been suggested that the release onto the market of the accumulated Achaemenid treasure, valued in the sources at 180,000 talents of silver or more,[67] produced price inflation. For the Mesopotamian staple, barley, at least, there is no evidence of such inflation, if the extremely high prices in the late- and post-Alexander period can be attributed to war and unrest alone, as I believe. It was suggested in chapter 3 that the Achaemenid bullion probably did not find its way into the pockets of Babylonians as coinage, but mainly into those of Macedonian veterans and Greek and Balkan mercenaries, who did most of their spending much further to the west, in the Aegean world.

Firstly, Slotsky included in her data the extremely high prices of the last quarter of the fourth century BC, which I have argued were aberrations due to serious disturbances in or near Babylon. Any mathematical method would undoubtedly show a decreasing trend from these very high prices. Secondly, a mathematical method looking for seasonality would be searching for a pattern appearing regularly every twelve months. The Babylonian calendar, however, was lunar, with a shorter year of about 354 days, which means that the harvest season could shift between the twelfth, first and second months of the year and the periodically interposed intercalary thirteenth. Thus a computer-aided search for a harvest occurring regularly in a particular month would be unlikely to find it.

[66] There is only circumstantial evidence for such a second barley harvest. Firstly, low mid-year barley prices are recorded in the *Diaries* in years 203/2 BC, 190/189 BC, 188/7 BC and also 183/2 BC, when the price is even less than that immediately after the main harvest. This obviously could have occurred for other reasons, e.g. because of dumping of stored barley onto the market by the great producers (Spek 2000a: 297–8), but this would be more likely at a time of high price. Secondly, the expression that is used with the price for month eight of year 204/3 BC, notably that the barley was 'very good', is unlikely to be describing more of the same crop that had appeared at the start of the year, following the main harvest, unless this had been further refined before sale, e.g. after removal of the husks.

[67] A total of 180,000 talents-worth of gold and silver is said to have been collected eventually at Ekbatana from the different Persian treasuries (Strabo 15.3.9).

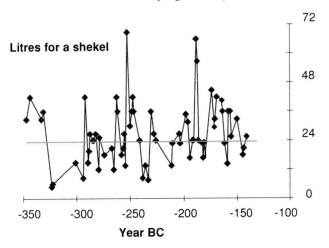

Litres for a shekel

Figure 5.3 Sesame prices

Other abnormally high barley prices in the *Diaries* are probably evidence of trouble in or near Babylon, but one may also be seeing the occasional crop failure and the *Diaries* do refer to famine and locust attacks from time to time.

Sesame (figure 5.3) behaved in much the same way as barley, with an underlying price of about 24 litres for a shekel. So too did **cardamom/cress**, at about 54 litres for a shekel (figure 5.4).

Wool also showed exceptionally high prices in the early period of troubles in Babylonia, at about 0.5 kilograms for a shekel (figure 5.5). Then the price gradually fell to 2 kilograms for a shekel as flocks recovered slowly, but probably not to the level of abundance of the end of the Achaemenid period, when the price of wool had been considerably lower, at about 3 kilograms for a shekel. For more than a century the price oscillated around 2, but *c.* 158 BC it increased rapidly again to only 1.25 kilograms for a shekel.

This sharp price change can, again, be explained by war. This time it was the Parthian invasion, which culminated in the loss of Babylon in 141 BC, and, what is more important, the raids of the king of Elam, which are mentioned with horror in the *Astronomical Diaries*. In November 145 BC, for instance, the Elamites 'marched around victoriously among the cities and rivers of Babylonia, they plundered this . . . [and] carried off their spoil. The people . . . their . . . their animals . . . for fear of this Elamite to the house(?). There was panic in the land . . .'[68]

---

[68] Sachs and Hunger 1996: no. -144.

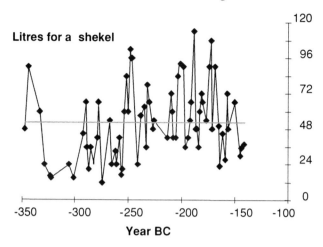

Figure 5.4 Cardamom/cress prices

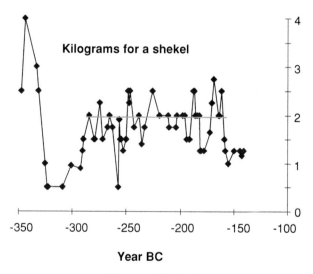

Figure 5.5 Wool prices

For any invading army bent on plunder, herds and flocks in the countryside would be a prime target, with resulting shortage in the cities and corresponding price increases.

There are now two commodities where something unusual appears to have taken place. The graph for **dates** (figure 5.6) shows a dramatic decrease of average price from 6 or 12 to about 120 litres for a shekel after the troubles

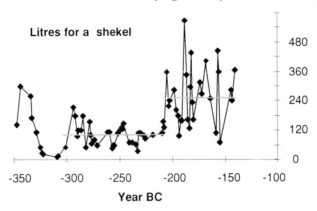

Figure 5.6 Date prices

of 311–308 BC, possibly as destroyed date plantations were replaced, but the price never reached the Achaemenid low of 240 litres for a shekel. Then quite suddenly, sometime between 208 BC and 205 BC, there was a dramatic price drop to about 240 litres for a shekel, or half of what it had been before. Indeed, this was now the same price as that prevailing at the end of the Achaemenid period. This cannot be explained by a single good harvest, because date prices seem to have oscillated about this new level for the next seventy years or so.

Looking now at **mustard** prices (figure 5.7), the graph shows similar behaviour, a decrease after 311–308 BC to about 240 litres for a shekel and then a sudden drop to around 480 litres for a shekel some time in or just before 208 BC.

Taking dates and mustard together, 208 BC seems to be the key date. A possible explanation for such a dramatic price drop is an administrative decision to remove tax on these commodities and this will be considered in ch. 8.1f.

But, apart from this, there is a remarkable stability of commodity base prices in Babylon under Seleukid rule. Whether this picture was true elsewhere in the East is unknown, but the possibility that it held in all of southern Mesopotamia, where cheap water-borne transport could even out price differentials, is high.

b. Comparative prices

In the regional economy of Delos, barley prices were considerably higher at this time, varying between 2 and 5 drachms per *medimnos* (1 Attic

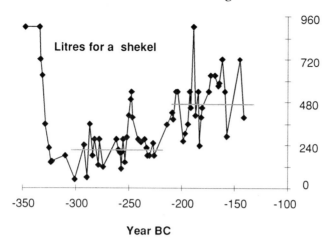

Figure 5.7 Mustard prices

medimnos = 51.8 litres) in the years 282 BC to 174 BC.[69] In Egypt, prior to the onset of inflation after about 222 BC, wheat prices varied between 1.2 and 3 drachms per *artaba* (1 Ptolemaic *artaba* = 40 litres), while barley prices were typically three-fifths of these and so the equivalent of between 0.9 and 2.3 drachms per *medimnos*.[70] These prices can be compared with the just under 0.9 drachms per *medimnos* average or base price at Babylon.

c. An assessment of Mesopotamian commodity price levels

The lower prices in Mesopotamia probably reflect the greater agricultural productivity of this region and the relatively modest cost of transport by river and canal compared to that in the Mediterranean. The fact that base commodity prices did not rise in almost two centuries indicates that there was no shortage of land. If population increased in some areas, more land could easily be brought under cultivation to feed it by an extension of the canal network. Similarly, the fact that commodity prices did not fall in the long term suggests that any population decreases that may have occurred, for example along the Euphrates to people Seleukeia-Tigris and the other new foundations, were evenly balanced between cultivators and urban residents.

[69] Reger 1994: 306.
[70] Heichelheim 1930: 118–21; Maresch 1996: 181; Cadell and Le Rider 1997: 25, 59.

What is revealing in Seleukid Babylon is the workings of a monetary economy where price levels in the market seem to have been determined by the interaction of supply and demand. Clearly, however, this was a market where only part of the commodity produce of the region was traded, a 'shallow' market in modern terms, where small changes in supply could affect prices dramatically.

CHAPTER 6

The granting of land

It was suggested as a hypothesis in chapter 3 that the founding of new cities by the first Seleukid kings and the policy of land grants to cities, temples and individuals were part of a systematic effort to intensify economic activity and generate more silver revenue for the royal exchequer.

I. LAND OWNERSHIP

The starting point in any discussion of land ownership is the arrival of Alexander in Asia. In his edict to Priene (*OGIS* 1)[1] Alexander made clear to a Greek city what he considered the status of land in its vicinity would be:

Βασιλέως Ἀλ[εξάνδ]ρου, τῶν ἐν Ναυλόχωι κ[ατοικούν]των ὅσοι μὲν εἰσὶ [Πριηνεῖ]ς, αὐτο[νό]μους εἶναι κα[ὶ ἐλευθ]έρους, ἔχ[οντ]ας τήν τ[ε γῆγ κ]αὶ τὰς οἰκίας τὰς ἐν τ[ῆι π]όλει πά[σα]ς καὶ τὴγ χώραν, ὥ[σπερ οἱ] Πριηνεῖ[ς αὐτοὶ] ... αἷς ἄν δέω[νται ...] τὸ δὲ ... καὶ Μυρσ[ηλείωγ κ]αὶ Πε[διέωγ ...] χώραγ [γ]ινώσκω ἐμὴν εἶναι, τοὺς δὲ κατοικοῦντας ἐν ταῖς κώμαις ταύταις φέρειν τοὺς φόρους· τῆς δὲ συντάξεως ἀφίημι τὴμ Πριηνέωμ πόλιν ...

From King Alexander. Of the inhabitants of Naulochos, those who are Prienians will be autonomous and free, possessing all their land and houses in the city and its countryside (chora), *just like the Prienians themselves . . . as to what they might desire. The . . . and the . . . of the Myrselieis and Pedieis I make known to be my land and those who live in these villages will pay tribute. I free the city of the Prienians from the syntaxis . . .*

In Alexander's edict the Prienians of Naulochos are clearly distinguished from the Prienians of the city itself, but are to receive exactly the same treatment, whereas the non-Greeks of Naulochos will be considered tributary. The picture one has is of a city and its surrounding *chōra*, plus a patchwork of outlying plots of land that belonged to its citizens, all this constituting city land. Everything else was to be the king's land and pay

---

[1] Sherwin-White 1985 for a commentary.

tribute, including the patchwork of land plots in Naulochos that did not belong to Prienians. Whether this policy was to be applied only in the case of Priene or generally throughout his empire, Alexander did not make clear. What he did, however, imply was that this was a concession, a grant by him, that preserved the tradition of the city's autonomy, but only because he so desired.

The question of land ownership is a tricky one. The idea expressed in Alexander's Priene edict may have been that of 'spear-won' territory: all the land belonged to the king by right of conquest and he could dispose of it in any way he wished. It will be recalled that Alexander is reputed to have thrust his spear into Asian soil upon crossing the Dardanelles, and Ptolemy was awarded Egypt at the settlement of Triparadeisos 'as if it had been won by the spear' (Diod. 18.39.5).

However, between such symbolic gestures and actual practice, there lay a huge gulf, created by long tradition and considerations of policy, which effectively restricted the power of the king to dispose of any land in his realm in whatever way he wished, although ultimately the royal will could prevail, if the king was sufficiently powerful.

To begin with, land in the Persian empire seems to have been distinguished between that which personally belonged to the king, to serve his own needs, and that which paid tribute.[2] The existence of a separate royal economic domain within each satrapy is also brought out in the analysis of ps.-Aristotle's *Oikonomika* (ch. 7.1b, in connection with *exagōgima* and *eisagōgima*). In the *Persepolis Fortification Texts* (ch. 9.1a), there is clear evidence of the workings of two separate economies, with the epithet 'royal' often applied to a commodity, and transfers sometimes taking place between satrapal and royal storehouses and stockyards. In Achaemenid Babylonia, the king and members of the royal family were treated as private landowners, much as any other, albeit on a grander scale.[3]

Alexander and the Seleukid kings inherited this situation and were constrained by it. Evidence for the continuing distinction between the kings' private property and all other tributary land is perhaps to be found in the terms sometimes used of *basilikē chōra* ('royal land') and *phorologoumenē chōra* ('taxed land') or just plain *chōra* ('land'), as can be seen, for example, in the Aristodikides inscription (section 3b below), where the two types of

---

[2] Briant discusses the matter at length, referring to the two types of land as *terre de la couronne* ('crown land') and *terre tributaire* ('tribute-yielding land') (1996: 427–33, 961–2).

[3] See Stolper for Achaemenid Babylonia (1974: 61–110; 1985: 36–69). Spek considers 'royal land' as only the private domain of the Seleukid king, who was a property owner no different in a legal sense from any other (1995: 195–7; 2000b: 27).

land may well be distinguished. Clearly the land of a Greek city was not considered royal land, although it might be taxed, while a long tradition made it the absolute property of its citizens. In most respects, a Babylonian or Phoenician or any other city of the empire was no different.[4] A king would be foolish indeed to confiscate its land and thereby lose its political support. Furthermore, temples also possessed land and movable property in the name of their gods, so that, whatever their legal situation, it would have seriously upset the religious sensibilities of the local population had the kings made any attempt to usurp these possessions. Indeed there is no record of confiscation of temple land by the Seleukid kings, but quite the opposite (section 4 below).

When a Seleukid king made a grant of land, it might well come from royal land or from tributary land, or both, as the case of Aristodikides may show (section 3b below). Sometimes this is not clear in a text dealing with a land grant, perhaps because the distinction was immaterial in practice, for example if there was no city or temple powerful enough to impose a practical restriction on the king's power.

2. THE NEW CITIES

The prevailing view is that the new Seleukid foundations were created primarily to satisfy political and military needs, that is, in order to control population centres or areas with important resources or strategic routes, although commercial considerations may also have played a part.[5] But there are problems with this view.[6]

Firstly, the Achaemenid empire did not require Persian settlements for control. It administered quite effectively, for about two centuries, a considerably larger territory, relying on a minimal presence of Iranian settlers, but with a strong satrapal administration, an extensive network of military garrisons, little interference in local affairs and co-option of the non-Persian

---

[4] Sarkisian notes that the Babylonian cities were given a privileged position, just like the Greek cities, so as to act as partners with the king in exploiting the rural population (1969: 313–17). Spek points out that the Greeks used the term *polis* for non-Greek cities too. Furthermore, Seleukid policy towards the Babylonian cities was to allow them to continue with their own traditional life and institutions. This included the free disposal of property, as numerous legal documents of the period show (1987: 58–9). Sometimes the property in question lay outside the city walls, in the *pahatu* ('district') of a city, such as Babylon or Uruk (Spek 1995: 173–91). It is possible that this might coincide with the *chōra* of a Greek city.

[5] Rostovtzeff 1941: 475–6; Seyrig 1970: 310; Cohen 1983: 67; 1995: 21, 64; Grainger 1990a: 67; Golenko 1993: 79.

[6] Aperghis (forthcoming) provides an overview of the Seleukid city-building process and its effect on the underlying economy.

elite into government. In the background there always lurked the threat of military intervention by the central power.[7] Would not Seleukos Nikator and his immediate successors have had this example before them? If anything, it was not indigenous populations that needed to be controlled, but the separatist tendencies of Greeks, for example Diodotos in Baktria, Andragoras in Parthia, Achaios in western Asia Minor, Molon in Media or the independence-seeking Greek cities of the Aegean coast. With the exception of the Maccabean revolt, no serious local rising is evidenced in the sources. The supposed breakaway of Persis was perhaps no more than a granting of local autonomy under Seleukid suzerainty to a native dynast (ch. 2).

Secondly, the pattern of many Seleukid cities does not seem to fit the criteria expressed in the prevailing view. An investigation into where cities were founded and of what size might help to resolve the issue.[8]

a. City locations

Northern Syria, for example, at the time of the foundation of the major *poleis* there (Antioch, Seleukeia-Pieria, Apameia and Laodikeia), was not a major population centre, perhaps only a tenth in size in comparison to Mesopotamia (ch. 4.1, 3), but rich in agricultural potential. It did indeed control two strategic routes from Mesopotamia, one to Asia Minor via the Kilikian Gates and the other to Egypt, at a time, just after Ipsos (301 BC), when this was a vulnerable frontier area, but surely four large cities plus several medium-sized ones (e.g. Chalkis, Beroia, Kyrrhos, Seleukeia-Zeugma) were far more than required for this task?

Along the lower Euphrates, in Babylonia, with its major population and economic centres, not a single new city was created, excepting only the inclusion (perhaps much later) of Greek communities in Babylon and Uruk, whose presence there may have been primarily for commercial reasons.[9] In fact, a relatively non-urbanized fertile region to the east along the Tigris and its tributary, the Diyala, was selected for development, with the foundation of a capital, Seleukeia-Tigris, and other cities, for example Apollonia, Artemita and Antioch-Sittakene.

The urban centres of northern Mesopotamia had suffered during the Assyrian collapse and, at the start of the Seleukid period, the region was still relatively sparsely populated (ch. 4.1), but it was fertile, dry farming

---

[7] Tuplin 1987a; Briant 1996: 369–528.   [8] Tscherikover 1973; Cohen 1978; 1995; Grainger 1990a.
[9] Spek 1987: 66–70; 1993a: 99–100; 1998a: 206.

was possible (ch. 5.1a) and a number of Seleukid foundations soon appeared in this area: an Alexandria, a Demetrias and perhaps two Seleukeias, while Edessa and Nisibis were refounded.[10]

In the far south-east of the Mesopotamian plain, in Susiane, Susa did receive the dynastic name Seleukeia-Eulaios and a Greek *politeuma* (*SEG* 7.2), but there is no indication of any overwhelming Greek settler presence there. Apparently there was room for new foundations, for example Seleukeia-Hedyphon and Apameia-Seleia, while along the coast of the Persian Gulf at least two cities of some importance were established, Antioch-Persis and Antioch-on-the-Erythraean Sea (a refounded Alexandria), along with a number of minor foundations.

The picture for northern Syria and Mesopotamia is thus one of extensive city-building, which started almost as soon as Seleukos I had consolidated his hold on these regions and was continued by his son, Antiochos.

A similar pattern is observed in Baktria and Margiane, although perhaps a little later, after Antiochos was dispatched there as viceroy to the Upper Satrapies about 291/0 BC (e.g. Antioch-Margiane, Antioch-Termez). It is tantalizing that we do not know the ancient name of Aï Khanoum, but its growth probably also belongs to the early Seleukid period.

If ever a region required supervision, it was the Persian heartland. Why was no city founded in the Persepolis plain, for example, if it was felt necessary to control this region by means of a city?[11] In fact, this part of Persis, quite densely inhabited as the *Persepolis Fortification Texts* and settlement surveys clearly show (ch. 4.2), was probably granted some form of independence, albeit under Seleukid suzerainty, early on (ch. 2).

In Media, a major population centre existed at the satrapal capital, Ekbatana, and the Seleukid administration seems to have quite happily made use of this, as had the Achaemenids earlier, to govern the satrapy. But, one also hears of new foundations in the remoter areas of the satrapy, such as Laodikeia-Nehavend, positioned off the strategic route from Babylonia to Ekbatana on a plateau in the Zagros, and Apameia-Rhagae, which took advantage of eastern Media's fertile plain (Strabo 11.9.1).

In Parthia, cities were founded in the chain of oases south of the Elburz and Kopet Dag ranges and north of the Dasht-i-Kavir desert, and also in the fertile Hyrkanian plain, for example Hekatompylos, Apameia-Choarene and Syrinx.

---

[10] Tscherikover 1973: 84–90, 96–7; Chaumont 1982.
[11] Polyainos 7.40 refers to the slaughter of 3,000 colonists in Persis, but where these were established is unknown; the only recorded fact is that they were led to a populous area, where the act was committed.

There is mention in the sources of Alexandrias in Aria and Drangiane, but only the former can firmly be attributed to Alexander.[12] Artacoana and Phra, which may have been renamed Alexandria-Areia and Alexandria-Drangiane respectively, both probably served as satrapal capitals in the Achaemenid period. One draws a complete blank on Karmania, but the terrain there is similar and space for a new city is likely to have been insufficient.

In the examples given above, a common thread seems to emerge, that the new cities were established in regions which were relatively little urbanized, but with rich agricultural potential or, if this was insufficient, with access to the sea or a river system.[13] Conversely, well-developed areas, such as western and southern Asia Minor and Kilikia, seem to have been avoided, or existing cities there simply refounded with dynastic names.

Kilikia is a good test case for Seleukid city-building. Seleukos I had ample opportunity in his thirteen years of rule there (294–281 BC) to build cities on the model of northern Syria and people them with Greek settlers. If strategic reasons had been the driving force for his city-building, in order to protect his territory from external and internal threats, why not now in this new frontier zone with his potential enemy, Lysimachos? Instead, existing cities were simply refounded with dynastic names, for example Antioch-Kydnos for Tarsos, Antioch-Pyramos for Megarsos, Antioch-Saros for Adana, and Seleukeia-Pyramos for Mopsuestia.[14]

What all this seems to show is a strong economic motive for the new city foundations, linked closely to the development of agricultural land, but political/military considerations undoubtedly also played some part.

b. City sizes

What determined the size of a new city foundation?

Doura-Europos on the middle Euphrates, built by Seleukos I, is a good example. The city's plan can be traced on the ground and is roughly rectangular, with an area enclosed by fortifications of some 45 hectares. One wall follows an escarpment running parallel to the river, but the other three do not utilize any natural features and were simply laid out to enclose an area of a desired size. Doura is probably one of the smallest Seleukid city foundations and, with a population density of 100–200 persons per hectare (ch. 1.5a), could have contained 5,000–10,000 inhabitants.[15] A maximum population of 10,000 requires about 5,000 hectares of irrigated land

---

[12] Fraser 1996: 171–90. [13] Leriche 1987: 59–61. [14] Cohen 1995: 358–72.
[15] Will estimates a population of 5,000–6,000 (1988b: 320–1).

(ch. 1.5a) to feed it, or 50 square kilometres. This much cultivable land is not available alongside the Euphrates in the immediate vicinity, but the necessary foodstuffs could be transported from further along the river without any difficulty. Another Hellenistic urban site on the middle Euphrates, at Djebel Khaled, is roughly the same size as Doura, about 50 hectares in extent.[16]

At the next level up were city foundations about twice as large, at around 65 to 100 hectares, for example Kyrrhos, Chalkis, Beroia and Seleukeia-Zeugma in northern Syria.[17] Populations in these cities may have ranged from 10,000 to 20,000 inhabitants.

In a different class of 20,000–50,000 inhabitants are likely to have been the major cities of the north Syrian tetrapolis, remnants of whose fortifications from the Hellenistic period give us an idea of what their approximate areas were: Seleukeia-Pieria 250–300 hectares; Antioch 225 hectares initially and expanding later; Apameia 205–255 hectares; and Laodikeia 220 hectares.[18] One can observe a certain uniformity in these sizes, any differences simply being those that would naturally emerge from the use of natural terrain features.

There is some independent evidence to suggest that the population figures are about right. Seleukeia-Pieria, when retaken by Antiochos III *c.* 219 BC, had about 6,000 free (male) inhabitants and more were added from the exiles who returned (Polyb. 5.61.1). Malalas gives 5,300 as the initial number of settlers for Antioch, presumably adult males, so 20,000–25,000 with their families (*Chron.* 201.12–16). Finally, it may be no coincidence that Plato considered that his ideal *polis* should possess 5,040 citizens (*Laws* 737E).

A new city foundation did not possess only Greek citizens and their families and slaves, but also a non-Greek population. Of the two quarters originally created by Seleukos for Antioch, roughly 150 and 75 hectares in area, the second was 'built for the multitude of colonists' (Strabo 16.2.4: τοῦ πλήθους τῶν οἰκητόρων ἐστὶ κτίσμα), which has sometimes been interpreted as a native quarter.[19] Assuming that Antioch had 5,000–6,000 Greek citizens initially, as suggested above, or 25,000 with their families, it is quite likely that slaves and non-Greeks made up a substantial part of the

---

[16] Leriche 1994: 533.   [17] Grainger 1990a: 92; Algaze *et al.* 1991: 206.

[18] Downey 1961: 78–9; Grainger 1990a: 91–2; Balty 2000: 459 and Will 1988a: 261–3, with less for Antioch. Downey gives 17,000–25,000 for the initial free population of Antioch (1961: 82), while Grainger estimates well over 50,000 free inhabitants for each of the major Syrian cities (1990a: 100).

[19] Downey 1961: 78. Briant regards separation of Greeks and non-Greeks within the cities as likely (1978: 88–9).

population if it approached the 50,000 mark, which seems to be possible, judging by its area.[20]

On a different scale altogether was the design of Seleukeia-Tigris, intended as a capital when it was founded, probably in about 305 BC. The area enclosed by the fortifications has been estimated at 550 hectares,[21] yielding a population of probably 50,000 to 100,000, about twice that of the cities of the Syrian tetrapolis, and implying a citizen body of as much as 10,000. However, it is unlikely that so many Greeks would have been available to Seleukos at the time, when he had no access to the Mediterranean, which could make the non-Greek population proportionately larger than in the Syrian cities, perhaps even as much as three-quarters of the total. There is, of course, the evidence of a move of some inhabitants of the cities of Babylon, Borsippa and Cutha to Seleukeia-Tigris (section 4b below).

What one may observe from these figures is a rough geometric progression in city size in multiples of two. That this could be pure coincidence is somewhat unlikely, but, rather, smacks of planning, as if decisions were consciously taken that cities should be built for civic bodies of standard sizes: about 1,250, 2,500, 5,000 and possibly even 10,000 adult male citizens.[22]

One should probably not refer to the new foundations as *Greek* cities. No doubt the Greek settlers were the dominant element politically, but it is likely that the bulk of the urban population was non-Greek.

c. City viability

To reach a decision on location and size, Seleukid planners must have given some thought to the viability of a city of a certain magnitude in a particular area, which meant looking to the surrounding land, royal land in the main, which needed to have both sufficient agricultural potential and no prior need to supply other major urban centres.[23] Alternatively, if the land was inadequate, there should be an easily accessed source of supply further afield.

One can see that this held true for all the large new foundations. Seleukeia-Tigris was positioned in essentially virgin territory along the Tigris, with the Diyala flood-plain ripe for development to the east and

[20] Kreissig points out that Antioch and Seleukeia-Tigris became large not because of the influx of Greeks, but that of non-Greeks (1976: 240).

[21] Will gives the area at more than 400 hectares (1988a: 259), while Invernizzi, conducting the Italian excavations of the city over several years, estimates 550 hectares (1993: 235).

[22] Also Downey 1961: 82.

[23] In the view of Briant, the land of Hellenistic cities was agricultural, whatever the later commercial development (1978: 61).

plenty of scope for growth. Antioch had the rich resources of its fertile plain to draw upon and Apameia those of the middle Orontes valley, both of which regions could support large cities once the necessary water-management works had been executed.[24] Similarly, Aï Khanoum was well placed at the junction of the Oxos and Kochba to take advantage of the extensive plain they formed, where agricultural production could be markedly improved. The oasis surrounding Antioch-Margiane offered some 300,000 hectares of irrigable land and was ripe for a large city. Even the Syrian ports of Seleukeia-Pieria and Laodikeia, despite their relatively small coastal plains, could rely on easily transported supplies by sea.

For the smaller cities, one gets the impression that the Seleukid planners attempted to fill every available piece of underdeveloped land with a city of the appropriate size,[25] as long as they could be assured of a supply of settlers. For example, the landscape of northern Syria was dotted with such foundations, placed in the gaps left in the zones of influence of the larger cities: along the coast (e.g. Balaneia, Paltos, Gabala) or the Orontes valley (e.g. Larissa, Arethousa), but especially north and east of the Orontes, to the mountains, the middle Euphrates and the desert (e.g. Chalkis, Kyrrhos, Beroia, Nikopolis, Doliche). Even along the middle Euphrates, with its relatively narrow cultivable strip of land, small cities of the size of Doura (e.g. Ichnai, Nikephorion, Anthemos) could be positioned at appropriate intervals along or near the river and be viable.[26] Inevitably, as each city in northern Syria grew, its economic hinterland would eventually infringe upon that of its neighbours and either growth of both cities would be arrested, or one would yield to the other. In the event, Antioch was the only Seleukid foundation that seems to have expanded steadily in the Seleukid period, at the expense of all the others.

In Asia Minor, a somewhat different pattern emerges. This was an area conquered at the very end of Seleukos' reign and immediately thereafter subjected to almost constant turmoil, with the Seleukids competing for its possession with Ptolemies, Attalids, Antigonids, Galatians, native kingdoms (Bithynia, Kappadokia, Pontos, Armenia), independent-minded Greek cities and one another (Antiochos Hierax, Achaios). Very soon, most of the coastal area had been lost and much of the central Anatolian plateau, leaving mainly a strip of territory extending from Kilikia to Lydia via Lykaonia, Phrygia and the northern parts of Pisidia, Lykia and Karia. Eventually this too was lost, until temporarily regained by Antiochos III. No large

---

[24] Leriche 1987: 61; Bernard 1995: 355.   [25] Also Grainger 1990a: 108.

[26] Cumont considers that exchange was also possible with the nomadic populations of the desert (1926: xxiv).

new Seleukid foundations are known from Asia Minor, although several existing cities appear to have been refounded, such as Seleukeia-Tralleis and Apameia-Kelainai.[27] This is probably because the region was already urbanized to a considerable degree and available land must have been somewhat at a premium.[28]

It is perhaps for this reason that the Seleukid kings adopted the policy of creating mainly smaller Greek settlements in this area, not cities but *katoikiai* or colonies. It is possible that this was due to the fluid frontier situation with the Attalids and other powers of Asia Minor, because of which a city could easily shift its allegiance, whereas a military colony would be more likely to stand firm. It has generally been considered that *katoikiai* were military settlements, established primarily so as to control vulnerable regions. But there is no conclusive evidence that all the inhabitants of *katoikiai* were military settlers or that they had a duty to respond to a call-up by the king.[29] Furthermore, one hardly hears of *katoikiai* outside Asia Minor and surely there were borders to defend elsewhere, in northern Syria or along the desert fringes of Mesopotamia or the north-eastern steppes? Thus the economics of available land probably determined, more than political or military considerations, the foundation of the mainly small new settlements of Asia Minor.

d. Seleukos as a founder compared to Alexander

Seleukos was credited in antiquity as having been the founder of many cities (Amm. Marc. 14.8.6), while Appian (*Syr.* 57) notes thirty-four foundations with dynastic names and twenty-five others as examples of the sort of name given. This has been dismissed by modern scholars as fiction, resulting from the inclusion of foundations of Alexander and other Seleukid kings, refoundations and a great deal of exaggeration. However, before these figures can be dismissed so lightly, one may consider what massive city-building took place in northern Syria alone in the few years immediately after its acquisition, or in northern Mesopotamia or along the Tigris or in Baktria in the reigns of the first two Seleukid kings. These are the regions the sources speak of and the silence from elsewhere may not be a silence of construction, but of documentation.[30]

---

[27] Cohen 1995.

[28] Marchese's survey of the Maiandros flood plain points to at least sixteen cities in this area in the Seleukid period, showing how densely occupied it was. Furthermore other large settlements also existed, which eventually turned into the eleven additional cities of the Roman period (1986: 307–20).

[29] Bikerman 1938: 82; Cohen 1978: 51–2.

[30] Cohen estimates that the Seleukid colonies probably exceeded seventy (1978: 11).

One may also consider how many of these cities grew and flourished in antiquity because of their sound economic base, compared with Alexander's foundations. Apart from Alexandria in Egypt, which was clearly intended from the very start to be a large city with a commercial future, most of the other Alexandrias, if they were indeed founded by Alexander himself, seem to have been conveniently located sites where veterans could be settled in order both to avoid the expense of repatriation and also to provide additional security along Alexander's lines of communications to India, although economic considerations also undoubtedly played a part.[31] The short life of many of these 'cities' shows that they may not have been truly organized as long-term projects, but chance naturally played its part in their survival. In several cases, refoundation by Seleukid kings was necessary for an Alexandria to survive (e.g. Antioch-Margiane and Antioch-on-the-Erythraean Sea).

e. Model of city creation

The creation of a new city, or the upgrading of an existing town or village, undoubtedly had a significant impact on the surrounding area, the more so the larger the new urban centre. For example, the establishment of Seleukeia on the Tigris probably gave the Diyala area to the east of the river such a powerful boost that its population increased severalfold in the Seleukid period.[32] While the traditional Mesopotamian cities on the Euphrates continued to flourish, they became, in a sense, peripheral to this new 'core'.[33]

For a new town or city, at least the nucleus of an urban population has to be imported, those specialized providers of services and manufactured goods that are not normally to be found in rural settlements. A city such as Seleukeia-Tigris could easily draw upon the old Babylonian centres for the necessary urban skills and it is possible that some population transfer from those nearest, such as Babylon, Borsippa and Cutha, did take place, perhaps not only when Seleukeia was founded (c. 305 BC) but also later.[34]

---

[31] See Fraser 1996 for the cities of Alexander the Great, particularly pages 171–90. Only six foundations can be firmly attributed to Alexander. Apart from Alexandria in Egypt, the remainder (Alexandria-Aria, Alexandria-Eschate, Alexandria-Susiane, Alexandria-Boukephala, Alexandria-Oreitai) were established on the sites of or very close to Achaemenid fortresses or satrapal capitals as synoikisms of Greek settlers with native populations, with the purpose of not only ensuring strategic control of territories but also encouraging the growth of settled agricultural life and trade.

[32] R. McC. Adams 1965: 63.   [33] Alcock 1993: 169.

[34] The original idea that a forced transfer from Babylonian cities had occurred, supported by some scholars, e.g. Briant 1978: 84; Spek 1987: 66 and Invernizzi 1993: 236, was based on the incorrect

In northern Syria the situation was quite different when the four major cities were created by Seleukos in about 300 BC, as this was a region with a low level of urbanization during the Achaemenid period (ch. 4.3). The solution, as evidenced in the sources, seems to have been threefold: (1) immigration from the Greek world, now that the Seleukid empire had access to the Mediterranean, (2) use of veteran soldiers in the aftermath of Ipsos (301 BC), including those who had already been settled in northern Syria by Antigonos at Antigoneia, and (3) inclusion of non-Greek populations. Also, one should not exclude the possibility that neighbouring Kilikia, with its numerous established semi-Hellenized cities, may also have served as a population reservoir for northern Syria once Kilikia became Seleukid in about 294 BC. Clearly an additional factor in the development of northern Syria was Seleukos' desire for an outlet to the Mediterranean, using his own ports, since those of Phoenicia were denied to him.[35]

But a town or city requires an agricultural hinterland to feed it (ch. 5.5a) and villages in the region must generate the surplus necessary for the city's survival. Although part of the urban population may itself be involved in agriculture and animal husbandry, there will be another part, increasingly important the larger the city, that lives off trade and industry or belongs to the administrative superstructure.

The observed pattern is of increasing density of rural settlements as one approaches the urban centre. Those villages are favoured which are nearest and can bring their produce to market more economically. As the urban centre grows, agriculture and animal husbandry are intensified in the villages closest to it, attracting inhabitants from further away, until the available land is fully utilized, with the result that the more remote settlements decline and are sometimes abandoned.[36]

For the surrounding villages, there can be both a 'natural' growth in activity and a 'mandated' one.

In the 'natural growth' model, the villager is attracted to the possibility of barter with the urban dweller, his agricultural produce in exchange for some specialized manufacture or unusual product of trade. But there is a limit to how much the surrounding villagers need and a city will grow only at the rate at which these needs can be increased. Obviously a city may rely on longer-distance imports of foodstuffs for its growth, but it is then still serving the needs of producing villages, albeit in remoter areas.

interpretation of an *Astronomical Diary* entry (Sachs and Hunger 1988: no. -273). Spek has now shown that there is no evidence for such a transfer (1993a: 98–9), followed in this by, for example, Kuhrt and Sherwin-White 1994b: 323 and Potts 1997: 281. It is likely, however, that inhabitants of Babylonian cities were persuaded to settle in the new foundation in the same way as Greeks were.
[35] Seyrig 1970: 310. [36] Gardin and Lyonnet 1978–9: 147–8 for Baktria.

In the 'mandated growth' model, the village is compelled to create a commodity surplus by the authority in command, which then extracts it as taxation. In the Achaemenid empire this was also the case, but the surplus was to a large extent stockpiled and used to feed the king, his administration and army.[37] This did not contribute materially to the growth of cities, virtually the only exceptions being the Achaemenid capitals. In the Seleukid case, however, the tax was to be collected in silver, which meant that a market had to be created where produce could be sold, an urban market. The more villages that could be supported on agricultural land of a particular area, the larger the required symbiotic urban centre, which perhaps explains the different sizes of the new Seleukid foundations.

f. Economic motive

Following the discussion above, I would suggest that the primary motive for Seleukid city-building was not political or military, but economic, the desire to open up relatively undeveloped land to economic exploitation.[38] There had already been experience in Macedonia, under Philip II and Alexander, of what it meant in terms of the royal economy to found new cities in rural areas, transfer populations to these and exploit local agricultural and other resources[39] and it is unlikely that this lesson was lost on Seleukos and his successors. Of course, an argument for a primary economic motive, which is based solely on a pattern of new city locations and sizes, cannot be conclusive, but more will be added on this score in subsequent chapters. And, no doubt, the idea that veterans had to be settled from time to time or that civilian Greek settlers were potential soldiers and supporters of the dynasty was not forgotten either.

3. LAND GRANTS TO INDIVIDUALS

a. Usufruct and outright concession

In the Achaemenid empire, the king regularly granted land to members of his family and deserving officials: an estate, a series of native villages

---

[37] The *Persepolis Fortification Texts* depict the procedure for collecting Achaemenid commodity taxation in satrapal storehouses and issuing it out again as rations (Aperghis 1998, 1999 and ch. 9.1a).

[38] Without suggesting that the primary motive was economic, Jähne considers that the really new thing in the East was the establishment of the new cities, which acted as a catalyst for a growing market economy, where the use of coinage was most important (1978: 141–7).

[39] Hammond describes the growth of the Macedonian economy under Philip II, based on the founding of new towns, the movement of people, the expansion of agriculture with irrigation works, flood control and land reclamation, and the exploitation of precious-metal mines (1992: 177–8). See also Hammond 1995 and Hammond and Griffith 1997: 657–71.

or even towns and cities. It is generally accepted that these land grants were made in usufruct, that is, that only the revenue from the land was transferred, and that there was nothing to prevent the king from reclaiming the land itself whenever he saw fit, either because the beneficiary's term of office had been completed or because he or she had fallen out of favour or because of the death of the recipient. Indeed it was customary for a new monarch to review and, in some cases, reinstate the land grants of his predecessor.[40]

Much the same practice continued in the Hellenistic kingdoms, the Seleukid empire being no exception.[41] It was in many ways simpler for the king to make the land grant rather than pay a salary or stipend to an official or member of the royal family. In this way he saved the expense and trouble of managing royal land and, at the same time, passed on any risk of a poor harvest or other potential problem to the grantee. As there was always the threat that the king could reclaim the property, this was also a good way of ensuring the loyalty of the official or relative concerned.

What is then puzzling is why, in some cases, the Seleukid king conceded land with the right of attachment to a city. Once the land had become city land, the king apparently no longer exercised direct control over it, as it effectively became private property. So why, then, did the Seleukid king make such concessions, which his Achaemenid predecessors had not felt compelled to make?

One reason that has been put forward is that kings who acted in such a manner did so because they found themselves in situations of weakness and sought to attract the political support of cities and temples by granting them land. But this line of argument breaks down when one considers that even under 'strong' Seleukid kings, such as Antiochos I and II, land grants with the right of attachment to cities were also made.[42]

Another possibility is that, by permitting attachment, the king was in effect increasing the value of his grant. But this is hardly the best way he could have chosen to do so, since increasing the amount of land in the grant would have worked equally well, without loss of royal control. So this is unlikely to be the true reason either.

In order to arrive at a solution, it will be necessary to examine whether the attachment to a city was mandatory in such cases or left to the discretion of a grantee. In other words, was the grantee permitted to retain private land outside the confines of city land or not?

[40] Briant 1985.   [41] Behrend 1973: 150–1; Funck 1978; Kreissig 1978: 40–6.
[42] For example, the Aristodikides grant by Antiochos I (Document 2) and the Laodike 'sale' by Antiochos II, which could be passed on to a third party (Document 3).

b. Aristodikides (Document 2)

In his first letter (no. 10) to his official Meleagros, Antiochos (I) issued orders that the first tract of land to be granted to Aristodikides be attached to either Ilion or Skepsis, whichever Meleagros thought best (δεδώκαμεν . . . προσενέγκασθαι . . . οὗ ἂν δοκιμάζηις). In this transaction the attachment to a city was clearly mandatory and the grantee had absolutely no say in the matter. Note also that the king was not particularly concerned about where the land was to come from, only that it be cultivable. No mention is made of 'royal' land and one may assume that this was probably 'tributary' land.

In the second land grant (no. 11), concerning the village of Petra, the king ordered, with regard to Aristodikides: 'and allow him to attach it to whichever city he wishes of those in [our] country and alliance' (καὶ ἐᾶσαι αὐτὸν προσενέγκασθαι πρὸς ἣμ ἂμ βούληται πόλιν τῶν ἐν τῆι χώρα[ι] τε καὶ συμμαχίαι·). When Aristodikides eventually decided upon the city, he would effectively become one of its citizens, since the owning of city land was seen by Greek cities as the prerogative of a citizen, with few exceptions. Note that there was absolutely no requirement in the king's orders that Aristodikides' land be attached to an *adjacent* city, although this would obviously have been convenient. What this means is that a city could possess land which was not contiguous to its existing land (*chōra*). Looked at in a different way, if all the land of a city was considered its *chōra*, this might well be made up of non-contiguous parcels (see also the case of Priene and Naulochos, discussed in section 1 above).

There was some improvement here for Aristodikides, as he was now being given bargaining power to negotiate concessions for himself and his land with the cities. As Meleagros' covering letter to Ilion (no. 13) makes clear, cities were indeed vying for this land: 'many others had spoken to him and presented him with crowns' (πολλῶν αὐτῶι καὶ ἑτέρων διαλεγομένων καὶ στέφανον διδόντων). Meleagros himself strongly recommended that Ilion should not fall short in the concessions race.

Here the village of Petra and its land were to be part of the grant, 'tributary' land it would seem, since an additional 2,000 *plethra* were to be added from the neighbouring land, which is referred to as 'royal'. There is a question too of the occupiers of this 'royal' land, referred to as the *basilikoi laoi* ('royal peasants'), being permitted to live in the village of Petra afterwards, if they wished.

Throughout, there is no indication that Aristodikides had received the right either to attach his land grant to a city or not to do so. Taken in conjunction with the first letter, the situation, in my view, becomes clear. The attachment to a city was mandatory in his case and what was conceded by the king was only the choice of city. This does not, by itself, prove that no private land could be held outside city (and temple) land, but the point will be discussed further below.

In the case of the first parcel of Aristodikides' land, the choice was possibly to be a political one, to be made by the king's representative in the region. For the second parcel, the king was effectively increasing the value of his land grant by opening up the way for concessions from the cities to the grantee. In the event, the second land grant fell through, as the land had already been conceded to another official, so the king replaced it with an equal tract elsewhere, which seems to have come partly from 'tributary' land and partly from 'royal' land (no. 12). As it was Meleagros, the king's official, who was to make the final choices from both 'tributary' and 'royal' land, it seems that the distinction between the two was in some cases quite blurred in practice.

The total area of land conceded to Aristodikides was 5,500 *plethra* of agricultural land (ἐργασίμου γῆς), or about 600 hectares. Its value as a grant had been enhanced by the right given to the new landlord to attach the land to a city of his choice, but seemingly at a loss to the king, who was relinquishing control over his property.

c. Laodike (Document 3)

The case of Aristodikides is repeated in Antiochos II's 'sale' of land to his estranged wife Laodike (no. 18): 'and [she] will have the right to offer [to attach the land] to whichever city she chooses' (καὶ κυρία ἔ[σ]ται προσφερομένη πρὸς πόλιν ἣν ἂν βούληται·). Again, I interpret this as a right to make a choice of city and not a right to decide whether or not to attach the land.

In Laodike's case, a clause in the agreement allowed her to sell or donate the land, in which case the right of selection of the city of attachment was to be passed on to the new landlord, unless Laodike had taken care of the matter herself: 'in the same way, those buying or receiving from her will also have the right to attach [the land] to the city of their choice, unless Laodike has made an earlier attachment to a city, in which case they will own the land as part of the city attached to by Laodike' (κατὰ ταῦτα δ[ὲ] καὶ οἱ παρ' αὐτῆς πριάμενοι ἢ λαβόντες αὐτοί τε ἕξουσιν κυρίως καὶ πρὸς πόλιν προσοίσονται ἣν ἂμ βούλω[ν]ται, ἐάμπερ μὴ Λαοδίκη τυγχάνει πρότερον προσενηνεγμένη πρὸς πόλιν, οὕτω δὲ κεκτήσονται οὗ ἂν ἡ χώρα ἦι προσωρισμένη ὑπὸ Λαοδίκης·).

In other words, Laodike was apparently given a grace period to settle matters with her land before she decided whether to hold on to it or to dispose of it.[43] Obviously, passing on to a potential buyer the right of city selection would considerably enhance the value of the land. Note that, as with Aristodikides, the city of choice did not have to be adjacent to the land granted to Laodike.

The particular way in which this land transaction was to be conducted may have been due to its special nature as a divorce settlement with an ex-queen. It will be argued later (ch. 8.1d) that Laodike was being given the revenue of two harvests with which to pay a nominal purchase price, set at the valuation of the land for tax purposes. Until the payment had been made, the land could remain part of royal land, as for any other land grant which did not have the right of attachment to a city. In fact, there may have been some difference in the way royal grants of land were handled, as between those to members of the royal family and those to deserving officials. In Achaemenid practice, as seen in the *Persepolis Fortification Texts*, the land of these two groups is distinguished as *ulhi* and *irmatam* respectively, but what the difference was is unclear, except that there must have been one.[44] One can speculate that *ulhi* were possibly intended to be lifetime grants, while *irmatam* were linked to the holding of an office.

Once the attachment had been made by Laodike to a particular city, it was not revocable. If she sold the land, the new owner was not permitted to remove it from the city and attach it to another, as the king made quite clear. Note that this is the only possibility envisaged by the king, presumably because this was something that he could do himself, if he so desired. He could obviously confiscate land from a city and either hold it as part of royal or tributary land or transfer it to another city. The other possibility, of course, would have been for the new owner to remove the land from the city to which it had been attached by Laodike and *not* attach it to any other, that is, to hold it privately outside city land, within the confines of royal or tributary land. But since the king, in his orders, had nothing to say about *this* possibility, it is unlikely to have existed.

d. Mnesimachos (Document 5)

This inscription will be used several times and discussed more fully in chapter 8.1a and e. It is clear that the land grant to Mnesimachos was in

[43] Haussoullier considers that this did not invalidate the rule of mandatory attachment to a city (1901: 33).
[44] Briant 1996: 458–60.

usufruct only, as there was the ever present danger that the king could take back his land from the Temple of Artemis, even if Mnesimachos had forfeited it to the temple by defaulting on his loan (line 13: ἐὰν ὁ βασιλεὺς ἀφέληται τῆι Ἀρτέμιδι διὰ Μνησίμαχον). This was the typical form of grant of the Achaemenid period (see above) and continued in the Seleukid.

e. Ptolemaios (Document 4)

So far, I have considered royal land held in usufruct or made private by being transferred to a city, and the question to be asked once more is whether there could be private land within the royal domain not attached to a city. The case usually quoted is that of Ptolemaios, Antiochos III's governor of Koile Syria, who referred in his letter to certain prerogatives (lines 23–4): 'in the villages that I own with right of inheritance and in those that you ordered be transferred to me' (εἰς τὰς ὑπ[άρχ]ουσας μοι κώ[μ]ας [ἐγ]γτήσει καὶ εἰς [τ]ὸ πα[τ]ρικὸν καὶ εἰς [ἃ]ς σὺ προ[σ]έταξας καταγράψ[αι]).

According to this view, *en ktēsei* refers to full ownership, while *eis to patrikon* shows that the land was inheritable. Since no attachment to a city is noted, this land of Ptolemaios was, presumably, privately held within the confines of royal land.

But, this terminology does not in fact prove private ownership. A land grant of Philip II needed to be approved several decades later by Kassandros (*Syll.*³ 332). Although the grantee's grandfather had 'received the land in inheritable ownership' (κεκτῆσθαι ἐν πατρικοῖς), and even with the 'right to sell' (ἀλλάσσεσθαι, ἀποδόσθαι), reconfirmation by the new ruler was necessary, showing that this land had not truly become private property in the widest sense.[45]

f. The case of Diotimos' land

One other case that is sometimes quoted as proof of private property out-side city land is that of the testamentary bequest by a certain Diotimos of land 'beyond the boundaries' to his city, Ariassos in Pisidia: 'I give and make

---

[45] Behrend analyses the use of *eis ta patrika* or *em patrikois* in various documents, e.g. from the temple of Zeus at Labraunda, the temple of Sinyri at Mylasa, the Ikaros inscription of Failaka and the Kassandros land-grant (*Syll.*³ 332), and concludes that these terms denote a hereditary lease (1973: 150). Likewise, Billows takes *eis to patrikon* in the Ptolemaios inscription as a variant with exactly the same meaning and considers that the Mnesimachos land grant would also have been such a hereditary lease (1995: 136). A different view, that the land had actually become private property when *eis to patrikon* is used, is expressed by Hatzopoulos in connection with a land grant of Lysimachos and also the Ptolemaios inscription (1988: 33–5). Robert concurs for the latter document (*BE* 1967, 651).

a gift to my dear fatherland of the property I own in the place Paunalla beyond the boundaries' (Δίδημι δὲ καὶ χαρίζομαι τῇ γλυκυτάτῃ πατρίδι μου κτῆσίν μου ἐνοῦσαν τόπῳ Παυνάλλοις ἐν ὑπερορίοις) (*IGRR* III, no. 1).[46] However, there is no proof here that this land was *not* considered part of the city's land. All the inscription indicates is that the land in question lay beyond the immediate geographical borders of the city and its surrounding *chōra*. If it belonged to a citizen, it would naturally be considered part of the city's land and did not necessarily have to be contiguous to the city itself, as was shown earlier when discussing the Aristodikides (Document 2, no. 12) and Laodike (Document 3) inscriptions. A further example of this is the Priene inscription quoted at the start of this chapter, which clearly showed that a city could own, through its citizens, a patchwork of land beyond the borders of its immediate *chōra*.

Thus the evidence does not permit one to conclude that private land – in the sense that it was totally alienable, without interference from the king – could be held outside the land belonging to Greek cities, but the case of non-Greek cities still remains to be examined and this will be done in connection with the Babylonian temples (below).

g. Advantage to a city

The desire of a city to acquire land can easily be explained. In my interpretation of the texts used above, Aristodikides was offering about 600 hectares of agricultural land to a city, enough to feed 600 people, at one person per hectare using dry-farming methods (ch. 1.5a). Laodike's land, valued at 30 talents, may have comprised a cultivable area of the order of 6,000–7,000 hectares and so been of huge interest to any Greek *poleis* in the vicinity.[47]

The agricultural land of the *chōra* of many a Greek city of western Asia Minor was too little to feed the city, which became dependent, sometimes heavily so, on grain imports. References to grain shortage (*sitodeia, spanositia*) are numerous in the sources, and cities were frequently forced to expend considerable sums of money on their provisioning, which they could hardly afford, or to rely on the generosity of a benefactor, or, finally, on the

---

[46] Kreissig 1978: 64.
[47] In chapter 8.1b it will be suggested that a typical village of the size of Mnesimachos' may have controlled an area of about 1,600 hectares, of which perhaps a third was cultivable, valued at about 750 gold staters or 2.5 talents. Laodike's land was valued at 30 talents, twelve times more. Its total area may have amounted to as much as 20,000 hectares or over 220,000 *plethra*, cf. Hatzopoulos' estimate of 15,000 hectares (1988: 52), a huge estate in any case. Of this, over 70,000 *plethra* may have been cultivable, which makes the 5,500 *plethra* received by Aristodikides seem puny by comparison.

'benevolence' of a Hellenistic monarch to donate or sell them grain from royal and tributary land nearby.[48] This 'benevolence' probably came with strings attached: a high price, pressure to buy from a near-monopolistic source, political dependence, and so on. In Antigonos Monophthalmos' letter to Teos (Document 1), for example, one can see how reluctant the Lebedians (and Teans) were to obtain grain from the royal stores and how unwilling Antigonos was to permit them to set up a fund to make purchases elsewhere.

For a Greek city within or on the borders of the Seleukid empire, the possession of enough land was not, in the end, a question of economics, but of survival. Expansion of the city *chōra* was at all times a major objective. Boundaries were disputed with neighbours,[49] the possession of native villages quarrelled over with royal administrators,[50] royal land grants hotly competed for[51] and even land purchases sometimes made from the kings.[52]

h. Advantage to the king

Outside city territories, in 'royal' and 'tributary' land, no such structural problem existed, although there might be an occasional bad harvest. As was noted earlier in the discussion concerning the new city foundations, rural areas were required to intensify agricultural production, so as to be able to sell a surplus to nearby urban centres, thus acquiring silver with which to pay their taxes and rents to the royal treasury. A Hellenistic monarch would need to ensure that any excess commodity production from his land, over and above the rationing requirements of his administration and army, could be speedily disposed of for silver (ch. 9.2), since goods left in store would eventually spoil.

The position then was that, compared to the Achaemenids, the Seleukid kings had less need of agricultural commodities from their land. As long as they could sell their surplus production to nearby cities and earn silver, there was no problem, but this was not always so easy. The independent-minded *poleis* or sanctuaries of Asia Minor and elsewhere would always be in search of less expensive or less politically dominated sources of food supply, if they felt they were being exploited, as the case of Antigonos and

---

[48] See Préaux for a discussion and examples (1978: 444–6). Note also the case of Herakleia-Latmos (Document 10).

[49] For example, Priene's disputes with Samos (*RC* 7) and Miletos (*RC* 46).

[50] For example, Apollonia-Salbake and its sacred villages (Document 7).

[51] For example, Aristodikides' land grant (Document 2).

[52] For example, Pitane's purchase of land from Antiochos I (*OGIS* 335).

Teos and Lebedos (Document 1) shows only too clearly. At the same time, the king could not be seen to be forcing himself too much, in the manner of a tyrant, on subject cities.

In the face of such a problem, a good solution, if you could not dispose of your produce, was to dispose of your land in an advantageous manner, which seems to have been done on a huge scale for the new Seleukid foundations. The intensification of rural agricultural activity to feed the cities, as well as the industrial and commercial activity of the cities themselves, probably meant more silver revenue for the king from taxation of different kinds (ch. 8). So, rather than becoming a loser by donating his land for the foundation of cities, the king probably came out a winner.

On a smaller scale, the same might be achieved by selling-off 'royal' or 'tributary' land or allowing a grant to be attached to a city. The king lost only if the land was highly productive and he had experienced no difficulty in selling its produce. But, if neighbouring cities were not turning out to be such a good market and the king was left with too much stock in his granaries and too little silver in his treasuries, he could pass on his administrative costs and problems to the cities. At the same time he need not suffer any significant loss in revenue, since the tribute of a city could justifiably be raised because of the increase in area of cultivable land. From the city's point of view, this might have appeared quite reasonable, if tribute were assessed at only one-twelfth of the nominal value of the land (ch. 8.1a), since it stood to gain much more. Where the royal treasury also collected certain city taxes, as at Sardeis (Document 9), these could be expected to show an increase, since more land meant more agricultural production, market transactions, people, animals, and so on. So a land grant attached to a city was not necessarily a loss for the king and could, in the end, have been what one would call today a 'win-win' situation, in which both parties benefit.

4. THE TREATMENT OF TEMPLES

a. Temples as economic units

Temples were, as economic units, very much like cities from the point of view of the Seleukid administration.[53] In some cases they were closely attached to cities, such as the sanctuary of Labraunda to Mylasa (at times),

---

[53] See Debord 1982 for the economic aspects of temple life in Asia Minor. Also Jones 1937: 39–41; 1940: 309–10; Broughton 1951; and Boffo 1985. McEwan 1981a deals with the Babylonian temples.

in others they were inextricably linked with them, such as the Temple of Jerusalem or the great temples of the Babylonian cities, in others still they formed self-administered entities within the empire, such as the sanctuary of Baitokaike in northern Syria. Temples frequently served as banks and centres of trade and industry, attracting pilgrims, organizing festivals and acting as meeting places for local tribes. The policy of the Seleukid kings seems to have been aimed at winning the support of the temples and was generally a benevolent one. No confiscation of temple land is recorded in the sources, but grants of several kinds, including that of land, are known (see below and ch. 10.4a). However, the Seleukid administration maintained a watchful eye on the temples and seems to have treated them, their land and economic activities, from the point of view of tribute and taxation, much as they did the cities.

b. The Babylonian temples

Very important in the economic life of Babylonia were the temples of the great cities: *Esagila* at Babylon, *Ezida* at Borsippa, *Emeslam* at Cutha, *Bit Reš* and *Irigal* (*Esghal*) at Uruk, *Ebabbar* at both Sippar and Larsa, and others.

The temples were proprietors of buildings and arable land and owned slaves, livestock and other moveable wealth. They earned revenue in money and kind both from contributions by individuals in respect of cult and from their own property. They also received financial support at times from the kings, particularly for building and maintenance. Temple revenue paid for the cult of the gods and for the maintenance of large numbers of personnel in the gods' service, some of whom manufactured the goods and foodstuffs that were required. An important part of temple revenue went towards prebend payments to a variety of officials and others associated with the temples and another part towards ration allotments to officials responsible for certain functions. Prebends and allotments might not even require the performance in person of the duties associated with the corresponding functions. They were, in essence the 'shares' of citizens of the cities in the enterprise 'Temple' and there was a lively market in the buying, selling and renting of fractions of prebends and ration allotments.[54]

The land possessed by temples may have been quite extensive,[55] but it is not clear how much was owned outright and how much may have been revocable grants by the kings to endow the temples with revenue.

---

[54] McEwan 1981a.   [55] McEwan 1981a: 121.

A document from Cutha refers to 'a share of arable land standing in stubble, the gift of the king on the bank of the Euphrates', which was claimed by the assembly of exorcists as a prebend for one of its members upon the intestate death of another. The exorcists were making the corresponding request to the full assembly of the temple. It is possible to see this as a case of ownership, in the sense that the temple authorities were the ones who decided who was to have the land. Here, perhaps, is an example of land attached to a temple, in much the same way as the king permitted land to be attached to a city. However, one should not exclude the possibility that the land had been granted by the king to the temple in inheritable usufruct only.

There may have been a net increase in temple land in the Seleukid period, although this is sometimes seen as the result of chance from the interplay between the interests of Babylonian cities and the kings.[56] In view of what has been seen above for Greek cities, it is likely that the granting of lands to temples was also part of the Seleukid policy of reinforcing those productive units that could eventually generate more revenue through tribute and taxation in silver than could the royal land, although the political advantages of eliciting support from the powerful civic-temple communities probably also played an important role.

A cuneiform text, *Astronomical Diary* -273 of 274 BC[57] may shed some light on the policy of land grants in Babylonia:

That month, the satrap of Babylonia made the fields which had been given in year 32 at the command of the king for sustenance of the Babylonians, Borsippaeans and Cuthaeans, (and) the bulls, the sheep and everything which [had been given] [to the citie]s and cult centres at the command of the king at the disposal of the citizens, [tributary to/confiscated property of(?)] the royal treasury . . .

Though temples are not specifically mentioned here, there is no reason to doubt that they were included with the Babylonians, Borsippaeans and Cuthaeans, since no real division probably existed between the civic authorities of a Babylonian city and the administrating bodies of the temples in Seleucid times.[58]

One view is that the text refers to a royal land grant, which was revoked after five years, and that the original granting of land to the cities was an attempt by Antiochos I to elicit support at the troubled start of his reign (ch. 2). The land may have lain beyond existing city land and was included within it in 279 BC. But in 274 BC Antiochos revoked this arrangement as he

---

[56] Spek 1993b: 76–7.   [57] Translated and commented upon by Spek 1993b: 67–70.
[58] Sarkisian 1969: 313.

was, according to this view, in desperate need of funds for the Galatian war and also to finance his intended campaign against Egypt for Koile Syria.[59] It is difficult to see, however, how the change in status of the land could have improved Antiochos' cash situation in the short term. A second view is that the reclaiming of land was connected with a corresponding granting of land at Seleukeia-Tigris to those citizens of the three Babylonian cities who were relocated there at this time, which does not appear unreasonable.[60] The relocation of urban settlers from Babylonian cities to the new capital was discussed earlier (section 2e above).

One may reconcile these two views and produce a third, as speculative as the first two. Initially the land may have been attached to these cities of northern Babylonia to reinforce their economy, which no doubt attracted political support as well. The land had been taxed previously as royal or tributary land and was now transferred to cities where a lower rate of taxation applied on city land, unless exemption had been granted, much as for any Greek city about which we possess information (ch. 8.1h). However, if a large number of citizens had moved or been moved to Seleukeia-Tigris, the cities could probably not use this land profitably any longer, because of the lack of hands to work it. But the tax remained, imposing an unfair burden on the citizens, so the land was possibly taken back by the king, who undertook once more to cultivate it himself. At the same time, of course, new land grants would have been made at Seleukeia-Tigris to the relocated citizens. This solution would seem to fit better with the generally benevolent policy adopted by the Seleukids towards the Babylonian cities and temples,[61] rather than any harsh confiscation.

What seems clear from this document is the idea of land belonging to a non-Greek city, available to its citizens and treated separately (for tax purposes?) from royal or tributary land, much as for any Greek city.[62]

c. Baitokaike (Document 15)

The grant of a village, its land and peasants (*laoi*) to the sanctuary of Baitokaike in northern Syria by a King Antiochos has all the characteristics of a land grant to an individual with the right of attachment to a city. The land was initially a grant in usufruct to a certain Demetrios and it was now to be given to the sanctuary: 'I have decided to grant to him [i.e.

---

[59] Spek 1993b: 68–9.   [60] Sarkisian 1969: 315–19.   [61] Spek 1985: 546.
[62] Sarkisian argues strongly for similarity between the treatment by the Seleukid kings of Greek and non-Greek cities in the empire, with a privileged position for *all* cities vis-à-vis the rural population, so as to elicit support for the dynasty (1969: 312–31). Also Spek 1998b: 138–40.

Zeus, the god of the sanctuary] for all time that from which the power of the god is derived, namely the village of Baitokaike, which Demetrios, the son of Demetrios, the son of Mnasaios formerly possessed . . .' (ἐκρίθη συνχωρηθῆναι αὐτῷ εἰς ἄπαντα τὸν χρόνον ὅθεν καὶ ἡ δύναμις τοῦ θεοῦ κατέρχεται κώμην τὴν Βαιτοκαι[κη]νήν, ἣν πρότερον ἔσχεν Δημήτριος Δημητρίου τοῦ Μνασαίου . . .).

'For all time' may be interpreted as a permanent transfer of the village and its land to the sanctuary, much as to a city.

There is nothing to prove that this is a late Seleukid document, describing a grant of land by a weak Seleukid king attempting to purchase the support of priests, as the later Ptolemies may have been compelled to do in Egypt.[63] Clearly, the Baitokaike temple's revenue was being increased by the grant, both from the proceeds of the land and also from those of the tax-exempted commercial fairs that the temple was authorized to hold twice a month. However, there is no mention of a general tax exemption in the inscription. One may suppose that Demetrios, who had held the land in usufruct earlier, was subjected to tribute and it is quite possible that the temple continued to pay it (ch. 8.1a and e for a discussion of the Mnesimachos inscription, which also deals with land held in usufruct). So the king need not have suffered any financial loss in passing on the land to the temple.

d. The question of the laoi

In the Baitokaike (above) and Laodike (section 1c above; ch. 8.1d; Document 3: no. 18, lines 8–9) land grants, the peasants living on the land, the *laoi*, were apparently transferred with it to the new landowner. There is a question about the status of these *laoi*, which has been addressed by many scholars in the context of the debate on the so-called Oriental or Asiatic mode of production or, as it developed with regard to the Achaemenid empire, the tributary mode of production. Were the *laoi* legally tied to the land or were they free peasants or were they free judicially, but effectively constrained to remain on their land by their tributary obligations to the king?

I will not enter into an analysis of the problem, since a recent treatment by Papazoglou[64] is both comprehensive and thoroughly convincing, while I am more interested in the financial aspects of the Seleukid economy rather than the social ones.[65] Papazoglou concludes that the term *laoi* ('people',

---

[63] *RC* 282. [64] Papazoglou 1997, especially 113–40, with full references.

[65] As will become apparent, particularly in the General conclusions, I view the Seleukid state from the standpoint of a 'modernist' and therefore feel entitled to make the separation of economy and society.

'subjects') was a technical term, adopted by Hellenistic administrations to denote all the native inhabitants subject to them, as distinct from the Greeks. It disappears after the Hellenistic period, in the sense in which it was then used. However, one should probably restrict the term *laoi* to just the native inhabitants of the countryside, not inhabitants of the cities, whether existing or newly founded. Land grants involving *laoi* are *not* to be interpreted as showing the transfer of ownership of populations, but of the revenue derived from these as part of their tributary obligation. The *laoi* were judicially free and at liberty to move. The phrase in the Laodike dossier which refers to the revenue the ex-queen would receive from her land grant is followed by (Document 3: no. 18, lines 11–13): 'and it will be the same if some people from this village had moved to other places' (ὁμοίως δὲ καὶ εἴ τινες ἐ[κ] τῆς κώμης ταύτης ὄντες λαοὶ μετεληλύθασιν εἰς ἄλλους τόπους). Thus some villagers had apparently departed from the village since the time when its tributary obligation as a collective unit had been set, but the tribute, which was now to be Laodike's revenue, was to remain unchanged. Obviously, if the tributary obligation of a village was high – as I hope to show (ch. 8.1f) – social pressure could impose some practical restraints on the departure of productive villagers. On the other hand, my model of city creation (section 2e above) suggests a natural gravitation of population from more distant villages to those nearest to urban centres, which was encouraged by the Seleukid kings.

5. CONCLUSIONS ON THE GRANTING OF LAND

The Baitokaike inscription shows land granted to a temple, which was to be considered its private property. The other land grants to temples mentioned earlier might also be interpreted in this way. Certain land grants to individuals (Aristodikides, Laodike) clearly indicated that attachment to a city was mandatory. But others, where no city was apparently involved (Ptolemaios, Kassandros), could not be proved to have been held unconditionally by the grantees. Considering all the available evidence, there is nothing which, in my view, shows that private land – in the sense that it was completely alienable, without interference from the king – could be held outside city and temple land.[66]

---

[66] Among those who support the idea that private land could not be held outside a city's land are Haussoullier 1901: 32; Rostovtzeff 1910: 249 and 1941: 495; Bikerman 1938: 183; Cohen 1978: 66; and Papazoglou 1997: 127; also Jones 1937: 45–6, although he finds it difficult to say how far the theory of royal ownership was actually put into practice. In Kreissig's view, the existence of private land outside a city is not proven, but possible (1978: 69–70). Spek makes the distinction between

The policy of the Seleukid kings with regard to the disposal of royal and tributary land seems to have been governed mainly by economic considerations and less by political and military ones. Recipients of land grants were first and foremost the new city foundations, which seem to have been established, of the right size, in areas with underutilized agricultural land and low existing levels of urbanization. The new cities and the refounded older ones created the conditions for the development of a monetary economy and spurred on the rural areas surrounding them to greater production and exchange, particularly that requiring the use of silver.

Land grants to individuals continued to be offered in usufruct, as in earlier times, but the practice of permitting attachment of the land to a city (or a temple) and thereby effectively allowing it to be held privately, was also introduced, with advantages for both the city (and temple) and the king.

Temples were treated by the Seleukid kings very much like cities, as economic centres to be reinforced, sometimes with land grants, apart from any advantages arising from their political support.

The overall pattern is one of royal and tributary land being put to more effective use in order to support a developing monetary economy and to help to generate more silver revenue for the royal treasury.

---

land held privately by the king, *chōra basilikē* ('royal land'), and the remainder (*chōra*), that was not included in city land and in which private property could, according to him, exist (1998b: 140–7). It is true that numerous Babylonian texts record transactions in which properties are freely alienated, but nowhere does any evidence appear, to my knowledge, that these properties lay outside recognized boundaries of city land. See also Spek 1995: 189–97.

PART III

The royal economy

CHAPTER 7

Ps.-Aristotle's Oikonomika, Book 2

Book 2 of the *Oikonomika* is presented in two sections, as a manual for would-be financial administrators. In the first, the theoretical part (1.1–8), the four types of 'economies' are described: royal, satrapal, city and household, along with their constituent elements. 'Economy' is, of course, to be understood here in the sense of a sphere of financial administration: a kingdom, a province, a city and its land (*chōra*) or an individual household (*oikos*). In the second section, the practical part (2.1–41), a number of financial stratagems of the past are presented, as examples both of ways in which funds were actually collected in times of need and of imaginative financial management. The first section ends with a bridging passage to the second (1.8), which explains why it was thought necessary to add the practical examples to the theoretical discussion.

It is now widely accepted, following van Groningen 1933, that Book 2 was written in the last quarter of the fourth century BC and that it was probably a treatise of an Aristotelian scholar intended to provide instruction on the efficient management of financial matters at different levels. As such, and in line with the Peripatetic school's practical approach to the study of the human and the natural world, it looked for real-life models. For what interest us here, the royal and satrapal economies, these models were apparently found in the financial organization of the Achaemenid empire and those of Alexander and his early successors, exposed to detailed study by Greek intellectuals for the first time. However, this view will be challenged in what follows.

The text of the first section of Book 2 is a difficult one to understand because of its 'technical' language and brevity.[1] My own translation is provided and, to begin with, contrasted with others solely from the point of view of language, principally with the translations of the Loeb edition of

---

[1] The text adopted here is that of van Groningen and Wartelle 1968, with comments on alternative readings in the Loeb edition.

the *Oikonomika*, which is commonly used, and that of van Groningen and Wartelle 1968, along with van Groningen's commentary of 1933. Then the problems of date and author are considered and what may have been, in my opinion, the real-life model for the royal and satrapal economies. In following chapters, each aspect of these economies will be analysed in detail, with reference to the sources.

1. TEXT AND TRANSLATION (BOOK 2, SECTION 1)

a. Introduction

§1 Τὸν οἰκονομεῖν μέλλοντά τι κατὰ τρόπον τῶν τε τόπων, περὶ οὓς ἂν πραγματεύηται, μὴ ἀπείρως ἔχειν, καὶ τῇ φύσει εὐφυῆ εἶναι καὶ τῇ προαιρέσει φιλόπονόν τε καὶ δίκαιον· ὅ τι γὰρ ἂν ἀπῇ τούτων τῶν μερῶν, πολλὰ διαμαρτήσεται περὶ τὴν πραγματείαν ἣν μεταχειρίζεται. Οἰκονομίαι δέ εἰσι τέτταρες, ὡς ἐν τύπῳ διελέσθαι (τὰς γὰρ ἄλλας εἰς τοῦτο ἐμπιπτούσας εὑρήσομεν)· βασιλική, σατραπική, πολιτική, ἰδιωτική.

He who will be involved in some form of financial administration must not be unacquainted with the places with which he has to deal and [must be] intelligent by nature and industrious and just by inclination. For whatever he lacks of any of these qualities will cause many problems for the task he undertakes. There are four economies, as they are divided by type – for we will find that the others are included in these – royal, satrapal, city and household.

§2 Τούτων δὲ μεγίστη μὲν καὶ ἁπλουστάτη ἡ βασιλική, <...>, ποικιλωτάτη δὲ καὶ ῥᾴστη ἡ πολιτική, ἐλαχίστη δὲ καὶ ποικιλωτάτη ἡ ἰδιωτική. Ἐπικοινωνεῖν μὲν τὰ πολλὰ ἀλλήλαις ἀναγκαῖόν ἐστιν· ὅσα δὲ μάλιστα δι᾽ αὐτῶν ἑκάστῃ συμβαίνει, ταῦτα ἐπισκεπτέον ἡμῖν ἐστιν.

Of these, most important and simple is the royal [economy], . . . , most varied and easy the city [economy], least important and most varied the household [economy]. In most cases it is necessary for these to interact. Whatever is the situation with each in turn, that is what we shall examine.

Πρῶτον μὲν τοίνυν τὴν βασιλικὴν ἴδωμεν. Ἔστι δὲ αὕτη δυναμένη μὲν τὸ καθόλου, εἴδη δὲ ἔχουσα τέτταρα· περὶ <τὸ> νόμισμα, περὶ τὰ ἐξαγώγιμα, περὶ τὰ εἰσαγώγιμα, περὶ τὰ ἀναλώματα.

First we will look at the royal economy. This exercises power over the whole and has four aspects: relating to coinage, to exagōgima [= goods that can be sent out], to eisagōgima [= goods that can be brought in] and to expenditure.

The translation in the Loeb edition refers to four departments of the royal administration. However, there is no idea in the text of a fixed organizational division, but rather of four main decision areas for financial management that affect the king directly (also van Groningen's *quatre aspects* or 'four aspects'). For *exagōgima* and *eisagōgima*, the Loeb uses 'exports' and 'imports', perhaps taken in the modern sense of these terms, which would seem to imply that the king was directly involved in matters of foreign commerce. Van Groningen also translates here *articles d' exportation et importation* ('exports and imports'), but qualifies this later (see below). It will be argued that this is not what should be understood. The ending *-imos* normally conveys the sense of 'can be' or 'able to'[2] and it will be best, for the moment, simply to consider that what is meant in the text is the movement of goods, of whatever nature, that could be brought out of or into something.

b. The royal economy

§3 Τούτων δὲ ἕκαστον. Περὶ μὲν τὸ νόμισμα λέγω ποῖον καὶ πότε [τίμιον ἢ εὔωνον] ποιητέον·

[Let us take] each of these separately. With regard to currency, I mean what to mint timion *or* euōnon *[= of large or small denomination] and when;*

Here the Loeb translation seems to be a long way off the mark when rendering this passage as 'I assign to currency the seasonal regulation of prices.' *Timion* and *euōnon* can literally be translated as 'expensive' and 'good-value' or 'cheap' respectively, which I have linked to denominations in a general sense. Van Groningen considers the terms a later gloss and translates this passage: *pour les monnaies il s'agira de savoir de quel type il faut en faire et quand* ('regarding coinage, the question will be to know what type to make and when'). 'What type' can then indicate 'what material' or 'what value'. In the case of the Persian king, van Groningen regards these as being exactly the same, because the latter minted, in his view, only gold darics and silver *sigloi*. It should be pointed out here that van Groningen's model of the ps.-Aristotelian economies is the Achaemenid empire, with Alexander as its inheritor.

περὶ δὲ τὰ ἐξαγώγιμα καὶ εἰσαγώγιμα πότε καὶ τίνα παρὰ τῶν σατραπῶν ἐν τῇ ταγῇ ἐκλαβόντι αὐτῷ λυσιτελήσει διατίθεσθαι·

with regard to goods that can be sent out or brought in, which of them, having been received from the satraps in their tagē *[= province], were to be profitably disposed of on his [i.e. the king's] behalf and when;*

---

[2] Buck and Petersen 1944: 186. For example, *ergasimon* is frequently used for agricultural land that is 'cultivable', 'workable', but not necessarily being cultivated at the moment.

This passage is translated in the Loeb edition: 'to imports and exports, the profitable disposition, at any given time, of the dues received from provincial governors'. Van Groningen is, to my mind, nearer the mark when he translates this passage: *Pour les articles d'exportation et importation, après les avoir reçus de la part des satrapes dans les contributions, il y aura lieu d'examiner à quel moment et sous quelle forme il sera advantageux d'en disposer* ('For export and import goods, after the satraps have received them as taxation, it will be necessary to examine at what moment and in what form it would be advantageous to dispose of them'). In his 1933 commentary (pages 34–5) van Groningen concludes that the king disposed of large quantities of goods from the *tagē* – which he understands as the tribute – all of which the king could not use for his own needs. The surplus was either collected at Susa, for example, to be sold, thus constituting the *eisagōgima*, or transported by the king's agents, for example the satraps, to a district to be disposed of there, thus constituting the *exagōgima*.

The first problem with this interpretation is the word *tagē*. This is not found elsewhere in connection with tribute, which is typically *phoros* or *dasmos*. In Hesychius (s.v. ταγή· βασιλικὴ δωρεά· καὶ ἡ σύνταξις πρὸς τὸ ζῆν ἀναγκαίων) the sense is quite the opposite, of a royal gift, or of the collection of the necessities of life. These cannot be related in any way to the use of the word in our text. The plural is more help-ful. Ταγοί in Hesychius (προστάται, ἄρχοντες, ἡγεμόνες), Pollux (1.129) and Harpokration (*reges Thessalorum*) are all commanders and rulers, while Harpokration (s.v. ταγαῖς· ἀρχαῖς, ἡγεμονίαις) points to their commands or areas of rule. In LSJ the translation 'command, province' is adopted for this passage of the *Oikonomika*.

So one is left with two possibilities: that *tagē* relates to tribute or to a satrapy. In van Groningen's interpretation, the satraps sent the king a stipu-lated tribute, from which a surplus might be left over, after the king's needs had been satisfied, which was then sold off by the king or returned to the provinces to be disposed of there. In my interpretation, one is not dealing here just with tribute sent to the king, but with the more general interaction between the royal and satrapal economies, that is, everything that moved between the two. One should visualize a part of the 'royal' economy within every province and the goods in question were simply able to move into it (*eisagōgima*) or out of it (*exagōgima*) from the other economies in the same province. That such an interaction did take place had been specif-ically noted in the text earlier. The provincial administration collected commodity and silver tribute and taxation (which will be considered in ch. 8 as part of the satrapal economy), and some of this served to cover its own expenses, while any surplus was directed to the royal economy (*eisagōgima*) – royal treasuries and storehouses – often within the province. The provincial administrators also managed royally owned land and natural resources, such as mines and forests, along with workshops and other royal properties in the cities. There were times when the produce of these, as well as the commodity surpluses already collected, needed to be disposed of on the king's behalf (*exagōgima*) and the local officials could see to it that this was done in a manner profitable for the king.[3]

This matter will be discussed at length in chapter 9, but here is an example of what I mean that supports the use of the specific language in the text. The city of Sardeis had suffered serious damage after its retaking by Antiochos III in 213 BC and the king wrote to give permission 'immediately to cut the (necessary) wood for the reconstruction of the city and to take it from the forests of Taranza' (Document 9, lines: 2–4: ε[ὐ]θέ[ω]ς δὲ καὶ ξυλὴν εἰς τὸν συνοικισμὸν τῆς πόλεως κόψαι καὶ ἐξαγάγεσθαι ἐκ τῶν ἐν Ταρανζοις ὑλῶν). The verb used is *exagagesthai*, exactly as in the *Oikonomika*, and the sense of the transaction is from the royal to the city economy.

περὶ δὲ τὰ ἀναλώματα τίνα περιαιρετέον καὶ πότε, καὶ πότερον δοτέον νόμισμα εἰς τὰς δαπάνας, ἢ ἀντὶ νομίσματος ὤνια,

with regard to expenditure, what is to be cut and when, and whether to meet expenses with coin or with goods in place of coin,

The text in the Loeb edition ends with ἢ ἃ τῷ νομίσματι ὤνια, which is a rather strange construction. Nevertheless it is rendered in the same general sense: 'and to expenditure, the reduction of outgoings as occasion may serve, and the question of meeting expenses by currency or by commodities', but van Groningen is again more accurate: *Quant aux dépenses, il faudra voir celles qu'on doit supprimer et à quelle date, et s'il faut regler en espèces ou en marchandises au lieu de monnaie* ('With regard to expenses, it will be necessary to know which one should cut and at what time and whether to settle accounts with coin or with goods in lieu of money'). The word

---

[3] Some quite different interpretations have been given to this passage, showing how difficult it is to translate. For example, Rostovtzeff relates it to the commercial policy of the king, i.e. how much of the merchandise received from the satraps he should sell and export and how much the kingdom needed in the way of imports (1941: 443). Corsaro sees *tagē* as the order of the king which determined the level of the satraps' contributions (1980: 1166). Andreades takes *tagē* as tribute, the king fixing what was to be delivered to him in precious metal and kind (1933: 91). Murray argues, correctly in my view, that in the royal economy the levying of tribute is not considered, as this is left to the satrapal economy. So *tagē* cannot be the word for tribute and the *exagōgima* and *eisagōgima* are the goods and bullion received from the satrapies, with whose reception, storage and disposal the king is concerned (1966: 151–3). In Briant's view, the *eisagōgima* and *exagōgima* represent the movement of goods in and out of royal storehouses (1996: 467).

periaireteon, which I have rendered as 'should be cut' is strictly translated as 'is to be done away with' in LSJ but this probably also implies a reduction of a total expenditure, when a part is discontinued. The goods given to meet expenses in place of coinage would normally be a commodity such as grain, for example as part of a soldier's pay. But this is too restrictive. One should envisage the king providing other than commodities in some cases, for example a land grant to an official in lieu of salary or a tax remission to a community, with the proviso that the community undertake to support a temple or royal cult, which may earlier have incurred actual expenses on the part of the king.

c. The satrapal economy

§4 Δεύτερον δὲ τὴν σατραπικήν. Ἔστι δὲ ταύτης εἴδη ἓξ τῶν προσόδων, [ἀπὸ γῆς, ἀπὸ τῶν ἐν τῇ χώρᾳ ἰδίων γινομένων, ἀπὸ ἐμπορίων, ἀπὸ τελῶν, ἀπὸ βοσκημάτων, ἀπὸ τῶν ἄλλων].

Secondly, the satrapal economy. This has six types of revenue: from land, from the private production in the country, from market centres, from dues, from herds and flocks and from the other [sources].

In the Loeb the second type of revenue arises 'from the special products of the country' and the translator may be implying that these include products of industry, but one should rather see revenue involving these included in that from market centres or dues.

Van Groningen considers the listing here of the six types of revenues as an annotation of a scholiast that was later included in the text. The ἀπὸ τῶν ἄλλων ('from the other [sources]') must have been included after the original text's sixth satrapal revenue, ἀπὸ τῶν ἀνθρώπων ('from people'), had become corrupted (see below).

Αὐτῶν δὲ τούτων πρώτη μὲν καὶ κρατίστη ἡ ἀπὸ τῆς γῆς, αὕτη δέ ἐστιν ἣν οἱ μὲν ἐκφόριον οἱ δὲ δεκάτην προσαγορεύουσιν.

Of these the first and most important [revenue] is that from land, which is what some call ekphorion *and others* dekatē.

In the Loeb translation, 'produce-tax' for *ekphorion* and 'tithe' for *dekatē* are completely general and do not clarify the difference, if any, between the two terms. An *ekphorion* is described in LSJ as 'a payment assessed on produce, especially a rent paid in kind'. Van Groningen translates as *impôt foncier* ('land-tax' or 'ground rent'), which is probably more correct. The term is rarely found in the sources, but *phoros* is usually applied to tribute, which is normally a pre-determined fixed amount. On linguistic grounds a *dekatē* is literally a 'tithe or tenth part', although it may sometimes be used in a general sense, as any fraction in connection with taxation. With regard to land, a proportion of the harvest should be understood.[4]

Since land is mentioned in general, it is reasonable to assume that all kinds of land are covered in this passage, including that belonging to the king, the cities, the temples and the subject dynasts and peoples (*ethnē*).[5]

There is a problem with the phrase 'which some call *ekphorion* and others *dekatē*'. Strictly speaking, this would imply that there was only one kind of revenue on land, with different names in different places,[6] but this is probably not how one should read the text. For the fifth and sixth types of satrapal revenue, those involving animals and people (see below), two names are also given for the tax. However, it would be difficult to accept that they have exactly the same meaning, for example that a *cheironaxion*, with its sense of an artisan tax, could be linguistically equated with an *epikephalaion*, a general head tax. Ps.-Aristotle may simply be trying to distinguish between the two forms that the revenue from land could take, the one based on a fixed assessment (*ekphorion*), the other on a proportion of the agricultural harvest (*dekatē*).

Δευτέρα δὲ ἡ ἀπὸ τῶν ἰδίων γινομένη, οὗ μὲν χρυσίον, οὗ δὲ ἀργύριον, οὗ δὲ χαλκός, οὗ δὲ ὁπόσα δύναται γίνεσθαι.

The second [revenue] is that produced from private property, in some place gold, in another silver, in another copper, in another whatever is available.

This is a very difficult passage to interpret and will always be the subject of much disagreement. For a better understanding, it needs to be analysed not only for what it says, but also for what it does not say. Furthermore, it should not be translated in isolation, but in the context of *all* the satrapal revenues.

Ta idia is certainly used in Greek texts to express the private property of individuals, as distinct from public property (cf. LSJ), while *ginomenē* conveys the idea of production. So something is being produced from private property, which generates revenue for the king in the satrapal economy.

---

[4] Also Rostovtzeff 1910: 245, n. 2.

[5] There is by no means agreement on how this passage should be interpreted. Some scholars consider that it refers only to royal land, while private land is dealt with in the second type of satrapal revenue, e.g. Rostovtzeff 1910: 241, Corsaro 1980: 1165; 1985: 86. According to Cavaignac, the *ekphorion* relates to royal land, the *dekatē* to private land (1923: 114).

[6] Rostovtzeff notes that the term *ekphorion* was only used in Egypt for the land tax, which was known elsewhere as the *dekatē* (1910: 241).

There are those that argue that what is meant here is the private land that supposedly existed outside city land – city land is taken to include the land of temples and of non-Greek cities. What was obviously generated, according to this theory, was agricultural and other produce, taxed by the king, preferably in gold, silver or bronze coinage, but, when this was not available, in kind.[7]

The problem with this view is, firstly, that there is no mention at all of land in the text, while land is clearly the subject of the first satrapal revenue, without any qualification whatsoever, leading one to naturally interpret this as 'all land'.

Secondly, if what ps.-Aristotle intended to convey was tax payments in coinage, it is likely that he would have expressed himself differently and not in terms suggesting that the coinage itself was *produced* (*ginomenē*) from the private properties. It is also unreal to expect that in some places these payments would be made in gold, in others in silver and in others in small bronze denominations, as the text would then seem to imply. An estate such as Mnesimachos', for example, had tax assessments that included fractions of a gold stater (ch. 8.1a, Document 5), which did not exist as coin.

Thirdly, why would the king desire to collect taxation in coin only from privately owned estates in the satrapal economy? There is no mention of the use of currency in the first source of revenue, only the form the tax on land took, whether lump sum or proportional. Is one to assume that this was only to be collected in kind from royal land? Yet it is clear from the Mnesimachos inscription that the tribute on his estate, which was held in usufruct only and not privately in the strict sense demanded here, was required in coin.

Finally, ps.-Aristotle has been careful to list all the various possible sources of revenue and, indeed, in what was apparently their order of importance (see below). Yet where then is the significant revenue the king must have derived from certain natural resources of his realm, which he undoubtedly controlled to a considerable extent: mines of precious metal, quarries, forests, salt pans, water in irrigation canals, special products such as balsam or asphalt, and so on (chs. 5.3; 8.2)? Such an omission would be incredible. Nor might these items have been included in the first source of revenue, as coming from land, since *ekphorion* or *dekatē* could hardly be used to describe a sale of wood from a royal forest or the output of a gold mine or the supplying of water on certain days for irrigation in Mesopotamia.

The examples given by ps.-Aristotle make clear that one is dealing here mainly with natural resources. At the same time *ta idia* does point to

---

[7] Rostovtzeff 1910: 241; Corsaro 1980: 1165; 1985: 86.

private ownership. Since the king was the owner of most important natural resources, *ta idia* must refer to these as the king's personal property. This fits in well with the distinction made in chapter 6 between *chōra basilikē* (royal land) and plain *chōra* (land), or *chōra phorologoumenē* (tribute-bearing land), that is, between the king's privately owned land within the satrapal economy and the remainder, as part of the general divide, discussed earlier in this chapter, of royal and satrapal economies. However, there is no reason why *ta idia* could not apply to natural resources owned by the king's subjects outside city land, if such a possibility did exist, as has not been proved (ch. 6.3).[8]

The obvious question arises as to why natural resources owned by the king should be included in the satrapal economy. This is the same as asking why royal land was also included in that economy and not mentioned in ps.-Aristotle's royal economy. In the case of the Seleukids, the answer is simply that the satrapal administration was responsible for both, as will be seen in numerous examples in chapters 8, 9 and 13.

Τρίτη δὲ καὶ ἡ ἀπὸ τῶν ἐμπορίων.

The third [revenue] is that from market centres.

Emporia is rendered in LSJ both as 'trading stations, market centres' and as 'merchandise', but the Loeb translation only considers the former and includes taxes on sales generally in the fourth revenue. Van Groningen translates more restrictively as *ports de commerce* ('harbours which are trading centres'), which is probably correct. An *emporion* or market centre, however, was not necessarily on the sea, although in the classical Greek world this would almost always have been the case. In Hellenistic Asia, any large inland city might have been an *emporion*, particularly those situated on major river systems, for example Seleukeia-Tigris or Antioch-Orontes. What is to be understood here, probably, is large-scale trading activity in cities, more often than not the result of transport of goods by water, rather than the usual market of a town or village.[9]

Τετάρτη δὲ καὶ ἡ ἀπὸ τῶν κατὰ γῆν τε καὶ ἀγοραίων τελῶν γινομένη.

The fourth [revenue] is that produced from tolls by land and sales taxes.

---

[8] Rostovtzeff initially interpreted the second type of revenue as that derived from private land, for which taxes were paid in precious metals, although he did consider the possibility of natural resources belonging to the king (1910: 241–2). This he later accepted as being correct (1941: 444).

[9] Again, the interpretation is difficult. For example, Rostovtzeff includes revenue from fairs along with customs dues and harbour dues (1941: 444).

In the Loeb *apo agoraiōn* is translated as 'from sales', while van Groningen's *marchés* may be taken as 'markets' or 'market transactions'. In LSJ, the translation 'market day' is also a possible one.

There is clearly a problem with the mention of 'land' here, as revenue from land had already been considered in the first source of satrapal revenue. The distinction is that *apo gēs* was used there, suggesting that taxation emanating *from land*, namely on produce, was what was to be understood, whereas *kata gēn* here may imply dues on land ownership and legal transactions *affecting land*. However, the preposition *kata* associated with land may also be understood in the sense of 'by' land and this would link nicely with the sales tax that immediately follows. First a product was transported by land and subjected to tolls along the way and then it was sold in a market, where a sales tax was collected. If this is the correct interpretation, it would make for a clear distinction between commercial traffic by water in the third source of revenue and by land in the fourth.

One inscription may be revealing in this context. At Herakleia-Latmos (Document 10), Antiochos III was called upon to grant the city and its port exemption from a number of taxes, including 'sales taxes and dues having to do with land as well as import and export custom duties . . .' (κ]αὶ τὰ τέλη καὶ ἔγγαια καὶ τὰ εἰσαγώγια καὶ ἐξαγώγ[ια]). Clearly there are two groups of taxes involved, each commencing with τὰ. The first group matches ps.-Aristotle's fourth revenue very well, if 'dues having to do with land' can be interpreted to include tolls, while the second group relates to port activities and so to the third revenue.

Dues on land transactions, such as land sales, might be included in the fourth revenue.

Πέμπτη δὲ ἡ ἀπὸ τῶν βοσκημάτων, ἐπικαρπία τε καὶ δεκάτη καλουμένη.

The fifth [revenue] is that from herds and flocks, called epikarpia *and* dekatē.

In the Loeb βοσκημάτων is rendered as 'from cattle', but this is too restrictive. Van Groningen's *troupeaux* ('herds' or 'flocks') is more general. An alternative manuscript reading of νομισμάτων ('of coinage'), that he simply points to without adopting, makes no sense and should certainly be rejected. In any case, coinage was treated under the royal economy.

In the Loeb *epikarpia* is translated as 'first-fruits', while in LSJ the specific meaning given to this passage is 'tithe paid for the pasturage of animals', but both seem unlikely. As with the tax on agriculture, what one probably has here is a tax on animal husbandry mirroring that on agriculture, which might be either a fixed amount (*epikarpia*) or a proportional amount of a herd or flock (*dekatē*). A pasturage due is generally described as an *ennomion*.

Ἕκτη δὲ ἡ ἀπὸ τῶν ἀνθρώπων, ἐπικεφάλαιόν τε καὶ χειρωνάξιον προσαγορευομένη.

The sixth [revenue] is that from people, called head tax and artisan tax.

In the Loeb *apo tōn allōn* ('from the others') is the reading here, instead of *apo tōn anthrōpōn* ('from the people'). This might naturally be expected to end such a list of revenue sources, implying the existence of a variety of others which it was not considered important enough, or general enough from the point of view of such a treatise, to enumerate. However, there is a problem, because the head tax and artisan tax then define this 'other' further. Rather than something vague, a kind of 'etcetera', this becomes a quite specific tax, on people. Van Groningen has rightly pointed this out and corrected to *apo tōn anthrōpōn*, which makes more sense. An instruction manual is designed to be specific and so, once land and animals had been dealt with in terms of a fixed or proportional tax, what remained were people.

In the Loeb *cheironaxion* is translated as 'tax on industry' and it may be implied that this tax was applied to the products of industry. However, it is preferable to see this as a particular form of head tax on a certain category of the population, the artisans, whereas *epikephalaion* may have been applied as a head tax more generally.

d. Summary of satrapal revenues

Despite the difficulty of interpreting precisely what each source of satrapal revenue in ps.-Aristotle was intended to comprise, it is clear that there were three basic groups: (1) land and its products, (2) goods and their transportation and sale and (3) animate objects: people and animals.[10]

e. Order of importance

A question that might be asked is whether the order of the six satrapal revenues is significant. If the author had simply wished to list revenues without any particular criteria, he had no need of *protē, deutera, tritē* ('first', 'second', 'third'), and so forth, so his selection probably has been made in terms of importance.[11] A point in favour of this is that the very first revenue, that from land, is termed *kratistē*, translated in LSJ as 'best, most excellent'. That agriculture was, by far, the most significant element of the underlying economy of the Near East has already been discussed in chapter 5. That it

---

[10] Rostovtzeff 1910: 241.   [11] Rostovtzeff 1910: 241.

was also the primary source of royal revenue, the author of the *Oikonomika* makes clear. There is thus a natural link between the two, which makes 'first' here equivalent to 'first in importance'.

If the order given by ps.-Aristotle is meaningful, as I believe,[12] here is how the different elements of the underlying economy would rank as sources of revenue: land and agriculture, natural resource extraction from the king's private properties (mostly), trading activity at market centres served mainly by water, tolls and trading activity by land, animal husbandry and people.[13] It is possible that this was the order recommended to his students by the author of the *Oikonomika* because he had a specific state in mind, since it is quite unlikely that each and every one, if there were several, would have had the same priorities. Which this state may have been and when will be considered later.

f. The continuation

In §5 and §6 the city and household economies are described and this first section of Book 2 effectively closes with:

§7 Ἐπεὶ τοίνυν τὰς διαιρέσεις εἰρήκαμεν, μετὰ τοῦτο πάλιν νοητέον ἡμῖν ἡ σατραπεία, περὶ ἣν ἂν πραγματευώμεθα, ἢ πόλις, πότερον ἃ πάντα ἄρτι διειλόμεθα ἢ τὰ μέγιστα τούτων δυνατὴ φέρειν ἐστί· <εἰ δ᾽ ἐστί, > τούτοις χρηστέον.

So, having discussed the divisions [of financial administration], we must next consider whether the satrapy, with which we may be dealing, or the city, is able to support all [the revenues] we have just detailed or most of them and, if so, to make use of them.

Μετὰ δὲ τοῦτο ποῖαι τῶν προσόδων ἢ τὸ παράπαν οὐκ εἰσί, δυναταὶ δ᾽ εἰσὶ γενέσθαι, ἢ μικραὶ νῦν οὖσαι μείζους οἷαί [τινες] <τε> κατασκευασθῆναι, ἢ τῶν ἀναλωμάτων τῶν νῦν ἀναλουμένων, τίνα τε καὶ πόσα περιαιρεθέντα <τὰ> ὅλα μηθὲν βλάψει.

And after this [we must consider] which of the revenues that are not present at all can be made to exist, or that are now small can be increased, or which of the expenses that are now incurred should be cut and by how much without damaging the whole [administration].

What is suggested (also §8 below) is that the financial administrator of either a province or a city needed to study the different types of revenue from his particular area of jurisdiction carefully and increase those that

---

[12] Also Briant and Descat 1998: 81–2.

[13] Rostovtzeff considers that the main income came from royal land, private land and, possibly, natural resources (1910: 243).

were present, but he also needed to determine if other sources of revenue could be tapped. There seems to be the sense here of a duty to maximize revenue (which is what I have considered in chapter 3 to be a cardinal point in the financial policy of the Seleukid kings). With regard to the other side of the balance sheet, expenses were to be cut where possible, but not if this would be damaging overall. One could imagine, for example, a reduction in military expenses to a level which might prove harmful for the security of a province.

2. INTENDED AUDIENCE

Book 2 appears to have been intended as an instruction manual for would-be financial administrators (also §8 below). In the introduction, the programme of the treatise is set out clearly, that there were certain fundamentals which could be learnt, but which required natural intelligence, industriousness and a sense of justice in order to be applied. The fundamentals would be taught, as becomes apparent in the development, by describing the different types of financial administration possible and the matters each dealt with. As for intelligence, industriousness and justice, these would not be taught, but examples of their application would apparently serve instead and indeed did, in the continuation of Book 2.

For the would-be financial administrator studying the manual, it is likely that suitable employment was envisaged and, therefore, the *Oikonomika* probably describes the conditions and opportunities of its time.

3. DATE OF THE WORK

It is accepted by most scholars, following the analysis in van Groningen 1933, that Book 2 of the *Oikonomika* dates to the last quarter of the fourth century BC,[14] but it is worth examining the basis for this, with the help of the history of the work given by van Groningen himself.[15]

---

[14] For example, Bikerman dates the work to the immediate predecessors of the Seleukids (1938: 120). Corsaro opts for the period between 323 BC and 305 BC, sometime in the transition from the empire of Alexander to the kingdoms of the Successors (1980: 1164–73; 1985: 84). Rostovtzeff prefers the last years of the fourth or the first years of the third century BC, with the Antigonid empire probably serving as a model, although very similar to the Seleukid empire (1941: 441). But other scholars place the work later, e.g. Musti: a possible reference to the Seleukid empire (1987: 135); Andreades: in Syria under the Successors, although whether Antigonos or Seleukos is not clear (1929: 3); Hornblower: probably Seleukid conditions with Persian features (1994: 62).

[15] Van Groningen 1933: 37–48.

Commencing with Niebuhr in the nineteenth century, scholars uniformly ascribed the work to the third century BC, differing only in whether it had been written towards the beginning, middle or end. Wilcken was the first to point out that the collection of financial stratagems contained in the second section had been presented essentially in chronological order, but that none dated to after Alexander's death, which, in his view, implied that the collection had been made at about that time or slightly later. However, there was a problem in connecting the stratagems to the first, theoretical section. The key lay in the linking phrase of §8:

§8 Τὰ μὲν οὖν περὶ τὰς οἰκονομίας τε καὶ τὰ μέρη τὰ τούτων εἰρήκαμεν· ὅσα δέ τινες τῶν πρότερον πεπράγασιν εἰς πόρον χρημάτων, εἴ <τε> τεχνικῶς τι διῴκησαν, ἃ ὑπελαμβάνομεν ἀξιόλογα αὐτῶν εἶναι, συναγηόχαμεν· οὐδὲ γὰρ ταύτην τὴν ἱστορίαν ἀχρεῖον εἶναι· ἔστι γὰρ ὅτε τούτων ἐφαρμόσει τις οἷα ἂν αὐτὸς πραγματεύηται.

So we have investigated the [different forms of] financial administration and their parts. And we have gathered together [examples of] whatever some of those in times past did to collect funds or of matters which they managed skilfully, which we considered to be worthwhile, for we do not believe that describing these would be useless. It may be possible for someone to apply some of these [examples] at some time in matters with which he deals.

Here Wilcken agreed with his predecessors that *tines tōn proteron*, whose stratagems were now going to be described by the author of Book 2, referred to 'people who had been living some time in the past'. Therefore, the first section of Book 2 must have been written later by a different person to the one who had made the stratagem collection. If the latter worked at the time of Alexander's death or just after, the former must have written in about 250 BC. The suggestion was that a student of the Lykeion had made a collection of stories to serve as practical examples in what was to be a treatise of Aristotle, which either never materialized or existed only in the form of teaching notes or was lost. This collection was discovered many years later and added to a short theoretical treatment of the subject by some other Aristotelian, perhaps with the help of the original teaching notes.

This idea of two separate sections was further developed by later scholars. Andreades pointed out that there was no connection between the two, the first having a scientific basis and showing the mark of a well-informed author, the second being simply intended to divert. More importantly, §7 promised a further development of certain topics, which never materialized or were lost, and, to replace these, the collection of stratagems was added with the bridging §8. However, Andreades reversed the chronological order of the sections, maintaining that the first had been prepared right at the end of the fourth century BC, exactly at the time when there were no tyrants about, since no 'tyranny' economy is mentioned, and that the second had been added at the end of the third century. This does not seem to be a valid argument, as we are told in §1 that other economies were included in the four principal ones and so were not considered by the writer.

Van Groningen attempted to reverse scholarly opinion, by trying to show that Book 2 of the *Oikonomika* was not an epitome, that both sections formed a unity, that they dated to the fourth century BC and that there was only one author. This has now been accepted by the majority of scholars, but it will be useful to re-examine van Groningen's arguments.

A fourth-century BC date is based on the argument that the king whom the author had in mind must have been the Achaemenid king or one who had inherited from him, but no reason is given for this. Apparently the fact that a Persian king ruled over an empire divided into satrapies was reason enough. However, countering this is a serious objection regarding coinage, which was certainly not the exclusive prerogative of the royal economy in the Achaemenid empire. The fourth century BC, right down to the last years of Achaemenid rule, saw the minting of numerous satrapal, provincial and city silver coinages all along the coasts of Asia Minor, Phoenicia and Palestine, in which regions hoard evidence indicates that the royal issues, the darics and *sigloi*, circulated in a distinct minority. Yet coinage is not mentioned in the satrapal economy and, therefore, the Achaemenid empire cannot have been the specific model for the *Oikonomika*, Book 2.

Van Groningen's alternative model was the kingdom of Alexander, as inheritor of the Achaemenids. He pointed out that in about 325 BC the reader of the treatise would have known of only one kingdom, that of Alexander, which bore some resemblance to the Achaemenid empire. Since, according to him, the empire of Alexander did not exist after 306/5 BC (with their self-promotion as kings by the principal Successors), and indeed after the death of Alexander IV in 310 BC, the work could not be representative of the situation then, therefore Antigonos Monophthalmos' short-lived kingdom (to 301 BC) was not the model for the *Oikonomika*.

My earlier point about coinage, that it was also part of the satrapal economy under the Achaemenids, is now no longer valid, since Alexander did in fact put an effective end to independent satrapal issues. However, there is another problem, namely that the latest stratagems in the second part of the *Oikonomika* date to not earlier than 325/4 BC.[16] Thus, if the author were visualizing Alexander's empire and writing a manual for its would-be administrators, this would have been prepared in just the two years remaining until Alexander's death. After this, what sort of a royal or satrapal administration could one speak of when the Successors vied for power, satrapies became in effect little kingdoms and Alexander's heirs were kings in name only? If anything, the only candidate at this time as a model is the one whom van Groningen rejects, Antigonos.

Van Groningen's point that the author must have been influenced by the world situation at his time is, of course, valid. But he then argues that, since the mercantile character of the Ptolemaic economy is not reflected in the treatise, the work cannot have been written at a time when this was in effect, presumably from the start of the third century. It is difficult to see why Ptolemaic Egypt should be excluded as a model for this reason, particularly if the second and third aspects of the royal economy, as described by ps.-Aristotle (*exagōgima* and *eisagōgima*), are considered to mean exports and imports, which were very much an area of activity controlled by the kings. The Ptolemies also certainly possessed an empire in the third century BC, which included several overseas provinces run by provincial governors. However, in one sense this differed from the Seleukid empire. Whereas the latter was the direct inheritor of the Achaemenid empire, in terms of much of its territorial subdivisions, Egypt had been just one satrapy before, to which the Ptolemies added parts of others. Would someone living in Asia Minor or Syria at the time have really considered the Ptolemies inheritors of the Achaemenids? Would he not have looked at something closer to home, for example the Seleukid empire? A model for would-be administrators is unlikely to have been based on the unique situation of Egypt.

Van Groningen suggests that an author writing in about 275 BC would not have known of one kingdom but of several, with nothing in common with the Persian empire. In the case of the Seleukids, he considers that satrapies are simply *mentioned*, without much greater significance, but this is not true, since satrapies, as organizational units, come very much into play in both literary and epigraphic sources. I hope to show in chapter 13 that the financial administration of the Seleukid empire inherited a great deal from that of the Achaemenids, as I expect a corresponding study of Ptolemaic Egypt and its empire will also show, but probably to a lesser extent.

---

[16] Stratagem 34: Antimenes in Babylon, appointed after the flight of Harpalos; stratagem 33: Kleomenes in Egypt, with whom Alexander would have communicated after his return from India.

Turning now to the different sources of revenue noted in the *Oikonomika* for the satrapal economy, one can find evidence for only a few in the Achaemenid empire[17] and hardly any in Alexander's. On the other hand, every single type of revenue is to be found in texts referring to the Seleukid empire (and will be discussed in chapter 8 in the order presented by ps.-Aristotle). Perhaps this is simply due to a lack of Achaemenid source material and the Seleukids, in fact, copied what they had found, rather than innovating themselves. But there is evidence to show (ch. 13.10) that significant financial changes did take place early in the reign of Antiochos I and that the sources of revenues tapped then were more varied than in earlier times.

The unity of the two sections is proved, according to van Groningen, because both were written from a practical point of view. This is a rather surprising evaluation of the first section, with its strict listing of the different types of economy and the constituent parts of each, the contrast with the later 'case studies' being most marked.[18] But there is an important argument in favour of two different authors. The first section starts off with the statement that the would-be financial administrator must possess natural intelligence, industriousness and *a sense of justice*. In many of the stratagems this last quality is totally lacking, hardly training for the kind of administrator that the author of the first section may have had in mind. Van Groningen concedes this point, but argues that the pupils of the treatise would be administering barbarians, so there would be less consideration for these! He forgets, first of all, that Greeks would have been amongst those governed and, secondly, that the administrators themselves were in some cases 'barbarians', representatives of indigenous populations. The modern view of the Hellenistic kingdoms of Asia is not the one that prevailed in van Groningen's time, that is, of a Greek colonial elite rigidly separating itself from barely civilized natives.

The objection raised by many scholars concerning the *proteron* (πρότερον) linking the two sections of Book 2 is not a significant difficulty for van Groningen, who does not consider this word an exact term. True enough, if it is taken in isolation, but not so in the present context. The text in §8 reads: ὅσα δέ τινες τῶν πρότερον πεπράγασιν. An aorist active participle is implied between πρότερον and πεπράγασιν as

---

[17] Briant notes these and then comments that Achaemenid-Hellenistic continuities lead one to suppose that other taxes known in the Seleukid period could have had their origins in the Achaemenid, but the documentary proof is lacking (1996: 410–11).

[18] According to Andreades, the second part of the book is not seriously trying to instruct, but to entertain (1929: 3).

the object of τῶν with the sense of 'living', such as βιοσάντων, so the translation should read 'those things which some who lived in the past had done'. Such a description could not normally be considered to apply to a person currently alive and one would expect the writer who had produced such a statement to belong to at least the next generation after the last person referred to in a stratagem, who must have been one of Philoxenos (stratagem no. 31), Kleomenes (nos. 33 and 39), Antimenes (nos. 34 and 38) or Ophellas the Olynthian (no. 35), with stratagems dating to *c.* 325–323 BC. If one generation is taken as twenty-five years, the first section of Book 2 cannot date to before 300 BC. We do know that Kleomenes was put to death by Ptolemy in 322/1 BC.[19] Of the other three, a Philoxenos is mentioned in 321 BC as having received the satrapy of Kilikia in the Triparadeisos settlement (Arr. *Ta meta Alexandron* 1.34) and is probably the same as the earlier satrap of Karia in the stratagem,[20] but we have no knowledge of his fate after this, nor of that of Antimenes[21] or Ophellas.[22] At the time when we hear of these men, however, they occupied important positions in the administration, probably in the prime of their lives and it is not unreasonable to suppose that one or more may have lived much longer and that *proteron* could be understood as 'long since dead'. In that case, the date of the first section of Book 2 could be brought forward still further, to about 275 BC.

I will accept van Groningen's point about the author living at a time when he could observe a kingdom that exhibited all the traits he was writing about, and particularly a fully developed satrapal organization comparable to that of the Achaemenid empire with, in addition, widespread use of coinage and a comprehensively varied system of collecting revenue. The kingdom of Lysimachos might appear too small to fit the bill, that of Ptolemy too restricted and that of Seleukos prior to Korupedion (281 BC) too remote to serve as an example. It was only when most of Achaemenid Asia came together under one master, Seleukos, in 281 BC, that the conditions were again right to allow one to speak of a 'royal' and a 'satrapal' economy.

But there is another point. The distinction of revenues emanating from water-borne and land-borne trade can only have had meaning for a Greek writer viewing the land-locked East at a time when the new cities founded there had had time to develop into important trading centres, since trade in the old Greek world had been almost entirely conducted by sea. By the reign of Antiochos I, this was certainly the case, as Seleukeia-Tigris, Antioch-Orontes and Seleukeia-Eulaios (= Susa, now connected by river to the

[19] Berve 1988: no. 431.   [20] Berve 1988: no. 794.
[21] Berve 1988: no. 89.   [22] Berve 1988: no. 599.

Persian Gulf) had become nodal points of both overland and river-borne commerce, as was also the case with several smaller cities. Furthermore there is evidence that important changes took place in financial administration in the early years of Antiochos I, which will be discussed in chapter 13.10. Thus the 270s BC seem to be the likeliest period, in my view, in which the first section of Book 2 was written, the second section having been prepared soon after the death of Alexander, but whether it was added to the first from the very beginning or later is not clear.

Van Groningen's strongest argument for dating the whole of Book 2 to the fourth quarter of the fourth century BC is its attribution to Aristotle. So, according to him, it must have been prepared in or near his time. This is true of the preparation of just under 90 per cent of the book, the part that deals with the stratagems, for which I have accepted an early date, and it is not impossible that Aristotle himself was aware of the collection. It is also likely that, faced with a new scholarly problem, the best method of administering Alexander's empire, Aristotle and his school would have been devoting some thought to this and probably preparing notes at the time. It would not be unusual for a later scholar of the Aristotelian school to observe that the conditions of his own time had again reverted to those of Alexander's, with a similar empire in existence, and so use whatever he could find on the subject, update it for the current situation, add the stratagems already collected and produce what we now have as Book 2. Since the bulk of the work was already linked to Aristotle, and most of the ideas of the first part also, it is not strange that Aristotle's name continued to be associated with it.

4. CONCLUSIONS ON THE *OIKONOMIKA*, BOOK 2

My conclusion, then, is that the first section of Book 2 of ps.-Aristotle's *Oikonomika*, the theoretical treatment of the four types of economy, is likely to date after 300 BC and probably to *c.* 275 BC, when it seems to be describing the administration of the Seleukid empire under Antiochos I. The order of satrapal revenues is indicative of their relative importance then. The second section, which details the financial stratagems, had probably been compiled several years earlier and added on to the first either when this was written or possibly even later.

In the chapters that follow, each theoretical aspect of the royal and satrapal economies in the *Oikonomika* will be dealt with from the practical point of view of the Seleukid empire and I will attempt to show that there is an excellent fit between theory and practice.

CHAPTER 8

Revenue

In this chapter the regular sources of income of the Seleukid kings are identified and, wherever possible, the manner in which these were tapped, with the description of the satrapal economy in ps.-Aristotle's *Oikonomika* (ch. 7) serving as a useful guide. Following this, various cases of *ad hoc* revenue generation are discussed. The question of what form the revenue mainly took, whether in silver or commodities, is also addressed, but the assessment of the total level of revenue at different times is left to chapter 12.

I. REVENUE FROM LAND

Of these the first and most important [revenue] is that from land, which is what some call *ekphorion* and some *dekatē*.

In the overwhelmingly agricultural economies of the ancient Near East, taxation of land and its produce was a major source of revenue for ruling powers.[1]

Two well-known inscriptions of the third century BC are the starting point when trying to determine the manner in which revenue was generated by the Seleukid administration from royal and tributary land and land grants. This is followed by a study of inscriptions relating to the taxation of city and temple land.

a. The Mnesimachos inscription (Document 5)

Mnesimachos listed the land grants he had received from Antigonos (Monophthalmos) and the annual tribute (*phoros*) assessed on each.[2]

---

[1] See Briant 1996: 399–487 for a review of tribute and taxation in the Achaemenid empire; Postgate 1974 and Kuhrt 1995a: 532–5 for the Neo-Assyrian empire.

[2] The inscription has been thoroughly analysed by Billows (1995: 111–45), with some differences of interpretation to my own, as will be noted later.

Specifically, the villages of Tobalmoura, Periasasostra and Iloukome paid 50, 57 and $3\frac{1}{4}$ gold staters respectively, while the land allotments (*klēroi*) in Kinaroa and Nagrioa paid 3 and $3\frac{1}{3}$ gold staters, the total *phoros* amounting to $116\frac{7}{12}$ gold staters each year. Out of all the villages and land allotments, two persons, Pytheos and Adrastos, had received an *exairēma*, a portion set apart (ἐκ πασῶν οὖν τῶν κωμῶν καὶ ἐκ τῶν κλήρων ... ἐξαίρημα ἔλαβεν Πυθέος καὶ Ἄδραστος), which may have been the two *klēroi* mentioned previously, but I shall argue against this.

The loan that Mnesimachos had obtained from the temple of Artemis, with the land serving as security, amounted to 1,325 gold staters and this was very possibly equal to the value of the land. Could this have been just an estimate made by the temple? Unlikely, as there was no real-estate market that could be referred to, this being a royal land grant to Mnesimachos in usufruct. Note that, further along in the inscription, the temple safeguarded itself just in case the king decided to reclaim his land. So there must have been some official valuation on which the temple could base itself and such could possibly have been the one for taxation purposes. The clue, of course, is in the amounts of annual tax noted for each land parcel, which are very precise numbers, suggesting that the land had been carefully assessed before the tax liability was set.

But why mention the *exairēma* of Pytheos and Adrastos, unless this land was *not* part of the arrangement between Mnesimachos and the temple, at least in so far as its revenue was concerned, which is what would have primarily interested the temple authorities? If one assumes, for the moment, that the *exairēma* consisted of the two independent *klēroi*, the total tribute assessment of the three villages alone would have amounted to $110\frac{3}{12}$ gold staters and the value of this land, 1,325 gold staters, would have been almost exactly twelve times as much as the tribute. In fact, at a rate of one-twelfth, the tribute on 1,325 staters should have amounted to $110\frac{5}{12}$ staters, only $\frac{2}{12}$ of a stater difference. Such a close fit is encouraging, suggesting that a one-twelfth rate of tribute is correct, but is not good enough.[3] Exactness is required, since a valuation of property for the purposes of a one-twelfth tax would simply not allow for wasted fractions. There are four other reasons why the isolated *klēroi* are not likely to have been the *exairēma* of Pytheos and Adrastos. Firstly, the text does not say so, as it could easily

---

[3] Alternatively Descat, who suggested the equivalence of the *exairēma* with the two *klēroi* and determined the one-twelfth tax rate, regards the very slight difference as resulting from a daric–stater conversion when the original Achaemenid assessment was converted into Greek currency (1985: 100–2). Cavaignac also took 1,325 staters as the value of the land and assessed the rate of tribute as 8–9 per cent (1923: 122–5).

have done. Secondly, the wording is clear that the land was included within the village areas of Tobalmoura and Periasasostra. Thirdly, Pytheos and Adrastos are not distinguished as separate landholders, but apparently held the two properties jointly, as only one *exairēma* is mentioned. Fourthly, the two pieces of land seem to have been of totally different sizes, the one in Tobalmoura containing a country house, dwellings of slaves and peasants (*laoi*) and cultivable land of an area requiring 15 *artabai* of seed, the other in Periasasostra with housing plots and cultivable land of areas requiring only 3 *artabai* of seed each. Clearly the part of the *exairēma* at Tobalmoura is about three times larger than the one at Periasasostra, yet the tax paid by the two independent *klēroi* is about the same. The conclusion then is that the *exairēma* is not the two *klēroi* mentioned in the text.[4]

The position then is this. For his total property, Mnesimachos was assessed for $116\frac{7}{12}$ gold staters. Excluding the *exairēma* of Pytheos and Adrastos in the two main villages, the assessed value was 1,325 staters and the tribute would have been $110\frac{5}{12}$ staters. So the tax assessment of the *exairēma* was probably $6\frac{2}{12}$ staters, almost exactly equal to that of the two independent *klēroi*, which amounted to $6\frac{4}{12}$ staters. In other words Pytheos and Adrastos, two individuals, effectively received the *total area* of two *klēroi* within the village territories.

b. The ekphorion

Here then is evidence of a ps.-Aristotelian *ekphorion*, a fixed amount of tribute assessed on land, essentially a ground rent owed to the king. One can also see that a detailed assessment of land value must first have been made and an annual tribute rate of one twelfth then applied on this, at least in this region of Lydia at this time.

Now it would be extremely interesting to know on what basis the assessment had been made. A clue comes from Herodotos (6.42), when describing the method of tribute assessment of the Ionian cities in 493/2 BC by Artaphernes, who 'measured their land by parasangs, which the Persians take as equivalent to thirty stadia, and after having measured in this way, set the tax for each' (καὶ τὰς χώρας σφέων μετρήσας κατὰ παρασάγγας, τοὺς καλέουσι οἱ Πέρσαι τὰ τριήκοντα στάδια, κατὰ δὴ τούτους μετρήσας φόρους ἔταξε ἑκάστοισι). It has been suggested that the parasang of area here would be the perimeter enclosed by a parasang of length (= roughly

---

[4] Also Billows 1995: 121–2.

5 kilometres), and so about 160 hectares, on which an assessment of 1 gold *mina* was made.[5] But the argument, although useful and thought-provoking, is too speculative.[6]

A different approach might work better. Let us assume that Mnesima-chos' two main villages were much like those one might find in the Aegean world today. These are nearly always of a nucleated pattern, separated from their neighbours by about 4 or 5 kilometres, depending on the terrain, so that a farmer need not spend more than an hour in travel time to service his most distant fields. Thus, a village's land usually occupies an area of some 1,300–1,900 hectares and the question, of course, is how much of this could be cultivated, with 20–40 per cent probably typical.[7] Using the mid-range figures and assuming cereal cultivation with a biennial fallow system, the area sown each year would amount to about 250 hectares. Barley was the main cereal grown in the ancient Near East because of the limited rainfall of the region (ch. 5.1a). At a rate of around 1,200 litres per hectare,[8] a Mnesimachos-type village might be expected to produce about 300,000 litres of barley a year, assuming for this exercise that only barley was grown on the land as a kind of equivalent of all foodstuffs.

Returning once more to Herodotos (6.42), one can envisage how Arta-phernes' measures may have been applied in practice. Officials of his admin-istration are likely to have visually inspected the land belonging to the Ionian cities and estimated or actually measured different homogeneous areas, assessing the quality of each mainly for agriculture, but also for ani-mal husbandry and other economic activities.[9] Done at the macro level of

[5] Descat 1985: 106–7.
[6] A parasang of area is more likely to be a square with a side of length 1 parasang, on the analogy of the Greek *plethron*, or about 25, rather than 1.6 square kilometres. Elsewhere, Herodotos (2.6) characterizes the units of land measurement in Egypt as an *orguia*, a *stadion*, a *parasangē* and a *schoinos*, as appropriate respectively to increasing sizes of land ownership. A city's territory was more likely to be estimated in larger parasangs than smaller. Furthermore, although only land measurement is noted in Artaphernes' measures, obviously the necessary first step in any assessment, additional factors must have been taken into account. Indeed, different types of land are unlikely to have been uniformly rated, as their crop-bearing capacity, and so tax-paying ability, could vary considerably.
[7] Descat gives 1,500–2,000 hectares for Turkish villages in the region, with 30 per cent cultivable (1985: 107), so 225–300 hectares each year under a biennial fallow system. Doxiades and Papaioannou estimate an average village area of 2,100 hectares in antiquity (1974: 49). Kramer's survey of ninety-six villages in western Iran gave an average village population of 488 (1982: 157). At 1 hectare per person under dry farming conditions (ch. 1.5a), such a village would require nearly 250 hectares under cultivation each year.
[8] Garnsey 1992: 148.
[9] Kreissig accepted that land was taxed according to population, area, productivity, location and other factors (1978: 42). Hatzopoulos noted that in third-century BC Macedonia vine-land generated twice the revenue of olive-land and four times that of grain-land (1988: 51). Andreades calculated that, on the basis of land area alone, Egypt would have paid Persian tribute of 270, Lydia 75 and Ionia 65

a city's territory rather than for each citizen's land plots, this would have been a manageable task and one can envisage that a city (or village) would have been characterized as being capable, under normal conditions, of producing so much grain (essentially barley in the ancient Near East, but some wheat in western Asia Minor) and so much wine and supporting so many animals. The objective of the Achaemenid authorities was presumably to impose a fair total tribute on the community, a city in one case, a village in another, and leave the community to decide for itself how to distribute the burden equitably amongst its members.

But the next step was the crucial one, the substitution by silver of whatever part of a community's agricultural and other production was to be taken as tribute by the Achaemenid administration. This probably coincided with the tributary reorganization attributed to Darius in about 519/18 BC (Hdt. 3.89–95). Since Darius' fiscal reform applied to the whole empire, Ionia included, it is likely that Artaphernes was simply making an up-to-date reassessment in 493/2 BC of the tribute-bearing capacities of the different cities in the wake of the Ionian Revolt, so as to redistribute the total tribute burden of his satrapy more equitably. Thus, at the time of the original reform, some evaluation of the productive capacity of different territories must have been made, albeit *grosso modo*, and estimates of production expressed as values in silver.

Commodity exchange for silver was, of course, being carried out in some places in the Achaemenid empire at this time on a significant scale, for example Babylonia or the cities of the Mediterranean fringe, but in most regions barter would have been the norm. For Darius, a certain quantity of barley or wine or a given number of sheep or goats as tribute was the same wherever they came from, so it might make sense to apply a uniform rate of exchange to convert a commodity assessment into a silver value. There is some evidence in the *Persepolis Fortification* and *Treasury Texts* for the rates that he may have used and that these were imposed by edict, albeit in the restricted area of Persis. For 504/3 BC the rates in effect seem to have been 1 Babylonian shekel (of around 8.33 grams) = 1 *irtiba* of barley (very nearly 30 litres) = 1 *irtiba* of fruit = 1 *marrish* of wine (very nearly 10 litres) = one-third of a sheep. There is evidence that the rates for wine and sheep remained stable well into the reign of Xerxes, but for barley the situation then is not clear-cut. For the only year for which we possess data,

---

drachms per square kilometre (1933: 92). This certainly points to productivity as the key factor, in this case essentially the difference between irrigated agriculture and dry farming.

the rate seems to have varied during the year in relation to the time of the harvest.[10]

Let us assume that the barley-to-silver exchange rate in Persis (1 Babylonian shekel = 1 *irtiba of* barley, or 30 litres) was applied empire-wide in the assessment of a silver tribute, or at least in Lydia, and see where it might lead us. Then our Mnesimachos-type village, producing 300,000 litres of barley-equivalent annually, would have been assessed for roughly 10,000 shekels. In terms of weight, a Babylonian shekel was almost exactly equivalent to a gold stater. With a one:thirteen gold to silver ratio in effect at the time,[11] the valuation of the village would have been about 750 gold staters and, at a tax rate of one-twelfth, the annual tribute due about 60 staters. As can be seen from the inscription, Tobalmoura paid 50 and Periasasostra 57 staters, suggesting that the line of reasoning followed above may not be too far off the mark.

What I am suggesting, then, as a possibility is that the Achaemenid administration assessed the land in terms of the values of the quantities of major commodities which they estimated could be produced in a normal harvest. The number of animals – principally sheep and goats – in a given region was probably also taken into account and the system may have been uniform empire-wide. Annual tribute was then calculated at one-twelfth of the total assessed value. The Mnesimachos inscription indicates that this system may have been carried forward into the Hellenistic period.[12]

c. *The* dekatē

It is just possible that ps.-Aristotle may have been implying in the wording he uses – 'this is what some call *ekphorion* and some *dekatē*' – that the ground rent on land and the tithe on agriculture were one and the same thing (ch. 7.1c). But there are clearly two different mechanisms at work in the Mnesimachos inscription. After detailing his landholdings, Mnesimachos listed all his assets (out of which Pytheas and Adrastos had received a part): 'So, from all the villages and from the allotments and the housing plots associated with them and the *laoi* with their households and possessions, the jars of the wine-tax and the money-tax and the labour-tax and the other things which are generated from the villages . . .' (ἐκ πασῶν οὖν τῶν κωμῶν καὶ ἐκ τῶν κλήρων καὶ τῶν οἰκοπέδων προσκυρούντων καὶ τῶν λαῶν πανοικίων σὺν τοῖς ὑπάρχουσιν καὶ τῶν ἀγγείων τῶν

---

[10] Hallock 1960; Aperghis 1997b: 284–8.   [11] Descat 1985: 104.
[12] Billows also suggested that the tribute in Mnesimachos' case was 'a fixed and known percentage of the land's mean annual produce', payable in cash (1995: 123).

οἰνηρῶν καὶ τοῦ φόρου τοῦ ἀργυρικοῦ καὶ τοῦ λητουργικοῦ καὶ τῶν ἄλλων τῶν γενομένων ἐκ τῶν κωμῶν . . .).

First come what one might call the producing assets: land, people and their possessions (e.g. agricultural implements). Then, the revenues derived from these: wine in jars (*oinēra*), a tax paid in coin (*argurikos phoros*), a corvée duty that could be imposed on the villagers (*leitourgikos phoros*) and, finally, 'the other things which are generated from the villages', presumably other products of agriculture due to the landowner.

One idea is that the *argurikos phoros* mentioned was the tribute to be paid to the king, as detailed earlier, and that the *leitourgikos phoros* was, likewise, corvée labour, perhaps on the road network of the empire. But both of these items are listed in what Mnesimachos clearly now considered *his own revenues*, since he then went on to identify that part of the total property which Pytheas and Adrastos had received as an *exairēma*. So it seems that he did receive these revenues in the first place.

However, if these were imposts due to the king, as the term *phoros* ('tribute') clearly indicates,[13] what advantage would there have been for Mnesimachos in holding the land? The idea of a royal land grant was that it should convey some benefit to the grantee for services that had been or were being rendered to the king, since a grant frequently served, in both the Achaemenid and Hellenistic periods, as a way of paying a salary or stipend to an official or a member of the royal family. Rather than go to the trouble of managing a royal property, extracting a surplus from it, converting this into silver and then making a salary payment, the king often found it more convenient to pass on both the revenue of the property (usufruct) and its expenses to the official concerned. The possibility that Mnesimachos did derive additional revenue from his villages and *klēroi* and then did not bother to mention this in the inscription will not hold in view of the detail he went into on other apparently less important matters, such as providing the names of slaves. And surely the creditor, for whom this was being written, the temple of Artemis, would have been more than interested.

So the position seems to be this. The land grant of Mnesimachos was assessed for tribute to be paid to the king, probably by the grant holder himself, and various imposts to be levied on the villages and *klēroi* for the benefit of the landowner.[14] Compulsory corvée labour was also to be provided by the villagers, probably under Mnesimachos' supervision, but

[13] Spek 1998b: 144–5.
[14] Also Rostovtzeff 1941: 495; Golubcova 1972: 148–9; Kreissig 1977a: 11; 1978: 42–3; Hahn 1978: 26; Descat 1985: 108. Billows, however, considers that the tribute was paid by the villagers to the

also perhaps on parcels of cultivable land set aside for his own needs, possibly the two *klēroi*, which cannot have been given to Pytheas and Adrastos, as we saw earlier.[15]

Whereas the amounts of tribute were listed precisely, the imposts due to Mnesimachos were left rather vague and it is as if the readers of the inscription, primarily the officials of the temple of Artemis, were expected to know these. There is thus a strong possibility that the imposts had been fixed for the region as a certain proportion of the harvest (*dekatē*) for agricultural produce (or different proportions for different commodities) and so many days in the month for corvée duty.[16] Some kind of regulation must have applied, otherwise there would undoubtedly have been a tendency for the grantee to try to extract as much as possible from his (precarious) land grant in his own short-term interests, but at the expense of the villagers' and the king's (as ultimate owner of the land) long-term interests.

For the moment then, one is left with the following revenue situation, that Mnesimachos' land was burdened by both a fixed tribute, due to the royal treasury, and a proportional share of the produce, due to himself as landowner, so both *ekphorion* and *dekatē*. One must suppose that the king had been entitled to both of these revenues, before conceding the land, but, once he had done so, the level of the *ekphorion* may have been set at one-twelfth of the value of a typical harvest. For the *dekatē*, one other inscription could possibly yield a clue.

d. The Laodike dossier (Document 3)

In the land sale to his ex-wife, Laodike, the assets being transferred by Antiochos II, villages, land, peasants (*laoi*) and their possessions, were once again listed, followed by the statement that the revenue of the fifty-ninth year was also being granted (σὺν ταῖς [τοῦ ἐ]νάτου καὶ πεντηκοστοῦ ἔτους προσόδοις). Further along in the inscription, Laodike was apparently offered a complete tax exemption (ἐφ᾽ ὧι οὐθὲν ἀποτελεῖ εἰς τὸ βασιλικόν), but it is not immediately clear whether this applied to tax on the sale or on the revenue from the property or, in all probability, on both.

In this inscription, there is no mention of tribute (*phoros*), as in Mnesimachos' case, but its presence is implied in the total exemption from tax.

---

chiliarchs, the estate owner's involvement being only incidental (1995: 126). My response to this is that it would not then have been necessary for Mnesimachos to note the tribute of the villages in his property declaration.

[15] Also Kreissig 1978: 99.

[16] This is accepted by Billows, who also estimates that the estate owner could extract at least another *dekatē* from the villagers after they had sold their produce (1995: 128).

Here one is dealing with revenue that was due earlier to the king as landlord, but was now to be collected by Laodike.

The king was definitely parting with his land, as, unlike Mnesimachos, Laodike had obtained the right to attach it to a subject city of her choice (ch. 6.3c). However, this does not seem to have been a true sale, but rather a divorce settlement camouflaged as a sales transaction.[17] The 'price' was 30 talents of silver and, if one accepts the evidence of the Mnesimachos inscription, this is likely to have been the valuation of the land for tax purposes, set equal to the value of its average annual agricultural and other revenue.[18] The king's real intentions may have been that the 'price' be paid by Laodike from the revenue of the land itself, as is implied by (a) Laodike's specified right to the revenue of the fifty-ninth year and (b) the timing of the three payment instalments in the sixtieth year in the months of *Audnaios* (December), *Xandikos* (March) and up to three months later, which, not so curiously, immediately follow the wine, olive and grain harvests respectively of that year. If two years' earnings were to suffice for Laodike, this means that her payments of 15 talents a year would come from exactly 50 per cent of the estate's estimated average annual revenue, that is, this was the ground rent on this particular royal land paid by the peasants (*laoi*) who worked it.

e. *Mnesimachos, again*

If in about 254 BC Antiochos II was collecting 50 per cent of the produce as rent on the land he was about to 'sell' to Laodike, there is no guarantee that in the earlier period in which Mnesimachos received his land grant from Antigonos, the situation was the same, but let us assume for the moment that it was and see where this might lead us.

Assuming that the assessed value of Mnesimachos' land was 1,325 gold staters, which represented the average value of a year's harvest, and he received 50 per cent of this from his villagers, or $662\frac{1}{2}$ staters, while he himself paid $110\frac{5}{12}$ staters in tribute to the king, Mnesimachos' net revenue would have amounted to about 550 gold staters or 11,000 drachms annually or 30 drachms a day. The grant may have been given to Mnesimachos in lieu of salary for some office that he held. By way of comparison, the Ptolemaic general in charge of the forces that faced Antiochos III in Phoenicia and Palestine, Skopas, received 1000 drachms a day and each of his staff officers 100 drachms (Polyb. 13.2.3), three times as much as Mnesimachos, but, of course, this may not have been Mnesimachos' only income.

---

[17] *RC* 97 for references.   [18] Also Rostovtzeff 1910: 263–4; Hahn 1978: 16.

f. An interim conclusion on royal land

What one may conclude then is this. Royal land was subject to a rent from its tenants, for example the *laoi* of villages in western Asia Minor, which in some cases amounted to 50 per cent of the harvest. When the king granted the land to some other party, he might choose to charge tribute on it, essentially a ground rent, perhaps set at one twelfth of the estimated average harvest. The grantee could then dispose of the remainder.

Obviously two cases, Mnesimachos' and Laodike's, will not permit one to generalize, so more evidence is sought for rates of taxation of land and its produce in the Seleukid empire.

Later in this chapter the development of taxation in Judaea after the Seleukid conquest in about 200 BC will be studied and it will be seen that, at some point in time, both tribute and a tax of one-third of the grain crop and one-half of the fruit crop were being applied simultaneously. This rate of taxation has been considered punitive, because of the Maccabean revolt,[19] but it does not now appear unreasonable in the light of what has been seen above or of Ptolemaic practice.[20]

A text from Babylonia dating to *c.* 308 BC apparently concerns a dispute between the Šamaš temple at either Sippar or Larsa and the royal administration about the use of some land, which the administration eventually conceded to the temple at a rent of half the crop.[21]

In ch. 5.6a, prices of commodities in Babylon in the Seleukid period were analysed and it was noted there that a sudden halving of the base price of dates took place in about 208 BC and remained in force for seventy or more years, subject only to fluctuations because of good or bad harvests and the time of the year in relation to the harvest. This may well have been due to an administrative decision, such as an exemption of this commodity from a 50 per cent tax (ch. 13.10). Exactly the same applied to another commodity, mustard.

From the point of view of the king it was desirable to generate as much revenue as possible from the land without placing the producer in jeopardy (and so killing the goose that laid the golden egg). The amount of ground rent on royal land (or tribute and tax on other land) could be set at an appropriate level depending upon the productivity of the land. In irrigated

---

[19] Bikerman 1938: 179–80; Goldstein 1976: 407; Hengel 1981: 28.
[20] Abel points to the *tritē* (one-third) and *hemiseuma* (one-half) taxes on viticulture in the Ptolemaic kingdom (1949: 186–7). Préaux notes that the Ptolemies could take more than half of a royal tenant's harvest in taxation or impose import duties of 50 per cent (1939: 134, 182, 375).
[21] Spek 1995: 238–41.

Mesopotamia, for example, with its higher productivity, 50 per cent of the grain crop might appear reasonable as the king's share and also perhaps on a choice property such as the land granted to Laodike. Elsewhere, the proportion collected by the king could well have been less, such as in dry-farming Judaea, at one-third of the grain harvest. But, one is left with the impression that, overall, royal and tributary land and its produce were heavily taxed and may have been the principal source of the king's revenue.[22]

By way of comparison, in Mauryan India all land is said to have belonged to the king and seems to have been equally heavily taxed, with a ground rent and a produce tax totalling not less than 50 per cent.[23]

Finally, there was one other source of revenue from royal land: by outright sale, for example the 330 plus 50 talents earned by Antiochos I from Pitane (*OGIS* 335, lines 132–4). This may reflect the policy suggested in chapter 6 of a cost-benefit approach to the disposal of royal land, rather than simple generosity. To work the land in Pitane's case may have been considered unprofitable by the king and there was still the question of extra tribute to be received from the city, perhaps at the one-twelfth rate.

g. Klēroi

Two *klēroi* (land allotments) were included in Mnesimachos' land grant, each subject to a different tribute, suggesting once more that great care had been taken in assessing the value of even the smallest land-parcel based

---

[22] *For low taxes on land.* Cavaignac estimates that taxation on land was more than 10 per cent, but considers that the one-third and one-half rates in Judaea were high, perhaps a remnant of Ptolemaic practice (1923: 114). Kreissig maintains that Judaean taxation had worsened after Magnesia (1978: 112), while Freyne regards Judaean land taxes as exorbitant (1980: 185–6).

For high taxes on land. According to Shipley, the primary aim of the satrapal economy was the raising of tribute through exploitation of the non-Greek *laoi* (1993: 275). Briant supports the idea of a very heavy tribute (*phoros*) on the village communities (1973: 116). Foraboschii regards the central function of taxation as that of skimming off the surplus from the producers (2000: 39).

[23] *For Indian taxation.* From Strabo 15.1.40 (= Megasthenes fr. 33.5): ἐστὶ δ' ἡ χώρα βασιλικὴ πᾶσα· μισθοῦ δ' αὐτὴν ἐπὶ τετάρταις ἐργάζονται τῶν καρπῶν [οἱ γεωργοί] ... ('and the whole country is royal land. And [the farmers] cultivate it for a quarter of the produce as their wage ...' or, more probably, 'for a rent in addition to a quarter of the produce ...').

From Diodoros 2.40.5 (= Megasthenes fr. 1.46): τῆς δὲ χώρας μισθοὺς τελοῦσι [οἱ γεωργοί] διὰ τὸ πᾶσαν τὴν Ἰνδικὴν βασιλικὴν εἶναι, ἰδιώτῃ δὲ μηδενὶ γῆν ἐξεῖναι κεκτῆσθαι· χωρὶς δὲ τῆς μισθώσεως τετάρτην εἰς τὸ βασιλικὸν τελοῦσι ... ('and the rent of the land is paid [by the farmers] to the king because the whole of India is royal property, it not being permitted for any private individual to own land. Apart from the rent, they pay a quarter [of the produce] to the royal treasury').

Considering both texts together, the rent was 25 per cent, or possibly even 50 per cent, and the agricultural tithe a further 25 per cent. Stein compares the evidence of Megasthenes and Kautilya's *Artašastra*, in which the Mauryan king was expected to receive one-quarter or one-third of the harvest under dry-farming conditions, so probably even more from irrigated land (1922: 95–6).

on its agricultural potential and then applying a factor of one-twelfth. No distinction is made between the *klēroi* and the villages when detailing the revenue and corvée labour owed to Mnesimachos and it is therefore quite possible that the *klēroi* were actually cultivated by the *laoi* of the villages for Mnesimachos' personal needs.

Elsewhere, however, there is direct evidence of a tax on the production of *klēroi*. At Magnesia-Sipylos, Seleukid *klēroi* were to be free of the tithe (ἀδεκάτευτοι) (*OGIS* 229, line 101), while a tax rate of one-twentieth on wine and one-tenth on grain and other crops was applied to Attalid cleruchs.[24] This appears very lenient compared to the harsh treatment of native land, but then the purpose of a *klēros* was to give its holder a reasonable income as compensation for services rendered or being rendered to the king.

h. City land

Since the empire was considered 'spear-won', all its land was subject one way or another to the authority of the king. The boundaries of the land (*chōra*) of existing cities, Greek and non-Greek, had been reconfirmed in the main after Alexander's conquest and his successors made no serious attempt to change the *status quo*. The new foundations that had been established made extensive use of non-city land, probably including that privately owned by the king (*basilikē chōra*). In all these cases, what was implied was a land grant by the king to the cities, in return for which he might demand tribute and taxation on the produce of the land. In principle this did not differ from a grant to an individual, such as Mnesimachos or Laodike, but, in each particular case, the king would decide at what level to set tribute and land taxes, if at all. Bearing in mind that a city could generate important revenue for him in other ways, such as from taxation on agricultural produce entering the city – emanating from royal land for example – or trade and industry in general, he could afford to be lenient in dealing with city land.

It is perhaps for this reason that one frequently finds cities granted *aphorologēsia* or *ateleia* or *aneisphoria* or the right not to be subject to the *suntaxis*.[25] The terminology is unfortunately not used consistently, so in many cases one cannot tell what exactly was being exempted. Normally *phoros* refers to tribute, whether of a city or a native village, and was considered the sign of subjugation,[26] but it sometimes included taxes on agriculture

[24] *RC* 51.   [25] Hahn 1978: 13–16.   [26] Bikerman 1938: 108.

and other activities, often the plural, *phoroi*, being used then, which may imply just this wider range of imposts. *Telē* are mostly applied to indirect taxes, whether due to the royal treasury or a city, but not always. *Eisphorai* (or *epitagai* or *epigraphai*) are typically special contributions of citizens to city revenue, but could sometimes be demanded by the royal authorities (e.g. *I. Labraunda*, no. 42). The term *suntaxis*, literally 'contribution', often replaces *phoros* for a city, really a kind of euphemism for tribute to create the impression that there was no subjugation, but an alliance between king and city instead. When Alexander 'liberated' the Ionian cities, he did away with the *phoros*, but imposed an equal *suntaxis* for the war against the Persians, as the inscription from Priene (*OGIS* 1) mentioned earlier shows. In this sense, the special 'contribution' imposed by Antiochos I on the cities of Asia Minor to help to finance the war against the Galatians, the *galatikon*, may have been estimated in exactly the same way as tribute, proportionally to the size and wealth of a city and its land.[27]

That subject cities were sometimes subject to a tax on agriculture may be inferred in an inscription from Mylasa:[28] 'and those that lease land will cultivate it as do the rest who cultivate their own land, and will pay all the contributions, both the taxes due to the royal treasury and the city, exactly like those who cultivate their own land' ([καὶ γεωρ]γῶνται οἱ μισθωσά-μενοι τὴν γῆν καθάπερ καὶ οἱ λοιποὶ τὰς ἰδίας γεωργίας ἐ[ργάζον]ται, καὶ τάς τε εἰσφορὰς διορθώσονται πάσας [καὶ τὰ] προσπίπτοντα ἐκ τοῦ βασιλικοῦ ἢ [πολι]τικοῦ καθάπερ καὶ οἱ τὰς ἰδίας γεωργίας γεωργοῦντες).

An inscription from Aigai in Aiolis clearly shows royal taxation on agricultural land: a *dekatē* on what is probably grain production and a one-eighth tax on fruit (*xulinos karpos*), but there is no mention of whether or not a *phoros* was also applied.[29] Since fruit was generally taxed more heavily than grain, the *dekatē* here may literally have been a tenth of the crop.

In concessions of Antiochos III to Teos,[30] the *suntaxeis* are distinct from the tribute and must imply all the other forms of taxation levied on Teos, including perhaps a tax on agriculture (First decree, lines 17–20): 'coming to the Assembly in person, he declared our city and *chōra* sacred and invi-olate and free of tribute and promised that he would free us of the other imposts that we had been burdened with by king Attalos' (παρελθὼν εἰς τὴν ἐκκλησίαν αὐτὸς ἀνῆκε τὴ[ν] πόλιν καὶ τὴν χώραν ἡμῶν ἱερὰν καὶ

---

[27] *RC* 15; Bikerman 1938: 110.   [28] Le Bas and Waddington 1972, no. 404.   [29] Malay 1983.
[30] Herrmann 1965; Ma 1997; 1999: nos. 17 and 18.

ἄσυλον καὶ ἀφορολόγητον [κα]ὶ τῶν ἄλλων ὧν ἐφέρομεν συντάξεων βασιλεῖ Ἀττάλωι ὑπεδέξατο ἀπολυθήσεσθαι ἡμᾶς δι' αὐτοῦ).

The king apparently kept his promise and granted some benefits immediately and others later, upon which the grateful citizens of Teos honoured the king again (Second decree, lines 50–3): 'because not only did the king offer us peace, but also brought relief for the future from the heavy and harsh burden of taxes and made profitable and secure the work and the harvests [of the city]' (ἐπειδὴ οὐ μόνον εἰρήνην ἡμῖν ὁ βασιλεὺς παρέσχεν, ἀλλὰ καὶ [τῶν] βαρέων καὶ σκληρῶν ἐκ<κ>ούφησιν εἰς τὸ μετὰ ταῦτα τελῶν παραλύ[σας] τῶν συντάξεων καὶ λυσιτελεῖς τὰς ἐν τῆι χώραι μετ' ἀσφαλεί[ας π]εποίηκεν ἐργασίας καὶ τὰς καρπείας). No doubt a harvest would be more profitable if a tax on it were removed.

A petition of Herakleia-Latmos to Antiochos III (Document 10) makes a specific request for exemption from taxes (*ateleia*) on all agricultural produce (ἀξιώσαντες δὲ καὶ ἀτέλειαν συγχωρῆσαι τῶν ἐκ τῆς γῆς καρπῶν πάντων). The Herakleians had already received other concessions previously from the king, which they pleaded should be retained (καὶ παρακαλέσοντας τά τε ὑπὸ τῶν βασιλέων συγκεχωρημένα [συνδιατηρηθῆν]αι).

Since *aphorologēsia* is not mentioned in the new 'shopping list' of the Herakleians, it is not unreasonable to suppose that it had been granted in the first batch of royal concessions, as in the case of Teos above, which reinforces the argument for the Teans requesting tax exemption also on agriculture at their second attempt.

An inscription, possibly from Seleukeia-Tralleis of the same period,[31] mentions the concession of a *dekatē* by Antiochos III in response to a petition of the city: 'we have released you from the *dekatē* that is owed to the royal treasury concerning . . .' (ἀφήκαμεν ὑμῖν τὴν ἀποτελουμένην εἰς τὸ] βασιλικὸν δεκάτην τῶ[ν – c. 29 –]). By analogy with Aigai, Teos and Herakleia, this may well have been a tithe on agriculture. Indeed, what would fit well in the *lacuna* is 'grain and fruit crops' ('καρπῶν τῆς γῆς καὶ ξυλίνων καρπῶν').

The time and place of all these inscriptions is about the same, the period of reconquest of western Asia Minor by Antiochos III, and their similarity is striking. It might not be unreasonable to suppose that they reflect a royal policy of graded concessions to enlist and maintain city support. Fixed tribute, psychologically onerous, was done away with first, while the removal of proportional taxation on agriculture followed later.

---

[31] *RC* 41.

i. Temple land

A temple and its land might be assessed for the purposes of tribute as part of a city's territory or separately. In fiscal terms, an independent temple was treated no differently from a city and subject to tribute and taxation in the same way on its land, with the possibility of exemptions.[32]

A *dekatē* was charged by the Seleukid administration on the land of the sanctuary of Apollo at Tralleis.[33] The kings may not have interfered much with the land of Babylonian temples, but they expected part of the yields,[34] and indeed 50 per cent in at least one case (see above). We may have parallels at Jerusalem regarding the efforts of Heliodorus, Seleukos IV's minister, to expropriate part of the Temple treasure that was purportedly being withheld from the king (2 Macc. 3.6). Later, a lump-sum annual tribute of 5,000 shekels, or 10,000 drachms, had been applied to the Temple, which Demetrios I relinquished (1 Macc. 10.42; Jos. *AJ* 13.55), and this is probably the tax that Lysias had intended to put up for tender to tax-contractors, 'as for all other native sanctuaries' (2 Macc. 11.3: καθὼς τὰ λοιπὰ τῶν ἐθνῶν τεμένη).

j. Scope of taxation on agriculture

No doubt the major commodities (grain, olives, wine, fruit, dates and sesame) yielded the bulk of taxation revenue from land, but the administration seems to have had a fiscal interest in every agricultural product. In early second-century BC Telmessos there was a lightening of the taxation burden on fodder (χόρτος) and straw (ἄχυρα), although whether under a local dynast, Antiochos III or Eumenes II is unclear.[35] In Babylon the *Astronomical Diaries* show a sudden halving of the price of mustard in about 208 BC at the same time as that for dates noted above, again suggesting the removal of a tax (chs. 5.6a; 13.10).

k. Rates of tribute and taxation of cities and temples

In all the cases of cities and temples considered above, the level of tribute is not mentioned, as if it were something well known. With regard to the cities of western Asia Minor, these had been assessed in the past by the Persians in the manner described by Herodotos (6.42). No doubt the assessment

---

[32] Kreissig 1977b: 377; Debord 1982: 176–7; Ma 1997: 108; 1999: 134.
[33] Piejko 1988: 55–6.   [34] Spek 1995: 194.   [35] Wörrle 1979: 83.

might have changed from time to time, as land, population and economic activity increased or decreased, but for large periods it was likely to have remained constant in the books of the imperial administration.

If the land grants of the kings are anything to go by, the level of tribute may not have been high, perhaps only one-twelfth of the silver value of an average harvest (section 1b above), which is perhaps why *aphorologēsia* was such a relatively frequent and early concession. Direct taxation of agriculture also seems to have been quite modest, perhaps no more than one-eighth of the harvest, with the *dekatē* that is frequently mentioned in inscriptions perhaps being just that, a tenth. But the king was not a philanthropist by nature. He balanced economic and political considerations and, indeed, my thesis is that he strove to maximize his revenue within the limits imposed by politics (ch. 3). In the case of a subject city he expected to earn more from indirect taxation on trade and industry and could afford to be generous on land taxes.

l. Summary of revenue from land

To summarize then, all land in the Seleukid empire may have been subject to tribute (or ground rent), as a sign of submission to the king, as well as to a proportional tax on agriculture, in ps.-Aristotelian terms an *ekphorion* and a *dekatē*.[36] In the case of royal land, however, these might be combined into one proportional rent to the king as landlord. When land was donated to a city, a temple or an individual, tribute and tax were separated and the king retained the right to set the level of each, often reducing or abolishing one or the other, or sometimes even both. There was probably no fixed policy governing the king's actions, only a specific calculation each time of the political and economic implications. In general, cities and temples seem to have received favourable treatment and their burden is likely to have been considerably less heavy than that imposed on rural populations.

2. REVENUE FROM NATURAL RESOURCES

The second [revenue] is that produced from private property, in some place gold, in another silver, in another copper, in another whatever is available.

It has been suggested (ch. 7.1c) that the private property implied here consists essentially of the natural resources, excluding land, owned by the king.

---

[36] Pompey prided himself that he had replaced fixed tribute with a proportional tithe (Appian, *B. Civ.* 5.4).

The Seleukids probably substantially controlled the most important, such as metals, timber, salt, irrigation water and a number of special products (also ch. 5.3).[37]

a. Mines

Although there is no direct evidence for control of mining and quarrying by the kings, it must be considered highly probable. Not only does ps.-Aristotle place precious-metals production near the top of his list, but comparative evidence suggests that this was common practice for imperial powers, for example Rome and the mines of Spain, Philip II and the gold of Pangaion, the Mauryas and their royal monopoly of mining.[38]

b. Forests

Evidence for royal forests at Taranza and on Mount Lebanon, from which timber was to be cut for the reconstruction of Sardeis and Jerusalem respectively, has already been referred to (ch. 5.3c; Documents 9 and 12). For Jerusalem, there is explicit mention of the fact that the timber would be toll-free, but not that it would actually be provided *gratis* by the king. In the case of Sardeis, there is perhaps an indication that a gift was being made to the city, because of the serious damage that it had suffered, a similar situation to the grant of warships, timber and pitch to Rhodes after its destructive earthquake (Polyb. 5.89.8–9). In all these cases, royal philanthropy was probably conditioned by practical economic sense and the sooner a subject city or trading partner found its feet, the sooner royal revenues could return to their previous levels, hence 'free timber for now', but a return to 'business as usual' when the customer could afford it.

Comparative evidence from the Achaemenid empire, the Macedonia of Philip II and Mauryan India again suggests that the concentration of good timber stands in royal hands was common practice.[39]

---

[37] By way of comparison, Stein notes royal monopolies in Mauryan India for mines, quarries, salt pans, forests for wood and elephants, alcohol manufacturing and weaving (1922: 99).

[38] According to Stein, the *Artaśastra* informs us that the mines of Mauryan India were in the hands of the state, which rented them out to private operators (1922: 63). Strabo refers to a tax that was even applied to the gold dust brought down by the rivers (15.1.57, quoting Megasthenes). See also Sartre for royal mines and quarries in Asia Minor (1995: 84).

[39] Briant 1996: 456–8; Hammond 1992: 179; Stein 1922: 99.

c. Salt

Because of its vital role in daily life, other empires, such as the Maurya[40] and the Ottoman,[41] have tried to control the production and distribution of salt and the Seleukid was probably no exception.

Evidence for the handling of salt by the Seleukid administration in Judaea comes from Antiochos III's concessions to Jerusalem after the taking of the city in about 200 BC (Document 12), where two actions are listed with regard to salt. The first was to supply seventy-five *medimnoi* to the Temple for the sacrifices and the second to exempt the Jewish senate (γερουσία), priests and scribes of the Temple and temple-singers, that is, the upper classes of Judaea, from a tax 'regarding the salt pans' (περὶ τῶν ἁλῶν). The first concession suggests that the king may have controlled a salt supply in the region, possibly from the Dead Sea (ch. 5.3d), while the second relates to a tax in connection with salt that was imposed as a head tax.

Later Demetrios I also promised relief from 'the price of the salt pans' (Jos. *AJ* 13.49; Document 13: τὴν τιμὴν τῶν ἁλῶν; 1 Macc. 10.29: τῆς τιμῆς τοῦ ἁλός), which his son, Demetrios II, actually fulfilled regarding 'the lakes of the salt pans' (1 Macc. 11.35; Document 14: τὰς τοῦ ἁλὸς λίμνας). The precise nature of this Judaean salt tax has been much debated,[42] but, before this problem can be tackled, the evidence from Mesopotamia must be considered.

Seal impressions on *bullae* from Uruk relating to salt pans (ἁλικαί) typically have the legend 'ἁλικῆς | year | name of city',[43] as does only one *bulla*, dating to 286/5 BC, from the Michigan excavations of Seleukeia-Tigris. Then there is a gap and, from 214/13 BC, ἐπιτελῶν (*epitelōn* = 'taxed') or ἀτελῶν (*atelōn* = 'tax-free') was consistently added. Of the *bullae* found at Seleukeia in the 'Great House', a private building, those in archive B have only *atelōn* stamps, the majority dating from 188/7 BC to 153/2 BC in an almost unbroken series. Archive A, largely destroyed, has only *epitelōn* stamps, dating from 208/7 BC to 191/0 BC, and the suggestion is that it contained a complete series of *epitelōn* stamps preceding those in archive B.[44]

---

[40] Stein 1922: 99.   [41] Potts 1984: 236–41.

[42] Rostovtzeff regards this as a compulsory contribution to the management of the salt pans that entitled each person to receive a quantity of salt, which he paid for separately (1941: 470). Bikerman considers that the Jews were expected to deliver salt to the royal authorities, which they had to buy back at a price. Perhaps two taxes were involved, one on persons, the other on production (1938: 112–13). But later he revised this to a salt tax or perhaps an obligation to purchase a certain quantity at a fixed price (1988: 126).

[43] Rostovtzeff 1932: 81.   [44] McDowell 1935: 180–4.

The 30,000 or more *bullae* found in the Italian excavations of the 'archives' building at Seleukeia-Tigris also consistently show *epitelōn* or *atelōn* on the salt-tax stamps,[45] the essential difference with the Michigan excavations being that these *bullae* were found in what appears to have been a public, probably municipal, building.[46]

The Michigan *bullae* show considerable variation in inner diameter, indicating different lengths of document. They also have up to three or four private seal impressions and the suggestion has been made that they did not enclose simple receipts for salt purchases, which would not have required the seals of contracting parties and witnesses. Thus, it has been argued that the *bullae* probably enclosed annual contracts between merchants and importers or producers of salt, in connection with which a tax was levied or not, and that, consequently, there was no royal monopoly, but only a tax on the sale of salt, with exemptions for certain parties.[47] But I will propose a different solution:

(1) There was an attempt by the royal administration to exercise a salt monopoly in those areas where this was feasible, which goes back to at least 287/6 BC and so to the reign of Seleukos I, or rather Antiochos I's presence as co-ruler in the East.

(2) There was a requirement that every household purchase a certain quantity of salt annually at a fixed price from the royal salt pans or mines, hence the terms 'of the salt pan' (ἁλικῆς), 'regarding the salt pans' (περὶ τῶν ἁλῶν), 'the lakes of the salt pans' (τὰς τοῦ ἁλὸς λίμνας) and 'the price of the salt pans' (τὴν τιμὴν τῶν ἁλῶν), on which an additional sales tax was applied.

(3) At some point in time, probably under Antiochos III, certain persons and their households were exempted from paying the additional tax, but not the fixed price of the salt.

(4) The householder of the 'Great House' at Seleukeia-Tigris became such a person at some stage. Each year, a document was prepared listing his dependants (who might vary from year to year), the quantity of salt compulsorily purchased and the tax due or not. This was witnessed as to its accuracy and sealed by the tax-officer responsible for salt.

(5) Since the sale and taxation of salt were probably an important source of revenue, the administration no doubt wished to check that a household had complied with the law, and one needed to be able to produce past

---

[45] Mollo 1996 has produced a first analysis and considers that the salt-pan stamp (ἁλικῆς) probably does relate to a salt tax, but will not speculate how.
[46] Invernizzi 1994: 353.   [47] McDowell 1935: 185–8.

salt-purchase documents upon request, hence the need for safe-keeping in a private or public archive.

(6) When Judaea was acquired, a Ptolemaic head tax on salt already existed there[48] that may have been similar. Antiochos apparently relieved the Jewish elite of the tax, but not of the purchase price, and his successors probably extended this measure later to the entire population.

There is a certain similarity here to the manner in which another royal resource, timber, was handled by Antiochos III for the reconstruction of the Temple at Jerusalem (above). Relief was given on the timber tax at Mount Lebanon, but not, apparently, on the purchase price of the timber.

d. Water

The suggestion has already been made that the large-scale supply of water for irrigation was treated as a royal monopoly (ch. 5.3e). Although the evidence is lacking for the Seleukid period, one may argue on the reasonable assumption of continuity with the Achaemenid.

In the *Murašu Archive* (ch. 1.4d) a typical contract records water leased to farmers in return for one-third of the harvest, when watering was done directly, or one-quarter, when bucket-irrigation was used, plus silver that was equivalent to about another 5 per cent of the harvest.[49] It will be recalled that the Murašu leased water rights from the administration and subleased them to their tenants, along with land, seed and equipment. A study of the archive shows that the costs of agricultural production for good land may have been divided somewhat as follows as percentages of the harvest, without taking taxes into account: land only 5–10 per cent; seed 5–10 per cent; water 15–35 per cent; equipment (plough and oxen) 30–35 per cent; and labour 15–35 per cent.[50]

For comparison, the *Artašastra* records water taxes in Maurya India of one-fifth, one-quarter and one-third of the crop when water was carried by hand, animals and mechanical means respectively.[51]

e. Other natural resources

One does not know how other special products, such as asphalt, balsam and purple dyes (ch. 5.3f), were handled, but, as for timber and salt, a sales price plus a tax, from which there might be exemptions, is likely. For example, a tax is attested in Ptolemaic Lykia which apparently related to a

---

[48] Bikerman 1938: 112.   [49] Stolper 1974: 78.   [50] Stolper 1985: 125–43.   [51] Stein 1922: 23.

royal monopoly of the purple dye from murex shells (πορφυρικόν)[52] and is likely to have been taken over by the Seleukids when they acquired this region.

f. Pasture land

Royal land that was suitable for grazing might be leased to a city or village upon payment of an ἐννόμιον (*ennomion*) or pasture rights, which were probably assessed on the extent of the land or the number of animals using it.[53]

g. Urban properties

Whether ps.-Aristotle would have considered this item under land or the king's own property, the king was also the owner of revenue-earning urban properties. Antiochos III chose to relieve Sardeis of the rent of workshops (ἐργαστήρια) that he owned in the city, having probably built the *stoa* containing these in the first place.[54]

3. REVENUE FROM MARKET CENTRES

The third [revenue] is that from market centres.

When discussing this source of satrapal revenue in ps.-Aristotle (ch. 7.1c), I suggested that it may have referred mainly to bulk trade by water. In Seleukid Asia many important inland cities were located on major navigable rivers, such as Seleukeia-Tigris, Antioch, Susa and Aï Khanoum.

a. The case of Uruk

One market centre for which we possess some information, from the *bullae* found there and the stamps impressed on them, is Uruk on the Euphrates, a thriving city in the Seleukid period (ch. 1.5c).[55] A *bulla* stamped 'of the port of Uruk' (λιμένος Ὄρχων) may point to an *emporion* (trading centre) established in the city to attract commercial river traffic, particularly that moving up from the Persian Gulf.[56] The stamp is likely to indicate the

---

[52] Bagnall 1976: 108–9.
[53] *OGIS* 55 and Bagnall 1976: 109, for this tax in Lykia under a local dynasty.
[54] Gauthier 1989: 81, 101–7; Ma 1997: 129; 1999: 156. [55] Rostovtzeff 1932.
[56] Rostovtzeff considers that 'port' (λιμήν) here signifies fiscal district since, according to him, there was no port at Uruk (1932: 79–80, *bulla* 51). He is supported by Bikerman (1938: 116). But

application of port dues – known elsewhere as an *ellimenion* (ἐλλιμένιον) – on shipping for the upkeep of the harbour. A stamp 'of ships of the Euphrates' (πλοίων Εὐφράτου), appearing without other official stamps, could represent a fee paid by ships registered at Uruk that were authorized to conduct river trade.[57]

Most frequently found is a 'sales tax' stamp (ἐπωνίου) or 'sales tax of the port of Uruk' (ἐπωνίου Ὀρχηνοῦ λιμένος), but on what goods a sales tax was applied is unclear. On some *bullae*, this stamp is associated with a 'slave tax' stamp (ἀνδραποδικοῦ). It is interesting that no other commodity – for a slave was considered such – is mentioned in connection with a sales tax, suggesting that an additional tax may have been imposed on slave sales,[58] unless of course this was not a tax but a registration fee. Whatever the 'slave tax' stamp may signify, an organized slave market in any major emporium is likely.

Many *bullae* with a 'sales tax' stamp, or with this stamp together with a 'slave tax' stamp, have a '*chreophulax*' (χρεοφυλακικός) stamp as well. The *chreophulax* (ch. 13.7f) is well attested in the Greek world as the official responsible for the registration of private contracts and it has been suggested that he was also involved in registrations where fiscal considerations were involved.[59] A case has been made for taxation of slave sales and mandatory registration introduced under Antiochos I,[60] but the problem is that not all the *bullae* with a 'slave tax' stamp bear the '*chreophulax*' stamp. An ingenious solution that would account for the latter, when missing, is that registration was only compulsorily carried out by one of the parties to the transaction, the one paying the tax. So, in the *bullae* we possess are supposedly reflected some transactions in which the temple of Anu and Antum, the presumed owner of the Uruk *bullae*, was the other party.[61] But this might lead to

this ignores the importance of river-borne trade in Mesopotamia and is rejected by McDowell (1935: 174).

[57] Rostovtzeff 1932: 89–90.   [58] Rostovtzeff 1932: 66.

[59] Rostovtzeff 1932: 58–9; McDowell 1935: 131.

[60] Doty 1977: 323; 1978: 85; 1979: 195–7. Doty also notes a change in the method of recording, from cuneiform to Greek. In the last cuneiform transaction from Uruk, of 274 BC, he reads an official Seleukid seal impression as *kar-um-pu-lik*, so possibly *chreophulax*. However, McEwan deciphers this as *sa-um-bu-lu*, or *sumbolon* (1982: 51–3). See also McEwan 1988: 419–20. Oelsner considers that Greek contracts would have been necessary if slave registration became compulsory (1977: 79), but Stolper (1989: 88) and Kuhrt and Sherwin-White (1994b: 315) argue for the obligation to register slave sales in the royal tax office as an Achaemenid innovation.

Regarding registration, Rostovtzeff considers this mandatory for transactions relating to slaves, but used for other documents only in order to improve security (1932: 66, 72). McDowell takes registration as probable for slaves (1935: 178). Bikerman believes that it was widespread for all private contracts (1938: 117–18). Bagnall notes that in *C. Ord. Ptol.* 21–2, from Ptolemaic Koile Syria, slaves had to be reported, or they were liable to be confiscated (1976: 18–19).

[61] McDowell 1935: 7–9, 134.

the conclusion that every sale involving a 'sales tax' stamp on its own had to be registered as well. It is difficult to imagine for what purpose this needed to be done, when surely the main aim was to collect taxes at the quayside? This could be handled on the spot by Seleukid officials, after which a registered record of the transaction itself would not be of much interest to the authorities.

b. The case of Seleukeia-Tigris

Another important *emporion* was clearly Seleukeia-Tigris, the nodal point of overland trade routes from the East and the Persian Gulf and water-borne commerce. *Bullae* from the Michigan excavations (ch. 1.5c) show the impression of a 'port' stamp (λιμένος), again possibly relating to the payment of port dues.[62] A '*chreōphulakes*' stamp (χρεωφυλάκων) never appears with a tax stamp, but with other apparently official stamps, and once with a 'registration' stamp (καταγραφῆς), confirming that the *chreophulax* was indeed involved in acts of registration. No 'sales tax' stamp is used, unlike at Uruk, which is surprising.

A number of stamps appear in connection with slaves. Apart from the normal 'slave tax' stamp (ἀνδραποδικῆς), a second stamp (ἀνδραποδικῆς| [ἐ]πιιη[or [ἐ]πιφη[) has led to the suggestion that, since ἐπίφημι = 'to agree', ἐπιφημίζω = 'to pledge, to declare', this implies an official appraisal of the value of the slave prior to payment of tax in order to avoid collusion of buyer and seller with a low declared price.[63] A third stamp, 'slave tax on imports' (ἀνδραποδικῆς εἰσαγω[γῆς or -γικῶν), points to a special tax on imported slaves, perhaps different from that on home-raised slaves.[64] The fourth stamp, 'registration' (καταγραφῆς), clearly indicates an act of recording, probably of slaves.[65]

Considering Uruk and Seleukeia-Tigris together, what seems likely is that dues were charged for the use of an *emporion*, and a general sales tax was levied on transactions that took place there. Perhaps only one commodity, slaves, was subject to an additional tax, which may have differed between imported and home-raised slaves. The Seleukid authorities also sought to collect revenue on related transactions, such as official assessments and registration.

---

[62] McDowell 1935: 173–5; Bikerman 1938: 117.   [63] McDowell 1935: 138–41.

[64] McDowell, following Rostovtzeff 1932, considers the possibility that at Uruk the general sales tax (*eponion*) was levied on home-raised slaves (1935: 176).

[65] McDowell 1935: 144.

c. Ports of cities

A city might be distinguished from its port with regard to taxation, since, from the king's point of view, the port, as an *emporion*, could bring in important revenue from indirect taxes. In the case of Iasos, when taken over by the Seleukids, exemption was separately granted for city and port taxes.[66]

Port dues seem to have been a common source of revenue, as at Uruk and Seleukeia-Tigris. At Herakleia-Latmos (Document 10) these dues had been specifically allocated by the city earlier for the purchase of oil for the gymnasium and Antiochos III made no change, when ordering: 'and let the oil fund that was allocated from the port dues for the young men (in the gymnasium), continue' (καὶ τὸ ἐλαιοχρίστιον δ[ι]αμένηι τὸ ἀποτεταγμένον τοῖς ν[έοις, ὃ] ἐπεκηρύσσετο τῆι ὠνῆι τοῦ λιμένος).

Another important tax at ports is likely to have been customs duty, charged separately on both imports and exports, referred to often in Mediterranean trade as the 'one-fiftieth tax' (πεντηκοστή).[67] At Herakleia-Latmos (Document 10) different terms were used, *eisagōgia* (εἰσαγώγια) and *exagōgia* (ἐξαγώγ[ια]), for the dues collected by the king on imports and exports through the harbour. Customs duty on trade with the Seleukid empire is also attested in the exemptions granted by Seleukos III to Rhodes (Polyb. 5.89.8).[68]

4. REVENUE FROM TRAVEL AND TRANSPORT BY LAND AND FROM SALES

The fourth [revenue] is that produced from tolls by land and sales taxes.

a. Tolls and sales taxes

Lesser in importance than revenue from market centres (in the order given by ps.-Aristotle), this source of revenue seems to refer to tolls on overland trade and sales taxes.[69]

In Herakleia-Latmos (Document 10), 'the [sales] taxes and taxes relating to land' (τὰ τέλη καὶ ἔγγαια) – close to ps.-Aristotle's 'tolls by land and sales taxes' (τῶν κατὰ γῆν τε καὶ ἀγοραίων τελῶν) – were clearly distinguished from 'the import and export dues' (τὰ εἰσαγώγια καὶ ἐξαγώγ[ια]) of the harbour.

---

[66] Wörrle 1979: 110.   [67] Moretti 1977: 333.
[68] Bikerman 1938: 115–16; Moretti 1977: 332.   [69] Also Descat 1997: 259.

There was a good reason for putting tolls and sales taxes together, since a toll at a city gate might immediately be followed by a sales tax in the marketplace. At Herakleia-Latmos, free wheat had been requested from Antiochos III, along with a tax exemption for both imported wheat entering the city and wheat sales in the marketplace: 'that free grain be supplied to the city and tax exemption (be granted both) on that imported into the city and that sold there' (ὅπως σῖτος δοθῆ τῆι πό[λ]ει δωρεὰν καὶ ἀτέλεια{ν} τοῦ τε εἰσαγομένου εἰς τὴν πόλιν καὶ τοῦ πωλουμένου).

Tolls were probably applied at provincial boundaries and city territory limits or city gates, as can be seen from the exemption on tolls for timber brought to Jerusalem from the Lebanon, Judaea and other places.[70] Also, Antimenes, Alexander's financial officer at Babylon after about 325 BC, imposed a toll on all goods brought by travellers to Babylon, which had previously fallen into abeyance under the Achaemenids (ps.-Arist. *Oik.* 2.2.38).

The exemption 'from the *dekatē* and taxes' (ἀπὸ τῆς δεκάτης καὶ τῶν τελῶν) promised by Demetrios I for the city of Jerusalem 'up to its boundaries' (Document 13) probably applied to merchandise entering the city as well as to sales and other taxes within the city. The 'boundaries' implied here are probably those of the city's land, corresponding to the *chōra* of a Greek city. Normally one would expect *dekatē* to refer to a tax on agricultural produce, but this is dealt with elsewhere in Demetrios' letter (section 7 below for the case study on Seleukid Judaea), so one is led to the conclusion that a toll is implied here, indeed one of exactly one-tenth of the value of the goods.

However, a toll was not necessarily always set at one-tenth of the value of the merchandise,[71] nor need the sales-tax rate have been a fixed proportion, but both probably depended on the particular item involved.[72]

As to what the other taxes may have been, it is reasonable to suppose that some of these were applied on legal transactions, for example those dealing with houses, land or slaves, which might also require official registration (section 3 above).

But the royal treasury seems to have had a say in aspects of private dealings that one might have regarded as being beyond its jurisdiction. Two interesting Greek Parthian-period private contracts from Avroman,[73]

---

[70] Document 12; Bikerman 1938: 116–17; Ma 1997: 107; 1999: 133.   [71] Bikerman 1938: 116–17.

[72] Stein notes variable tolls at city gates in Maurya India, as recorded in the *Artašastra*: 4 or 5 per cent on grain, wood and grease, 6 or 10 per cent on textiles, 16.7 per cent on fruit and 20 per cent on imported articles (1922: 263). Strabo mentions a one-tenth sales tax in Indian cities (15.1.51).

[73] Minns 1915: 28, 30.

possibly reflecting earlier Seleukid practice, show that in case of violation of the agreement, not only was the injured party to receive a penalty payment from the other party, but the royal treasury also, an *epitimon* (ἐπίτιμον), which is perhaps an indication of how pervasive the taxation system was.

One wonders also if a toll was imposed at customs posts on travellers and their animals in addition to their goods. The captive Jews to be liberated without ransom by Demetrios I were granted tax exemption, as noted in 1 Macc. 10.34: 'and every Judaean who was taken prisoner from Judaea to any part of my kingdom, I set free without payment and all will be exempt from tax, (for themselves) as well as for their animals' (καὶ πᾶσαν ψυχὴν Ἰουδαίων τὴν αἰχμαλωτισθεῖσαν ἀπὸ γῆς Ἰούδα εἰς πᾶσαν βασιλείαν μου ἀφίημι ἐλευθέραν δωρεάν, καὶ πάντες ἀφιέτωσαν τοὺς φόρους καὶ κτηνῶν αὐτῶν). These Jews had apparently been deported earlier and, as captives, what taxes would they have borne and what animals might they have possessed? Head taxes and taxes on flocks cannot be excluded, but what is more likely, in my view, is that the erstwhile deportees were to return to Judaea, with pack-animals to carry their families and belongings, and were effectively being given a toll-free journey. And since these Jews were to be found in 'the whole kingdom', this suggests that tolls on travellers may have been applied empire-wide.[74]

Relatively important, probably, were tolls imposed on goods that crossed from royal land into city land, for example the timber from Mount Lebanon to Jerusalem mentioned earlier. At Herakleia-Latmos (Document 10) exemption was requested from tolls applied on grain leaving royal land, whether for private use or for resale: 'those exporting from the king's land to the city for their personal use and for sale shall be exempted from tax' (οἱ ἐξάγοντες ἐκ τῆς τοῦ βασιλέως εἰς τὴν πόλιν ἐπὶ τὰς ἰδίας χρείας καὶ εἰς πρᾶσιν ἀτελεῖς ὦσιν). With this added to the price paid to the king for the grain, the tolls charged for entering the city and the taxes for sale in the marketplace, the unfortunate Herakleians had reason to plead with the king for a lightening of their burden. And their case may not have been untypical of a subject city of the empire.

b. Religious festivals

One particular case of markets where taxes were levied by the administration was the commercial fairs associated with religious festivals or *panēgureis* (πανηγύρεις). Tax exemption (*ateleia*) was sometimes granted

---

[74] Stein notes a travel tax in Maurya India, as recorded in the *Artašastra* (1922: 98).

to a sanctuary for a *panēguris* for one or more days in the month or for the few days preceding and sometimes following the festival.[75]

The temple of Baitokaike in northern Syria was exceptionally favoured with *ateleia* on the fifteenth and thirtieth days of each month (Document 16),[76] while a sanctuary of Apollo was granted tax exemption for the commercial fair on its feast day (τὴν] πανήγυριν ἐν τῶι γενέ[σθαι ἀτελῆ])[77] and Herakleia-Latmos was also given exemption for its *panēguris* (Document 10).

The grant of *ateleia* does not make clear what taxes were involved at a *panēguris*. Perhaps dues for participating in the fair were one impost, analogous to the port dues of an *emporion*, but sales taxes were probably also levied on transactions and, perhaps, tolls on merchants and goods travelling to a *panēguris*.

The grant of *ateleia* was not wholly motivated by social considerations. A commercial fair attracted traders and customers from a wider region, particularly in rural areas which did not have easy access to large markets. The fair, in essence, became a temporary *emporion* and generated sales that might otherwise not have taken place, which meant more taxed production and transport.[78]

5. REVENUE FROM ANIMALS

The fifth [revenue] is that from herds and flocks, called *epikarpia* or *dekatē*.

There is some evidence for both fixed-amount (ἐπικαρπία) and proportional taxes (δεκάτη) on animals.[79] An inscription from Aigai in Aiolis, when it was probably Seleukid, refers to a royal treasury and a one-fiftieth tax levied on sheep and goats, yearlings being excluded, plus a lamb and a kid, along with a one-eighth tax on beehives, presumably on the honey collected. Furthermore a charge was made on deer and boar of a leg from each animal hunted.[80] At Herakleia-Latmos (Document 10), Antiochos III exempted a pasturage tax (ἐννόμιον) on animals and beehives, while a tax on flocks (προβατικόν) is referred to for an unknown city of Asia Minor *c.* 200 BC which used Macedonian month names.[81] At the sanctuary of Apollo Tarsenos, an additional tax exemption on sheep had been granted by Eumenes II, to add to earlier ones by Antiochos III: 'and let the god

---

[75] See Debord 1982 for the commercial importance of the sanctuaries of Asia Minor.
[76] Bikerman 1938: 117.   [77] Piejko 1989: letter A.   [78] Kuhrt and Sherwin-White 1994a: 452.
[79] Bikerman can, surprisingly, find no evidence of a tax on animals (1938: 118).
[80] Malay 1983.   [81] Robinson 1958: 75.

have tax exemption on flocks as well' (καὶ ὑπάρχειν τῶι θεῶι ἀτέλει]αν καὶ προβά[των).[82] The liberation and tax exemption offered to Jewish captives and their animals by Demetrios I (1 Macc. 10.33) may indicate a tax on the possession of animals (but also a toll, as discussed in section 4a above).

For comparison, in the Mauryan empire shepherds and cowherds paid tax from their animals (Arr. *Ind.* 11.11) and the *Persepolis Fortification Texts* show Achaemenid tax-collectors on their rounds gathering sheep or goats from specific tax-payers.[83]

6. REVENUE FROM HEAD TAXES

The sixth [revenue] is that from people, called both *epikephalaion* [= 'head tax'] and *cheironaxion* [= 'artisan tax'].

What might be considered head taxes are the 'crowns' or 'wreaths' (στέφανα) or 'crown tax' (στεφανιτικὸς φόρος) attested in a number of sources. What probably started as a voluntary gift from a city, a golden wreath with which to crown a royal benefactor, changed with time into a fixed annual contribution in coin, with the golden wreath sometimes added on top, as for example in Antiochos II's letter to Erythrai (*OGIS* 223, lines 4–5): 'and they brought us the wreath, with which you had crowned us, as well as the money that is given as a gift' (καὶ τὸν στέφανον ἀνήνενκαν, ὧι ἐστεφανώσατε ἡμᾶς, ὁμοίως δὲ καὶ τὸ χρυσίον τὸ εἰς τὰ ξένια), or the Jews to Demetrios II (1 Macc. 13.39).[84] That certain classes of the population could be exempted by royal decree is attested in Antiochos III's letter to the Jews (Document 12), in which two other head taxes are also mentioned. The first is described as 'those which they are liable to as head taxes' (ὧν ὑπὲρ τῆς κεφαλῆς τελοῦσι), the plural suggesting a number of taxes or, perhaps, different levels, depending on population categories. The second head tax is the salt tax, attested also in Mesopotamia and discussed earlier (section 2c).

The liberation and tax exemption offered to Jewish captives by Demetrios I (1 Macc. 10.33) may also indicate a head tax (if not a toll; see section 4a).

The Larichos inscription[85] of the time of Antiochos I refers to benefits offered by the city of Priene to Larichos: 'tax exemption on his person and

---

[82] Piejko analyses the inscription and suggests that this may not have been a tax on flocks, but rather a sales tax on sheep or a special tax on sacrificial sheep (1989: letter B, 400). Kreissig locates this temple on royal land (1977a: 15).

[83] For example, texts PF2025 and PF2070 in Hallock 1969.   [84] Bikerman 1938: 111–12.

[85] *I. Priene* no. 18, lines 5–7, 24–6; Gauthier 1991: 50.

that which he brings into or out of his own household . . . tax exemption on the animals and slaves located both on his estates and in the city' (ἀτέλειαν τ[οῦ] σώματος καὶ ὧν ἂν εἰσάγηται ἢ ἐξάγηται εἰς τὸν ἴδιον οἶ[κον] . . . ἀτέλεια καὶ τῶ[γ] κτηνῶγ καὶ τῶν σωμάτων ὅσα ἂν ὑπάρχη ἔν τε [τ]οῖς ἰδίοις κτήμασ[ι] καὶ ἐν τῆι πόλει).

Two interpretations are possible: exemption from a head tax on Larichos and his slaves and animals or, as is more usually considered, exemption from military service and the requisitioning of animals.[86] The former, however, is to be preferred since a tax exemption on the movement of goods intervenes, suggesting that the subject of the text at this point is indeed taxation.

Although the taxes here are city taxes, these could be wholly or partly taken over if the city became subject to a Hellenistic king, as noted for Telmessos and Iasos.[87] Then there is a frequent distinction between taxes due to the royal treasury and 'those over which the city retains control' (ὧν ἡ πόλις κυρία ἐστί),[88] which might sometimes involve the sharing of the same tax, presumably collected by the city and then partly paid to the king.[89] Therefore a royal head tax (ἐπικεφάλαιον) on a city's citizens and slaves is quite possible, although not attested.

For a village, however, a royal head tax is certainly known, one that was to be paid by the Kardakes near Telmessos in 181 BC, just after Magnesia, when the region had passed to the Attalids. Its level had been set at 4 Rhodian drachms and 1 obol for each adult. These were presumably *plinthophoroi* drachms at this time, so the tax was equal to exactly 3 Attic drachms, which strongly suggests a Seleukid tax originally.[90] If such a tax had been imposed on our Mnesimachos-type village of section 1a–b above, the village's annual 50-stater tax would have been borne by about 300 adults, a not unreasonable number for a medium-sized village.[91] This indicates that the head tax may have been an alternative, easier way of assessing tribute on a village, although perhaps not a usual one, since this form of taxation might then have ranked higher in ps.-Aristotle's estimate. Perhaps the strength of the village of the Kardakes did not lie in agriculture, but in animal husbandry,[92] while it

---

[86] Atkinson 1968: 50; Gauthier 1991: 55, 60. [87] Wörrle 1979: 107, 110.

[88] Bikerman 1938: 110; Moretti 1977: 327; Ma 1997: 128; 1999: 155.

[89] Gauthier (1989: 33–6) and Ma (1997: 128) note the one-tenth city tax of Sardeis, from the proceeds of which Antiochos III was entitled to a half, but did not actually exercise his right.

[90] *SEG* 19.867; Allen 1983: 95; Ashton 1994.

[91] Doxiades and Papaioannou estimate 700 inhabitants as the average village size in antiquity, so about 350 adults (1974: 48).

[92] Descat wondered whether Achaemenid tribute may also have been established on the basis of the number of people (1997: 258).

is interesting that the head tax here is euphemistically referred to as a 'contribution' (σύνταξις).

Turning now to the artisan tax (χειρονάξιον), a *cheironaxion* was applied to non-citizen artisans of Telmessos; they would be relieved of this if they undertook to patrol the mountain borders of the city. The city taxes of Telmessos had been taken over at the time by a local dynast or, possibly, the Seleukid king.[93]

In the sources there is also mention of a *cheirotechnion* or 'tax on industry' (χειροτέχνιον) in mainland Greece, which seems to have been the same tax,[94] the difference in terminology possibly reinforcing the idea that the author of the *Oikonomika* lived in Asia Minor or further east.

By way of comparison, in the Mauryan empire artisans, traders and wage-labourers paid tax and were subject to corvée labour, while armourers, shipwrights and those that manufactured implements for agriculture were exempted (Arr. *Ind.* 12.1; Strabo 15.1.46; Diod. 2.41.1).

7. CASE STUDY – SELEUKID JUDAEA

For no other province of the Seleukid empire do we possess so much detailed information concerning taxation as for Judaea in 200–140 BC. The questions, of course, will be whether the system of taxation in Judaea was similar to that in other provinces of the empire and whether it also applied in the third century BC.

a. Antiochos III's letter concerning Jerusalem (Document 12)

After he had conquered and taken Judaea from the Ptolemies in about 200 BC, Antiochos ordered, amongst other things, tax relief for Jerusalem, which had suffered during the war. Specific taxes are noted in his letter.

For the transportation from Judaea, other regions and Lebanon to Jerusalem of timber and other materials that were necessary for the repair of the Temple, no *telos* was to be imposed. This would imply that a toll was normally levied at the city gates of Jerusalem, at the borders of the province of Judaea and at the exits of the royal forests of Lebanon for certain goods.[95]

Three head taxes seem to have been applied, as some sections of the population were to be exempted. These have been discussed above (section 6).[96]

---

[93] Wörrle 1979: 106–7. Bikerman can, surprisingly, find no evidence of a tax on professions (1938: 118).
[94] Daux 1934; Flacelière 1935.   [95] Bikerman 1935: 16.
[96] Bikerman considers that the ὧν ὑπὲρ τῆς κεφαλῆς τελοῦσι ('that which they are liable to as head taxes') may refer to different head taxes according to local custom (1935: 18). Tscherikover notes, as

A three-year exemption from taxes (*ateleia*) was to be granted to the inhabitants of Jerusalem and all those who returned to the city by a certain time. This probably does not include the head taxes already mentioned, since the concession to the Jewish ruling classes would then have been of no value. So one must suppose that the taxes implied are those that were normally levied within the city for legal and economic transactions, such as sales taxes and registration fees. The distinction is being made between *telos* here and *phoros* in what follows, between taxation and tribute, which one will see being repeated in other documents concerning fiscal matters in Judaea.

The same inhabitants of Jerusalem were being granted a permanent one-third reduction in tribute.[97] There is a problem here, since it has generally been considered that tribute was applied as an annual sum to a collective entity, for example a Greek polis, a village in royal land, a temple, a dynast, an *ethnos* or nation, which in turn distributed the burden amongst its members as it saw fit. So why is Judaea not mentioned here, but only Jerusalem? It is quite clear in the text that the Jews were considered an *ethnos*, but apparently only in so far as their own laws and customs were concerned: 'the people of the nation shall have a form of government in accordance with the laws of their ancestors' (πολιτευέσθωσαν οἱ ἐκ τοῦ ἔθνους κατὰ τοὺς πατρίους νόμους). As far as the Seleukid fiscal authorities were concerned, however, Judaea seems to have been treated very much like any other province of the empire and Jerusalem like any other subject city, with a tribute assessment and a range of appropriate taxes.[98]

There is not a single tax concession in Antiochos' letter for the rest of the population of Judaea, unless a few of the members of the Jewish ruling classes, who benefited from the head-taxes exemption, happened to reside in the countryside. Indeed it is very probable that Judaea would continue to pay tribute, assessed on its towns and villages, as well as head taxes and transaction taxes. Perhaps most important of all, taxes on agricultural production and animal husbandry are not mentioned in Antiochos' letter, probably not because they were not applied, but simply because they did not affect the city of Jerusalem as much as the countryside (see the letters of Demetrios I and II below).[99] Since the only tolls suppressed were for

an example, the half shekel paid annually by each Jew to the Temple for the daily rites (1959: 155). But this is unlikely, in my view, because Antiochos had clearly stated that he would not interfere in local custom.

[97] But Hahn takes this, along with the previous concession, as tribute remitted for three years and then reduced by one-third (1978: 18).

[98] Also Schäfer 1995: 29. Kreissig (1978: 73) and Bikerman (1988: 126), on the other hand, consider that tribute was paid collectively by all Jews as an *ethnos*.

[99] Also Avi-Yonah 1978: 220–1. Bikerman accepts the possibility of some kind of tithe (1988: 126–7).

building materials entering Jerusalem for the repair of the Temple, including those from the rest of Judaea, one must suppose that tolls on all other goods, for example agricultural produce, would still be levied at the city gates.

In this light, Antiochos' gesture does not appear to have been quite so generous. In the position of strength in which he found himself in about 200 BC, the Seleukid king had no particular need to make concessions, nor did he probably have any desire to reduce his revenues more than was absolutely necessary. Indeed he would have preferred to increase them, if he could, which seems to have been the consistent policy of the Seleukid kings all along. Antiochos' decisions regarding the Jews were probably based on short-term political and financial considerations. The main beneficiaries were to be the Jewish ruling classes and the Temple, whose political support was desirable and would be paid for by the concessions. The rest of the population of Judaea was, in this respect, a negligible quantity. As for the Temple, it was central to the economy of the province. By repairing it, and in particular its commercial porticoes (τάς τε στοάς), and providing temporary relief from a number of transaction taxes in the city, the economy of Judaea could be stimulated. After three years, when the tax exemption no longer applied, Jerusalem would be expected to produce a satisfactory return for the royal treasury. There was also likely to be an improvement in the revenue-generating capacity of the countryside, as the city's economy, with which it was closely linked, grew stronger.

The position then, at the time of Antiochos III, seems to have been that Judaea paid tribute, assessed separately on Jerusalem and the different towns and villages, plus tithes on agriculture, head taxes of various kinds, tolls and other transaction taxes and perhaps taxes on animals. There is no mention of how the tax was collected, whether by the royal authorities or by tax farmers.

b. Taxation in the reign of Seleukos IV

At the time of Seleukos IV the tribute and taxes of Judaea are said to have amounted in total to 300 talents a year (Sulpicius Severus, *Chron.* 2.17.5). Either this is an estimate or, more probably, in the light of subsequent events, a lump sum promised by a tax-contractor.

c. The tax-farming concessions of Antiochos IV

The next reference to taxation is when tax-farming contracts were conceded by Antiochos IV to two high priests. Onias had earlier acquired the right to collect the taxes of Judaea, presumably the 300 talents above, but was outbid by Jason, who 'promised the king 360 talents, plus 80 more for any other revenue', but what this was is not clear from the text (2 Macc. 4.8: ἐπαγγειλάμενος τῷ βασιλεῖ δι' ἐντεύξεως ἀργυρίου τάλαντα ἑξήκοντα πρὸς τοῖς τριακοσίοις καὶ προσόδου τινὸς ἄλλης τάλαντα ὀγδοήκοντα). Possibly the larger amount comprised tribute and taxation on land, while taxes on people, animals and commercial and legal transactions made up the smaller amount. This would be in keeping with the idea that ps.-Aristotle has listed sources of revenue by importance and the very high taxation noted on land generally, but also specifically in Judaea (see below).[100] Menelaos exceeded Jason's offer by 300 talents (2 Macc. 4.24: ὑπερβαλὼν τὸν Ἰάσωνα τάλαντα ἀργυρίου τριακόσια), but does not seem to have been able to meet his quota (2 Macc. 4.27), which suggests that the fiscal capacity of Judaea may well have reached its limits.

d. Demetrios I's letter to Jonathan (Document 13, with slight differences in 1 Macc. 10.25–45)

Fiscal matters come up once more in about 150 BC, when Demetrios I promised the Jews that he would free them from most of the tribute (τοὺς φόρους) and taxes (τὰς συντάξεις) that they had paid his predecessors. His situation was quite unlike Antiochos III's in that he found himself in a position of weakness, in need of Jewish support against his rival, Alexander Balas.

The major difference with Antiochos is that there was to be no special treatment of Jerusalem, as what was offered by the king applied to the whole of Judaea, including recently added districts from adjacent provinces. Demetrios was compelled, so to speak, to lay his cards on the table and one can thus obtain a full view of the range of taxation in Judaea.

In Demetrios' letter, immediate exemption was to be granted both from tribute (τοὺς φόρους) and the tithe on agriculture: 'and of the value of the third part of the grain crop and the half of the fruit crop which was my due' (καὶ ἀντὶ τῶν τρίτων τοῦ καρποῦ καὶ τοῦ ἡμίσεος τοῦ ξυλίνου καρποῦ τὸ γινόμενον ἐμοὶ μέρος). Ἀντί is to be translated here as 'in place of', 'the value of' and understood as the equivalent value in silver of the amount of the commodity concerned that was to be collected as tax.[101]

---

[100] Abel regards the 80 talents as relating specifically to the collection of customs duties and tolls (1949: 331).

[101] Also Goldstein 1976: 402, 406–7.

It is quite certain that there were two different tax burdens, as the tithe is linked to the tribute with πρὸς τούτοις ('on top of this').[102] This helps to reinforce the idea that a tithe on agriculture also existed under Antiochos, but was not relieved, and is what the Mnesimachos and other Greek inscriptions showed as possibly being standard fiscal practice in the Seleukid empire for revenue from land, namely tribute (*ekphorion*) plus a tithe (*dekatē*) on agricultural produce.

Demetrios also promised relief from the 'price of the salt pan(s)' (τὴν τιμὴν τῶν ἁλῶν / τῆς τιμῆς τοῦ ἁλός in 1 Macc. 10.29) and 'the price of the crowns' (τὴν τιμὴν τῶν στεφάνων) and, separately, 'from the head tax on each person, whatever was owed to me' (ὑπὲρ κεφαλῆς ἑκάστης ὃ ἔδει μοι δίδοσθαι). These are exactly the same head taxes from which Antiochos had exempted only the Jewish upper classes earlier and confirms that there were indeed three. In fact, the phrasing of the last head tax does suggest that different rates may have been applied to different sections of the population. The nature of the salt tax has already been discussed (section 2c above).

Continuing with Demetrios' promises, Jerusalem, up to her boundaries, was to be relieved of the *dekatē* and the *telē* (ἀπὸ τῆς δεκάτης καὶ τῶν τελῶν). Freedom from *telē* – sales and transaction taxes – within the city probably matches the exemption granted earlier by Antiochos for three years, but the use of *dekatē* is puzzling. The terminology might suggest a tithe on agriculture for Jerusalem, but this would be absurd if the tithe had been abolished in Judaea as a whole. In any case, the terminology used previously for the agricultural tithe is quite different and it is more likely that the *dekatē* was specifically a toll, to be distinguished from the sales and other transaction taxes in the city.[103] It had not been mentioned in Antiochos' letter simply because no general relief from tolls at the city gates of Jerusalem had been granted then, but only relief on materials for the repair of the Temple, so one presumes that Demetrios had continued to levy tolls for goods crossing the frontiers of Judaea.

There was also 'to be no requisitioning of the animals of the Jews' (μηδὲ ἀγγαρεύεσθαι τὰ Ἰουδαίων ὑποζύγια), while the Sabbaths and feast days, and also three days before each feast day, were to be free of taxes (ἀτελεῖς). These last are likely to have been dues for holding a commercial fair (*panēguris*) and sales taxes, much as happened elsewhere in the empire

[102] Also Schäfer (1995: 54), *contra* Mørkholm, who suggests that Antiochos IV introduced fixed tribute and then replaced it with proportional land taxes (1966: 145–6). Freyne considered that land taxes replaced tribute after the Maccabean revolt (1980: 185–6).

[103] Bikerman 1938: 115–17; Goldstein 1976: 408.

(section 4b above). However, if the correct interpretation has been given to this document, sales taxes would not have been incurred within the city of Jerusalem anyway, so what seems to be implied here is the rest of Judaea.

There is, finally, the case of the liberated Jewish captives (1 Macc. 10.33) discussed earlier, who would be freed of tax along with their animals. Two possible interpretations were given (sections 4–6): either exemption from a head tax and a tax on animals or, more probably, from tolls on persons and animals, when these Jews travelled back to Judaea.

e. Demetrios II's letter to Jonathan (Document 14)

In a position of weakness once more, a Seleukid king again sought support from the Jews. It is likely that Demetrios I's earlier promise had not been fulfilled, as the high priest, Jonathan, seems to have preferred to side with Alexander Balas (1 Macc. 10.47).

This time Jonathan's demand was that Judaea and the attached three districts of Samaria be made tribute-free (*aphorologētos*) in return for 300 talents (1 Macc. 11.28), but this should not be taken literally, as the king would still earn 300 talents a year using the Jewish high priest as tax-farmer.[104] Demetrios II agreed and, as part of the package, ordered that the tithe on the products of agriculture – 'from the crops and fruit trees' (ἀπὸ τῶν γενημάτων τῆς γῆς καὶ τῶν ἀκροδρύων) – be abolished. He also granted tax relief from tolls and transaction taxes (δεκάται and τέλη), the salt tax (τὰς τοῦ ἁλὸς λίμνας) and 'the crowns which were due to him' (τοὺς ἀνήκοντας ἡμῖν στεφάνους). Compared to the 360 plus 80 talents or more that the high priest Jason had paid the Seleukid treasury in the reign of Antiochos IV for Judaea alone, Jonathan must have been getting quite a bargain, but his was definitely the stronger position.

8. EXTRAORDINARY REVENUE

In the theoretical section of the *Oikonomika*, ps.-Aristotle attempted to categorize the regular income of kings via their satrapal administrations. He did not make provision there for any *ad hoc* revenues, but these were dealt with in the practical examples that followed.

Seleukid kings raised funds from time to time by resorting to extortion and plunder. Such cases have found their way into the mainly hostile sources for their reigns, for example Polybios for temple-plundering by

---

[104] Also Schäfer 1995: 54.

Antiochos IV (31.9) or 1 and 2 Maccabees for the treatment of the Jews, and tend to create the impression that this activity was widespread. But given the fact that there were very few wars of conquest outside the borders established by Seleukos I, except for those persistent and mostly inconclusive Syrian Wars, the opportunities for plunder seem to have been fairly limited. In those cases where erstwhile Seleukid provinces or cities were reconquered, which occurred only rarely, it did not pay the king to inflict excessive damage, as this would have ruined his future revenue-earning prospects from tribute and taxation. So, more often than not, he settled for an indemnity (see below).

From time to time, a defeated enemy or a rebel city or people were treated harshly and plundered and enslaved, but this was legitimate practice in the eyes of the Greek world: to the victor belonged the spoils of war and he could impose his will on the defeated. Nevertheless, the cities and peoples of the Seleukid empire lived a relatively peaceful existence, when compared to the turmoil of the old Greek world in the last three centuries BC.

a. Indemnities

An indemnity might be imposed on a defeated enemy. Antiochos III exacted 300 talents from the Armenians plus 1,000 horses and 1,000 mules (Polyb. 8.23.5). Euthydemos of Baktria made concessions to this king, including the provisioning of his troops and the supply of elephants, but also 'on other matters' (Polyb. 11.39.10). Sophagasenos of the Paropamisadai was similarly imposed upon for elephants, but also for treasure (Polyb. 11.39.11–12), which suggests that this may also have been Euthydemos' 'other matters'. Gerrha avoided a military confrontation by paying 500 talents of silver, 1,000 talents of frankincense and 200 talents of myrrh (Polyb. 13.9.5).

As a variation on this theme, Antiochos VII demanded 1,000 talents from Simon, the Jewish high priest, unless he delivered up the cities and lands (mainly Joppa and Gazara), along with their tribute, which he had taken outside the borders of Judaea (1 Macc. 15.30).

A city within the empire might be fined for rebelling or supporting an opponent of the king, for example the 1,000 talents imposed by Antiochos III on Seleukeia-Tigris for supporting Molon, graciously reduced to 150 talents (Polyb. 5.54.10–11), possibly also a fine on Sardeis after its recapture in 213 BC from Achaios,[105] while Selge in Pisidia paid 400 talents to Achaios to cease hostilities, with a further 300 talents to come (Polyb. 5.76.10).

---

[105] Gauthier suspects that an indemnity was mentioned in the illegible first line of the inscription (Document 9), to be settled within three years (1989: 13, 19–21).

An indemnity may be a pointer to annual revenue from a province or city. In Greek tradition, a fine was often levied for late payment or violation of an agreement equal in value to the transaction itself. In the Mnesimachos inscription (Document 5), for example, twice the value of the loan was to be paid if Mnesimachos violated his agreement. At Aspendos, Alexander doubled the tribute of 50 talents to 100 when the city did not pay up immediately (Arr. *Anab.* 1.26.2, 27.4). Thus the fine of 150 talents imposed on Seleukeia-Tigris may possibly have equalled the city's annual tribute (also ch. 12.2).

b. Plunder

Captives were an important element of plunder in warfare. During the Maccabean revolt the Seleukid official Nikanor calculated that he could raise 2,000 talents from the anticipated sale of the Jewish population (2 Macc. 8.10; Jos. *AJ* 12.299), while Antiochos IV apparently enslaved 40,000 people when he suppressed a Jewish revolt and took Jerusalem (2 Macc. 5.14), although such a figure is highly suspect.

The looting of temples of their valuables appears with somewhat greater frequency in the sources, but should not give one the impression that the Seleukid kings plundered for plunder's sake, although it is true that short-term financial difficulties may have made temple treasuries attractive targets.[106]

An attempt was made by Heliodoros, the minister of Seleukos IV, apparently to rob the Temple of Jerusalem of the savings of widows and orphans valued at 200 talents of gold and 400 talents of silver, but was frustrated by divine intervention, according to Jewish tradition (2 Macc. 3.7–40). There is some question, though, whether this was quite such a wanton act, given the fact that Seleukos IV had for some time been supporting the Temple (2 Macc. 3.3): 'with Seleukos, the king of Asia, covering from his personal funds all the expenses that were necessary for the conducting of the sacrifices' (καὶ Σέλευκον τὸν τῆς Ἀσίας βασιλέα χορηγεῖν ἐκ τῶν ἰδίων προσόδων πάντα τὰ πρὸς τὰς λειτουργίας τῶν θυσιῶν ἐπιβάλλοντα δαπανήματα). It was signalled to the Seleukid authorities by their local supervisor of the Temple (προστάτης τοῦ ἱεροῦ) that the contents of its treasury (2 Macc. 3.6) 'did not match the accounts for the sacrifices' (καὶ μὴ προσήκειν αὐτὰ πρὸς τὸν τῶν θυσιῶν λόγον) and thus it is quite possible that Seleukos, believing that the funds that he had been supplying for a specific purpose had been misused, demanded their return.

---

[106] Debord 1982: 271.

The temple of Aine at Ekbatana was despoiled by Antiochos III of gold and silver ornamentation valued at nearly 4,000 talents (Polyb. 10.27.13). Here we know of no cause given by the temple, other than the unfortunate fact of being in possession of wealth at the precise moment when the king, faced with the pressing financial needs of his Anabasis, was passing through.

Some years later Antiochos IV, on his return from Egypt, captured Jerusalem by assault, took many captives and plundered the Temple of possessions valued at 1,800 talents. However, the Jews had apparently revolted, misled by a false report about the king's death in Egypt (1 Macc. 1.20–3; 2 Macc. 5.5–21). In Greek eyes, subjects who rebelled were forfeit along with their possessions and this was normal treatment. An alternative explanation is the enforced collection of arrears of the annual tribute of 660 talents promised by the high priest Menelaos in 172 or 171 BC, but never delivered (section 7c above).[107]

Antiochos III died attempting to plunder the temple of Zeus-Bel in Elam (Diod. 28.3, 29.15; Strabo 16.1.18) and Antiochos IV may have suffered a similar fate after an attempt on the temple of Artemis-Nanaia, also in Elam (Polyb. 31.9; Diod. 31.18a), which is how a hostile tradition has coloured these events. One may, however, consider them simply in the context of military campaigns, whose objective was to bring back into the Seleukid fold provinces that had broken away in the aftermath of Magnesia, as the normally hostile 1 Maccabees has presented this for Antiochos IV (3.31): 'and he wished to go to Persis in order to collect the tribute of these countries' (καὶ ἐβουλεύσατο τοῦ πορευθῆναι εἰς τὴν Περσίδα καὶ λαβεῖν τοὺς φόρους τῶν χωρῶν). Perhaps resistance just happened to be met at important local sanctuaries, which also served as treasuries.

Sometimes, temples were not robbed but required to give 'gifts' to the king. In a sense, they acted as his (probably unwilling) bankers, repaying him for his support over the years. In 188/7 BC Antiochos III was presented with a crown of gold weighing 1,000 shekels (valued at nearly 7 talents of silver) by the temple authorities of Babylon, along with an unknown quantity of gold (*Astronomical Diary* -187). This may well have been a regular crown tax, such as was paid by other subjects of the king (section 6 above), but it is unlikely. Only a couple of years after Magnesia, the Seleukid king was probably feeling the pinch of the Roman indemnity and calling in his favours.

---

[107] Mørkholm 1966: 142–3.

Yet another Babylonian temple, that of Nabu in Borsippa, seems to have yielded the huge sum of 113 talents to Seleukos I in 302/1 BC, funds which the king probably needed to help to finance his march west in the war against Lysimachos.[108]

c. *Other sources of revenue*

The king might acquire revenue by the act of granting a charter to a Greek *polis*. There were advantages to being a citizen, fiscal and otherwise, which someone would be willing to pay for. Jason, the high priest, was apparently quite aware of this when he offered Antiochos IV 150 talents for the privilege of enrolling citizens in Antioch-Jerusalem (2 Macc. 4.9), which no doubt he felt he could recoup quite easily. One wonders if this practice had also been applied in other city foundations. In a similar vein, Demetrios I was paid 1,000 talents by Olophernes for helping to place him on the Kappadokian throne (App. *Syr.* 47).

Finally, the sale of royal land to the city of Pitane has already been mentioned (section 1f). Although this is an isolated case, it might be indicative of a more widespread Seleukid practice of generating revenue from unprofitable land.

d. *Conclusions on extraordinary revenue*

The various cases of extraordinary revenue collection described above often do show high amounts, but one questions what these might have represented compared to regular annual revenue. If, for example, the indemnity of Seleukeia-Tigris was actually set at one year's tribute from the city, as has been suggested, one should consider the remaining 160 years when the city provided regular revenue of this order. If the Temple of Jerusalem yielded 1,800 talents in plunder (and not tribute owed) after more than thirty years of Seleukid rule, this represented only a small fraction of what the province had generated in revenue in this time. Although extraordinary revenue did help with temporary cash-flow problems, particularly those created by the need to finance military campaigns, it probably constituted overall and in the long run a negligible proportion of the income of Seleukid kings.[109]

---

[108] Spek 2000a: 302.
[109] Green believes that booty constituted a major item in the revenue account (1990: 362), which I have questioned.

9. REVENUE IN SILVER OR COMMODITIES?

Having dealt with the different sources of income of the Seleukid kings, I must now consider whether the bulk of the revenue was collected in silver or in kind. The evidence comes from various parts of the empire and from the Graeco-Baktrian kingdoms of the second century BC, where it is not unreasonable to postulate a continuation of earlier practice, from the time when this region was subject to the Seleukids.

a. The Jewish tribute

The tribute demanded by the Seleukid kings from Judaea is often expressed in the sources as a lump sum of silver, to be provided by the high priest, acting as tax-contractor (section 7 above). It is difficult to see how the high priest could have obtained this silver, if not through tax contributions from the population. There is no evidence to suggest that he collected commodities as tax, which he himself then sold in order to raise the necessary silver, although this may have occurred to some extent. In fact, one does know that each Jew was expected to make a regular annual contribution of half a shekel for the Temple rites,[110] so why not a Seleukid silver tax at the same time? Even when a proportion of the grain or fruit harvest is mentioned as the tax (e.g. ἀντὶ τῶν τρίτων τοῦ καρποῦ), the ἀντί ('in place of') should probably be interpreted as the equivalent value in silver (section 7 above). Judaea was by no means a highly urbanized region and yet the evidence is strong that taxation was mainly collected there in silver.

b. Rural Asia Minor

One would have expected commodity taxation to be more prevalent in rural areas, but this is not the picture we have from documents of Asia Minor. In the village of the Kardakes (section 6 above), a head tax, at least, was imposed in silver. This was set at 3 Attic drachms per adult, seemingly, that later became 4 Rhodian drachms and 1 obol, the exact equivalent, when the region was lost to Rhodes after Magnesia. Furthermore, the villages and *klēroi* of Mnesimachos had tax assessments in gold staters in the early third century BC (section 1a above), which does not definitely mean that they paid in coin, but strongly suggests it. The fact that a silver tax (ἀργυρικὸς φόρος) is noted in the text, irrespective of whether this was payable to

---

[110] Tscherikover 1959: 155.

Mnesimachos or the king directly, makes this more than just a strong suggestion. And again, my interpretation of the Laodike dossier (section 1d) concluded that the estate donated to the ex-queen was taxed at the rate of 15 talents annually, probably another tax in silver.

c. Urban areas

When it comes to urban areas, lump-sum city taxes or indemnities are some-times mentioned in silver, for example Aspendos' 50 talents, Kaunos' and Stratonikeia's 120 talents together, Seleukeia-Tigris' 150 talents indemnity (ch. 12.2).

With regard to royal revenue from trade and industry and the head taxes discussed earlier in this chapter, these must have been mostly collected in silver. How else might a 'slave tax' or a 'registration fee' on slaves be construed at Mesopotamian cities, or port dues, or dues for ships using the Euphrates (ch. 3a–b)? All the customs duties, sales taxes and tolls at provincial borders, harbours and city gates and in the marketplaces of the cities can obviously be interpreted as both impositions in kind and in silver, but some curious results would be obtained with the former interpretation. For example, could one really expect the king's timber to travel from the royal forests of Lebanon and elsewhere to subject cities (section 7a above), with quantities deducted at the forest exits, the borders of provinces and city gates, or consignments of exotic products arriving from Arabia and India being gradually whittled away by customs inspectors on their way to the Mediterranean? And why would a salt tax be referred to in connec-tion with 'the price of the salt pans', if it were not to be paid in silver? And, finally, could the wreath of precious metal that originally represented the crown tax have been replaced by anything other than a contribution in precious metal, probably coined? Even when the king received a frac-tion of the agricultural produce from a city as tax, might this not have been, in most cases, the equivalent value in silver, much as for Judaea (above)?

d. The royal properties

There is one area where it is likely that a significant part of tribute and taxation may have been paid to the king in kind and that is from the royal land, either exploited on the king's behalf or leased to tenants, such as the Ebbabar temple in Babylonia, which was compelled to pay a rent of half the crop (section 1f above). But in some cases, for example Mnesimachos' villages and *klēroi*, which had been granted to him by the king in usufruct (section 1a), a tribute assessment in silver probably meant exactly that, that the onus was on the tax-payers to produce the silver.

Wood, water, salt and other important or rare commodities were treated to a considerable extent as royal monopolies (ch. 5.3) and the evidence for their sale and taxation has been presented (section 2 above). What could the Seleukid kings have obtained in return? Hardly agricultural produce, as this they seem to have produced in more than abundance from royal land, the evidence even suggesting that the kings made strenuous efforts to dispose of surpluses by sale or gift (chs. 9.2; 10.4a–b), which leaves mostly silver as a candidate. Furthermore, when an indemnity was demanded of a foreign state after a successful reimposition of Seleukid sovereignty, it was silver that was required as tribute, or animals, or luxury items, not agricultural produce (section 8a above).

e. Evidence from Baktria

It is all very well to argue with logic that the Seleukid kings could not have collected this or that form of taxation other than in silver, but some concrete evidence is required that will show silver used in a tax-collection transaction. Such evidence may be forthcoming from the Graeco-Baktrian successor-state of the Seleukids, where it is not unreasonable to postulate that Seleukid administrative practices continued.

In one case,[111] an inscription found on a jar fragment from the treasury of Aï Khanoum reads: 'From Zenon. Were counted by Oxeboakes and Oxubazos 500 drachms. Oxeboakes sealed [this container]' (παρὰ Ζήν-ωνος ἠρίθμηνται διὰ Ὀξηβοάκου καὶ Ὀξυβάζου δρχ φ· ἐσφράγισται Ὀξηβοάκης).

There are several other inscriptions like this (ch. 13.5k) and it is possible that Oxeboakes and Oxubazos were carrying the proceeds of silver taxation from a district collector, Zenon, to a central treasury.

A text on parchment[112] refers to a Graeco-Baktrian kingdom, probably in western Baktria, and is dated to *c.* 170 BC. It is presented and discussed more fully in chapter 13.6c, in connection with the roles of the officials involved, and is probably a tax receipt by a tax-collector for 20 (silver) staters from a tax-payer in the presence of two royal officials.

---

[111] Rapin 1983: 326, no. 4a.
[112] Rapin 1996; cf. Bernard and Rapin 1994; Rea, Senior and Hollis 1994.

10. CONCLUSIONS ON REVENUE

The picture of taxation in the province of Judaea in 200–140 BC shows taxes applied to most economic activities that match very well with the six sources of revenue in the satrapal economy of ps.-Aristotle's *Oikonomika*. One can observe:

(1) tribute on corporate entities, such as the city of Jerusalem, and a tithe on agriculture that varied according to the product,

(2) revenue generated from royally owned natural resources such as forests and salt-pans,

(3) tolls on goods crossing provincial boundaries or city gates or exiting from royal forests, as well as tolls on persons and animals, plus sales and transaction taxes in the city and countryside and during religious fairs,

(4) taxes on animals,

(5) head taxes that were both general and also selectively applied to certain categories of the population.

Only some special taxes of an *emporion* are missing, such as port dues, but that is simply because Jerusalem and Judaea received no water-borne trade.

The same picture has been observed in the study of the documents examined earlier in this chapter, which came predominantly from Asia Minor. Again, every single form of revenue described by ps.-Aristotle was identified and, in one case at least, that of Herakleia-Latmos (Document 10), most could be found together.

Since ps.-Aristotle was describing the picture that he could observe in Asia Minor or northern Syria in the early third century BC and one cannot detect any significant differences in Judaea of the first half of the second century BC, it is quite possible that this Seleukid system of taxation was general in both time and space. It seems also to have been a very comprehensive system, leaving no area untouched where the Seleukid kings could derive revenue, whether from native populations or Greeks, in keeping with the policy of maximization of income which I have considered to be one of their objectives (ch. 3).

As to whether the income of the Seleukids, from tribute, taxation and the exploitation of royal properties, was increasingly collected in silver rather than in commodities, the evidence presented earlier suggests that the changeover to a monetary economy had proceeded rapidly, which will be borne out in subsequent chapters, when the handling of royal surpluses, expenditure and coinage are more fully discussed.

CHAPTER 9

The handling of surpluses

With regard to goods that can be sent out or brought in, which of them, having been received from the satraps in their provinces, were to be profitably disposed of on his [the king's] behalf and when.

In chapter 7.1b on the *Oikonomika* it was suggested that the second and third aspects of the royal economy represented the interaction between this and the other types of economy in terms of goods and silver that crossed their respective boundaries in either direction. Although the terms εἰσαγώγιμα (*eisagōgima*) and ἐξαγώγιμα (*exagōgima*) can indeed denote imports and exports in the modern sense, of a Greek *polis* for instance, here the meaning is more specific. It concerns the management of the surplus collected by the king from tribute and taxation and the natural resources he controlled. It includes items transported even within a province to and from royal land, treasuries and storehouses.[1]

Fortunately there is a source which can show how the management of surplus was handled in detail at some point in time and place in the Achaemenid empire. This may help to illuminate several Hellenistic-period texts and Seleukid administrative practice.

I. EVIDENCE FROM THE ACHAEMENID EMPIRE

a. *Surplus, exchange and price in the* Persepolis Fortification Texts

It will be recalled (ch. 1.4b) that the *Persepolis Fortification Texts* of the time of Darius I deal with the movement of commodities to and from storehouses in

---

[1] Briant also refuses to translate the *exagōgima* and *eisagōgima* of ps.-Aristotle as *exportations* ('exports') and *importations* ('imports'), but rather as *sorties* ('exits') and *entrées* ('entries'), which concern the surplus that had to be managed intelligently by the administration (1994b: 74). His original idea was that this referred to grain transported from one satrapy to another to balance surpluses and shortages and build up stocks on the great strategic routes (1986: 42), but this developed into any exits and entries of products out of and into royal storehouses (1996: 467) and a categorical denial by Briant and Descat that this had anything to do with exports and imports (1998: 91). Murray also takes the view that the terms have to do with the reception, storage and disposal of goods and bullion received from satrapies (1966: 151).

an administrative area centred on Persepolis, which probably coincided with the later Seleukid satrapy of Persis. The chief administrator at Persepolis and his deputy controlled the entire operation with an organization that will be discussed in chapter 13.1. Slightly later in time, the *Persepolis Treasury Texts* (ch. 1.4b) record payments made in silver to officials and workers at Persepolis in lieu of part of their ration allowance.

The *Persepolis Texts* provide us with a glimpse of the workings of a satrapal economy, but the royal economy intrudes from time to time and there is evidence that similar operations may have been conducted at Susa and in Arachosia, which raises the possibility that the system may have been general.[2]

Here is an example of how the surplus between commodity taxation receipts and ration-issuing requirements was handled at a satrapal storehouse according to the *Fortification Texts*. This matter has been discussed elsewhere at length.[3]

Part of an Account[4] for years eighteen and nineteen of Darius I (504/3 BC) at the Hištiyanuš fortress reads as follows:

And again, in that fortress, an account was made for Maraza the assistant fruit-handler, Umaka the *haturmakša*, Hindukka the *etira*, total three [persons]. They withdrew $27\frac{22}{30}$ [*irtiba*] of fruit. Then they made a *sut* [for] an adult female ass of lowest quality, the payment [being] $16\frac{20}{30}$ [*irtiba*] of fruit. Then the ass was entrusted to Bakaparna in the twentieth year, on the twelfth day [of] the first month. [As] balance they were withdrawing $11\frac{2}{30}$ [*irtiba*]. Of that they did not expend [for] what they were to make *sut*. Then [for?] each 55 *šaumaraš* [and] one-third *šaumaraš* were brought in, in [accordance with] the former law.

At this storehouse there were stocks of grain, wine and fruit, which had apparently been collected from taxation of the surrounding district. Maraza was the storekeeper responsible for fruit, while the role of the other two officials in the text will be discussed in chapter 13.1.

It was decided that a certain quantity of fruit was surplus to the storehouse's requirements and this was 'withdrawn' in accordance with a general policy of bringing commodity stocks down to zero or very low values by the end of the year in preparation for taxation receipts from the following year's harvest. This 'withdrawal' essentially belonged to the king and now entered the royal economy from the satrapal.

A certain part of the amount withdrawn was exchanged for an ass at a price that had actually been pre-set for this type of animal and quality, and, some time later, an official, Bakaparna, on a round of collection, picked

---

[2] Briant 1996: 462.   [3] Aperghis 1997b.   [4] Hallock 1969: PF1980, lines 21–31.

up the ass, as he did various animals from other storehouses. Such officials also collected surpluses of grain and other commodities and brought them to royal storehouses or estates.

But at Hištiyanuš some fruit still remained and this was sold for so many *šaumaraš*, again at a pre-set rate of five to an *irtiba* (= 30 litres) of fruit. It was noted that on this particular occasion the transaction was not carried out at the current official rate for some reason, but at the previous one. The *šaumaraš*, it turns out, were very possibly so many units of silver, which were also collected from the storehouses and brought to Persepolis.

The *Treasury Texts* show us that silver was used at Persepolis to make partial payments to officials and workers and it then presumably found its way back to the storehouses in exchange for supplies. A trading post (*zamataš*) is where this exchange may have taken place. In one text,[5] 78 *irtiba* of barley were withdrawn from a storehouse and 'Antarma received and took it [to] the *zamataš* of Harriyauzaka at Manada; he removed [it] by road. It was deposited to his [account and] he will be making *sut*.'

One can envisage Antarma carting 2,340 litres of the king's barley, which might otherwise have rotted in the storehouse, to the *zamataš* or trading post where it could be profitably exchanged or sold on the king's behalf.

Sometimes one can see the process reversed, a transfer back from a royal to a satrapal storehouse:[6] 'Tell Piratamka, Ziššawiš spoke as follows: Flour, which from the [royal] stores went to him [at] Uzikurraš in the twenty-second year, out of that flour 49½ BAR [of] flour [is] to be issued [as] rations to Skudrian [and] Ašketian workers, whose apportionments are set by Baraddumawiš.'

Ziššawiš was the deputy-head of the Persepolis administration and Piratamka a storekeeper in charge of a travel station on the Royal Road between Persepolis and Susa. Flour rations were normally provided to travellers passing through, sufficient only for one day, whereas workers in the vicinity had to be content with raw barley. This was obviously an exceptional situation, perhaps a bonus of some sort, as one often finds in the *Fortification Texts*, and at the usual rate of 1 litre per worker per day, this amount of flour would have fed 495 workers for one day. This and more flour had apparently been issued to the travel storehouse from some royal store where, presumably, surplus grain had been collected and milled.

Here is how a transfer between satrapal and royal storehouses was typically recorded on a transaction tablet:[7] '29 marrish of wine Appirmarsha

---

[5] Hallock 1969: PF1956, lines 27–9.   [6] Hallock 1969: PF1813.   [7] Hallock 1969: PF42.

acquired and took [it] from [the place] Rashinuzza [to] Bashrakada [for] the royal stores'.

There are also occasional references to the 'sheep of the king', the 'cattle of the king', the 'royal horses', and suchlike, which allow us a glimpse of the royal economy.[8]

b. Other Achaemenid evidence

But, on a more general level, one should ask oneself how the Persian satraps obtained the silver that they sent as the tribute of their respective provinces to the king (Hdt. 3.89–95),[9] if not to some extent through the sale of their surplus stocks. An example is to be found in an Athenian decree honouring the Persian satrap Orontes for having sold grain to the Athenians for silver (*IG* ɪɪ² 207, a–d).[10]

In fifth-century BC Babylonia the *Murašu Archive* (ch. 1.4d) shows quite clearly that taxes were owed to the Persian treasury in silver on land granted by the king to *hatrus*, which were groupings of fiefs of soldiers, artisans, and the like. These *hatrus* may have found it difficult to cultivate their land and raise the necessary silver, so the Murašu firm undertook to lease the land from them and pay the taxes. They then subleased the land to cultivators, along with water rights, equipment and seed, in return for a rent in barley or dates. One is not told how they converted these commodity receipts into silver, but it is not unreasonable to suppose that this was done through bulk sales in city markets, perhaps partly after conversion into other products, such as barley beer or date wine. As far as the royal administration was concerned, its objective had been achieved and an intermediary had undertaken to convert what was originally commodity taxation into silver.[11]

The examples discussed above show a system in operation exactly like that described by ps.-Aristotle regarding 'goods that can be sent out or brought in'. Not only was there movement of commodities between the royal and satrapal economies in both directions, but the surpluses of satrapal storehouses were exchanged for something else or sold for silver in a way that was apparently advantageous for the king.

---

[8] Hallock 1969 notes 'royal' sheep (PF775, 1442), cattle (PF1942, 1965, 1991) and horses (PF1668–9, 1784), for example.

[9] Briant discusses the Persian tribute in silver (1996: 402–6), as does Descat 1985 and 1989.

[10] Briant discusses the decree in detail and concludes that the sale of grain surpluses was *une pratique courante et normale des satrapes* ('a current and usual practice of the satraps') (1994b: 72–3).

[11] See Stolper 1974; 1985 for the Murašu.

2. EVIDENCE FROM HELLENISTIC TEXTS

a. Antigonos' letter to Teos regarding the synoikism with Lebedos (Document 1)

In a letter addressed by Antigonos Monophthalmos to Teos in western Asia Minor regarding a union with Lebedos, Antigonos appeared upset by the request of the Lebedians, seconded by the Teans, that they be allowed to import grain because of an anticipated shortage. He pointed out that this was unnecessary, 'as the taxed land is close by, so that, if there were need for grain, we believe that as much as necessary could be easily obtained from it' (πλησίον οὔσης τῆς φορολογουμέ[νης χώρας ὥστε ἐὰν χρεία γ]ίνηται σίτου, εὐχερῶς οἰόμεθα εἶναι μεταπέμπεσθαι ἐκ [ταύτης ὁπόσο]ν ἄν τις βούληται).

Looked at from the perspective of ps.-Aristotle, the 'taxed land' (*phorologoumenē chōra*) belonged to the satrapal economy, which is where taxation and rents were collected (ch. 8.1). It was the surplus over and above the needs of the satrapy, both in silver and in kind, which could be disposed of on the king's behalf. So what Antigonos was implying is that, on his orders, the Teans and Lebedians could receive grain from this surplus.

One can see that Antigonos was protesting his good intentions too much and the reality was probably quite different. Teos and Lebedos were probably tied customers for Antigonos' surplus grain and justifiably wanted a less expensive supplier, but had to be diplomatic about suggesting this to their nominal ally, but actual overlord, Antigonos. If they could have bought grain at a low cost from him, why look elsewhere? 'As everyone knows' in Antigonos' letter suggests that the sale of commodities from royal land must have been common practice and Antigonos himself declared that it was his policy for all subject cities to restrict grain imports. Thus one should not doubt that Antigonos Monophthalmos kept his one eye very firmly on the market and took advantage of his near-monopolistic position. In the end, however, he acceded to the request of the Teans and Lebedians, presumably attaching more value to long-term political advantage than to short-term financial gain.

b. Eumenes and the mercenary agreement

In this text (*OGIS* 266), a contract with mercenary soldiers is laid out in detail, which, though from Attalid Asia Minor, is probably relevant to Seleukid practice as well. There are some special circumstances relating to a mutiny that had just taken place, but these do not affect the present discussion. Mercenaries were normally given a daily wage (ὀψώνιον, μισθός) and a food ration or allowance (σῖτος, μέτρημα) (ch. 10.1e). In the agreement (line 1) here is how the Attalid king was to handle the question of food: 'to set a price for wheat of 4 drachms per *medimnos* and for wine of 4 drachms per *metrētēs*' (σίτου τιμὴν ἀποτίνειν τοῦ μεδίμνου δραχμὰς τέσσαρας, οἴνου τοῦ μετρητοῦ δραχμὰς τέσσαρας).

It has been suggested[12] that what the text means is that the king paid these sums, presumably on a monthly basis, so that the soldiers might themselves purchase their grain and wine supplies. However, there is a problem here. If the king were indeed specifying payments that he had contracted to make, what of the normal wages of the mercenaries, which should logically have appeared at this point in the agreement and do not? In my own interpretation, the king was fixing prices for his soldiers, so that they could make purchases at royal storehouses.[13] A *medimnos*, equal to 48 *choinikes*, was the normal soldier's ration in antiquity for forty-eight days and one can envisage soldiers' messes, their 'household economies', making regular bulk purchases from the royal economy. It is interesting that the wheat price, at which Eumenes had agreed to sell produce from the royal stores to his mercenaries, if this interpretation is correct, seems to have been lower than the prevailing price in this period.[14] The fact that such a price option was included in the agreement suggests that the price must indeed have been intentionally low. One can speculate that perhaps one of the reasons for their revolt may have been the fact that the mercenaries, as tied customers of the king, were being compelled to purchase supplies at rather high prices, thereby effectively returning to their paymaster much of what they had earlier received from him in pay. Eumenes was perhaps using a near-monopolistic position to sell his produce no differently from Antigonos and so, in all likelihood, would have been the policy of a Seleukos or an Antiochos.

c. Demetrios I and the Jews

In the competition between Seleukid contenders for Jewish support in about 152 BC, the offer of Demetrios I included the following (1 Macc.

[12] Grote 1913: 86–7; Griffith 1935: 282–8.

[13] The verb ἀποτίνειν is normally translated 'to pay' or 'to repay'. However, the meaning 'to make one the price' is also given in LSJ.

[14] Also Launey, who discusses the meaning of ἀποτίνειν and draws attention to the higher prices at Delos in the first half of the third century BC of 5.7 to 9.9 drachms per *medimnos* for wheat and 10 to 11 drachms per *metrētēs* for wine (1950: 738–46). Eumenes' mercenaries were apparently getting a good deal.

10.40): 'and I will give each year 15,000 shekels of silver from the king's account from the places belonging to me' (κἀγὼ δίδωμι κατ' ἐνιαυτὸν δέκα πέντε χιλιάδες σίκλων ἀργυρίου ἀπὸ τῶν λόγων τοῦ βασιλέως ἀπὸ τῶν τόπων τῶν ἀνηκόντων).

Obviously it is not possible to pay silver from land, and what is probably referred to here is the value of a certain amount of agricultural produce from royal land. A sale would have to be made in the satrapal or city economies and the proceeds entered into the royal treasury, before payment to the Jews could be effected.

d. The Laodike letter to Iasos (Document 6)

Laodike, the wife of Antiochos III, wrote to the city of Iasos concerning a gift of grain that she had made to the city: ' I have written to Strouthion the *dioikētēs* to bring to the city and deliver to the representatives of the city each year for ten years a thousand Attic *medimnoi* of wheat' (γεγράφεικα Στρουθίωνι τῶι διοικητῆι ἐφ' ἔτη δέκα κατ' ἐνιαυτὸν πυρῶν χιλίους μεδίμνους Ἀττικοὺς εἰς τὴν πόλιν παρακομίζοντα παραδιδόναι τοῖς παρὰ τοῦ δήμου).

As will be argued in chapter 13.5, the *dioikētēs* was responsible for the financial administration of a satrapy, or sometimes a region within one, including the management of the king's own property, and took his orders directly from the king. Here it is the queen who issues the command, which suggests that this grain was coming from a royal storehouse, and the text goes on to inform us that the city was expected to sell the grain so as to provide dowries for daughters of poor citizens. Naturally, Laodike could have provided the silver herself, but it was probably more convenient to shift the problem of the grain sale onto the city.

One can see a similar picture in the *Persepolis Fortification Texts*, where estates belonging to members of the royal family are called *ulhi*, whereas those granted to officials of the administration are *irmatam*. Here is an example of an Achaemenid queen's orders to issue commodities from her estate:[15] 'Tell Šalamanna [the woman] Irtašduna spoke as follows: From my *ulhi* [estate] [at] Kuknaka 100 *marrish* [of] wine [is] to be issued to Kamšabana the accountant. Irtima [is] the *hirakurra*. In the twenty-second year [this] sealed document [was delivered].'

Irtašduna was Artystone, the wife of Darius I (Hdt. 3.88), Irtima the *hirakurra* may have been the bailiff of her estate and Šalamanna, who crops up a number of times in the *Fortification Texts* arranging for provisions

---

[15] Hallock 1969: PF1837.

to be supplied, is likely to have been a financial official in the satrapal administration.

e. Other texts

Wood from the royal forests of Taranza and Lebanon for the rebuilding of Sardeis (Document 9) and the Temple of Jerusalem (Document 12) are other examples of transfers from the royal to city economies. Free grain supplies and oil for the gymnasium of Herakleia-Latmos (Document 10) probably originally arrived at royal storehouses as the surplus of rent from royal land or taxation from cities. And so on.

3. CONCLUSIONS ON THE HANDLING OF SURPLUSES

The Achaemenid kings received much of their income from commodity taxation, but, although they paid many of their expenses as commodity rations, a surplus was still left over, which needed to be disposed of for two reasons. The first is that commodity stocks would eventually spoil if left in storage for too long, the second that other useful items were also required for the running of the empire, most notably precious metals.

For the Seleukid kings it has been suggested (ch. 3) that they strove to convert more of their taxation receipts and administrative expenses into silver. But, although the volume of incoming and outgoing commodities in the satrapal economy may have been lower than for the Achaemenids, since taxation in coin was becoming more the norm, the problem of a surplus and its disposal continued to exist.

In both empires the solution seems to have been the same: satrapal officials had the responsibility of disposing of the surplus by sale or royal grant. In the Seleukid empire, however, one has the impression that the king was more directly involved in the decision-making (also ch. 13). One thing is clear, that the commodity surpluses of the king, whether Achaemenid or Seleukid, were not left idle.[16]

---

[16] According to Briant, a tributary economy had need of access to a market where it could dispose of its surpluses for silver. Exchange could be initiated by officials of the administration or private merchants acting as intermediaries (1994b: 76).

CHAPTER 10

Expenditure

> With regard to expenditure, what is to be cut and when, and whether
> to meet expenses with coinage or with goods in place of money.

The main regular expenses of the empire concerned the maintenance of
armed forces and satrapal administration and the upkeep of king and court.
Ad hoc expenditure aided the kings' foreign and domestic policies and
included the funding of city construction, grants of tribute and taxation
relief and gifts to cities, temples and individuals. And one should not forget
losses suffered in war, in particular the Roman indemnity after Magnesia.

Expenditure was incurred both in silver and in kind and my theme has
been that, increasingly, it took the form of silver, as this was what its major
destination, the Seleukid armed forces, required. An attempt will be made
in chapter 12.4 to estimate total expenditure.

1. MILITARY EXPENSES

No figures are given in the sources for the military costs of the Seleukids at
any time and yet, as will be seen below, this represented the major expense
item of the royal economy.[1] This was a 'spear-won' empire, retaining its hold
on the land, as its predecessors had done in the Near East, primarily through
the threat and application of military force. An army was maintained in
order to exact tribute and fed off the process of this tribute. This was, in
essence, the practice of the Roman Empire too – for which there is a great
deal more numerical information – where a professional army and navy
consumed perhaps two-thirds or more of the state budget at times.[2]

To arrive at a total cost, it is necessary to know basically three things: the
size of the army and navy, the average rate of pay of a soldier or sailor and

---

[1] Also Andreades 1933: 99.
[2] Duncan-Jones estimates over 70 per cent *c.* AD 150 and *c.* AD 215 (1994: 45).

the period during the year when he was paid. Clearly there is oversimplification here. Army numbers could differ significantly between 'peacetime' conditions and those of a major campaign or war lasting several years. Rates of pay would vary for different classes of soldier or sailor and might also depend upon the status of the troops, whether Greek settlers, Greek or native mercenaries, native levies or 'allies', while they may also have changed during the two and a half centuries of Seleukid rule. Finally, length of service could involve anything from year-round garrison duty to short summer expeditions with the fleet.

Despite all these uncertainties, an attempt will be made to arrive at an approximate total cost of the Seleukid armed forces in two conditions: in 'peacetime' and during a major campaign. The period for which there is most information regarding army size spans the reigns of Antiochos III and his successors to the defeat of Antiochos VII by the Parthians in 129 BC, after which, and the resulting loss of Mesopotamia, one can no longer speak of a Seleukid empire. As for the earlier period, it is possible only to extrapolate backwards with caution.

a. The army

The starting point is the detailed figures in the sources for two major battles, Raphia against Ptolemy IV in 217 BC (Polyb. 5.79) and Magnesia against the Romans in 190 BC (Livy 37.37.9; 37.40; App. *Syr.* 32), and the procession (πομπή) at Daphne in 166 BC (Polyb. 30.25). The table below shows the approximate make-up of the army in each case.[3]

---

[3] I essentially follow Bar-Kochva 1979, with some differences in allocating troops to the different categories. What he has termed 'military settlers', I have called 'regulars'.

The 1,000 Thracians at Raphia I consider mercenaries, whereas Bar-Kochva regards them as military settlers from Persis. But why should *Thracian* military settlers in particular be singled out and no other nationality?

At Magnesia the detailed figures in Livy for contingents (37.40) do not add up to his total of 60,000 infantry and 12,000 cavalry (37.37.9), but only to 45,200 infantry and 11,700 cavalry. However, the missing figures can be supplied with some confidence. The number of 'Tarentine' mercenaries in the cavalry is not given, but was probably about 500 (also Bar-Kochva 1979: 169), the *arguraspides* in the Seleukid infantry normally totalled 10,000 (also Bar-Kochva 1979: 9) and the remaining 5,000 or thereabouts are likely to have been the troops guarding the Seleukid camp and the 'lights' supporting the fifty elephants. Bar-Kochva assumes that the camp was guarded by 3,000 Thracian military settlers (1979: 51), but one notes that Alexander also seems to have used Thracian mercenaries in this role at Gaugamela (Arr. *Anab.* 3.12.5).

In the Daphne procession 3,000 Thracians are noted and this time Bar-Kochva *does* consider them mercenaries (1979: 52). As for the 'lights' supporting the fifty elephants, these would be about 2,000 trained regular troops. Finally, Bar-Kochva assumes that the 2,500 Mysians were allies (1979: 51), rather than mercenaries, as I do, bearing in mind their appearance in the procession at Daphne.

Table 10.1 *Seleukid army numbers in major campaigns*

	Raphia 217 BC		Magnesia 190 BC		Daphne 166 BC	
	Infantry	Cavalry	Infantry	Cavalry	Infantry	Cavalry
Regulars	30,000	6,000	28,000	8,000	25,000	6,500
Mercenaries	13,500		14,000	4,200	16,000	
Native levies	8,500		16,200			
Allies	10,000		2,000			
Total	62,000	6,000	60,200	12,200	41,000	6,500

The figures in the table are for field armies only, as garrisons, navies and support personnel will be dealt with later.

The battle of Raphia was the culminating major action of the fourth Syrian War, which followed immediately upon the suppression by Antiochos of Molon's revolt in the East. At the time, the king could not draw upon the full resources of the empire, since western Asia Minor was effectively lost to the usurper Achaios, southern Asia Minor was controlled by the Ptolemies and, beyond Media and Persis, Seleukid control was either weak or non-existent (ch. 2). Thus, the 68,000 troops of Raphia represented only a part of Seleukid military potential.

At Magnesia, an army of some 72,000 was deployed. But two years earlier Antiochos had crossed over to Greece with a force of 10,000 infantry and 500 cavalry, which faced the Romans at Thermopylai (Livy 35.43.6; 36.15.3; App. *Syr.* 17), but only 500 escaped the battlefield (Livy 36.19.11; App. *Syr.* 20). In all probability, Antiochos' losses were mainly in mercenaries, which he seems to have recouped quickly for Magnesia.

The purpose of the Daphne procession has always remained unclear. Was it, as a hostile Polybios (30.25) has tried to persuade us, a response to the games celebrated by Aemilius Paulus, a declaration of the wealth and strength of the empire, essentially an image-building effort?[4] Or was it simply a victory procession after the invasion of Egypt?[5] Or was it, as I am inclined to believe, the festive commencement of the expedition of Antiochos IV against the Parthians, the gathering of the main forces in preparation for the eastward march the following year?[6] The Roman inspectors, who had anxiously arrived, could find nothing threatening to the interests of Rome (Polyb. 30.27) and one may suppose that they were not unhappy that Antiochos' ambitions were directed away from the Mediterranean.

---

[4] Sherwin-White and Kuhrt 1993: 220. [5] Gruen 1984: 76.
[6] Also Bunge 1976: 71: Will 1982: 346.

The absence of non-Greek levies and 'allies' at Daphne is not surprising, if a military expedition was in preparation. It would have been normal for such auxiliary troops to join the army on its march east, at a staging centre such as Seleukeia-Tigris nearer their area of recruitment. If the battle of Raphia can be considered a guide, serving in the Seleukid army then were 5,000 Medes, Kissians, Kadusians and Karmanians, as well as 2,000 'Agrianian' and Persian bowmen and slingers (Polyb. 5.79), a total of 7,000 native auxiliaries from the eastern provinces.[7] The indications are that Antiochos IV may still have retained some sort of control over Media and suzerainty over Persis (ch. 2). So, it seems quite possible that native levies from the east may have totalled 7,000 men or more, giving a total army size for this campaign of not less than 55,000.

At the same time, however, substantial Seleukid troops were engaged in Palestine in suppressing the Maccabean revolt. The fanciful figure given for the battle of Ammaus (165 BC) of 40,000 infantry and 7,000 cavalry in 1 Maccabees 3.39 can be discarded, but the 20,000 in 2 Maccabees 8.9 may well be a reasonable figure, if Edomite and Philistine 'allies' are included.[8] Thus, a total force of around 75,000 in two Seleukid field armies at this time is a not unreasonable figure.

There is some support for such a number in the later campaign of Lysias against the Maccabees to quell what had by then become a dangerous situation for the Seleukids in Palestine, which culminated in the battle of Beith-Zacharia in 162 BC. In Josephus' account of the campaign (*BJ* 1.41–6), the figures of 50,000 infantry and 5,000 cavalry given for the Seleukid army may well be reasonably accurate.[9] These could have represented a substantial part of the forces that had travelled east with Antiochos IV a few years earlier, but certainly not all, if one considers that the situation there had been left unresolved by his sudden death, with the Parthian threat undiminished.

From the detailed figures in the sources for the specific periods of Raphia, Magnesia and Daphne, spanning about fifty years, one may arrive at the conclusion that the Seleukid kings could and did raise field armies then of 70,000–80,000 troops when required.

There are no equally reliable figures for other major campaigns in this period, but one can nevertheless reach some conclusions. It is possible that a larger Seleukid army was deployed in the victorious battle of Panion in 200 BC during the fifth Syrian war than in the earlier defeat at Raphia. In

---

[7] Bar-Kochva regards the 'Agrianians' as possibly Persians armed in the style of the Agrianians of Alexander (1979: 51).
[8] Bar-Kochva 1979: 13.   [9] Bar-Kochva 1979: 177.

the Book of Daniel (11.13): 'the king of the north shall again set forth a multitude, greater than the former', which possibly refers to the fourth and fifth Syrian wars.

For the eastern Anabasis of Antiochos III (212–205 BC), one should not reject Justin (41.5.7) out of hand, when he quotes 100,000 infantry and 20,000 cavalry, although these figures have obviously been rounded up.[10] Polybios also writes of a large force (10.28.1). One may consider the importance and difficulty of this campaign in recovering lost and distant territories, which so added to the prestige of the king that he was granted the title 'Great' by his contemporaries. One may also note the relative quiet at this time on the Mediterranean political and military front, which would have permitted a maximum effort in the East. Finally, the analysis of mint output at Seleukeia-Tigris in chapter 11.5e suggests that huge amounts of coinage were minted there, far greater than any 'peacetime' needs of the region, indicating very high military expenditure. So it is not unreasonable to consider that Antiochos was able to gather a rather large army for the Anabasis, probably not smaller than those of his other campaigns and a figure of 70,000 or more, approaching Justin's, may not in the end be unreasonable.[11]

For the period after Antiochos IV one other figure in the sources should be noted, the 80,000-strong army raised by Antiochos VII in a last-ditch effort against the Parthians, which culminated in his defeat and death in 129 BC (Justin 38.10.1–2). Such a number should not really surprise one in view of what has already been seen of Seleukid military potential and the critical importance of Mesopotamia to the empire.[12] Diodoros (34/35.17) hints at a massive recruitment drive when he speaks of the loss suffered by every family in Antioch after the defeat. Justin's account has Antiochos receiving the submission of several native 'kings' on his march east, victoriously occupying Babylonia and having all the people of the region pass over to his side until nothing was left to the Parthians. What one may read between the lines is the recruitment of substantial Greek and non-Greek forces from erstwhile Seleukid territory in Mesopotamia and western Iran[13] to which may also be added the potentially large Jewish contingent led by Hyrcanus (Jos. *AJ* 13.250). There is no reason to doubt that the army that finally faced the Parthians may have been of the size given by Justin.

[10] Bar-Kochva 1979: 10.
[11] Grainger maintains that only half of these forces could be used on extended campaigns and that these thus constituted the standing army (1996: 339).
[12] Also Bar-Kochva 1979: 11. A study of numerical distortion in Roman writers by Duncan-Jones 1997 shows that numbers beginning with high digits are considerably less frequent than those beginning with low digits, as they tend to be rounded upwards, e.g. 90 to 100. In my view, this means that a number starting with 9 or 8, being relatively 'unpopular', has a greater chance of being accurate.
[13] Sherwin-White and Kuhrt 1993: 224.

The earlier period from Seleukos I to Antiochos III is the most difficult for any estimate, since the only precise numbers we have are for Seleukos' army on the march to Ipsos, which consisted of 20,000 infantry and 12,000 cavalry, along with 480 elephants (Diod. 20.113.4). The relatively small numbers of infantry are not indicative of Seleukid military potential then, as it is likely that Seleukos would have put together only a picked force for the long march west at a time when the eastern satrapies of the empire had recently been conquered and a potential threat from Chandragupta, the Maurya emperor, still existed, despite the peace treaty between the two kings. On the other hand, the size of the cavalry in the army is revealing, as it is completely out of proportion to infantry – the normal ratio in Hellenistic armies being more like one to ten, as at Raphia – and equal to the largest number we know of, that for the battle of Magnesia. No doubt this was due to the inclusion at the time of Ipsos of Baktria within the Seleukid empire, with its large resources of horsemen.[14] One may suppose that Seleukos could, if he had so wished, have mobilized a force as large as those raised subsequently by Antiochos III or IV and this probably applied to his immediate successors. Whether they did so or not in any of the numerous campaigns of the third century BC is unknown.

Returning to the fifty-year period spanning the reigns of Antiochos III to Antiochos IV, Seleukid field armies of 70,000–80,000 men, engaged in campaigns which usually lasted for a few years, have been regularly noted. The core of these armies seems to have been about 35,000 'regulars', as I have termed them in table 10.1 of Seleukid army numbers. According to several scholars,[15] these were mainly military settlers, with a duty to serve when called up by the king,[16] but I question whether this was a regular policy, as there is no direct evidence to this effect in the sources. It seems to me that the Greek settlers in the new Seleukid foundations were more valuable to the kings when left in place, generating revenue for the royal exchequer through their productive activity, although undoubtedly some of their sons might be serving as conscripts in the regular Seleukid army.[17] The number of mercenaries normally employed was at least 15,000, but it

---

[14] Ten thousand Baktrian horsemen under Euthydemos later faced Antiochos III's invasion of Baktria (Polyb. 10.49.1).

[15] For example, Griffith 1935: 162–4; Bar-Kochva 1979: 59–62; Billows 1995: 172–8; Foulon 1996: 60–1.

[16] Briant believes that this essentially replicated the call-up obligation of military colonists in the Achaemenid empire (1986: 35–6).

[17] Bikerman regarded the army as consisting essentially of mercenaries and permanent recruits, with conscription only used when necessary. For example, in the Maccabean war it was regular troops who fought, not colonists. Land allotments (*klēroi*) given to settlers did not, in his view, entail an obligation of military service (1938: 78–88). Cohen stresses that there is no evidence that military obligations were tied to settlers' lots (1991: 41; 1995: 63), as does Corsaro 1980: 1216–17.

is possible that more were used in the Anabasis. The remaining troops were non-Greek levies and 'allies', although it is difficult to see how the latter, at least, differed greatly from mercenaries.

What may be considered surprising is that no non-Greek troops were apparently utilized in the Seleukid 'regular' infantry. Syria and Mesopotamia, for example, are not noted as having supplied specific contingents in any of the major Seleukid campaigns. The explanation given,[18] that this was for reasons of security, because to arm troops from areas so close to the heartland of the empire was considered dangerous, is not convincing. The human resources existed and the Achaemenids certainly had no qualms in using them, when one considers, for example, the huge contingents from the provinces that found their way into the Persian battle line at Gaugamela (Arr. *Anab.* 3.11.3–7). The truth must lie elsewhere, probably in the designation given to certain troops that were 'armed in the Macedonian fashion', and I suggest that this is where the missing Syrians and Mesopotamians, and possibly Persians too, may lie. It is interesting to note in *Astronomical Diary* -273 a statement concerning the First Syrian War: 'That month [March 273 BC] the general [of Babylonia] gathered the troops of the king, which were in Babylonia, from beginning to end, and went to the aid of the king in month I [April 273] to Transpotamia [i.e. Syria].'

The 'troops of the king' here seem to be regular troops, based in the satrapy, as the king was already in Syria with his army. 'From beginning to end' may refer either to the month or to Babylonia or to the completeness of the gathering, one cannot tell. It is quite possible that many of these soldiers were garrison troops, mostly Greeks, but it is not improbable that some were locals.

It will be recalled that Alexander had set the trend by creating first a mixed cavalry[19] and then, shortly before his death, a mixed phalanx of Macedonians and Persians, in which the Macedonians were given the senior positions (Arr. *Anab.* 7.23.3–4) and this is likely to have been continued by the Seleukids. As for the 'regular' cavalry, this is definitely noted as a mixed force at Magnesia, where the *agēma* and the royal squadron are described by Livy (37.40.5–6, 11) as comprising Medes and races from the same region: Syrians, Phrygians and Lydians.

One other point is worth noting, that the 'regular' infantry consisted essentially of phalanx-type troops, a force that required special training to function effectively, not one that could be put together hurriedly. I have

---

[18] Bar-Kochva 1979: 52.   [19] Aperghis 1997a: 143–8.

already questioned the view[20] that European military settlers were constrained to provide troops in return for their land grants when required to do so. This view sees the settlers' sons serving for a time in the *arguraspides* units or in the elite cavalry squadrons of the Companions and the *agēma* and then being transferred to a reserve and called up when required for other cavalry and phalanx units. I myself consider that the *arguraspides* and the elite cavalry squadrons were permanently manned units, in which settlers' sons may have enlisted, if they so wished. I have also suggested that phalanx troops 'armed in the Macedonian fashion' refer to substantial numbers of non-Greeks, particularly from Mesopotamia and Syria, while there are clear references to non-Europeans even in the elite cavalry.

In the fifty-year period that has been considered above, 30,000 or so infantrymen and 6,000 cavalrymen seem to have been almost continuously employed on campaign. If these were essentially Greeks, there was hardly any respite for them. But would it have made sense for the Seleukid kings to have relied so exclusively on their subjects of European origin when they had so many Asians to draw from? In the last resort, the Greeks were the pillar supporting the dynasty, and dissatisfaction due to constant campaigning or losses in a single crucial battle, such as Raphia or Magnesia, might destroy this support at one blow; this the kings could surely see. Yet the dynasty survived, with military forces that could reach their former levels even after major defeats, which suggests that the Seleukids did indeed draw their 'regular' forces from a virtually inexhaustible reservoir of subject populations.[21] Perhaps only the 10,000-strong *arguraspides* corps and the elite squadrons of the cavalry were mainly composed of Greeks.

What of the mercenaries in the army? Again, one must consider the almost continuous campaigning of the fifty-year period that has been considered and the relatively steady number of mercenaries that keeps cropping up in the sources for the great battles, at around 15,000. Given the distances involved, which would have made recruitment and transportation of mercenaries from beyond the borders of the empire a lengthy and costly process, it would be far more sensible for the Seleukid kings to maintain a steady number of mercenary troops for their almost continuous military needs and utilize some of these on garrison duty in times of peace. A clue to this possible preference for a regular mercenary force is offered by Josephus

---

[20] Bar-Kochva 1979: 59–62.
[21] Compare this with the British, who controlled India mainly with native troops and British officers.

(*AJ* 13.129) in describing the action of Demetrios II who, upon concluding peace with the Jews, 'dismissed his army and reduced their pay (presumably below agreed levels) and continued to give their pay only to the mercenaries who had come up with him from Crete and from the other islands'.

What, then, is the conclusion one may reach? In my view, the Seleukid kings, or at least Antiochos III and IV, maintained a more or less permanent army of about 50,000 men, 35,000 'regulars' and 15,000 mercenaries, excluding garrisons,[22] but no doubt some of these troops served on garrison duty in the brief intervals of peace. For the needs of major campaigns, garrisons could be reduced, more mercenaries recruited, levies raised from subject populations and 'allies' called upon and, in these circumstances, army size could increase substantially. I am not convinced that the troops I have called 'regulars' could be markedly augmented by a call-up of Greek settlers, nor that these settlers had any obligation to respond to such a call-up. In my view the essential Seleukid army, 'regulars' and mercenaries, was, effectively, a permanent professional force.[23]

But, the question will naturally arise as to what the difference was between a 'regular' and a mercenary soldier. Perhaps it was a question of pay (but see below). Perhaps it related more to the type of soldier, the heavily armed 'regular' cavalryman or phalangist compared to the 'light' mercenary infantryman. In my view, the distinction is more likely to have been between a soldier who was already a subject of the Seleukids and one who had come to serve from outside the empire. It will be noted that Demetrios II (above) differentiated between the rest of his army and 'the mercenaries who had come up with him from Crete and from the other islands'. It is quite possible that, because of the restrictions imposed by the treaty of Apameia (188 BC) on the recruitment of western mercenaries, the rest of Demetrios' army was mainly 'home-grown'.

b. The navy

With regard to the navy, the source information is even scarcer than for the army. Until Antiochos III, the Seleukids apparently made no serious

---

[22] In the view of a number of scholars, the standing force would only have consisted of the 10,000 *arguraspides* and some cavalry, for example Foulon (1996: 60–1) and Bar-Kochva (1979: 59–62). But, since there was continuous fighting of the Seleukid phalanx, Griffith concludes that this too was effectively part of a standing army (1935: 164).

[23] Austin regards Hellenistic armies as substantially professional, always with a mercenary element (1986: 464). Allen also supports the idea of a professional army for Attalos I, another Hellenistic king (1983: 85).

attempt to challenge the Ptolemies or Antigonids in the eastern Mediterranean and, consequently, probably maintained only token naval forces there.[24]

The situation changed with Antiochos III, whose drive into Asia Minor from spring 197 BC began with a combined operation of army and fleet against the Ptolemaic possessions along the coast of southern Asia Minor. One does not know the size of his initial fleet, part of which may have come from the recently conquered Phoenician cities,[25] but a few years later, in 192 BC, forty 'decked' and sixty 'open' warships, along with a few others that had been on patrol in the Aegean, escorted the expeditionary force that landed in Greece (Livy 35.43.3–4). Again, it is likely that the Greek coastal cities of Asia Minor, newly taken over or brought into alliance, may have supplied some of the vessels and crews. An 'open' warship here is likely to have been a trireme, with a complement of about 200 men, or perhaps a bireme or triaconter, while most 'decked' warships at this time were quadriremes and quinqueremes, with 300 or more rowers and marines each. Thus, the total numbers in Antiochos' fleet for his Greek expedition must have been of the order of 20,000–25,000. This was, naturally, a fleet put together for a specific campaign and the treaty of Apameia (188 BC) later permitted only ten 'decked' warships, no triremes, but some smaller vessels to the Seleukids (Polyb. 21.42.13), presumably with reference only to the Mediterranean, and thus a force of no more than 5,000 men, probably employed mostly during the sailing season.

The situation was different in the Persian Gulf, where a war fleet had probably safeguarded Seleukid interests since the time of Seleukos I. The fort at Ikaros (Failaka) dates to the early third century BC and probably protected a naval station, while a Seleukid presence at Tylos (Bahrain) seems likely.[26] Antioch-Persis appears to have been an important foundation on the Gulf, perhaps at modern Bushire, while Pliny (*HN* 6.159) gives us the names of three otherwise unknown Seleukid settlements in this area (Arethousa, Larissa and Chalkis), which may have been naval stations similar to the probable one at Failaka.

Seleukid naval activity in the Gulf appears to have increased markedly with the arrival of Antiochos III on the scene, following his return from the Anabasis in 205 BC, when he exacted tribute from Gerrha and sailed as far as

---

[24] The opposite view is taken by Bikerman (1938: 98).

[25] Musti considers that the Seleukid navy really developed after the battle of Panion in 200 BC (1984: 184). But note the forty Ptolemaic warships captured earlier in Ptolemaïs, in 217 BC, which included twenty 'decked' ones (Polyb. 5.62.2–3).

[26] Salles 1987: 102–8; Le Rider 1989: 248–50.

Bahrain (Polyb. 13.9.5). One notes the creation of a satrapy of the Erythraean Sea, with its own mint, at about this time, testifying to real interest in the Gulf trade, which persisted down to the mid second century BC.[27] There is also the report of a naval battle conducted by Numenios, admiral of a king Antiochos, perhaps Antiochos IV, off cape Ras-Musandam on the very same day that a land battle was fought at the cape (Pliny *HN* 6.152). That this episode was considered worthy of mention suggests a not insignificant Seleukid expeditionary force.

There is no way of knowing the size of the Seleukid fleet in the Gulf or the types of vessel it contained. Since no significant Arab naval force apparently opposed it, the number of warships need not have been high. If twenty or so triremes were deployed, one might suppose that the total force could have amounted to around 5,000 men.

Although numbers for the Seleukid navy are highly conjectural, a figure of not more than 10,000 under 'peacetime' conditions seems likely, which was virtually all of the time, in marked contrast to the use of the army. Only after Antiochos III's conquest of the ports of Phoenicia and Palestine is the Seleukid navy likely to have been of much consequence and the total naval forces of the empire may have briefly reached the level of 30,000 sailors and marines or so during Antiochos III's campaign to Greece.

c. *Garrisons*

References to Seleukid garrisons (φρουραί) or garrison commanders (φρούραρχοι) appear from time to time in Greek sources, frequently connected with the citadels from which subject cities were dominated, or also with guard posts (σταθμοί, φυλακαί).[28] Clearly the purpose of garrisons was to guard against possible uprisings, to provide security for the local population, so that it could go about its daily activities, and to ensure that tribute was collected by financial officials of the administration. Perhaps every city was garrisoned,[29] even a theoretically 'safe' one like Babylon in the third century BC,[30] and the Seleukid 'supervisor' (ἐπιστάτης) noted in many cities was probably supported by troops.[31]

The citadels and forts in which garrisons were based might also serve as local administrative centres, treasuries (γαζοφυλάκια) and depots of supplies and material for the administration and army. It was frequently the case for the troops themselves to be billeted on the civilian population,

---

[27] Salles 1987: 91–9; Sherwin-White and Kuhrt 1993: 65–6.
[28] Bikerman 1938: 53–5, with references.   [29] Bagnall 1976: 220.
[30] Sherwin-White 1982: 55, 70.   [31] Ma 1997: 93; 1999: 118.

which must have imposed a heavy burden, hence the almost persistent request of the Greek cities to be freed from the obligation of billeting (ἐπισταθμεία).[32]

Clearly the garrison of an important subject city of the Aegean could amount to several hundred men, whereas a guard post was probably manned by only a few dozen soldiers. The number of 30,000 Jews requested by Demetrios I for garrison duty (1 Macc. 10.36–7) may not be taken seriously, but an offer was probably made and then repeated by Demetrios II (1 Macc. 13.40). The 2,000 Jewish settler-soldiers from Babylonia that Antiochos III ordered to be sent to Phrygia and Lydia were intended to reinforce 'the forts and strategic points' there (Jos. *AJ* 12.149: τὰ φρούρια καὶ τοὺς ἀναγκαιοτάτους τόπους).

One can perhaps consider the Seleukid garrison network as an extension of that of the Achaemenids, faced with exactly the same problem of control, where several hundred garrisons must have existed, probably at least one in every important city and more concentrated in frontier regions.[33] One may also note the very considerable use made by Alexander of mercenaries for garrison duty in a somewhat greater area, with estimates of their numbers ranging from 36,000 to over 100,000.[34]

Troops manning garrisons might be not only western mercenaries, but also soldiers brought from other parts of the empire, a regular practice also of the Achaemenids.[35] Apart from the 2,000 Jews mentioned above, a force of Persian cavalry under Omanes is noted at Palaimagnesia near Smyrna (*OGIS* 229).

All one can say about numbers is that, given the huge area and population to be controlled, there must have been several hundred garrisons and large numbers of troops required. I will venture on a figure at the time of Antiochos III that is somewhat less than the minimum estimate for Alexander's mercenaries, or about 20,000–30,000 for the hard core serving garrison duty, increased in 'peacetime' conditions by mercenaries not on active service.

---

[32] And not only cities, but villages too (cf. Ptolemaios' request in Document 4). Also Hennig 1995: 267–78.

[33] Tuplin lists Persian garrisons appearing in the sources, but the distribution is quite uneven, because of different source quality from different areas (1987b: 235–41). Better-documented western and southern Asia Minor gave fifty-six garrison sites, Palestine nineteen and Persis also nineteen, which creates the impression of a quite dense network.

[34] Milns reproduces the estimates of Griffiths (36,000), Thomas (54,000) and Wirth (over 100,000) (1987: 250–1).

[35] Briant 1996: 620–5.

d. *Total armed forces*

Under 'peacetime' conditions then, the Seleukid armed forces possibly numbered about 70,000–80,000 soldiers, that is, 35,000 regulars, 15,000 mercenaries and 20,000–30,000 garrison troops, with a cavalry to infantry ratio of approximately one to ten, and about 10,000 sailors and marines, giving 80,000–90,000 men in all. For an important expedition, such as the Anabasis, recruitment of more mercenaries, 'allies' and subject levies could raise this number by at least another 20,000–30,000 to a total of 100,000–120,000, or even more when a large fleet was involved, as against the Romans.

e. *Rates of pay*

Hellenistic armies were on the whole more professional than their predecessors of the Classical period. The Seleukid kings in particular relied, as discussed earlier, on a mostly standing army of some size, a network of garrisons in the satrapies and a regularly employed mercenary force, which might serve garrison duty in (rare) 'peacetime' conditions. All these troops most probably required regular pay.[36]

There were various ways of paying one's soldiers, the standard method being to provide a wage (μισθός, ὀψώνιον) plus a ration allowance (σῖτος, σιτομετρία, σιτώνιον, σιταρχία), or money in lieu, although sometimes these terms confusingly seem to cover both forms of payment. There was also the possibility of allowing purchases from royal storehouses at low prices and offering soldiers fiscal immunities for themselves and their goods.[37] One method used for troops posted to garrisons for lengthy periods was the provision of *klēroi* or land allotments, which would naturally reduce the administration's expenditure in silver.[38] In this respect, however, there does not seem to have been general application of the Ptolemaic practice of awarding *klēroi* to soldiers under the obligation to report for active duty when called up.

There is no direct evidence for rates of military pay in the Seleukid kingdom, only for those in the Mediterranean world at this time, but one

---

[36] Austin 1986: 464–5.

[37] Griffith 1935: 282–8; Launey 1950: 738–46. See also the contract of the Pergamene king with mercenary soldiers (*OGIS* 266), discussed in chapter 9.2b.

[38] *Klēroi* are noted for the garrison of Palaimagnesia (*OGIS* 229), the Jewish soldiers sent to Phrygia and Lydia (Jos. *AJ* 12.149–52) and the Parthian-period garrison of Susa (*SEG* 7.13; Cumont 1931: 241). See also Cohen 1978: 7–9 and Bar-Kochva 1979: 21.

may suppose that soldiers could be attracted for service in the East at going rates, which at the time of Antiochos III seem to have been about 1 drachm (= 6 obols) per day for the average infantryman, plus a ration allowance or money in lieu, while a cavalryman could expect to earn at least twice as much.[39]

For recruits serving in the Seleukid army, the evidence suggests that they were also paid and that their rates of pay did not differ from those of mercenaries, as can be deduced from Demetrios I's offer to enrol 30,000 Jews in his army at the same pay as for his other troops (1 Macc. 10.36). When Demetrios II disbanded his soldiers after his Jewish campaign, retaining only the mercenaries, he provoked dissatisfaction because his predecessors had paid troops even in 'peacetime', so as to be ready for a call-up (Jos. *AJ* 13.130).

An *ostrakon* or pottery sherd from third-century BC Babylon may provide some concrete evidence on the level of pay of garrison troops. *Ostraka* were often used as temporary records of monetary transactions, until the proper accounting had been done. Here, a unit under Ballaros and another under Artemon each apparently received a sum of 249,[40] which is likely to have been the monthly pay in drachms of each unit. The question now is 'How many men belonged to each unit?' The normal depth of the Macedonian phalanx file, the smallest unit, the *lochos*, numbered sixteen men (Polyb. 18.30.1; Arr. *Anab.* 7.23.3–4),[41] but these soldiers on garrison duty are unlikely to have belonged to the phalanx. Instead, they may have been mercenaries, lighter-armed infantry, where the depth of a file was exactly half that of the phalanx, that is, eight men (Arr. *Tact.* 14). Their daily pay then works out at almost exactly 6 obols each, as in the old Greek world at this time, while a unit leader probably earned twice as much as

[39] Launey lists the epigraphic evidence and concludes that the pay for a mercenary in the third century BC was about 8 obols per day plus 3 or 3⅓ obols for rations, if paid in silver, but probably lower in the second century BC (1950: 750–8). Pritchett makes use of much the same information, but interprets ὀψώνιον and σιταρχία in two cases as composite pay, arriving at 6–8 obols per day (1971: 22–3). In one case (Thermos *IG* IX², 3 of 263/2 BC), he is not justified in doing so, since the composite rate for a light infantryman (ψιλός) of 4⅔ obols per day would seem to be far too low, if it were to include a 2–3 obols per day ration allowance. Griffith, likewise, opts for 6–8 obols per day, which he regards as composite pay, and considers that mercenaries probably received the same as citizen soldiers (1935: 300–6). Moretti takes 1–2 drachms per day as the standard pay for a mercenary (1977: 323), Cavaignac 20–25 drachms per month for a foot soldier (1951: 142) and Bar-Kochva 1 drachm per day as the mercenary wage in Judaea (1977: 173). Callataÿ estimates 8 obols as the daily pay of an hoplite in the third century BC and considers this to have remained roughly the same into the early first century BC (1997: 404–5).

[40] Sherwin-White 1982: 55–61.   [41] Bar-Kochva 1979: 66–7.

the ordinary soldier.[42] However, the cost of living in Babylon, as reflected in the market price for barley (ch. 5.6a), was seen to be less than half of that in the Aegean and it might, consequently, be argued that a mercenary's daily pay in Mesopotamia may also have been half as much, namely 3 obols, in which case one could estimate that Ballaros' and Artemon's units numbered sixteen men each. All one can say is that the pay of a Seleukid soldier, whether 'regular' or mercenary, is likely to have depended to some extent on where he served, with those in Mediterranean provinces tending to receive higher pay. At the time of Antiochos III and IV, most military activity was taking place in these regions and, consequently, average daily pay of 5–6 obols is more likely. If the normal daily ration allowance in the Aegean was 2–3 obols, the average in the Seleukid empire should have been slightly lower, when paid in coin, for the same reasons given above, so probably about 2 obols.

There is no evidence for sailors' pay in the Seleukid empire or, for that matter, anywhere else in the Hellenistic period, but, on the analogy of the Classical period, it is likely to have been somewhat lower than that of a foot soldier.

f. Period of pay

Two inscriptions (*I. Cos* 10; *OGIS* 266), depending on how they are interpreted, suggest that wages of mercenary troops may have been paid for only nine or ten months of the year,[43] or perhaps for the full year, but with service demanded for less.[44] This might equally apply to soldiers in the regular army, on the assumption that they could not be actively engaged in winter, but perhaps not if they were on campaign at the time.

With regard to most sailors and marines, it is likely that they would have been paid only when on active duty, that is, mostly during the summer sailing months.

g. Method of payment

The military resources of the Seleukid kings could be augmented at the time of a major campaign by tapping the reserve constituted by Greek and other settlers, by recruiting more mercenaries on the open market,

---

[42] Double pay is noted by Allen in a Cretan inscription of the time of Attalos I (1983: 209). There is also the reference in Arrian to Alexander's διμοιρίτης or double-pay man (*Anab.* 7.23.3–4).

[43] Griffith 1935: 283–4.   [44] Grote 1913: 86; Launey 1950: 741, 755–6.

by calling upon 'allies' for troops and by raising levies from amongst the subject populations.

For a mercenary it is very likely that an advance payment was necessary in order to attract him to royal service for a particular campaign, since a professional soldier had no guarantee that he would finally be paid off if his paymaster were defeated. If he were fortunate, he could expect a final settlement when his services were no longer required, in addition to any booty that he might have acquired. Given, however, the fact that the Seleukid kings were at war much of the time, or had need of soldiers for garrison duty, a mercenary might continue to be employed indefinitely. In such a case, he could expect regular pay and the *ostrakon* from Babylon (above) suggests that it was provided on a monthly basis, which could apply also to the regular army.

Evidence for advance payments to mercenaries may come from an interesting hoard of fifty-eight gold Ptolemaic coins (*trichrusa*) buried in northern Syria west of Antioch at the time of the second Syrian war. On about ten of the coins are small incisions, forming distinguishable Greek letters, made there after striking. It has been suggested[45] that these marks identified the owners of the coins, who were mercenary soldiers. A hypothesis that would fit the picture of the hoard is that an initial advance of Ptolemaic forces from Seleukeia-Pieria towards Antioch brought a company of mercenaries to this point, where, in the face of some danger, their funds were buried and never recovered after the Ptolemaic retreat. The high-value gold coins being carried by the soldiers do point to their having been received as advance payments for this campaign.

An even stronger piece of evidence for such advance payments to mercenaries is provided by the coinage issues of Mithridates VI Eupator.[46] The entire series is dated by regnal year and month, and die studies enable one to estimate the volume minted at any time. Two clear peaks in production are noted. The first occurs in 89 and 88 BC, at the very start of the First Mithridatic war, which was forced upon the Pontic king by the Romans, and his preparations for war, particularly the recruitment of mercenaries, must therefore have been hurried. The second peak is noted in 75 and 74 BC, *before* the start of the Third Mithridatic War, which Mithridates himself provoked. The impression one obtains is of the putting together of a huge war-chest of coinage, ready to be opened at the right moment for the recruitment of troops and their regular pay.

---

[45] Davesne and Yenisoganci 1992: 33.   [46] Callataÿ 1997: 52.

h. Total cost of the armed forces

So far, best estimates have been made of the sizes of the 'peacetime' and 'wartime' Seleukid armed forces, of around 80,000–90,000 and 100,000–120,000 men respectively, but only fighting men.

At 5–6 obols per day for infantry and sailors and twice that for cavalry, the annual cost of the wages of the 'peacetime' Seleukid armed forces at the time of Antiochos III would have amounted to about 4,000–5,000 talents per year in silver. At 2 obols per day for rations, the additional cost would have been about 1,500 talents, but no doubt as much of this as possible was supplied in kind from the royal storehouses. To these figures one should add the cost of support personnel (commissariat, baggage handlers, grooms, servants, etc.) and the overheads (clothing, equipment, pack-animals, housing, maintenance of the war-elephants and cavalry horses, commissioning of war-ships, etc.), although some of these ancillary expenses would undoubtedly have been settled in kind. A total annual cost of 7,000–8,000 talents for the 'peacetime' armed forces should not surprise one.[47] If a major campaign, such as the Anabasis or the conquest of Asia Minor, was under way, military expenses might rise to 9,000–10,000 talents a year.

For comparison, estimates of the annual cost of Alexander's army reach as high as 15,000 talents in the last phase of his campaign,[48] while the Romans set the 15,000 talent indemnity after Magnesia at the level of what they claimed had been the cost of the war to them (Polyb. 21.17.4) and the army of Augustus is thought to have cost about 445 million sesterces annually, or nearly 19,000 talents.[49]

2. COST OF THE PROVINCIAL ADMINISTRATION

The Ptolemaic general in charge of the forces that faced Antiochos III in Phoenicia and Palestine, Skopas, received 10 minas a day and each officer of his staff 1 mina (Polyb. 13.2.3). Generals could and did change sides and become governors of provinces (e.g. Ptolemaios, Document 4) and, perhaps, this is an indication of pay scales of senior officials in the Seleukid empire as well.

---

[47] Milns calculates a cost of 2,200–4,800 talents per year for the mixed phalanx and 6,000 talents per year for 100,000 mercenaries, paid at the rate of 1 drachm per day. He also adds 30–50 per cent for food and overheads. This would give a total of more than 10,000–15,000 talents a year (1987: 254). Cavaignac estimates that a 100,000-man army would cost 6,000 talents a year (1951: 142). Cavaignac also puts the cost of a fleet of the period, consisting of eighty or ninety ships, at about 2,000 talents per year (1923: 118).

[48] Bellinger 1963: 73–4; Milns 1987: 254.   [49] Hopkins 1980: 124–5.

However, for many officials a large part of their earnings, and perhaps even all, may have been indirect, from the land granted to them by the king, while they remained in office or even afterwards. One does not know what services Mnesimachos had rendered, but following the argument in chapter 8.1a and e, his own revenue from the land grant may have amounted to about 30 drachms per day. Aristodikides' land grant (Document 2) ultimately contained 5,500 *plethra* of mostly cultivable land, or about 500 hectares, roughly equal in fact to the estimated cultivable area of one of Mnesimachos' two main villages and so perhaps yielding half his revenue. By way of comparison, a governor of the minor Achaemenid province of Judaea earned 40 (Persian) shekels daily from 'the satrap's table' (Nehemiah 5.15–17), equivalent to about 50 drachms.

These are isolated rates of pay, which really give only an indication of what some administrative personnel of a satrapy may have cost. So, to arrive at a total cost of the provincial administration, one is reduced to 'educated speculation'.

The financial and, indirectly, civil administration of a satrapy is discussed in chapter 13. Let us assume that the chief officers of a satrapy, the *stratēgos* and the *dioikētēs*, received half of Skopas' daily pay, namely 500 drachms.[50] Each of the twenty or so satrapies of the empire at its peak may have been divided into three or four hyparchies or *oikonomiai*, on average.[51] Let us assume that the hyparch and the *oikonomos* were each paid 50 drachms per day, half the salary of Skopas' officers. Garrison commanders are not taken into account, as their pay has been considered part of military expenditure, but there were other senior officials in a satrapy, such as one or more *eklogistai* ('tax assessors'), probably an *epi tōn hierōn* ('supervisor of the sanctuaries') and certainly *epistatai* ('supervisors') for some cities (ch. 13.4–7). Again, let us assume that each of these middle-level officials earned 50 drachms per day.

So, two chief officers and about ten at the next level made up the 'senior management' of a satrapy and may have cost up to 1,500 drachms per day or roughly 90 talents per year. At least one large satrapy (Koile Syria) possessed intermediate administrative subdivisions, the meridarchies, with a meridarch and a *dioikētēs* in command of each, which would have increased their cost (ch. 13.5a). So, for twenty satrapies in the empire at its peak, the

---

[50] Plutarch exaggerates, no doubt, when he considers that the servants of a Seleukid satrap were wealthier than all the Spartan kings put together (*Agis* 7). The assumed daily pay of 5 minas for a satrap would have amounted to 30 talents a year, the revenue of a good-sized city of Asia Minor; cf. the annual revenue of 50 talents that Themistokles apparently received from Magnesia (Thuc. 1.138.5).

[51] The seventy-two provinces attributed by Appian (*Syr.* 62) to Seleukos I were in all likelihood hyparchies. See chapter 13.5i for the coincidence of hyparchy and *oikonomia*.

total annual cost of senior personnel works out at about 2,000 talents, although a substantial part of this may have effectively been covered by land grants (from which the king could even expect taxation revenue in silver). At more junior levels of the administration, individual personnel costs would have been appreciably lower, probably nearer the 0.5–1 drachm daily pay of the average soldier. Taking into account other expenses of the satrapies that could not be met by requisitions or corvée labour, the total cost of the provincial administration in silver may have been of the order of 2,000–3,000 talents annually at the empire's peaks *c*. 281 or 190 BC, purely based on 'educated speculation'.

3. COST OF THE KING AND HIS COURT

Here too one is unfortunately reduced to 'educated speculation', since a figure must be derived, however approximate.

The Persian king, we are told (Athenaios 4.145a), spent 20 or 30 talents or more a day for his maintenance, for which there is some confirmation in the huge quantities of commodities listed by Polyainos (4.3.32) for the 'King's dinner'.[52] In both of these cases, it was clearly not only the king and his courtiers who wined and dined, but also that part of the army which was permanently attached to the court and travelled with it. On the assumption that half of the cost was borne by the army, the expenditure of the Persian king and his court would have amounted to about 5,000 talents annually.

One cannot apply this directly to the court of the Seleukid king,[53] of course, even if the figures were accurate. Nevertheless, to consider that the king spent 2,000–3,000 talents a year on himself and his entourage does not appear unreasonable, since, as part of the ideology of kingship, he was expected to give the impression of great wealth.[54] For example, even at a time of financial strain after Magnesia (ch. 12.4), Antiochos IV could be regarded as surpassing all previous kings in his public displays (Livy 41.20).

4. EXTRAORDINARY EXPENDITURE

a. Benefactions

The Seleukid kings used some of their wealth in acts of benefaction (εὐεργεσία), with which they sought to create goodwill (εὔνοια), which can essentially be interpreted as the gaining of political support. This aspect

[52] Lewis 1987.   [53] Bikerman 1938: 31–50.   [54] Sherwin-White and Kuhrt 1993: 129–32.

of their rule has been discussed by others[55] and it is the intention here only to assess its economic implications.

Sanctuaries were prime targets of benefactions, partly because of the religious sensitivities of the kings and partly because they influenced large sections of the population. Sanctuaries received outright grants of land,[56] or revenue from land,[57] or tax exemptions,[58] or financial and material assistance with construction and maintenance,[59] or goods and subsidies for the performance of cult.[60]

There is no evidence of *regular* contributions by the royal administration to the running costs of the Babylonian temples, as was the case in Ptolemaic Egypt.[61] There is, however, evidence of royal involvement in building and maintenance on an *ad hoc* basis, for example Alexander's work on the Esagila temple, continued by Seleukos I and finished by Antiochos I. The Seleukid kings also provided funds and sacrificial animals as offerings to the gods, or their officials did on their behalf.[62]

The scale of some royal gifts is impressive. The temple of Apollo at Didyma, a pan-Hellenic sanctuary, whose influence spread far in the Greek world, was presented by Seleukos I with gold vessels weighing 3,248 drachms and silver vessels weighing 9,380 drachms, a total value in precious metal alone of almost 7 talents, plus large quantities of frankincense, myrrh and other valuable items.[63] The Temple of Jerusalem was granted by Antiochos III, for the performance of the rites, a number of animals and substantial quantities of wine, oil and frankincense, to the value of 20,000 shekels of silver (nearly 7 talents), plus large quantities of flour, wheat and salt (Document 12; Jos. *AJ* 12.138–44). Demetrios I promised 150,000 drachms for the sacrifices, or 25 talents, and that he would also relinquish the 10,000 drachms which he collected annually from the temple as tax (Jos. *AJ* 13.55).

Greek cities were also important targets of benefactions, but it is sometimes difficult to distinguish between motives that were political, such as the acquisition of prestige or influence, or economic, although there was often

[55] Sherwin White and Kuhrt 1993: 132–6; Ma 1997: 147–201; 1999: 179–242.
[56] For example, Baitokaike (Document 16; ch. 6.4c).
[57] For example, the temple of Apollo Toumoundos (Meriç and Nollé 1985: 21).
[58] For example, the commercial fairs held at religious festivals (ch. 8.4b).
[59] For example, the great temples of Babylonia (Horowitz 1991; Kuhrt and Sherwin-White 1991) and the Temple of Jerusalem (Document 12).
[60] For example, the provision of flour, wheat and salt for the daily sacrifices of the Temple of Jerusalem (Document 12).
[61] McEwan 1981a: 199.
[62] For example, Grayson 1975: no. 13b and Sherwin-White 1983b, with regard to offerings by Seleukos II to the Esagila temple at Babylon.
[63] *RC* 5; Bringmann and von Steuben 1995: no. 280.

something of both. One of the largest gifts, worth several hundred talents, was that by Seleukos III to Rhodes after its devastating earthquake: ten fully equipped quinqueremes, 200,000 *medimnoi* of grain, 10,000 cubits of timber and 1,000 talents in weight of hair and resin, plus duty-free status (*ateleia*) for trade with the empire (Polyb. 5.89.8–9). Obviously, to place a trading partner on its feet, and one that performed the very useful function of combating piracy in the eastern Mediterranean as well, made good economic sense. And the Rhodians, it seems, were Seleukid favourites, for Antiochos IV also lavished attention on them (Livy 41.20) and Demetrios I presented them with 200,000 *medimnoi* of wheat and 100,000 of barley (worth 300–400 talents) (Diod. 31.36).

Other Greek cities, both inside and outside the empire, came in for a wide range of benefactions, such as the building of a commercial stoa at Miletos,[64] the repair of an aqueduct and the supply of oil for the gymnasium at Herakleia-Latmos (Document 10), grain to be sold to raise money for dowries for daughters of poor citizens at Iasos (Document 6), the repair of the walls of Jerusalem (1 Macc. 10.45), and so on. Sometimes a city had suffered damage because of war and needed assistance. At other times, it was mainly a question of keeping it on one's side in the politics of the time. Often it was purely a demonstration of the king's wealth, for example the gift of a tiger to Athens by Seleukos I.[65] One aspect of benefactions to cities was the granting of political subsidies to allies, for example those by Antiochos III to the Aitolians (Livy 36.26.5) and the Byzantines and Galatians (App. *Syr.* 6). There was no place where a Seleukid king's presence might not be felt. A good example is the very wide range of benefactions of Antiochos IV,[66] which were much praised by Livy (41.20) and even drew a reluctant acknowledgement from a normally hostile Polybios (26.1.10).

The overall impression is that the Seleukid kings must have regularly spent several hundred talents annually on benefactions, but much of what they offered was in kind, from the royal properties or storehouses. At times it made more sense to dispose of one's surplus commodity stocks by gift, earning an intangible return in goodwill, if the possibility of selling the commodities was not on the cards.

b. *City- and colony-building*

Each time a new city or colony was founded, a considerable expense was incurred. In my view, however, most of what a city or colony needed – land,

---

[64] Rehm 1997: no. 270; Bringmann and von Steuben 1995: no. 281.
[65] Bringmann and von Steuben 1995: no. 20. [66] Mørkholm 1966: 55–63.

building materials and grain to feed the settlers initially and provide them with seed – could have been supplied in kind and may have been surplus to the kings' own requirements anyway. For example, the 2,000 Jewish settlers whom Antiochos III transported to Phrygia and Lydia were to be given land and grain, until they could produce enough themselves, with tax exemption for ten years (Jos. *AJ* 12.149–52), but no mention whatsoever is made of silver. But that is not to say that there were no silver expenses involved in the building of the new Seleukid foundations, only that they may have been quite manageable and, in any case, of short duration.

c. Tax exemptions

Clearly, when revenue was lost as a result of a land grant or a tax exemption offered to a city or temple, a cost was effectively incurred indirectly. It has been suggested (ch. 6.3h and above) that land grants may have been one way of cutting down on silver payments to officials and, whenever there was attachment to cities, this may actually have resulted in more silver revenue for the kings through increased economic activity and taxation.

With regard to tax exemptions, it is hardly ever that a Seleukid king made a subject city totally tax-free, although perhaps Jerusalem (and Judaea) approached this condition when faced with weak kings (Demetrios I and II) vying for support. In most cities of Asia Minor about which there is information, only one or a few of a wide range of taxes were usually exempted and typically the tribute on land first. This may not, however, have been such a heavy burden after all, compared to some of the other taxes (ch. 8.1).

d. Indemnities

An extraordinary expense of considerable magnitude was the 15,000 talent Roman indemnity, which, after the initial payments of 500 and 2,500 talents, became a regular disbursement of 1,000 talents annually for twelve years and did cause problems for the Seleukid treasury (ch. 12.4).

e. Productivity improvements

We know very little about productivity improvements undertaken by the Seleukids in the underlying economy and nothing at all about any expenditure that they may have incurred for these in silver. Certainly the new city-building activity probably required the construction or expansion of irrigation networks in some places, for example along the Diyala in Mesopotamia or in Baktria (ch. 4.1–2), but considerable effort must also have gone into the maintenance of existing systems. The scale of activity required to dam the outlet of the Euphrates into the Pallakottas canal every year, recorded as requiring the labour of 10,000 men for two months in the Persian period (Arr. *Anab.* 7.21.1–5), may well represent an extreme case, but something of this order was probably required regularly nevertheless, while the *qanat* system of Iran was also maintained.[67]

The linking of the Eulaios river to the sea by the Seleukids can be seen as a productivity improvement to facilitate trade[68] and one may also suppose that the Persian road network was kept in working order for the same purpose and for reasons of communication.

However, all these activities probably used corvée labour in the main (the *leitourgikos phoros* of the Mnesimachos inscription in ch. 8.1a) and one may justifiably question whether the silver expense was considerable.

Finally, one should note once more the reputed attempt by Seleukos (I) to introduce exotic products, *amomum* and *nardum*, and perhaps cinnamon, from India (Pliny, *HN* 16.135).[69]

5. CONCLUSIONS ON EXPENDITURE

The evidence suggests that the greater part of the expenditure of the Seleukid kings, particularly in silver, was ear-marked for the armed forces, certainly not less than half in 'peacetime' conditions and probably considerably more when a major campaign was under way. Most of the remainder supported the provincial administration and the king and his court. A non-negligible amount was used in benefactions in the interests of foreign and domestic policy. Although the information is scarce, it is difficult to accept that much, in silver certainly, was spent on what one might call today productivity improvements in the underlying economy.

---

[67] Sherwin-White and Kuhrt 1993: 70; Spek 2000b: 29.
[68] Le Rider 1965: 267. [69] Rostovtzeff 1941: 1164–5.

CHAPTER II

Coinage

> With regard to currency, I mean what to mint of large or small denomination and when.

That is how ps.-Aristotle reduced the king's coinage problem to its essentials. But one might also add 'and where and why'. Or, in other words, what was the Seleukid coinage policy and how was it administered?

It has been suggested, as a hypothesis (ch. 3), that the kings' primary objective was to ensure an adequate supply of coined money from tribute and taxation with which to meet military and administrative expenses.

The first task will be to examine what the Seleukids actually coined, the mints and their production. Here Newell's two catalogues[1] are invaluable, although they reach only to the reign of Antiochos III and new issues have been added and new attributions made since then. The picture has somewhat changed and a revised and much more extensive catalogue has now been published.[2] Mørkholm has also contributed a detailed analysis of the coinage of Antiochos IV, while a number of articles deal with the production of specific mints or issues and will be referred to where appropriate.

Next I shall consider the different categories of coinage and their uses and it will become apparent that the silver tetradrachm was by far the most important denomination.

Finally, the circulation of tetradrachms within the empire will be studied, based on hoard and die evidence, and a picture should hopefully emerge of Seleukid coinage policy and its application.

---

[1] *WSM* and *ESM*, with revisions by Mørkholm.

[2] Houghton and Lorber 2002. I am grateful to the authors for providing me with a draft of volume 1 of the *Catalogue* prior to its publication. This deals with the issues of the early kings down to Antiochos III. The major improvement, with regard to Newell's catalogues, is the much clearer identification of each coinage series, including all the primary and secondary control marks that it uses.

I. MINTS

When Alexander died in 323 BC, only the mints of Babylon and, perhaps, Susa existed in the whole of Mesopotamia and the Upper Satrapies. The nearest mints were located in Phoenicia and Kilikia[3] and it is clear why this was so. The ports in these regions served to ferry reinforcements of mercenary troops to Alexander and discharged soldiers back to Greece, while Babylon was where his veterans were mainly being paid off after the return from India and where the bulk of the bullion captured in the Achaemenid treasuries was stored. At the same time, Babylonia was used to a monetary economy involving weighed precious metal, since this is how taxes had partly been paid to the Achaemenid administration, as evidenced by the *Murašu Archive*.[4] The mint at Babylon issued some coins on the local standard to ensure continuity, but, essentially, it served a military need.

Seleukos I faced a different problem, as has been suggested (ch. 3). The Achaemenid bullion had mostly been coined and the bulk of this coinage probably circulated in the West, which was the main theatre of conflict of the Successors. Apart from Babylonia, with its economy based partly on precious metals, the East does not seem to have progressed much, at the time, towards a monetary economy. Commodity taxation had served the Achaemenid king well, since it would do to pay officials and troops, but this was not what western mercenaries required. As has been argued, the need to make payments in silver led the early Seleukids to restructure the economies of their different provinces in such a way that silver could be collected through the taxes paid to the administration. And an adequate supply of coinage was ensured by the creation of a number of mints, each supplying the needs of a specific region.[5]

A major mint was opened by Seleukos at his new capital, Seleukeia-Tigris, to serve Babylonia, and that at Babylon seems to have been gradually phased out by the end of his reign. Mints appeared at other provincial centres, as the new measures were gradually introduced: Karrhai for northern Mesopotamia and at one or more unknown locations in Kappadokia, northern Mesopotamia or northern Syria, while the mint at Ekbatana is probably pre-Seleukid. In some eastern regions progress seems to have been slower and it took Antiochos (I)'s presence in the Upper Satrapies, as co-ruler from *c.* 291/0 BC, for a mint to be established at Baktra, another at Aï Khanoum and possibly even a third.

---

[3] Price 1992: 72.   [4] Stolper 1974; 1985.

[5] For the mints of Seleukos I and Antiochos I, I have relied on the catalogue of Houghton and Lorber 2002.

In the West, the process of monetization appears to have been easier, as the Greek inhabitants of the new city foundations of northern Syria were already accustomed to the use of coinage. Mints were introduced at Antioch, Seleukeia-Pieria and Laodikeia immediately (from 301/0 BC). In Kilikia and western Asia Minor a number of mints already operated, which simply switched to production for their new master when Seleukos acquired these regions (Tarsos in 294 BC, Sardeis and Pergamon in 281 BC).

Under Antiochos I, certain ephemeral mints with very limited production were opened in eastern regions, perhaps in Drangiane, western Arachosia and Aria.[6] In the West, Magnesia-Maiandros and Smyrna probably coined for the king at this time, Doura-Europos and Edessa in northern Mesopotamia supplied some bronze, and there were more, as yet unattributed, mints from this general region.

Many more mints were created by Antiochos II in Asia Minor: Kyme, Phokaia and Myrina, Aigai and perhaps Temnos, Lampsakos possibly, Alexandria-Troas, Ilion and Abydos, Lysimacheia and perhaps Kabyle in Thrace, Mylasa, Ephesos for some bronze and a few others, as yet unattributed, while in the East an important mint was established at Artakoana for Aria. The transformation of a commodity-based barter economy to a monetary one seems to have been proceeding quite rapidly in most areas, but it cannot have been a simple task in the Upper Satrapies, if one considers the delay in setting up major mints in Baktria and, even more so, in Aria.

The picture, then, is one of a proliferation of mints, each seemingly serving a particular region. Normally a mint would be located at a satrapal capital, but, where Seleukid city-building was being conducted on a significant scale, additional mints might be set up, for example in northern Mesopotamia at Karrhai or in Baktria at Aï Khanoum or, much later under Antiochos IV, when the eastern trade had became important, in southern Mesopotamia at Antioch-on-the-Erythraean Sea.[7] If, however, a satrapy did not possess a sufficiently important monetary economy, perhaps because of poor agricultural resources and lack of urban centres, it was apparently served from the mint of a neighbouring satrapy. Thus, the mint at Ekbatana may have supplied Parthia and Hyrkania with the necessary coinage, that at Artakoana, Drangiane, that at Baktra, Margiane and Sogdiane, while the mint at Susa almost certainly covered Persis, until the local *frataraka* coinage was produced in this region, and possibly Karmania.[8]

---

[6] Houghton and Moore 1984: 5–9.   [7] Mørkholm 1970: 44.
[8] Newell's identification of a mint at Persepolis has been shown to be incorrect by Houghton 1980.

But why so many mints? Could not the Seleukids have solved the problem of issuing coinage in the way the Romans and Ptolemies did, mostly from one central mint? To suggest that overland distances in the empire were too great for the economic transportation of coins is not the answer. In Kilikia alone, three mints operated simultaneously at the death of Antiochos III: Tarsos, Soli and Seleukeia-Kalykadnos,[9] when one could probably have served the province quite adequately with regard to distances. This question will be addressed later, after a discussion of what coinage was produced at the mints and what uses it had.

2. COINAGE ISSUES

Newell has listed what he considers to be different coinage issues. Frequently the difference between these is simply a control mark or control-mark arrangement on the reverse of the coin, while the obverses may have been struck from the same die.[10] That is not what one would really call now an 'issue'.

A summary picture of the number of Newell-type issues by region and king for the early Seleukids is given in table 11.1, where coinage has been divided into four major categories: gold, large silver (mainly tetradrachms, but also any other silver coin larger than a drachm), small silver (drachms and fractions) and bronze. For each king, the percentage distribution of his issues is calculated across regions and shown in column eight.

It is recognized that issues, as defined by Newell, are clearly not equal in size, nor can even an average volume of coinage be assigned to one. So, of what use might this picture be? It so happens that when one compares the percentage distribution of Newell-type silver issues across regions for each king with the actual distribution of silver coins, mainly tetradrachms, worked out by Golenko,[11] based on coin hoards, publications and private collections known to him and shown in column nine, the correlation between the two sets of data is quite high, with a correlation coefficient of 89 per cent. To some extent this is to be expected, since Golenko worked with Newell's classifications, but not perhaps to such a high degree. What this means is that Newell's picture is valid in so far as *relative approximate* volumes of coinage are concerned, that is, if one king had fewer Newell-type issues in a particular region compared to another, he is likely to have produced *roughly* proportionally less coinage there.

[9] Mørkholm 1984: 93.
[10] For example, *ESM*: nos. 48 and 49, 52 and 53, 57 and 62. [11] Golenko 1993; 1995.

Table 11.1 *Pattern of Seleukid coinage issues*

Region	King	Gold	Large silver	Small silver	Bronze	Yrs	% LS Newell	% silver Golenko
MESOPOTAMIA	Seleukos I	17	137	76	25	31	61	66.8
	Antiochos I	4	38	8	42	20	35	59.2
	Antiochos II	1	15	–	11	15	15	35.6
	Seleukos II	–	22	3	32	20	27	23.3
	Seleukos III	–	5	–	4	3	23	25.9
	Antiochos III	2	76	3	42	36	41	35.2
UPPER SATRAPIES	Seleukos I	8	42	53	3	31	20	16.6
	Antiochos I	9	24	19	15	20	24	17.0
	Antiochos II	4	7	5	4	15	8	10.8
	Seleukos II	–	11	12	16	20	16	5.6
	Seleukos III	–	1	–	–	3	5	2.6
	Antiochos III	–	18	15	48	36	11	16.0
N. SYRIA-KILIKIA	Seleukos I	4	40	5	29	31	17	9.2
	Antiochos I	–	21	2	36	20	19	8.6
	Antiochos II	4	28	3	10	15	29	24.8
	Seleukos II	8	37	10	31	20	46	54.2
	Seleukos III	–	16	2	13	3	73	71.4
	Antiochos III	2	71	12	50	36	40	46.3
ASIA MINOR	Seleukos I	–	6	1	3	31	2	4.9
	Antiochos I	–	25	2	12	20	23	15.1
	Antiochos II	1	47	1	30	15	48	28.8
	Seleukos II	–	8	4	9	20	11	16.8
	Seleukos III	–	–	–	–	3	0	0
	Antiochos III	3	15	–	1	36	8	2.4
KOILE SYRIA	Antiochos III	–	–	–	13	36	0	0
TOTAL EMPIRE	Seleukos I	29	225	135	60	31		
	Antiochos I	13	108	31	105	20		
	Antiochos II	10	97	9	55	15		
	Seleukos II	8	78	29	88	20		
	Seleukos III	–	22	2	17	3		
	Antiochos III	7	180	30	154	36		
GRAND TOTAL	All kings	67	710	236	479	125		
% of value	All kings	18	78	3	<1			

Columns 3–6: numbers of Newell-type series by king and region in four coin categories.
Column 7: total regnal years of king. Column 8: percentage distribution of large silver across
regions for each king, by Newell-type series. Column 9: percentage distribution of all silver
across regions, by Golenko.

Were one to use Newell at the individual mint level, the discrepancies with Golenko would be greater, but agreement still quite good (correlation coefficient 84 per cent). As one consolidates the information at higher levels, the results become still closer.[12]

At the highest level, the total numbers of Newell-type series in each coinage category, for all the early Seleukid kings taken together, are likely to represent quite well the relative magnitudes of the coinage emissions in each category. If each number is multiplied by a weight factor reflecting the value of the coins in the category (where drachm = one value unit), one has the approximate relative values of the coinages in each category. There is a further consideration, as discussed in chapter 1.6b, that a gold die is assumed to have produced only half the number of coins compared to a tetradrachm die, while smaller silver and bronze dies may have produced more or less, but this does not materially affect the calculation because of the relatively small quantities involved. For this reason, the factors used are: gold staters: ten (not twenty); tetradrachms: four; small silver: one-half; and bronze: one-twentieth. With these factors, gold represented roughly 18 per cent of the total value of Seleukid coinage issued, silver tetradrachms 78 per cent, small silver 3 per cent and bronze only 1 per cent. What is important here is the overwhelming concentration by the Seleukid kings on high value coins, particularly tetradrachms, which probably accounted for about three-quarters of the total value minted.

There is one other consideration. Several of the early gold and silver coins minted during the reign of Seleukos I were 'Alexanders' in the name of Alexander. Newell has taken many into account in his classification, but not all.[13] What this will certainly do for Mesopotamia is to increase the percentage of Seleukos I's Newell-type tetradrachms minted there and bring this more into line with Golenko's estimate.

3. COIN CATEGORIES

a. Gold

When the king set out to mint gold staters, or the rare double stater, double and a half stater or octadrachm, he was clearly not catering for the everyday

---

[12] This is in the nature of comparative lists of positive numbers, with subtotals and totals. A large percentage difference at the level of a particular number is normally reflected in a smaller difference in the subtotal it affects and an even smaller one in the total.

[13] Price deals with the 'Alexanders' from Babylon, Seleukeia-Tigris, Karrhai, Susa and Ekbatana, noting coins he believes to have been minted in the period 311–280 BC (1992: 451–95). For about half of these coins, a reference in Newell is given. For the remainder it is not possible to estimate how many might have formed Newell-type series of their own.

currency needs of his subjects. With the gold to silver ratio at one to ten, a gold stater was worth 20 Attic drachms or 10 silver shekels on the Babylonian standard. Given that a shekel could purchase 120 litres of barley on average in Babylon (ch. 5.6a), a gold stater could feed a man for nearly twenty-seven months at a consumption rate of 1.5 litres of barley per day. Clearly a coin like this did not circulate much in the local market, although it could have been used by the royal treasury as the medium of large payments for services and supplies to the administration and of receipt of taxes (cf. the Mnesimachos inscription, Document 5, with its tax assessments noted in gold staters).

Gold may also have played a role in long-distance trade. It is possible that gold staters were used primarily for purchases from India[14] and their production ceased when the East was lost, that is, by the end of the reign of Antiochos II. This is not unreasonable and can be supported by an examination of where gold Newell-type issues were minted in the reigns of the first three Seleukids: in the East at Baktra (12), Seleukeia-Tigris (10), Ekbatana (9) and Susa (6); in the West at Karrhai (6), Antioch (2), Tarsos (4), Kappadokia or northern Syria (2) and Smyrna (1). If gold had been intended primarily as a medium of payment of taxes or for services and supplies to the administration, one would have expected a much more uniform distribution of gold production across mints to serve their respective regions, but in these figures there is a marked preponderance of the eastern mints. What is even more interesting is that Baktra, the nearest mint to India, outdoes even Seleukeia-Tigris in gold, whereas its tetradrachm production is considerably less (only 16 Newell-type issues compared to 110).[15] Indian trade was thus a probable destination for some of the gold.

Gold-coinage production in the East appears to have declined considerably with the next two Seleukids: a little perhaps at Seleukeia, Ekbatana and Susa for Seleukos II and none at all for Seleukos III. The significant gold issues by Antiochos III at Nisibis, Seleukeia-Tigris and Susa may be associated with advance payments and final settlements of soldiers' pay in connection with the Anabasis, supplied partly by the gold looted from the temple of Aine (Polyb. 10.27.13), which we do know was coined,[16] but there is also a probable connection with the revival of the eastern trade in this reign (ch. 5.5a).

---

[14] Bikerman 1938: 214.

[15] The presence of additional gold 'Alexanders', in the name of Alexander, of the reign of Seleukos I, does not invalidate the basic conclusion.

[16] Bikerman considers a similar use for the gold struck at Antioch (1938: 215). Payment in gold, when available, rather than silver, would represent a 90 per cent reduction in weight of the coins carried by a soldier.

In the West, gold seems to have become more of a prestige issue, to convey a message concerning the king, but it also served a practical purpose, more often than not for a military payment.[17] The gold stater struck by Antiochos IV, for example, can probably be associated with the festival at Daphne in 166 BC and may have been intended to demonstrate the wealth and power of the Seleukid king,[18] even after his setback at the hands of the Romans in Egypt. At the same time, however, there was probably a sound financial reason behind this issue, an advance in pay to the army then preparing for the expedition to the East (ch. 10.1g). The several gold issues at Antioch by Seleukos II are too many for prestige purposes and heavy military expenditure is again the most likely reason given the turbulent nature of this reign (Laodikeian war, conflict with Antiochos Hierax, expedition to retake Parthia, etc.).

b. Silver tetradrachms

A silver Attic tetradrachm was worth a fifth of a gold stater, so could purchase five and a half months' supply of barley for a man in Babylon at the rate of 1.5 litres per day. Thus it too was unlikely to have been common in the local marketplace. Yet, as was noted earlier, it probably represented about three-quarters of the total value of coinage issued by the Seleukids, at least up to and including Antiochos III. It is likely, therefore, that the tetradrachm served as the principal medium of exchange for economic transactions between the administration and its subjects.[19]

One may envisage the path a tetradrachm followed after it left the mint. To begin with, it would have been used to make payments by the royal authorities to officials, soldiers and suppliers of goods and services to the Crown and also to provide subsidies to cities, temples, local dynasts, and so on.[20] A soldier's pay, for example, might amount to 7 or 8 tetradrachms a

---

[17] Of the ten gold issues of the second century BC listed by Bikerman, most have a clear military purpose and this is not excluded for some of the others (1938: 214–16). Mørkholm includes emergencies with special occasions and propaganda as the prime reasons for gold issues (1984: 96). One would have to argue that large military expenditure might be considered an emergency, if one did not have the requisite amount of silver at hand to cover it, as there would be no point in simply hoarding the gold then.

[18] Mørkholm 1963: 33.

[19] Schönert-Geiss agrees that the tetradrachm constituted the bulk of Seleukid coinage issues and was used for large transactions (1978: 134). Howgego regards state expenditure as far and away the most important reason for circulating new coinage (1995: 34). Foraboschii takes the use of coinage as primarily for the purpose of paying armies and financing public building, secondarily only to facilitate trade (2000: 38).

[20] M. H. Crawford maintains that 'coinage was probably invented in order that a large number of state payments be made in a convenient form' (1970: 46). Mørkholm has no doubt that 'the prime

month, while a senior official could earn considerably more (ch. 10.2). The soldier or official would make certain purchases in the market, exchanging his tetradrachms for small silver and bronze, with moneychangers available in all likelihood to perform the conversion.[21] At some point, the producer and intermediate seller were called upon to pay taxes and these would probably be collected in tetradrachms, or even gold staters, by the authorities. For example, the Mnesimachos inscription (Document 5) shows a village being assessed annually for 50 gold staters, the equivalent of 250 tetradrachms. One may imagine the villagers selling their produce in the nearby cities either to a re-seller or directly in the marketplace and converting their small-change earnings into the right number of tetradrachms to meet the annual tax commitment of their village. Now, these coins might be Seleukid or other Attic-standard 'international' issues, such as 'Alexanders' or 'Lysimachi', which circulated freely in the Seleukid empire (see below). For the administration it probably made no difference, but there may have been a small premium on Seleukid issues or countermarking for a fee on some foreign issues to make them legal tender, although this was quite rare.[22] Some of the tetradrachms were now collected in a district treasury of the provincial administration, where they could be utilized to meet local expenses, with any surplus probably being transferred sooner or later to a provincial treasury.

The tetradrachm must also have been the coin used *par excellence* in intra-regional, inter-regional and long-distance trade, because of the greater value of the bulk transactions involved. Within the empire, it was accepted everywhere, as also in the Greek world to the west, with the exception of Ptolemaic Egypt, as is evidenced by coin hoards. Intra-regional and inter-regional trade have been discussed earlier and not considered significant when compared to local trade (ch. 5.5a–c). They therefore probably utilized a rather small proportion of the tetradrachms in circulation. The long-distance Indian and Arabian trade, on the other hand, may have been more important in terms of value. It was, at this time, in the hands of Arab middlemen, and that they too accepted Seleukid tetradrachms is shown by

---

motivating factor regulating the volume of coinage (of Hellenistic kings) was the rise and fall of public expenses', although there were also considerations of propaganda and prestige, commerce and profit (from the mint) (1991: 24).

[21] Merker notes that a fee for the exchange of copper coins (ἀμειψέως χαλκ[ῶν]) is attested in an inscription from Palestine, probably of the late second century BC (1975: 239–40).

[22] Mørkholm points out that countermarking is noted mainly in the period 175–170 BC (1984: 105, 108–9). Seyrig considers it an expedient at the time to save on re-minting expenses because of the severe drain on the Seleukid treasury of the Roman indemnity, the ceasing of revenues from Asia Minor and the cost of campaigns in the East (1958: 196). In my view, countermarking was a rather restricted phenomenon, probably due to temporary local difficulties rather than any general policy.

the copying of Seleukid coinage by Gerrha and other Arab principalities.[23] But the question again is how important this long-distance trade really was compared to local production and exchange between cities and their rural surroundings, which provided the bulk of taxation revenue.[24]

c. Small silver

When one considers small silver – drachms to hemiobols – one is probably looking at an everyday currency. But there seems to have been too little of it produced by the Seleukids, as seen by the number of issues in Newell: 236 compared to 708 tetradrachm issues (table 11.1). Indeed, if one excludes the coinage of Seleukos I, when some silver was also minted in the name of Alexander, the comparison becomes 101 to 483. To some extent, this is due to the accidents of discovery, as it is easier to find a large-denomination coin, especially in hoards, but there is clearly another factor at work. Taking the three major mints of Seleukos I, one notes that Seleukeia-Tigris produced 45 Newell-type issues of small silver, Ekbatana 41 and Susa 17. By the reign of Antiochos I the numbers are down to 6, 6 and 0 respectively and there is absolutely nothing under Antiochos II. Under Seleukos I only Seleukeia-Tigris, of these mints, coined bronze, a total of 24 issues. In the reigns of Antiochos I and II bronze appears for the first time at both Ekbatana (15 and 4 issues respectively) and Susa (2 and 1) while continuing at Seleukeia-Tigris (20 and 9). While coins of one ruler could be expected to circulate in subsequent reigns, albeit in reducing quantities because of wear and loss, what one sees here is clearly a picture of the replacement of one *category* of coinage by another for everyday use, bronze in place of small silver.

In the West, the great mint at Antioch started coining later in the reign of Seleukos I. Under him and his early successors only 11 issues of small silver, and then only drachms, were struck there compared to 127 issues of bronze and the picture is the same at other important mints. Tetradrachm production is associated with very few small-silver issues from Antiochos I onwards but considerable quantities of bronze (419 issues in table 11.1) and one should bear in mind that some subject cities also minted their

---

[23] Mørkholm 1976.

[24] Golenko has stressed the primary role of international trade and local commerce in the development of Seleukid coinage, going so far as to suggest that the kings tried to secure a monopoly on the sale of Mesopotamian grain and that dues from transit trade constituted their main income. In his opinion, this led the Seleukids to try to involve as large a part of the population in commercial relations as possible (1993: 88, 110; 1995: 96). What I will only accept is that the administrative-payments–tax-collection cycle did involve perforce most of the population in local commerce and the use of coinage.

own bronze coins, which tilts the balance even more in favour of the use of bronze compared to small silver. It would seem, then, that Antiochos I initiated a shift towards a bronze coinage for everyday use, which was followed by his successors.

However, that is not to say that small silver did not circulate. There were huge numbers of 'Alexander' drachms around, which, as will be seen, dominated the small-silver market and the Seleukids were apparently content that this should be so, since drachms were also a suitable denomination for the administrative-payments–tax-collection cycle. What they apparently restricted severely was fractional silver. It was as if they were experiencing at this stage some silver shortages and preferred to direct their more limited supplies to the tetradrachm, which served their coinage policy best.[25] It will be recalled (ch. 2) that, starting from the reign of Antiochos I, the Seleukids began to lose control of border areas in Asia Minor, Kappadokia and Armenia, and later Baktria and Karmania, where silver was mined. This must have been offset to some extent by net inflows of silver from a favourable balance of trade (see below; ch. 5.5d).[26]

d. Bronze

Seleukid bronze appears to have been a token currency, that is, its value was not dependent on its metals, copper and tin, but set by the issuing authority. This is clear firstly because coin weights were not controlled to nearly the same extent as for gold and silver. An analysis of the bronze coinage of Seleukos I from Seleukeia-Tigris in Newell shows weights ranging from 2.08–4.55 grams for one-unit pieces, 5.17–9.24 grams for two-unit pieces and 8.94–16.72 grams for four-unit pieces. What is even more revealing are bronze coins of Antiochos IV from the same mint marked with *AX*, *BX* and *ΔX*, probably specifying 1, 2 and 4 *chalkoi* respectively, whose respective weight ranges are 2.82–5.10 grams, 6.20–8.88 grams and 11.27–20.25 grams.[27] The very wide range of weights, on average more than 25 per cent about a mean, cannot be due to wear. Thus, when a bronze coin circulated, its value was probably known by its *approximate* size and not by its weight. To make matters absolutely clear, it might even be stamped with a letter giving its denomination, as seems to have happened after a halving of weight under Antiochos IV and again later under Alexander Balas.[28]

---

[25] Mørkholm 1984: 108.   [26] Mørkholm 1982: 302.   [27] *ESM*: no. 271.
[28] Newell considers bronze a mere token coinage (*ESM*: no. 273). Le Rider notes that bronze, after Antiochos IV's measures, represented only 20 to 25 per cent fiduciary value (1994a: 32). Mørkholm considers bronze a heavily overvalued fiduciary coinage (1984: 97).

For the second reason why Seleukid bronze was a token coinage, one must look at the relationship between silver and bronze in terms of their intrinsic values, which probably stood at about 1:120 to 1:96 in the third century BC and may have gone down to 1:60 by the second century BC. One can use the well-known equivalence from classical Athens of 1 drachm = 6 obols = 48 *chalkoi*, which was followed by the Macedonian kings. Thus, if a one-unit bronze of Antiochos IV, which weighed roughly as much as a silver drachm, was equivalent to 1 *chalkous* in the above relationship, its nominal value would have been one-forty-eighth of the equivalent silver, against an intrinsic value of only one-sixtieth, and so a nominal value mark-up of 25 per cent. But this was after Antiochos' halving of weight, which may have become necessary because of the rise in value of bronze.[29] And being a token coinage is probably one reason why so very little bronze seems to have been hoarded.

What needs to be examined now is the relationship which bronze production bore to small silver. Taking Seleukeia-Tigris as an example, one notes in Newell that the silver hemidrachms and obols of Seleukos I seem to have been discontinued in favour of four-unit, two-unit, one-unit and half-unit bronze pieces under Antiochos I. This pattern of changeover occurred at most eastern mints,[30] suggesting that the bronze was intended as a purely token coinage replacement of the small silver. Where a mint continued to produce small silver, as the Baktra mint did, there may have been no bronze coinage at all.

Now one can perhaps understand a passage in the *Astronomical Diary* of 274 BC.[31] After reference had been made to the collection of 'silver,

---

[29] Newell suggests a silver to bronze ratio in third-century BC Italy and Sicily that lay between 1:120 and 1:96 (*ESM*: no. 273). Price quotes prices at Athens from the end of the fifth century BC of 230 drachms per talent of tin and 35 drachms per talent of copper. Given that the greatest quantity of tin found in a Greek coin is just under 15 per cent, the silver to bronze ratio should not have been more than 1:93 and more probably in the region 1:120 to 1:100 (1968: 103), thus agreeing with Newell. However, any increase in the cost of copper and tin was likely to overvalue bronze coins and remove them from circulation. That is perhaps the reason why Antiochos IV doubled the denomination of the existing coins and then noted the new value on them. If Le Rider is correct, the nominal silver to bronze relationship would then have stood at 1:100, while that based on the cost of metals was more like 1:127 (1994a: 31), implying that prior to the revaluation of bronze the actual value stood at just over 1:60, which would have been substantially above the nominal value. Bikerman takes bronze at near its true value and considers that it must have borne a 1:50 relationship to silver in the second century BC (1938: 217).
  Most scholars accept the equation of one obol = eight bronze units (e.g. Schönert-Geiss 1978: 134; *ESM*: no. 271; Price 1992: 40; Le Rider 1994a: 20–1). Bellinger, however, takes one obol = one bronze unit (1963: 34).

[30] From table 11.1, in Mesopotamia and the Upper Satrapies respectively: 76 and 53 small-silver issues of Seleukos I to only 8 and 19 for Antiochos I, while bronze issues increase from 25 and 3 to 42 and 15, despite the much shorter reign of Antiochos.

[31] Sachs and Hunger 1988: no. -273.

cloth, goods and utensils [?]' by the satrap of Babylon to help the king (Antiochos I) pursue the war against the Ptolemies in northern Syria, the *Diary* continues: 'That year, purchases in Babylon and the [other] cities were made with copper coins of Ionia.'

The 'copper coins' referred to here are obviously the official Seleukid bronze currency, as the Achaemenids had not used copper in their coinage and this was to the Babylonians an 'Ionian' – that is, Greek – invention. If bronze had been a normal medium of exchange in the market of Babylon at the time, there would have been absolutely no need to mention it. However, what was happening was abnormal, according to the Babylonian astronomers. The small-silver coinage had apparently been collected by the authorities to help to finance the war, probably in exchange for bronze, and the inhabitants were now compelled to use the distasteful (to them) bronze coinage, distasteful because it was a purely token currency introduced into an area which had possessed a long tradition of exchange based on the value of precious metal, although bronze had been used in the distant past.[32] That mention should be made of a bronze coinage in these terms in the *Diary* suggests that the measure of replacing small silver by bronze had just been introduced in Babylon and one notes that the Babylon mint had never minted bronze under Alexander or Seleukos I.[33] The conclusion is that this may have been an emergency measure because of the war, but since a shift from small silver to bronze is detectable at all eastern mints, it is likely that it was planned as part of a general restructuring of the currency (also ch. 13.10).

Before leaving this question of bronze coinage, one may note that small-silver denominations continued to be produced, albeit on a very small scale, at the same mints with bronze. For example, Antiochos III issued a hemidrachm and an obol at Ekbatana alongside forty-eight bronze series ranging from six-unit to half-unit pieces. The question is why? Clearly some small silver from previous issues of the Seleukids and Alexander continued in circulation, but it was apparently felt necessary to 'top up' what would have been a declining volume because of wear and loss. Some transactions which may have been conducted mainly in silver, such as the payment of taxes, would also have required the small pieces for exactness.

e. Minting profit

Even silver coinage is in some respects a token currency, as the intrinsic value of a coin is always slightly less than its nominal value to

---

[32] Powell 1996: 227–30. [33] Price 1992: 72–5.

cover a minting profit, but how much this was so at Seleukid mints is unclear.[34]

An easier, although short-term way of making a profit was to lower coin weight. Under Antiochos IV, a reduction of tetradrachm weight is noted between the first and second Antioch series from mainly in the region of 16.90–17.19 grams to mainly in the region of 16.50–16.79 grams, a reduction of about 2 per cent, which can only have been due to an administrative decision.[35] This came at a time when competing coinages had also experienced weight reductions from the Attic standard of 17.2 grams most commonly achieved, for example Pergamon (16.90–16.99 grams *c.* 190 BC), Macedonia (16.80–16.89 grams *c.* 178 BC) and Athens (16.70 grams *c.* 166 BC). It would have been foolish for a state to continue to mint a heavier coinage than that of its competitors, which would be preferred in the market and eventually find its way out of circulation as bullion. On the other hand, too light a silver coinage would sooner or later find no acceptance with those providing supplies and services to the state.

There was, of course, not only a question of weight, since, in order to achieve a greater profit, one might also reduce the silver content. Until Antiochos IV, purity of 94–95 per cent silver was still maintained in tetradrachms, but a debasement commenced slowly with Alexander Balas (91 per cent purity) and reached quite low levels of silver by the first century BC (65 per cent purity).[36]

With regard to bronze, there was considerable profit to be gained by a mint, as it was very much a token coinage, and therefore a reason why cities avidly sought the right to mint bronze, even to the extent of paying for the privilege.[37]

4. COINAGE CIRCULATION

a. Analysis of coin hoards

An analysis of coin hoards can provide indications of the pattern of circulation of coinage in the Seleukid empire in different periods. In theory, a hoard should be a reasonably accurate cross-section of the money circulating in the area at the time when the hoard was buried and this may be true when there was war or some other violent disruption which caused a person to hurriedly hide the coins in his possession for reasons of safety.

---

[34] For the silver coinage of the early Seleukids, Golenko has suggested a minting profit of about 3.3 per cent, but it is difficult to accept his argument (1993: 96–7).
[35] Mørkholm 1963: 40. [36] Bikerman 1938: 216. [37] Mørkholm 1967: 82; 1982: 302.

However, in some cases, hoards appear to represent savings which had been accumulated over a number of years through selective retention of certain types of coins: perhaps the heavier specimens or those richer in precious metal or least worn or simply those most appealing to the hoarders, which one has no way of knowing.[38] In other cases, the coins in a hoard mostly belong to a particular issue and do not seem to have had time to find their way into general circulation before they were buried, for example payments to mercenary soldiers, coinage issued by a city for a particular local need, and so on. In situations such as these, the evidence of the hoard can be quite misleading and it is only when the data from several hoards from the same region and period have been set beside one another, that these anomalies can be ironed out and a reasonably coherent picture can emerge.

Care should also be taken to distinguish between gold, large silver (mainly tetradrachms, but also the occasional didrachms, shekels and larger issues) and small silver (mainly drachms, but also a few fractions), as significant differences in patterns of circulation may emerge because of the different uses to which different denominations were put (sections 3–4 in this chapter). With regard to gold, the rather rare issues were frequently commemorative of some special event, but that is not to say that they did not have a utilitarian function as well.

A computer-aided analysis has been undertaken using the *Inventory of Greek Coin Hoards* (*IGCH*) and *Coin Hoards*, volumes I–IX, with the following considerations:

(1) Only hoards found within what had at any time been Seleukid territory are considered.

(2) Only hoards are taken into account in which Seleukid issues, live and/or posthumous 'Alexanders' or live and/or posthumous 'Lysimachi' are present, as these represented the main currencies of the Seleukid empire. Occasionally a hoard contains only coins in the name of a city or, in one case (*IGCH* 1431), only Antigonid coins, but it is ignored as it was probably put together from issues minted for special purposes.

(3) For silver, only those hoards with twenty or more coins are regarded as likely to be, to any extent, representative of currency circulation.

(4) More weight is given to the evidence of hoards that the publisher would regard as complete, from the information at his disposal, or to coins found in excavations.

---

[38] M. H. Crawford regards a hoard as *normally*, but not *necessarily*, reflecting actual coinage circulation (1970: 40).

b. Gold

Hoards with gold coins are extremely rare (Appendix 1 – Coin hoards list 3), as are the number of known gold issues,[39] so one should not really speak of 'circulation'.

In Asia Minor, only 'Alexander' staters appear in the reign of Seleukos I, but, by the time of Antiochos III, Seleukid issues may have represented 20–30 per cent of the total gold in circulation. Further east, they predominate down to the end of Seleukid rule, often 100 per cent, and not less than 50 per cent, of the content of hoards of gold coins, while even in the Graeco-Baktrian kingdom *c.* 180–170 BC, 30 per cent of the gold circulating may have been Seleukid. One reason that has already been suggested for this interest in gold is the overland trade with India (section 3a above).

c. Large silver

Appendix 1 – Coin hoards list 1 presents the calculated percentage of large-silver Seleukid coins (almost entirely tetradrachms) in all selected hoards, grouped by wider geographical area and sorted by earliest estimated burial date. This includes 'Alexanders' in the name of Alexander, but issued by the Seleukids, when they are so identified in a hoard. The remaining coins in these hoards are mainly life-time and posthumous Alexander and Lysimachos tetradrachms. A rough pattern emerges, which is summarized in table 11.2 below. When the hoard evidence is missing or insufficient, a '?' after the percentage range indicates an 'educated guess' based on earlier and later periods and adjacent geographical areas.

From table 11.2, the circulation pattern of large-silver coins seems to have been roughly as follows in different areas:

i. Mesopotamia

The share of Seleukid issues increased steadily from probably only 10 or 20 per cent by the end of the reign of Seleukos I to perhaps 70 per cent by the time Mesopotamia finally fell to the Parthians in 129 BC. This gradual growth of 'market share' can most easily be explained by a policy of replacement of 'Alexanders' and 'Lysimachi', as coins dropped out of circulation through loss or wear. The relatively high percentage under Seleukos I is probably due to the inclusion of the 'Alexanders', in the name of Alexander, that he also minted.

---

[39] *WSM*; *ESM*; table 11.1.

Table 11.2 *Estimated percentage of large Seleukid silver within the circulation pool*

King	Dates BC	Mesopotamia	N. Syria Kilikia	Upper Satrapies	Asia Minor	Koile Syria
Seleukos I	311–281	10–20	5–10	10–20?	0–5	0
Antiochos I &II	281–246	20–30	5–10	20–40	0–5	0
Seleukos II & III	246–223	30–40	10–20	30–40?	10–15	0
Antiochos III	223–187	40–50	20–30	40–50?	20–30	0–10?
Seleukos IV & Antiochos IV	187–164	50–60	10–20	50–60?	5–10	10–30?
Antiochos V to VII	164–129	60–70	40–50	60–70?	0–5	30–70
Antiochos VIII & later kings	129–64	20–30	50–70	20–30?	0	70–90

The decay rate of a coinage – what is removed annually from circulation because of wear and loss – is normally taken at about 2 per cent.[40] For the total amount in circulation to remain the same, because of the needs of a stable economy, new issues must replace what is now missing. New Seleukid issues could clearly not have added 2 per cent to the market each year, for had they done so, the Seleukid share would have risen much faster, reaching 40 per cent after 25 years, 64 per cent after 50 years and 87 per cent after 100 years. A rate of replacement that would match the hoard evidence quite well is about 0.6 per cent annually, which would give percentage shares for Seleukid issues of 14 per cent after 25 years, 26 per cent after 50 years, 45 per cent after 100 years and 59 per cent after 150 years.

There are three possibilities as to why Seleukid coinage was not introduced in greater quantities. The first is that the decay rate of the coinage in circulation may have been less than 2 per cent. The main component of this figure is the actual wear in coins, estimated at an average of 5–6 milligrams per year for gold and 10 milligrams per year for tetradrachms, although loss and hoarding are other factors that should be considered.[41] Unfortunately, one does not know at what weight a tetradrachm would be considered substandard by mint officials, if there ever was any such rule, but one can attempt a calculation. If a weight reduction of 0.5 grams were considered the limit, the average life of a tetradrachm would have been

---

[40] Callataÿ considers this percentage valid, at least for Roman Republican coinage, and would accept even as much as 3 per cent (1995: 303–4).

[41] Davesne and Le Rider estimate a loss from wear of 5–18 milligrams annually in the Meydancikkale hoard (1989: 245, 256–8). See also Davesne and Yenisoganci 1992: 35.

50 years and the decay rate due to wear 2 per cent annually. For a 1-gram loss, the average life would increase to 100 years and the decay rate become 1 per cent annually. Given the considerable spread of weights of Seleukid tetradrachms one can observe in hoards, typically much more than 0.5 grams, a decay rate nearer 1 per cent is more likely.[42] But even if a decay rate of only 1 per cent in the mass of circulating coinage is accepted, which would increase by some unknown factor if coin losses and hoarding were to be added, new Seleukid issues by themselves would only have been able to partly offset the loss, since they could contribute on average only 0.6 per cent each year to the stock.

The second possibility is that there was a declining economy, and corresponding lesser need for coin, so a smaller quantity was introduced into circulation each year, only the 0.6 per cent or thereabouts provided by the Seleukids. But this would imply hardly any new coins from elsewhere, which was not the case (see below), and it would certainly not fit in with the idea of an economy becoming *more* monetarized as part of a conscious effort on the part of the administration.

The third possibility is that the Seleukids did not need to replace all the coins that dropped out of circulation, because there was a net inflow of foreign Attic-standard coinage to make up the difference, due to a positive balance of trade (ch. 5.5d). This must be quite likely, given the numerous new issues of posthumous 'Alexanders' that were being continuously produced in the cities of Asia Minor throughout the third century BC and finding their way into Seleukid hoards, apart from any other coins of mainland Greece that did so. Conversely, hardly any Seleukid coinage has been found in hoards outside Seleukid territory.[43]

What the Seleukid kings probably did was establish a policy whereby free circulation within the empire of all Attic-standard issues was permitted. No attempt was made to systematically replace the 'Alexanders' and 'Lysimachi' in circulation, which were just as much legal tender, along with other Attic-standard coinages, as Seleukid tetradrachms.[44] Furthermore, the supply of tetradrachms in the market was to be 'topped-up' with Seleukid issues whenever it fell below the level required by the economy. This must have occurred in a gradual and quite 'natural' way, without any kind of sophisticated planning. If there happened to be a need somewhere

---

[42] For example, in the Meydancikkale hoard, with its 5215 coins (Davesne and Le Rider 1989).
[43] A perusal of the *Inventory of Greek Coin Hoards* and *Coin Hoards*, volumes I to IX, is sufficient to show that this is indeed the case.
[44] Golenko agrees that the objective of the Seleukids was to maintain the supply of currency, not to reconstruct it (1995: 139).

to make an administrative payment and the supply of coinage in the provincial treasury proved inadequate, more could be minted from the bullion and melted-down substandard coins held by the treasury. Occasional large payments, particularly those for important military expeditions, could be left to major mints, such as Seleukeia-Tigris or Antioch (see section 5 below on 'peacetime' and 'wartime' coinage).

ii. Northern Syria and Kilikia

As can be seen in table 11.2, the 'market share' of Seleukid issues circulating in this region was much smaller than Mesopotamia's until the reign of Antiochos III, when it seems to have grown sharply to 20–30 per cent, though never reaching Mesopotamian levels. A significant increase in production can also be observed at this time, essentially at the Antioch mint, and Newell-type issues for the region account for 40 per cent of Antiochos III's total production, while Golenko's estimate is 46.3 per cent (table 11.1).[45] This is not justified by the economic needs of the region (see below on 'peacetime' coinage) and the most likely explanation is that the new coinage was required to finance several military campaigns, which used this area as a base: westwards to Asia Minor and southwards to Koile Syria, namely southern Syria, Phoenicia and Palestine.[46] Part of this coinage seems to have found its way into circulation in the northern Syria and Kilikia region, probably for purchases of military equipment and supplies and as expenditure of returning soldiers. Consequently, the sharp growth in the 'market share' of Seleukid coinage circulating in northern Syria and Kilikia in the reign of Antiochos III corresponds to a replacement rate substantially greater than Mesopotamia's, over 1 per cent.

Then comes a rather sharp drop in the twenty or more years following the death of Antiochos III, which may simply be due to the nature of the hoard evidence of this period, but, since the data come from five reasonably sized hoards (see Coin hoards list 1), a reason should be sought. One that rapidly comes to mind is the possible withdrawal from circulation of large quantities of Seleukid currency to pay the Roman indemnity. The Romans, it will be recalled, required payment of the 15,000 talents set by the treaty of Apameia (188 BC) in precious-metal coinage of a high standard of weight and

---

[45] Callataÿ also notes the sharp increase in production of the Antioch mint in this reign (Callataÿ, Depeyrot and Villaronga 1993: 24–5).

[46] Houghton points out that the mint of Soloi in Kilikia was opened at this time, with production matching that of the principal mint at Tarsos (1989b: 16).

purity, and Seleukid issues undoubtedly qualified as such,[47] but the scale of Seleukid production does not seem to have been affected.[48] At this time, the Pamphylian 'Alexanders' that had been entering the Seleukid market since about 220 BC[49] were joined by a spate of new Attic-standard issues from the recently liberated cities of western and southern Asia Minor, until the Attalids established numismatic control and a closed economy within their kingdom by switching to the production of the *cistophori* coinage, perhaps by about 175 BC, or even earlier.[50] Thus, for a few decades plenty of alternative Attic-standard coinage would have been available to fill any gap caused by the mass removal of Seleukid issues from circulation.[51]

Following the death of Antiochos IV, the sharp revival in Seleukid coinage in circulation can probably be attributed to reduced production of Attic-standard coinage from Asia Minor mints, following the general switch to *cistophori* in the Attalid kingdom, and the increased need to finance mercenary armies with coinage in one's own name in the internecine struggle of rival houses for the Seleukid throne. At the same time, the continuing debasement of Seleukid silver, which had started at about the time of Alexander Balas, would cause foreign coins of better quality to be withdrawn from the market as bullion.

iii. Upper Satrapies

There is very little hoard evidence for this region, and what there is comes mainly from the reigns of Antiochos I and II (Coin hoards list 1), but the indications are that somewhat more Seleukid royal currency may have circulated here than in Mesopotamia, until the time of the loss of Baktria. This is to be expected, given the fact that no mint had been opened in this region by Alexander, the nearest being at Babylon. But under Seleukos and Antiochos I, several mints were established, as discussed earlier, giving a new economic impetus to the region. Considering also the distance that posthumous 'Alexanders' and 'Lysimachi' minted in the West had to travel

[47] Le Rider maintains that the Romans were not interested in types, denominations or standards, but only in silver of high purity with which to reach the total weight required by the indemnity. And they preferred this in coin rather than bullion (1992: 268–75; 1993: 50–2).

[48] Howgego 1995: 37.

[49] Mørkholm 1982: 302. This spate of production by the Pamphylian cities is difficult to explain. It occurs at about the time when Ptolemaic control is loosening and before Antiochos III appears in full control. Could these have been tribute payments, after the early incursions Antiochos had made in Asia Minor? Or were the cities paying for Seleukid trade, particularly in eastern goods, that were now being carried along the southern coast of Asia Minor to the West?

[50] Mørkholm 1979: 50.

[51] Mørkholm also notes an acute shortage of Seleukid silver at this time, remedied by countermarking large quantities of Asia Minor coins with the Seleukid anchor (1966: 321).

and bearing in mind the arguments for relatively little inter-regional trade (ch. 5.5c), it is not surprising that Seleukid issues may have been more common here than further west.

After the loss of Baktria and the East, it is likely that coinage circulation in Media did not differ greatly from that in Mesopotamia. By this time, the semi-independent dynasts in Persis may have been producing their own coinage for several years.[52]

iv. Asia Minor

Seleukid coinage never really circulated in large quantities in Asia Minor, probably because of (a) the strong competition from numerous local issues of posthumous 'Alexanders' and 'Lysimachi', various city coinages and those of the most powerful states of the region, the Pergamene kingdom and Rhodes, and (b) the relative instability of Seleukid rule in Asia Minor in the second half of the third century BC. Even when western and southern Asia Minor were reconquered by Antiochos III, coinage production does not seem to have been stepped up, as one might have expected, for the economic needs of the region.[53] However, the hoard evidence in table 11.2 shows that, under Antiochos III, Seleukid coinage did acquire a more respectable share of the circulating currency and this should probably be linked to increased military expenditure in the region, but with coinage that had probably been minted further east, which matches well with the increased production noted in northern Syria and Kilikia at this time (see above). Just as for northern Syria and Kilikia, this sharp growth in the 'market share' of Seleukid coinage corresponds to a greater replacement rate than Mesopotamia's, over 1 per cent.

After Apameia and the loss of Asia Minor (188 BC), there was, not unexpectedly, a dramatic drop in the volume of Seleukid currency circulating in western and southern Asia Minor to virtually zero. This was also partly due to the role of the coinages of the Attalid kingdom and Rhodes in creating more or less closed monetary areas in their spheres of political and economic influence.

v. Koile Syria

After the conquest of this Ptolemaic province by Antiochos III, one can observe a very slow introduction of Seleukid coinage initially and no mint

---

[52] Koch 1988.

[53] Only 8 per cent of Antiochos III's production in Newell-type issues, or 2.4 per cent according to Golenko (table 11.1), comes from Asia Minor. Houghton and Lorber 2002 are hard put to it to identify any production from Sardeis, which had been an important mint earlier.

for silver issues has been identified in this area under Antiochos III, who was apparently content to allow Ptolemaic currency to circulate freely. Under his immediate successors, the royal mint at Ake-Ptolemaïs was opened and those of the major Phoenician cities also began producing Seleukid issues. The interesting thing, however, is that the bulk of the Seleukid coinage minted in the region was produced on the Ptolemaic standard, no doubt because the population was used to this for its monetary transactions.[54] Once more, a financial decision can be seen that aimed at promoting production and exchange in the most efficient manner. At the very least, one can view this as a *laissez-faire* attitude, which certainly did no harm to the Seleukid treasury.

The very high proportion of Seleukid currency in circulation in this region in the period after Antiochos IV can probably be linked, as in northern Syria and Kilikia, to the continuous need of the various contenders for the Seleukid throne to issue coinage for their soldiers' pay and to the debasement of the silver.

d. Small silver

With regard to small silver, mainly drachms, Appendix 1 – Coin hoards list 2 presents the hoard evidence. The picture for Asia Minor seems to be that hardly any Seleukid issues circulated there throughout the third century BC and up to the loss of this area after Apameia (188 BC), while lifetime and posthumous 'Alexander' and 'Lysimachos' drachms dominated the market. The pattern appears similar for Syria and Kilikia and it is only at the time of dynastic strife, from about 160 BC onwards, that perhaps as much as 20–30 per cent of the small silver in circulation consisted of royal Seleukid issues, again probably in response to the increasing need to finance armies and to the debasement of the silver. For Mesopotamia and the Upper Satrapies, the corresponding figure in the third century may have been of the order of 5–10 per cent, increasing gradually to 20–30 per cent by the time these areas were lost to the Parthians in the mid second century BC.

It seems clear, both from the hoard evidence and the small number of drachm and fractional silver issues minted (section 3c above) that the Seleukid kings had less call for small-silver coinage[55] than for tetradrachms,

---

[54] Mørkholm 1984: 96. However, Seyrig regards this as due to the strengthening of both political and economic ties with Ptolemaic Egypt from Alexander Balas onwards, since his predecessor, Demetrios I, minted only Attic-standard coins in the region (1973: 121).

[55] Le Rider estimates that in the third century BC perhaps 95 per cent of the drachms in circulation were 'Alexanders' (1994b: 470).

which better served their needs for payment of administrative expenses and tax collection.

e. Bronze

Finds of bronze coins in hoards are extremely rare, probably because of the token nature of this coinage, and thus it is not possible to produce an analysis similar to that above for silver.

There is, however, the question of whether bronze produced at Seleukid mints was intended to circulate only locally or over a wider area.[56] Two eastern mints, Seleukeia-Tigris and Ekbatana, minted large quantities of bronze under the early kings to Antiochos III (103 and 86 Newell-type issues respectively) while the other mints of Mesopotamia and the Upper Satrapies, including Babylon, Susa, Baktra and Artakoana, each produced nothing or very little (53 issues in all).[57] And yet, bronze coinage certainly circulated in Babylon, as we know from the *Astronomical Diary* of 274 BC, while coins of Seleukeia-Tigris of all the early sovereigns have been found in Susa[58] and there seems to be no reason why Ekbatana under Antiochos I needed 15 bronze issues for its local economy as against Susa's 2 issues. The picture that emerges is of two major eastern mints for bronze, that at Seleukeia-Tigris supplying Mesopotamia and Susiane and the other at Ekbatana supplying Media and most of the Upper Satrapies, where bronze coinage was still a relative novelty, probably not readily accepted and therefore not required in great quantities. In northern Syria and Kilikia, the Antioch mint seems to have produced the lion's share of the bronze coinage of the early Seleukid kings (126 out of 167 Newell-type issues), while Sardeis was the principal mint for Asia Minor, but with limited production (43 out of 53 issues), probably because many Greek and Hellenized cities of this region minted their own bronze coinage.

f. Summary of coinage circulation

This review of the evidence for the circulation of Seleukid coinage, when linked to that for its production, suggests that the basic policy of the kings was not to tamper with the Attic-standard precious-metal currency in circulation, principally 'Alexanders' and 'Lysimachi'. They simply attempted to keep the level of currency up to their payment needs, as wear and loss

---

[56] Locally: Bikerman 1938: 223. Over a wider area: Golenko 1993: 81; Mørkholm 1991: 6.
[57] *ESM.*   [58] Le Rider 1965: 446–7.

took their toll, by minting their own coins when and where required. The mints of Mesopotamia and the Upper Satrapies essentially performed this function for their respective regions, which resulted in a gradual, but very slow, natural increase in 'market share' of Seleukid coinage. Up to a point, the same situation prevailed in northern Syria and Kilikia and to a lesser extent in Asia Minor, which explains why there were so many mints, since each had the very limited but specific task of monitoring the needs of its own region and providing the necessary replacement coinage.

One can now complete the picture presented earlier of taxes arriving at local treasuries in tetradrachms (and some small silver) and being passed on to regional treasuries after the deduction of any sums required for local use. One may imagine mint officials sorting through the coins and setting aside those that were too worn to be allowed to circulate, thereby creating a reserve to be melted down and reminted whenever the needs of their region demanded it.

The campaigns of Antiochos III seem to have upset the balance somewhat, as the mints in northern Syria and Kilikia produced more coinage than was strictly necessary for their own regional needs in order to finance campaigns of conquest in Koile Syria and Asia Minor. The conquered regions, already highly monetized, were thus initially supplied with a replacement currency that could satisfy their needs for some time and did not require any new coinage. In due course, Asia Minor was lost, while Koile Syria followed the pattern of northern Syria and Kilikia, with a speeding up of Seleukid coinage production and increase in 'market share' primarily because of three factors: the greater isolation of the Seleukid economy, the intensification of military expenditure in the dynastic conflicts of this period and the debasement of the currency, which naturally caused purer foreign coins to be withdrawn from the market as bullion.

With regard to bronze, this was a coinage that attempted to replace Seleukid small-silver issues, but with no seeming urgency, particularly in the East. An adequate supply appears to have been provided from just a few major mints.

The two key factors of Seleukid coinage policy, the 'topping-up' of the precious-metal coinage in circulation and the bursts of military expenditure, now need to be discussed further.

5. 'PEACETIME' AND 'WARTIME' COINAGE

A die study allows one to estimate the volume of a particular issue of coinage, with a greater or smaller degree of accuracy (ch. 1.6b). When a mint can also be identified and a plausible chronology for the issue established, one has at one's disposal a piece of very useful data, that in a certain place at a certain time a particular quantity of gold or silver was minted. The next question is 'For what purpose?' And this is where literary sources or plain common sense may provide a satisfactory answer, which can throw more light on the coinage policy of the Seleukid kings.

a. The case of the Antioch mint of Antiochos IV

Mørkholm has carried out a detailed study of the silver coins of the mint of Antioch under Antiochos IV, grouping these into three series when major changes of type or legend occurred and, within each series, into a number of issues determined by denomination and type.[59]

The numbers of obverse dies used at Antioch were: 2 for gold staters, 55 for tetradrachms, 2 for drachms, 1 for a hemidrachm and 2 for diobols. As a rough indication of relative value, in drachm terms, the ratios between gold,[60] large silver, small silver and bronze were 20:220:2.5:0.7, the huge importance of tetradrachms issues being evident in these figures.

Mørkholm's analysis showed 23 tetradrachms produced from 4 obverse dies for Series I (175–173/2 BC), 89 from 17 dies for Series II (173/2–169/8 BC) and 136 from 36 dies for Series III (169/8–164 BC), although some dies span series. Using Esty's statistical method (ch. 1.6b), best estimates and 95 per cent confidence limits for the total number of obverse dies for the three Series are 4.3 (range: 4.0 to 8.3), 18.6 (range: 17.0 to 26.0) and 42.2 (range: 36.0 to 56.9) respectively. In terms of average annual usage, the best estimate for the Antioch mint of Antiochos IV is that it used slightly fewer than two obverse dies per year for Series I, about four and a half dies per year for Series II and about ten dies per year for Series III.

Series I represents the peaceful start of Antiochos' reign. One can associate Series II with the preparations for the war against Egypt and probably the first campaign. Series III is then linked with the second campaign against Egypt, the military effort to suppress the Maccabean revolt and the preparations for and expedition to the East in the last years of the king's reign (ch. 2).

I shall call Series I a 'peacetime' coinage. The needs of a population for an adequate supply of silver coins, so that the administrative-payments–tax-collection cycle could work, have already been discussed, and Seleukid

---

[59] Mørkholm 1963.
[60] Note that a die for gold coins is assumed to have had half the production capability of a tetradrachm die (ch. 1.6b).

issues essentially represented a 'topping-up' of the coinage supply because of normal wear and loss, that is, a replacement coinage. The marked increase in mint output in Series II and III would correspond to what I will term 'wartime' issues, which met the financial requirements of important military campaigns. Note that a 'wartime' issue at one mint might reduce or even supplant 'peacetime' issues for a number of years at the same or different mints, provided that those receiving payment (mainly soldiers and suppliers of military equipment and provisions) spent their earnings in the regions served by those mints. Thus, in Antiochos IV's Antioch, for example, it might be expected that soldiers returning from the Egyptian campaigns to the city, the staging point for these campaigns and for the expedition to the East, would contribute with their expenditure to the supply of circulating coins.

For the moment, one may simply note that the population of northern Syria was estimated at this time at about one and a half to two million inhabitants (ch. 4.3). Therefore, its 'peacetime' needs seem to have been met by a little over one tetradrachm obverse die per year per million of population, equivalent to 20 talents-worth of coins or slightly more (ch. 1.6b).

b. The case of the mint at Seleukeia-Kalykadnos

This minor mint in Kilikia Tracheia has been extensively studied.[61] Tetradrachm production commenced there with the conquest of the region by Antiochos III *c.* 197 BC, but was limited to the use of only one obverse die apparently. In subsequent reigns, up to and including that of Antiochos VII (to 129 BC), the same low-key operation seems to have continued, with production from one or two dies per reign and sometimes none, making eight dies in all, or one every nine years or so. So far, this clearly looks like a 'peacetime' coinage. If one obverse die per year at Antioch served as a replacement coinage for the needs of about one million people (see above), the region served by Seleukeia-Kalykadnos may have contained a population of about 100,000, or somewhat more, if one considers that Kilikia Tracheia was not as heavily urbanized as northern Syria or Mesopotamia or Kilikia Pedias and so had less need of coinage.

But then appeared a huge peak in production under Seleukos VI: 126 known specimens from 44 obverse dies, giving a best estimate of 58 dies. Clearly an extraordinary minting effort was going on, probably associated

---

[61] Houghton 1989a, also quoted by Callataÿ, Depeyrot and Villaronga 1993: 22–3.

with the arrival of Seleukos at Seleukeia-Kalykadnos in 98 BC(?) and the commencement of military preparations there for his bid on the Seleukid throne, which ended with the taking of Antioch in 94 BC(?).[62] So the mint was producing a 'wartime' coinage then and, at about twenty talents to an obverse tetradrachm die (ch. 1.6b), roughly 1,200 talents were coined in up to four years for Seleukos' war effort.

In chapter 10.1e–g soldiers' pay was discussed and it was suggested that in the Hellenistic period professional soldiers required an advance payment and regular pay thereafter. Therefore, preparations for a campaign probably involved a considerable amount of minting of new coinage, which might continue at a lesser intensity during the campaign itself, until another peak was reached, the paying-off at the end, if sufficient funds had not been coined already.

In Seleukos' case, one does not know whether his troops were paid off at Antioch with coinage minted at Seleukeia-Kalykadnos, but, on the assumption that they were and at the rate of 1 drachm per day per man (ch. 10.1e), 1,200 talents would have sufficed for 5,000 soldiers paid for four years or 10,000 for two years. The numbers sound about right for the force that Seleukos VI might have raised to take Antioch.

c. The case of the Mesopotamian mints of Antiochos III and Seleukos IV

Mints operated for Antiochos III (223–187 BC) and Seleukos IV (187–175 BC) at the Mesopotamian cities of Seleukeia-Tigris, Susa and Nisibis, and one may add Ekbatana just outside this region. The known specimens of tetradrachms at one time and the obverse dies used for this coinage are shown in table 11.3.[63] An estimate has been made using Esty's method (ch. 1.6b) of the probable total number of obverse dies used ($k2'$) and the 95 per cent confidence limits of this prediction (95% $k2'$).

Seleukos IV is not known to have organized any large-scale military operations in the East, so it might not be unreasonable to consider that his eastern mints coined only what was sufficient for the current needs of the eastern satrapies, that is, a 'peacetime' coinage. From table 11.3 the best estimate for Mesopotamia is that he used about 61 obverse dies or 5.1 per regnal year on average. For an estimated population of four to five million (ch. 4.1), this is again consistent with a level of about one obverse die per million inhabitants, as at Antioch above. In fact, the two regions seem to have been quite similar in their high degree of urbanization, which necessitated

---

[62] Houghton 1989a: 97–8.   [63] Le Rider 1993: 57–8.

Table 11.3 *Coin production at eastern mints under Antiochos III
and Seleukos IV*

King	Mint	Coins	Obv. dies	Est. total dies	Dies per year	95% Confidence limits
Antiochos III	Seleukeia-Tigris	55	49	343.8	9.6	143–783
(36 years)	Susa	23	17	51.1	1.4	17–121
	Nisibis	171	57	72.2	2.0	57–95
	TOTAL MESOPOTAMIA			467.1	13.0	
Seleukos IV	Seleukeia-Tigris	17	11	24.5	2.0	11–59
(12 years)	Susa	18	9	14.6	1.2	9–20
	Nisibis	38	16	22.2	1.9	16–38
	TOTAL MESOPOTAMIA			61.3	5.1	
Antiochos III	Ekbatana	78	36	54.4	1.5	36–80
Seleukos IV	Ekbatana	5	3	5.9	0.5	3–26

increased currency supplies. One can possibly be even more specific: northern Mesopotamia (Nisibis) required 1.9 dies per year on average, central Mesopotamia (Seleukeia-Tigris) 2.0 and southern Mesopotamia (Susa) 1.2. What is somewhat surprising here is the comparatively large production of the mint at Nisibis. Either northern Mesopotamia was more densely populated than the evidence suggests or Nisibis was conveniently supplying coinage to the Babylonian heartland cities along the Euphrates.

One may also consider Ekbatana, serving Media, with an output of half a die per year on average. In terms of population, Seleukid Media should have possessed about a quarter of Mesopotamia's population (ch. 4.7) and one would have expected roughly one die per year at Ekbatana. The smaller number, if not a statistical error, might simply be an indication of the lesser need for coinage in a region not so heavily urbanized, where much of payment, taxation and exchange were still being conducted in kind.

Under Antiochos III, the picture is virtually the same at two mints: Nisibis, requiring 2.0 dies per year on average, and Susa 1.4, and so equivalent to the 'peacetime' output of Seleukos IV. But there is a dramatic change at Seleukeia-Tigris, where the best estimate of annual obverse die usage has gone up to 9.6. Admittedly, the 95 per cent confidence limits of the prediction are quite wide, because of the small index ratio of coins to dies, but even at the lower limit (143 dies at four per year) the result is much higher than any 'peacetime' output. To a smaller extent, this is the picture at Ekbatana where there is a tripling from one-half to one and a half dies per year on average. Clearly an explanation is required.

It is not difficult to consider that the huge increase in production at the mint of Seleukeia-Tigris is a 'wartime' coinage issued to finance Antiochos III's Anabasis to the East between 210 and 205 BC. The size of the army has been discussed in chapter 10.1a and, for the purposes of this calculation, I shall take 50,000 troops (35,000 'regulars' and 15,000 mercenaries) paid in silver and 20,000 eastern levies and 'allies', who were not (in an attempt to be as conservative as possible). Assuming 4.5–6 obols per day for an infantryman and twice that for a cavalryman (ch. 10.1e), and allowing also for the possibility of lower pay for service far from the Mediterranean, the daily cost of paying troops in silver would have been about 7–9 talents, using a cavalry to infantry ratio of one to ten. This gives a total of some 10,000 to 13,000 talents over the five years of the campaign. To this should be added some expenses in silver for troop rations, support personnel and overheads (ch. 10.1h), even allowing for the possibility that the army lived mainly off the land or at the expense of local rulers (ch. 2). It is difficult, therefore, to envisage a total expense for the Anabasis amounting to much less than 15,000 talents.

Seleukeia would have been the logical staging point for the expedition and one may suppose that some payments were made there to the troops. Perhaps pay was issued at a reduced rate, or not at all, during the actual campaign or while Antiochos was returning via Karmania and Persis. We are not told where any troops were disbanded, but Seleukeia-Tigris seems a logical point and, again, its mint would have to come into play for any final payments. None of the other Mesopotamian mints, it was noted, shows any significant increase in silver output at this time, above any 'peacetime' currency needs.

From table 11.3, the entire production of Seleukeia-Tigris (best estimate 344 obverse dies) will be considered to have been devoted to the expenses of the Anabasis. At twenty talents to the die, this works out at about 7,000 talents, considerably less than the estimated cost of the expedition in silver. It is quite possible that Antiochos already carried with him a substantial war chest of coined money when he arrived at Seleukeia-Tigris at the start of the campaign. It is also probable that some payments were made in gold. One other possibility is that the actual number of dies used at Seleukeia-Tigris may have been higher than the best estimate, since the 95 per cent confidence limit can indeed take us up to 783 dies, or just over 15,000 talents, but the possibility is very small. A stronger possibility is that more coins than 30,000 were struck on average from an obverse tetradrachm die.

Perhaps Ekbatana also minted for the Anabasis, being on the direct route the expedition took and along which reinforcements and supplies might be expected to have travelled. It has been suggested[64] that the gold and silver obtained by Antiochos from the sacking of the temple at Aine near Ekbatana, which produced nearly 4,000 talents of coined money (Polyb. 10.27.13), were minted mostly there. But the die evidence goes against this. The best estimate of 55 obverse dies at Ekbatana for the whole of the reign of Antiochos III, discounting any need for 'peacetime' coinage, would amount to only about 1,000 talents of silver, far short of what Aine apparently produced. Nor is there any historical evidence that Aine yielded gold to the tune of nearly 3,000 talents, since Polybios is careful to detail the mainly silver ornamentation of the temple and the fact that other looters, Alexander, Antigonos and Seleukos, had already passed through earlier (when it might plausibly be expected that they would have availed themselves of any gold in preference to silver). Nor is there numismatic evidence that Antiochos minted such huge quantities of gold staters that would have required about 60 obverse dies, at the rate of fifty talents to a die (ch. 1.6b).

There is perhaps a simpler explanation for the increased output of the Ekbatana mint under Antiochos III, compared to under Seleukos IV. The re-establishment of Seleukid political control in the East after the Anabasis must have created the need for more coinage to fuel the administrative-payments–tax-collection cycle. Mints that had once served this area, Artakoana in Aria and others in southern Iran and Afghanistan (section 1 above), no longer functioned. The mint at Baktra, which had also probably contributed earlier, was outside Seleukid jurisdiction, in the hands of Euthydemos. Only Ekbatana was in a position to supply the necessary coinage to what was quite a large region, comprising not only Media, but probably also Aria, Drangiane, Karmania and perhaps Arachosia. If one considers these 'reaffirmed' provinces as similar in terms of degree of urbanization and economy to Media, the extra output from Ekbatana of one obverse die per year could serve roughly two million more people, which does not fit badly with the independent assessment of population in chapter 4.7 for these eastern provinces. After the defeat of Antiochos III at Magnesia, control of this area seems to have been lost once again. This could explain the reduction in mint output at Ekbatana under Seleukos IV.

---

[64] For example, *ESM*: nos 217–18.

6. THE SPECIAL ISSUES

a. The Seleukid 'Alexanders'

'Alexander' tetradrachms were minted by Seleukid kings alongside their own royal issues. This continued well into the second century BC and probably represented a substantial proportion of mint output.[65] This is not surprising in the light of the coinage policy that seems detectable, namely that the basic intention of the Seleukids was to maintain the currency supply at the right level and not to establish a Seleukid royal currency *per se*. What the coinage in circulation was appeared immaterial, as long as it was based on the Attic standard (with the exception of Koile Syria later).

But why 'Alexanders'? It may be that the Seleukid kings felt a need to reaffirm themselves to their subjects at the start of a reign, or when dynastic conflict or external problems posed a threat, or in newly conquered territories, and so issued 'Alexanders' at the time, which received greater acceptance. 'Alexanders' also probably helped to develop a primary habit of coinage in areas where such had not circulated before.[66] But a more detailed study is required, before the reasons for specific Seleukid 'Alexander' issues can be determined.[67]

b. The lion staters

The so-called lion staters were coined by Alexander at Babylon alongside his official Greek-style coinage and this practice was continued by Seleukos I (who also introduced the so-called elephant stater) at Ekbatana and Susa too. However, the weight of the lion stater is quite variable and this suggests that it may have circulated more as bullion, making it suitable for transactions in Babylonian markets when it was too soon to implement a Greek tri-metallic coinage.

The circulation of lion staters was restricted to Babylonia and parts of western Iran and, in one (erroneous) view, was terminated by 275 BC when Antiochos I removed the last remnants of the civilian population of Babylon to Seleukeia-Tigris.[68] Probably the lion staters ceased to be minted at about

[65] The very large Meydancikkale hoard from Kilikia Tracheia, with burial date *c.* 240–235 BC, is considered representative of what circulated in Asia Minor and Kilikia at this time. It has yielded 251 Seleukid tetradrachms, of which 147 are 'Alexanders', and 10 Seleukid drachms, of which 8 are 'Alexanders' (Davesne and Le Rider 1989: 230, 240).
[66] Golenko 1993: 87.
[67] This may well be possible today using Price 1992, but is likely to be facilitated by the new Houghton and Lorber 2002 catalogue.
[68] *ESM*: no. 104. See ch. 6.2b, and e on the founding of Seleukeia-Tigris.

this time not because of the supposed evacuation of Babylon, but in line with the increasing acceptance of Greek-style currency, although one could still think in terms of shekels. There is evidence from numerous Seleukid-period legal texts from Babylon and Uruk of prices expressed in shekels of silver and fractions of a shekel, frequently with the designation 'in staters of Antiochos (or another king) in good condition'.[69] A parallel existed in Greece until recently where the drachma was still sometimes called a franc in everyday speech, a throwback to pre-independence times, when foreign coins were used as a medium of exchange.

The main reason why such a currency may have been issued alongside the normal Attic-standard coinage could have been to facilitate coin-based transactions in an area with a long tradition of bullion-based exchange,[70] but somewhat sceptical of coins in the Greek sense, until public acceptance of the new system could be cultivated. As part of Seleukid coinage policy, it probably satisfied in the best way at the time the needs of the administrative-payment–tax-collection cycle in traditional Babylonia. However, the newly opened-up area to the east around Seleukeia-Tigris could be served better from the start by Attic-standard coinage.

c. The Ptolemaic-standard coinage

This has already been discussed briefly. It is the currency the Seleukids minted on a standard of 14.2 grams for a tetradrachm after the conquest of Koile Syria *c.* 200 BC from the Ptolemies, although not immediately. The region had, until then, entertained close commercial links with Alexandria, with mints at Berytus, Sidon, Tyre, Ake-Ptolemaïs and Joppa.[71]

It initially facilitated the Seleukid administration to make certain payments and receive taxes in the area from the already existing stock of Ptolemaic coinage, which did not disrupt the economy. That is probably why Antiochos III minted no silver in the region after his conquest and one has to wait for the reign of Seleukos IV for the first Attic issue at Ake-Ptolemaïs. Under Antiochos V, tetradrachms on the Ptolemaic standard were coined alongside Attic. This was not repeated by Demetrios I, but from Alexander Balas onwards several Phoenician mints were opened and Ptolemaic-standard coins began to predominate, along with the occasional Attic.[72]

---

[69] Doty 1977; McEwan 1981a. By the Parthian period, this terminology was no longer used and the shekel was simply the equivalent of 2 drachms (Spek 1998a: 246–7).

[70] Bellinger 1963: 65.   [71] Rostovtzeff 1941: 868; Seyrig 1973: 121.

[72] See Le Rider 1995 for a review of the monetary policy of the Seleukids in Koile Syria.

It has been suggested[73] that Attic-standard silver was eventually used in the new province only in the frontier areas and for certain payments the administration was obliged to make in this coinage to troops and administrative personnel temporarily based there. Indeed a compulsory change of Attic-standard coins may have been required of traders arriving from the rest of the empire. Although this is likely to have been inconvenient, what was important was that the economy of the province be served in the best way. An alternative suggestion is that, as Ptolemaic influence increased, because of the support given to different pretenders for the Seleukid throne, the region became more economically attached to Egypt and the Ptolemaic standard came to predominate.[74]

Perhaps the truth is that Ptolemaic-standard Seleukid coins were minted because the supply of true Ptolemaic coins in the area was dwindling due to natural wear and loss. In line with their general policy, the Seleukid kings showed no concern to establish their own coinage in Koile Syria and whatever could be shown to facilitate the administrative-payments–tax-collection cycle was acceptable: Ptolemaic-standard for the bulk of their needs, Attic-standard for the remainder.

7. CONCLUSIONS ON COINAGE

The aim of the early Seleukid kings was to monetize the economy of the empire to the greatest extent and as rapidly as possible, so as to ensure for themselves and their successors an adequate supply of silver for their expenses, principally military.

Numerous mints were established to serve different regions, their primary objective being to maintain the money supply at the desired level, so as to fuel the administrative-payments–tax-collection cycle (a 'peacetime' coinage). What coins were used for this purpose was immaterial, but tetradrachms were by far the most convenient. The Seleukids never made any effort to replace the 'Alexanders' and 'Lysimachi' completely, or indeed the numerous city and other silver tetradrachms and drachms that circulated within their domain, as long as they belonged to the Attic standard. In Koile Syria, they even relaxed this rule and minted on the Ptolemaic standard themselves, while permitting Ptolemaic coins to circulate at the same time, since this seemed to serve their needs more efficiently. In Babylonia,

---

[73] Le Rider 1995: 401–4.

[74] Bikerman 1938: 214. Le Rider considers that Ptolemaic coins were freely admitted to Koile Syria after 200 BC (1993: 54).

transactions were carried out for some years in coinage of a local standard, until familiarity with Attic-standard coinage had been developed.

The Seleukid 'peacetime' issues essentially replaced the coins that dropped out of circulation through wear and loss. The rate of production of tetradrachms, representing the lion's share of the coinage issued, seems to have been roughly the output of one obverse die per year, or about twenty talents, for the needs of one million people in more urbanized provinces and perhaps half of this in more rural ones.

At the same time, a reserve was kept of silver and gold in coin and bullion (from mine output or the melting-down of coins withdrawn from circulation as too worn). This was used when required for some major item of expenditure, almost always an important military campaign, and issued then as a 'wartime' coinage.

The pattern of circulation of Seleukid tetradrachms, as evidenced by coin hoards, shows the effect of a steady natural replacement of the original and posthumous 'Alexanders' and 'Lysimachi' in circulation within the empire, as wear and loss took their toll on these. This progressed faster in Mesopotamia and the Upper Satrapies and also after the Seleukid realm became more isolated from the Aegean world, following the loss of Asia Minor.

Finally, small-silver issues were not preferred and bronze seems to have taken their place in the market, mostly from the time of Antiochos I. This had two benefits for the royal exchequer. It saved on silver for the more important tetradrachm issues and it also yielded a greater minting profit, because of the token nature of bronze. Gold was minted rarely, because of its scarcity, and usually only when there was a serious shortage of silver or some particular message of the royal ideology needed to be expressed, alongside a utilitarian function such as the payment of troops.

CHAPTER 12

A model for the Seleukid economy

In previous chapters population, production and exchange, royal revenue and expenses and coinage were treated separately. Logically there should be certain relationships between these different elements of the Seleukid economy.

A very approximate model will be developed. Using source material and a measure of common sense, the magnitude of each factor of the economy will be estimated independently of the others and plausible relationships will also be found independently between them. Then if all the relationships actually hold between all the estimates, the model might be considered a reasonable one, since the several parameters involved will have been derived independently and the possibility that they could fit together in this way by chance is unlikely.[1]

I. POPULATION

It will be useful to retain some 'best estimates' of population from chapter 4. The Seleukid empire at its peaks *c.* 281 BC and *c.* 190 BC probably contained between fourteen and eighteen million inhabitants, compared to between perhaps twenty-five and thirty million in Alexander's empire at the time of his death. Mesopotamia's population was estimated at four to five million, northern Syria's at up to one and a half million by the middle of the third century BC and perhaps even two million by the middle of the second, Judaea's at just under a quarter of a million, while the inhabitants of Egypt at this time may have numbered between three and three and a half million.

---

[1] The need for models to describe ancient economies is stressed by Davies, who goes on to describe three levels of qualitative and descriptive model: from a simple household economy to that of a Greek city. Davies is essentially concerned with the flows of goods, services, money and intangibles within or between cellular structures (households, cities, provinces, etc.) (1998: 243–50). In my view, a qualitative model is a necessary first step in helping one to visualize the different interrelated aspects of an economy. It can be really useful only when it is quantified, which I have attempted to do. An earlier version of this analysis appeared in Aperghis 2001.

The average population of a Greek city of Asia Minor and its territory was taken as 15,000, but the range could have been quite wide, while the largest new foundation, Seleukeia-Tigris, may have been designed for about 100,000 inhabitants.

2. ROYAL REVENUE

a. Revenue examples

With regard to total revenue, the annual income of Alexander at his death is given as 30,000 (Attic) talents, but this must include a small contribution from the European provinces as well (Justin 13.1.9). Antigonos Monophthalmos is said to have received 11,000 (Attic) talents as that part of the revenue which ended up in his hands at the time (316 BC) when he had established a certain measure of authority over all the Asian provinces (Diod. 19.56.5). Ptolemy II reportedly obtained 14,800 (Ptolemaic) talents from Egypt alone, plus 1,500,000 *artabai* of grain (Jerome, *Daniel* 11.5), while the income of Ptolemy Auletes in the mid first century BC amounted to 12,500 (Ptolemaic) talents (Strabo 18.1.13).[2]

However, the total of 30,000 talents for Alexander's revenue given by Justin is quite different from that which can be derived from Herodotos (3.89–95) for Darius, namely 8,100 Babylonian talents, or a little over 9,000 Attic.[3] Consequently, Justin has been rejected as too high, although some growth in economic activity, and so taxation, by the end of the Achaemenid period has been allowed.[4] A simpler explanation, however, is that Herodotos and Justin are simply referring to different sides of the same coin, the former to that part of the revenue of the satrapies that was passed on to the king after the expenses of the satraps had been taken care of, that is, the surpluses discussed in chapter 9, the latter to the total revenue of the king and his administration from all sources, including royal land and natural resources. The 11,000 talents of Antigonos would then be more akin to the tribute of Darius, net rather than gross revenue.

b. Revenue rates

When these amounts of revenue are compared with the population figures derived earlier, certain relationships seem to emerge. The Ptolemies come

---

[2] Préaux 1939: 424–5.
[3] The 360 talent tribute assessment of the Indian nome is considered to represent the value in silver of the gold dust actually paid. This is also the view of Briant 1996: 402.
[4] Cavaignac 1923: 109–13.

out, as one would expect, given their very strict control of the Egyptian economy, as the most intensive generators of income. Their revenue of 14,800 Ptolemaic talents, or roughly 12,000 Attic, on a population of three to three and a half million works out at around 3–4 talents per thousand people. If the population of Alexander's empire was about twenty-five to thirty million, his revenue of 30,000 talents would represent a taxation rate of about 1 talent per thousand.

Looking now at different parts of the Seleukid empire, a certain pattern emerges. Revenue from Judaea was noted as 300 talents under Seleukos IV (Sulpicius Severus, *Chron.* 2.17.5). Earlier it had been higher, before Antiochos III reduced the tribute by one third and made other concessions, but later it was to go up to 440 talents under Antiochos IV (ch. 8.7a–c). On a population of 200,000–250,000, a revenue rate oscillating around 1.5–2 talents per thousand seems to have applied.

Regarding Seleukid Mesopotamia, which was probably not too different from that of the Achaemenids in terms of population, there is the interesting statement in Herodotos (1.192) that the satrap of Achaemenid Babylonia collected daily as the tax of the province a Babylonian *artaba* of silver, equivalent, according to Herodotos, to an Attic *medimnos* and 4 *choinikes*, or, in modern terms, to about 56 litres. A solid mass of pure silver of this volume would actually weigh about 590 kilos or nearly 23 Attic talents (at 10.5 grams per cubic centimetre), which corresponds to just over 8,000 talents annually. Obviously, neither is a sackful of pieces of silver a solid mass, nor is Herodotos likely to have been exact. Still, one is led to total annual revenue from Mesopotamia of the order of 5,000–6,000 talents. Almost all scholars have rejected Herodotos here, considering this to be one of his 'stories' and because this figure is in total disagreement with what he gives as the tribute of Mesopotamia of only 1,000 Babylonian talents. But it does happen to fit a population of four to five million taxed at the rate of about 1–1.5 talents per thousand inhabitants.

There is, of course, the need to explain the huge difference between the 5,000–6,000 talents total revenue of the satrapy and the only 1,000 talents apparently received by the king. Again, Herodotos is helpful because he informs us that one of the duties of the Babylonian satrapy was to 'feed' the king and his court for four months in the year, the remainder being provided for by the other satrapies of Asia (1.192). One reads in Athenaios (4.145a) that the daily expenses of the Persian king's table (read 'court') amounted to 20 or 30 talents, or sometimes more. Again, this may be just a 'story', but, if this rate were maintained for four months in the year, one can calculate that the total expense would be around 2,500–3,500 talents or more, making this probably the largest single item of expenditure for the satrap of Babylonia, greater even than that of administering his satrapy, and the idea of 5,000–6,000 talents total revenue and only 1,000 talents net tribute more plausible.[5]

Considering individual cities now, Aspendos was assessed for 50 talents by Alexander (Arr. *Anab.* 1.26.2), while the combined payment of Kaunos and Stratonikeia to the Rhodians was set at 120 talents (Polyb. 30.31.7), these figures probably comprising tribute and all taxes. All three were sizable cities, probably above the norm for Asia Minor and, with populations of say 25,000–30,000 each, their rates of revenue would have been about 2 talents per thousand. For comparison, Magnesia-Maiandros, which may have been larger, generated 50 talents for Themistokles in the Persian period, or probably nearer 1.5 talents per thousand (Thuc. 1.138.5). It was suggested (ch. 8.8a) that the indemnity of 150 talents finally imposed on Seleukeia-Tigris by Antiochos III (Polyb. 5.54.11) may have been set equal to the annual royal revenue from that city, which, on an estimated population of 100,000, would then have amounted to 1.5 talents per thousand.

For a rural community, one has the evidence of the 3 (Attic) drachms per adult head tax for the village of the Kardakes (ch. 8.6), which works out at only 0.25 talents per thousand of population, but this was probably not the only tax. Mnesimachos' villages (ch. 8.1a) ended up paying about 50 gold staters in tribute, or 1,000 drachms, at the one-twelfth rate. With a population of, say, 500 for a typical village, this would have amounted to 2 drachms per head or a third of a talent per thousand, but this was after the grant to Mnesimachos. Prior to this, assuming that the village had paid the king 50 per cent of its average annual income as rent, as I regarded likely (ch. 8.1b), the revenue generated would have been six times greater and reached 2 talents per thousand of population, while a population of 650 would have yielded nearer 1.5 talents per thousand.

Three points need to be made. The first is that revenue rates from subject cities seem to have been quite high, when tribute and taxation were fully applied, which supports the idea in chapter 8.1h that the king purposely made lighter the taxation of city land, since he expected to gain also from tolls and taxes on trade and industry. The second point is that many subject cities, temples and peoples did not pay the full rate, because of the exemptions granted them. The third point is that revenue rates in Asia Minor appear to have been higher than those in Mesopotamia, for which there is a simple explanation. The lower commodity prices prevailing in Mesopotamia (ch. 5.6c) would generate smaller amounts of silver compared

---

[5] See Lewis 1987 and Sancisi-Weerdenburg 1989: 133–5 for a discussion of the 'King's table'.

to Asia Minor from the sale of exactly the same quantities of commodities that represented the tax burden. For the eastern parts of the empire, one should also make allowance for the fact that there was less urbanization, with the possible exception of Baktria, and a smaller degree of penetration of a monetary economy, as evidenced by mint activity (ch. 11.2). Consequently, silver revenue rates there were likely to have been substantially lower.

What emerges from this very rough analysis is a spectrum of regional revenue rates ranging from about 1.5 talents per thousand of population in the Mediterranean provinces to nearer 1.25 talents per thousand in Mesopotamia and perhaps as little as 0.5 talents per thousand in most of the Upper Satrapies. Thus, for example, Mesopotamia's four to five million inhabitants could be expected to generate 5,000–6,000 talents in royal revenue annually.

c. Total revenue

Using the above conclusions on revenue rates, in conjunction with the population graph of chapter 4.7 (figure 4.1), presented below in figure 12.1 is a best estimate of total revenue of the Seleukid kings over time, expressed as a likely range.

A peak of 14,000–19,000 talents per year was probably achieved at the end of the reign of Seleukos I and an even higher one just before Magnesia, perhaps approaching 15,000–20,000 talents. While it may appear surprising that the Seleukid empire could have been more wealthy in the reign of Antiochos III than at the time of its founder, this can be explained by two factors: the addition of prosperous Koile Syria to the realm and the increase in population in northern Syria, as the new city foundations developed to their full capacity, both regions being considerably more monetized than the lost Upper Satrapies. As a comment, the loss of Asia Minor may have been equivalent in terms of population to the loss of Baktria and the East, but was probably considerably more important in terms of silver revenue.

3. PRODUCTION

a. Agricultural production

Agricultural production has been considered the most important economic activity – stressed also by ps.-Aristotle (ch. 7.1e) – and one must attempt to relate it to population and royal revenue.

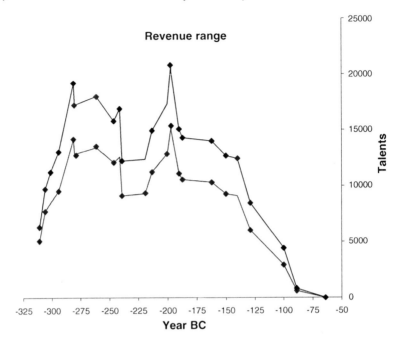

Figure 12.1 Estimated annual revenue of the Seleukid kings

Mesopotamia will be considered as an example, because it has the advantage of being an essentially 'closed' system from the point of view of agriculture, that is, it is difficult to envisage the transport of bulk agricultural commodities across its borders. To the east lay the Zagros range, to the north the Anti-Tauros and mountains of Armenia, to the west and south the Syrian and Arabian deserts and the Persian Gulf, and it was only in the north-western corner that a corridor of cultivated land extended from the Euphrates to the Mediterranean. Even assuming that grain could easily have been transported up or down the Euphrates, the seven-day overland trip to the Mediterranean would have been expensive (ch. 5.5b–c). It is clear that Mesopotamia in this period is not likely to have been either an exporter or an importer of bulk agricultural commodities, except in special circumstances, such as supplying provisions for a military campaign in Syria or Asia Minor.

What one can say about agricultural production, then, is that it must have been at least adequate to feed the Mesopotamian population, or about 20–25 per cent more, since an allowance must be made for seed set aside for the next year's sowing and for some loss during transportation to city granaries and while held there in storage.[6] Naturally one would expect a fixed running surplus to be kept in store to guard against a poor harvest, perhaps even a supply of a year or more, but average annual production must have about matched the needs of consumption over the long term.

b. Consumption

The usual way of estimating food consumption in a region is to define first the average person's energy requirements, then the diet that would satisfy these and finally multiply by the total population. Since the precise diet in antiquity is, of course, unknown, one may, with caution, use that of a population of more recent times whose living conditions were similar. In the case of Seleukid Mesopotamia, a useful comparison may be made with modern Iraq of 1960, where a detailed study of agriculture in the Hilla-Diwaniya area between the Euphrates and the Tigris (roughly in the region of ancient Nippur) included dietary habits and food intake of a sample of 195 farmer families, comprising a total of 1,197 persons, or 6.2 persons per family. The average energy consumption per person was 1,906 Calories per day, satisfied as follows: cereals 40.8%, dates 25.6% and other foodstuffs 33.6%.[7]

In ancient Mesopotamia, as also in modern Iraq, dates were the alternative staple to barley, as the *Astronomical Diaries* show (ch. 5.6a). Indeed, the prices recorded there indicate that, whereas barley and date prices fluctuated considerably, the difference between the two at any time was much less. This corresponds well with a market mechanism, whereby demand shifted from one product to the other when the first had become too expensive.[8] Given the different timing of the harvests (spring for barley, autumn for dates), barley shortages in winter, for example, could be covered from the new date crop. Both commodities have a similar energy content, but barley is much richer in protein, which makes it the preferred staple in any diet with a low meat intake, as the ancient Mesopotamian was (dates: 2,980 Calories per kilogram, 1.2% protein content; barley: 3,300 Calories per kilogram, 10% protein content,[9] although the *effective* figure per kilogram of unhulled barley is 20–25 per cent less because the hull and rachis have to

---

[6] From accounts of Old Babylonian Larsa, showing grain carried to the city from the surrounding district, Breckwoldt works out a 5 per cent maximum loss during transportation (1995/6: 78), while Adamson estimates that a 10 per cent loss of grain in storage is a probably conservative figure for the ancient Near East (1985: 7). Seed set aside for the following year's sowing amounts to a further 10 per cent roughly, or somewhat less when grain yields exceed ten to one, as has been argued for irrigation farming in chapter 5.1a.

[7] Poyck 1962: 66–9.   [8] Vargyas 1997: 340.   [9] Poyck 1962: 67, Table 4.21.

be removed before milling). Cereals and dates together provided 66.4% of
the daily energy intake of the Iraqi villager in 1960, 51.0% of the protein,
14.3% of the fat and 78.3% of the carbohydrates. With regard to the other
items in the diet, sugar made a rather high contribution (11.8% energy,
15.3% carbohydrates), which is probably particular to the modern era and
the Arab habit of drinking much sweetened tea. With this consideration,
the contribution of cereals and dates to the Mesopotamian diet in antiquity
is likely to have been higher and similar to that in the Graeco-Roman diet,
probably 70–75 per cent in terms of the energy requirement.[10]

Furthermore, the base prices of barley and dates, as recorded in the
Astronomical Diaries, were both about 120 litres for a shekel up to *c.* 208 BC,
after which the base price of dates dropped to roughly half its former level
(ch. 5.6a). For comparison, in Iraq of 1960, barley cost about 10 *fils* per kilo
versus 4 *fils* per kilo for dates.[11]

Taking calorie content and price into consideration, it is not unreasonable to consider dates the rough equivalent of barley, or slightly less. For
the calculation that follows, dates will be equated with barley.

The study of Iraq in 1960 showed that the average energy content of an
individual's daily diet was 1,906 Calories per day.[12] The total consumption
of the average family of 6.2 persons was thus 11,817 Calories per day, which
was compared to the minimum requirement of 13,300 Calories per day for
this family, using the Food and Agriculture Organization standard based
on an adult man of 60 kilos living in a subtropical climate. Figures for the
Graeco-Roman world tend to be somewhat higher, as one might expect
because of the colder climate.[13] I will work with a figure of 1,900 Calories
per day for the average person in Seleukid Mesopotamia.

It is difficult to know what form the barley took that was sold in the
Babylonian market. If it contained hulls and rachis, as is likely, 20–25 per
cent of the weight could be lost in the milling process. Since barley has
a calorific content of about 3,300 Calories per kilogram, this would leave
about 2,475–2,620 Calories after milling. Assuming that barley (substitut-
ing also for its near-equivalent, dates) satisfied 70–75 per cent of a person's

[10] Also Foxhall and Forbes 1982: 74; Gallant 1991: 68; Reger 1994: 87; Garnsey 1998: 230; Spek 1998a: 248.
[11] Poyck 1962: 67, table 4.21.
[12] This fits reasonably well with the minimum energy requirement noted by Clark and Haswell for the average person, which ranges from 1,625 Calories per day for the smallest-bodied people in the warmest climates, with men averaging only four hours of work per day, to 2,011 Calories per day for larger-bodied people in colder climates, with men working eight hours per day (1970: 58).
[13] Using the FAO guidelines, Foxhall and Forbes have derived a figure of 15,495 Calories per day for the average six-person family in the Greek world in the 'very active' category. If this is downgraded to 'moderately active', the corresponding figure becomes 13,243 Calories per day (1982: 49).

energy requirements – 1,330–1,425 Calories per day – 508–576 grams of unmilled barley would be required per day or 185–210 kilograms per year for the average person. The weight of a litre of un-hulled barley varies somewhat, but is usually taken at around 620 grams. Thus the average Mesopotamian would require 298–339 litres per year of barley, if it supplied 70–75 per cent of his daily energy requirement.

The problem, of course, is with the other ingredients of the daily diet and what their barley-equivalent might be. If one were to consider calorie content only, then the extra 25–30 per cent that the other ingredients provided would raise the total barley-equivalent of all foodstuffs to 397–484 litres per year for the average person. However, it is more correct to calculate a barley-equivalent based on price, since many of these other ingredients were probably more expensive than barley. While the ancient Mesopotamian diet was possibly quite similar to that of an Iraqi in 1960, which included chicken, meat, fish, eggs, animal fat, milk, yoghurt, legumes, fresh vegetables, fruit, and suchlike, the prices of these commodities are not known in the Seleukid period.

In order to solve this type of problem, the concept of a wheat-equivalent has been derived to cover all the other ingredients in the diet of a peasant society, by estimating their relative values compared to wheat.[14] Clearly there is the assumption that neither the diet nor the relative prices vary dramatically across such societies. In the case of an average daily energy requirement of 1,900 Calories, as I have been using, the wheat-equivalent would be as high as 277 kilograms per person per year.[15] To convert this to barley, the starting point is to recognize that barley and wheat flour have the same calorific content, roughly 3,300 Calories per kilogram. However, before the barley can be milled, husks and rachis, making up 20–25 per cent of its weight, must be removed. In terms of volume, wheat weighs around 775 grams per litre and barley only about 620 grams per litre, which makes the latter roughly 20 per cent lighter. Thus the energy content of a litre of unhulled barley is only about 60–64 per cent of that of a litre of wheat. Since the wheat-equivalent, converted into litres, is 357 litres per person per year, the barley-equivalent consumed per year by the average Mesopotamian person, using this method, should be 558–595 litres

---

[14] Clark and Haswell 1970: 57–83.

[15] Clark and Haswell give 230 kilograms and 275 kilograms of wheat-equivalent per person per year for a 1,625 and a 2,011 Calorie daily requirement respectively. These figures are increased to 245 and 290 kilograms respectively when textile fibres are included in the diet (1970: 83). By interpolation, a 1,900 Calorie daily requirement should require 262 kilograms of wheat-equivalent per person per year or 277 kilograms if textile fibres are included.

per person per year, or, rounding the numbers, 550–600 litres per person per year.[16]

One may check these figures. Earlier it was calculated that a diet supplying 70–75 per cent of the daily energy requirement with barley (and its near-equivalent, dates) would require 298–339 litres per person per year. If the remaining 25–30 per cent had been supplied solely by barley, this would have necessitated a further 113–136 litres. In terms of barley-equivalent, however, using the figures derived above and subtracting actual barley from total barley-equivalent, the other ingredients in the diet provide 219–297 barley-equivalent litres per person per year, which is roughly twice the amount of barley only that could have theoretically made up the remainder of the diet. Since the wheat- (or barley-)equivalent method is based on relative prices of the ingredients of the diet, what these figures seem to show is that the other ingredients cost roughly twice as much as the barley that could have satisfied the same energy requirement, which does not appear unreasonable.

There is yet another check. In the *Persepolis Fortification Texts* the regular barley ration of the normal male worker is 30 litres per month, or 360 litres per year, and of the normal female worker 20 or 30 litres per month, or 240 or 360 litres per year. Children receive less, on a scale determined by age.[17] These figures correspond reasonably well with the range of 298–339 litres of barley consumption per year computed earlier for the average person. The workers also received extra rations in other commodities from time to time, but it has been argued that this was a bare subsistence diet with a high mortality level for men. However, certain favoured workers, both male and female, were provided with as much as 50 litres per month or 600 litres per year. This rather high figure happens to match quite well a barley-equivalent of 550–600 litres per year for a total diet, the idea being, presumably, that the favoured worker could exchange some of his surplus barley for other, more expensive commodities.

It is, finally, no coincidence that administrative documents of the Neo-Babylonian period often record barley rations issued to workers at the rate of 1.5 litres per day or 548 litres per year.[18]

What is the significance of the barley-equivalent figure per person? When multiplied by population, it gives us an idea of what the average total annual agricultural production of Mesopotamia may have been. If a value could

---

[16] I owe the idea of Clark and Haswell's wheat-equivalent and its conversion to a barley-equivalent to Spek, who comes up with a range of 571–608 litres of barley per person per year for the conditions of Parthian Mesopotamia (1998a: 247–52).

[17] Aperghis 2000: 131–5, 140–1.   [18] Joannès 1997: 321.

be assigned to this, one would have an estimate of the economic base from which rent and tax were extracted by the administration.

c. Price

As discussed in chapter 5.6a, the *Babylonian Astronomical Diaries* record accurate commodity prices in the market of Babylon throughout the Seleukid period. The base price of barley works out at 120 litres for 1 shekel, or 60 litres for 1 drachm, subject to fluctuations because of good or bad harvests and the time of the year in relation to the harvest, but occasionally influenced by disturbances in or near Babylon.

The question is, of course, whether prices in the city of Babylon were representative of those in Mesopotamia generally. Certainly in southern Mesopotamia, Babylonia, where the bulk of the population was located (ch. 4.1), one would expect that river transport along the Euphrates and Tigris and the dense network of canals could move goods cheaply from areas of temporary surplus to those of temporary shortage and so probably even out price differentials.

d. The value of agricultural production

With a base price of 60 litres of barley for a drachm (above), the average inhabitant of Mesopotamia's consumption of 550–600 litres of barley-equivalent per year of foodstuffs would have been worth 9–10 drachms. This, increased by the seed set aside and the transportation and storage losses (about 25 per cent), would have made the value of the average agricultural production per inhabitant of Mesopotamia equal to 11–12.5 drachms, since self-sufficiency was the likely condition. With a population of four to five million, the total value of agricultural production in Mesopotamia works out at 7,500–10,500 talents annually.

e. Taxation of agricultural production

As noted earlier, at about 1.25 talents per thousand of population, the total annual revenue of the king and his administration from Mesopotamia was likely to have been about 5,000–6,000 talents. This, it will be recalled (ch. 8.1–6), included rent and taxation of various kinds, but also proceeds from royal land and the natural resources the king controlled, principally irrigation water.

One may now consider what the royal revenue may have been specifically from agricultural production. If the land was directly administered on the king's behalf, he obviously received the full revenue it could generate. If it was leased to tenants, he could expect perhaps 50 per cent of the crop as rent, as the text from the Šamaš temple showed (ch. 8.1f). But even if the land was owned by a temple or an individual, taxation and water rights probably represented a substantial proportion of the harvest, possibly as much as a third (ch. 8.2d). The overall impression is that the king's income from agriculture in Mesopotamia must have been high, probably around 40 per cent of the value of total agricultural production, which was put earlier at 7,500–10,500 talents annually, and so the royal revenue may have amounted to 3,000–4,500 talents.

The figure derived above constitutes the lion's share of the 5,000–6,000 talents that was estimated earlier to be the total royal revenue from Mesopotamia and provides support for ps.-Aristotle's statement that revenue from land was by far the most important (ch. 7.1e). Incidentally, it also shows that Herodotos' report about the satrap of Babylonia and his sack of silver may be a 'story' with some basis of fact.

f. Other productive activities

It was suggested in chapter 5.5b–c that, in relative terms, longer-distance trade was not as significant in the Near East as in the Mediterranean world. Ps.-Aristotle seems to have known this well enough, if he based his treatise on the Seleukid empire, as I have argued (ch. 7.3), and listed satrapal revenues in order of importance. The analysis of revenue from agriculture in Mesopotamia (above) also shows that perhaps not more than a quarter to a third of royal revenue may have been derived from other sources.

A similar picture can be obtained from inland Judaea, located well off important trade routes, where the high priest Jason had offered 360 talents for the tribute of Judaea and only 80 talents for 'the other taxes' (ch. 8.7c). It is tempting to see this as a distinction between the revenue that could be earned from land and that from taxes and tolls on people, animals, trade and industry.

Along the Mediterranean coast, the picture was undoubtedly somewhat different and intra- and inter-regional trade probably played a much more prominent role in both economic life and Seleukid taxation receipts, perhaps more so than land in some cases, as the many tribute concessions and low rates of taxation of agricultural produce of the Greek cities of Asia Minor (ch. 8.1h) seem to indicate.

4. ROYAL EXPENDITURE AND SURPLUS

The next element in the model to consider is expenditure. In chapter 10 an attempt was made to estimate the major expenses of the Seleukid kings. It might be useful to consider three points in time: just before Antiochos III's Anabasis (212 BC), just before Magnesia (190 BC) and at the end of the reign of Antiochos IV (164 BC).

From the revenue graph presented above (figure 12.1), the best estimate for Antiochos' revenue *c.* 212 BC is about 11,000–15,000 talents annually. In chapter 10.1h the cost of Antiochos' 'peacetime' armed forces was calculated at about 7,000–8,000 talents. The cost of the Seleukid administration at the empire's peaks in 281 BC and 190 BC was estimated at 2,000–3,000 talents, but the point in time being considered (212 BC) is before the full conquest of western and southern Asia Minor and Koile Syria and so the figure was probably less then, while the expenses of the king and his court amounted to perhaps as much again. So a small annual surplus probably existed. However, once the Anabasis was under way, 'wartime' expenditure would quickly have done away with this and eaten into the royal treasury's reserves. The 'conquest' of the East did not significantly improve the king's revenue in silver terms and it was only when Koile Syria and, more importantly, Asia Minor were acquired that revenue may have increased briefly to as much as 15,000–20,000 talents annually (fig. 12.1). But the cost of the 'wartime' army and navy were now much higher and administrative expenses had also increased because of the new acquisitions. I suspect that Antiochos must have been about breaking even at this point, as he seems to have been able to sustain high levels of military expenditure year after year until Magnesia (190 BC).

Then occurred the very important loss of Asia Minor and total revenue probably plummeted to around 11,000–15,000 talents (figure 12.1). Reduced revenue may have been matched by a temporary decrease in size and cost of the 'peacetime' army under Seleukos IV, but these were up again to nearly former levels under Antiochos IV (ch. 10.1a). Nor is there any sign of a cutting down of expenditure of the king and his court (Polyb. 26.1; ch. 10.3), while any reduction in the cost of administering those Asia Minor provinces held at the time of the Anabasis and now lost was partly balanced by the corresponding new expenses of Koile Syria. So let us say that Antiochos IV's costs were roughly what Antiochos III's had been before the Anabasis. Under these conditions there was unlikely to have been much annual surplus and, if any, it was required to pay the Roman indemnity of 1,000 talents annually – incidentally, the Romans probably had a very good idea of what the Seleukid kings could afford and no more. The signs of cash-flow problems are there until the end of the reign of Antiochos IV, for example the resort to temple-raiding and the scheme to sell the population of Judaea in 165/4 BC in order to raise the last (delayed) 2,000 talents owed the Romans (ch. 8.8b).

The plunder that Antiochos IV took from Egypt and the Temple of Jerusalem in 169/8 BC was probably intended to help to pay for his eastern Anabasis, since insufficient funds may have been available in his treasuries at the time. Had this campaign succeeded, the finances of the empire would have been placed on a better footing, but this did not happen, because of the king's death. It soon became clear that a powerful army could be maintained no longer, hence, possibly, the episode in which Demetrios I disbanded his regulars without full pay, keeping only the mercenaries and thereby provoking discontent (Jos. *AJ* 13.129–130).

A downward spiral now set in for the Seleukid kings. Insufficient revenue to maintain an adequate army, because it was squandered for the purposes of internecine warfare, led to loss of territory, to even less revenue and more loss of territory until the final collapse.[19]

5. COINAGE

The last element in the model of the Seleukid economy is coinage.

In chapter 11.5 the idea of a 'peacetime' coinage was introduced, those issues necessary to top-up the currency in circulation because of natural wear and loss and maintain it at the level required by the administrative-payments–tax-collection cycle. It was calculated that the output of one obverse tetradrachm die per year could serve the 'peacetime' needs of one million inhabitants in Mesopotamia and slightly fewer in northern Syria, probably because of the latter's marginally greater degree of urbanization and consequent adoption of a monetary economy. What is true of northern Syria probably also applied to other Mediterranean coastal regions that were similarly structured, but in the Upper Satrapies the need for coinage was likely to have been considerably less, as evidenced by the relatively low 'peacetime' output of the Ekbatana mint under Seleukos IV, of perhaps half an obverse die per year per million inhabitants. Overall, one obverse die per year per million inhabitants seems a reasonable empire-wide average.

---

[19] Austin notes that whereas an increase of territory led to an increase in revenue, a decrease sent Hellenistic dynasties into a spiral decline (1986: 461). In my view, this is true for the Seleukid empire at a certain point in time (140 BC), coinciding with the loss of Mesopotamia.

At its peak, then, the Seleukid empire's fourteen to eighteen million inhabitants would have required the output of roughly fourteen to eighteen obverse tetradrachm dies per year. Since each die was likely to strike 30,000 coins worth 20 talents (ch. 1.6b), the total value of tetradrachms put into circulation annually at the time was probably of the order of 300–350 talents.

It was estimated (ch. 11.4c) that, in the reign of Antiochos III, the Seleukid tetradrachms issued annually represented about 0.6 per cent of the total value of large-silver coinage in circulation in Mesopotamia and the Upper Satrapies and somewhat over 1 per cent in northern Syria, Kilikia and Asia Minor. An average rate of about 1 per cent appears reasonable.

Thus, if the 300–350 talents minted annually actually represented 1 per cent of the total value in circulation, the total value of tetradrachms circulating in the Seleukid empire may have been around 30,000–35,000 talents. Tetradrachms are considered to have accounted for about three-quarters of the value of all Seleukid coinage issues (ch. 11.2) and there is no reason to suppose that the figure would be significantly different for the total of all coinages circulating in the Seleukid empire, bearing in mind that the Seleukid tetradrachms essentially fulfilled a 'topping-up' function, as has already been argued. Consequently, the total value of coinage circulating within the empire at the time of Antiochos III may have been of the order of 40,000–45,000 talents. This does not appear to be an unreasonable figure for the Seleukid share of all Greek coinage at the time, when one considers what the starting point may have been: the 180,000 talents or more of the Persian booty captured by Alexander (Strabo 15.3.9), which was soon coined, plus whatever already circulated in the Aegean world at the time, giving a total of the order of 200,000 talents. Certainly, wear would have taken its toll on this mass, but new mining production may well have been able to make up the losses.

Earlier it was shown that the administration's annual revenue rate at the time of Antiochos III probably peaked at 15,000–20,000 talents, which would have been a very significant part of the total value of coinage that circulated in the empire (40,000–45,000 talents), perhaps as much as a half, and even more if tetradrachms only (30.000–35.000 talents) are considered. In other words, most tetradrachms found their way rather often into a Seleukid treasury. This lends support to the idea that coinage in the Seleukid empire was intended primarily for administrative payments and tax collection, that is, to serve the royal economy, rather than to facilitate private transactions.

6. CONCLUSIONS ON THE MODEL

The rather crude model that has been presented of the Seleukid economy makes use of estimates that have been derived from a set of separate analyses in this and preceding chapters. All its interrelated parts seem to fit together reasonably well, which could only be the case if the magnitudes of the different parameters and the nature of their interrelationships were roughly correct. What this means, I suggest, is that the various ideas and hypotheses and analyses, from which I have derived my picture of the Seleukid economy, are not unduly off the mark.

CHAPTER 13

Financial administration

In previous chapters a case was made for a Seleukid royal economy whose different elements – the foundation and support of cities, the policy concerning royal land and its produce, the system of tribute and taxation, and the manner in which coinage was used – were planned in such a way so as to ensure for the kings an increase in their revenue, primarily that in silver. What was required was an efficient system to collect this revenue.

In this chapter the rather limited evidence is examined in an attempt to produce an outline and assessment of the Seleukid system of financial administration.

To begin with, it will be necessary to review what one knows of the Achaemenid system and any changes introduced by Alexander. Administrative practices throughout history have been relatively insensitive to political change, as new masters are reluctant to replace something that works well, as long as they continue to benefit, just as their predecessors did before them. In principle, therefore, one would expect some continuity from the Achaemenids to the Seleukids (and, indeed, the Ptolemies), since the underlying problems of empire remained essentially the same and the method of administration had proved itself over two centuries. While this is likely to be true, it has been more of an assumption than a proven fact.

Fortunately one can make use of a so far underutilized source, the *Persepolis Fortification Texts* (ch. 1.4b), which provide many details of Achaemenid administration. It is interesting how much clearer some Hellenistic epigraphic data become when tested against the Achaemenid material, suggesting that the assumption of a degree of administrative continuity between the Achaemenid and Seleukid empires is correct.

One might also expect some aspects of the Macedonian kingdoms of Philip II and Alexander to be reflected in the Seleukid empire. In the early period this may well have been so. The influence of Macedonian soldiers in assembly in electing a king was certainly felt by Seleukos I and, probably, Antiochos I after the assassination of his father, but this soon weakened as

the ethnic nature of the army became diluted (ch. 10.1a). What remained
after a time was probably only lip-service to the concept of shared rule
between the king and his Macedonians, whereby the latter endowed the
king with absolute authority, but he included in his decisions the authority
of his 'Friends' and military forces. With regard to financial administration,
it is not clear what, if anything, was inherited by the Seleukids that was
originally Macedonian and not an aspect of the Persian system taken over
by Macedonian kings.[1]

1. ACHAEMENID PRACTICE

The *Persepolis Fortification Texts* (*PFT*) were discussed in chapter 9.1a in
connection with the handling of the surplus from taxation. It was suggested
that they provided evidence of the workings of a satrapal economy in the
Persian homeland – later to become the Hellenistic satrapy of Persis –
and so perhaps typical of how actual satrapies were administered. Parallel
to the satrapal economy could be distinguished traces of a royal economy,
siphoning off commodity surpluses for the king's own use, but occasionally
returning them when there was need.

The key to the workings of this satrapal economy in Persis was the more
than one hundred storehouses at which commodity taxation was collected
and from which rations were issued for the maintenance of the Achaemenid
king, members of the royal family, officials, workers and animals. The
storehouses came under the orders of the chief administrator of Persepolis,
Parnaka, and his deputy, Zissawis, in the period of the *PFT* (509–494 BC)
and an analysis of the texts indicates that there were three main departments
involved.[2]

The first department collected the commodity tax and managed the
storehouses, which were geographically grouped into districts under district
officers, while the districts themselves belonged to regions under regional
officers. Districts and regions tended to follow the major roads spreading
out from Persepolis.[3] Within the storehouse organization there seem to have
been two sections, the first looking after the commodity stocks, the second
seeing to their collection as tax. In the first section, storekeepers, sometimes referred to as 'grain-handlers' or 'wine-carriers', handled day-to-day

[1] See Hatzopoulos 1996 for a survey of Macedonian institutions under the kings. Hammond 2000
considers each successor state a Macedonian one, but is not convincing.
[2] Aperghis 1998; 1999. See also Tuplin 1987a and Briant 1996: 369–487 for the administration of the
Persian empire in general.
[3] Aperghis 1996.

storehouse operations under the district officer. In the second, commodity tax was brought in by tax-collectors, whom the texts refer to as 'deliverers', while a 'delivery man' (*ullira*) is noted, who may have been the tax-inspector or tax-estimator for the district. In the accounts of most storehouses, two officials are usually recorded as representing the storehouse, the district officer (or sometimes the storekeeper) and the 'delivery man', suggesting that the latter was not the subordinate of the former, but perhaps of the regional officer above him. The third official who is normally present in the account is the 'apportioner', on whose behalf the particular stock was being maintained.

The second department of the financial administration consisted of these 'apportioners', who managed the work-groups and animals and determined the ration entitlement of each junior official, worker and animal. Here too a three-level hierarchy seems to have been in place, using military titles: decurion apportioners reporting to centurions, with a handful of 'chiefs of workers' at the top. Between the two departments of the administration there appears to have been a regular interchange of personnel, a kind of sidestepping advancement up the ladder of promotion, from decurion to centurion and then, presumably, chiliarch, given that this was the system of command we know of in the Persian army.

The procedure for the receipt or issuing of commodities was a rather clever one. Senior apportioners maintained commodity accounts at many storehouses in anticipation of the rationing needs of the workers they controlled in the district, or who were likely to be transferred to it, perhaps in order to collect the grain or sesame harvest. Thus a storehouse's stock might be divided up into several such accounts. For most transactions, two seals were applied to the tablets recording them, one representing the storehouse, which physically controlled the commodity, the other the apportioner, who determined who was entitled to receive what. In this way, each department acted as a check upon the other. Only in the case of very senior apportioners, or other high officials, would one seal, their own, be sufficient for a commodity to be issued without the need of a storehouse's 'counter-signature'.

Finally, a third department of the financial administration collected the commodity surpluses and the products of exchange from the storehouses (ch. 9.1), along with the transaction tablets recording these, and brought them to Persepolis, where the storehouse accounts were prepared. In the texts one can recognize senior accountants, who wielded personal seals and 'signed' the storehouse accounts, and more junior officials who were sent to the storehouses for collections.

One thing immediately becomes clear from a study of the texts, which will be very relevant for Hellenistic practice: that the chief administrator of Persepolis not only supervised the workings of the satrapal storehouses, but also had the authority to requisition commodity stocks from the royal storehouses when he needed them. In other words, he acted as the king's representative not only in the satrapal economy, but in the royal economy too.

The satrap in the Achaemenid organization was responsible for financial administration in his satrapy, so the chief administrator in the *Fortification Texts*, Parnaka, should be the equivalent of a provincial satrap. This becomes clear also from the travel authorizations he was entitled to make, something that in travel-ration texts was reserved for the king, provincial satraps and, apparently, their deputies only. The deputy, Ziššawiš, attested in the *PFT* for the 'satrap', Parnaka, had very wide powers in managing the storehouses and apportioners and in issuing travel authorizations, matching those of the 'satrap' himself, and it is possible that he was the official actually responsible for financial administration on a daily basis.

2. THE CHANGE WITH ALEXANDER

Alexander introduced a major change in the workings of the empire. Because he apparently sought to give Persian nobles a share in government, he appointed several in command of satrapies. At the same time, however, he may have been concerned that his foreign satraps might wield too much power, so the financial administration of at least some satrapies was placed under Greeks, who reported directly to the king.

The situation is not clear-cut, as the sources identify some satrapies with their own chief financial administrator and others grouped together in what may have been larger financial jurisdictions. In many satrapies, no financial officers can be identified, particularly in those in the East.[4]

Firmly attested, as chief financial administrators of satrapies, are Nikias in Lydia in 334 BC (Arr. *Anab.* 1.17.1, 7) and Asklepiodoros in Babylonia in 331 BC (Arr. *Anab.* 3.16.4). In the same year, Kleomenes was made responsible

---

[4] The matter is discussed at length by Griffith 1964, who describes the curtailing of the financial powers of the satrap as 'an experiment in government' that did not survive Alexander's death. For the eastern satrapies he argues that no royal financial administrators were appointed, because it appeared more politic to Alexander, as part of his policy of *rapprochement* with the Persians, to leave the Iranian peoples in this area, and their taxation, to Iranian satraps as before. So, according to him, there is really no evidence one way or the other for the eastern satrapies. However, in my opinion, if Alexander's purpose was to curtail the power of the satraps, there is no reason why he should have excluded some, particularly those as far out of his reach as Baktria or India. See also Badian 1965.

for the revenues of all four *nomoi* into which the satrapy of Egypt had been divided (Arr. *Anab.* 3.5.2). At some point, Ophellas the Olynthian is noted as appointing a financial officer for an Egyptian *nomos* (ps.-Arist. *Oik.* 2.2.35) and, presumably, this could be done by the chief financial officer of the satrapy. A Krateuas is noted in Lydia – when Menandros was satrap there between 330 and 323 BC – authorizing a land grant (*Syll.³* 302) and it has been plausibly suggested that he was the chief financial officer of the satrapy, perhaps succeeding Nikias.[5]

Other situations involving financial administrators do not unequivocally point to single satrapies. In 331 BC Koiranos was authorized to collect the revenues of Phoenicia, and Philoxenos those of Asia Minor west of the Tauros (Arr. *Anab.* 3.6.4, 16.9), but these may have been short-term assignments, perhaps just to gather the contributions of the cities in these areas.[6] Harpalos is noted as being in charge of the central treasury in Ekbatana to begin with and then Babylon (Arr. *Anab.* 3.6.6, 19.7; Diod. 17.108.4), but this is unlikely to have involved financial administration of a satrapy.[7] This particular function may have been exercised later by Antimenes in Babylonia, although this official appears to have possessed authority in certain financial matters that extended beyond the borders of his satrapy.[8] But Babylon, no doubt, occupied a special position as a capital of Alexander's empire. Finally the appointment of Menes as *hyparchos* of Syria, Phoenicia and Kilikia is noted (Arr. *Anab.* 3.16.9–10) and it has been suggested that this was a financial appointment.[9]

Alexander also left in place the Achaemenid system whereby the king appointed and controlled the commanders of the garrisons in the satrapies. This had always been good policy, as it served to balance the military power of the satraps, but the new measure restricted their financial power as well.

Thus, at Alexander's death a tripartite system may have been in place in most, if not all, satrapies: a civil governor with some military capability, a financial administrator and one or more garrison commanders. That this is likely to have been so can be seen from the case of Eumenes (below).

3. THE PERIOD OF THE SUCCESSORS

Alexander's tripartite system did not survive him long. In the scramble for power amongst his generals, it was natural for these to attempt to control

---

[5] Griffith 1964: 30; Berve 1988: no. 447.   [6] Badian 1965: 168.
[7] Badian 1965: 172.   [8] Ps.-Arist. *Oik.* 2.2.34, 38; Andreades 1929.
[9] Griffith 1964: 24. Andreades suggests four large financial groupings of satrapies, adding three more: (1) Egypt with Arabia, (2) Asia Minor and (3) Mesopotamia with Susiane, Persis and Media (1929: 6).

the finances of their respective satrapies in order to make these serve their political aims, when there was no central power strong enough to check them. A number of examples point in this direction.

Plutarch reports (*Eum.* 3.6) that, when Eumenes took over his satrapy of Kappadokia soon after the settlement at Babylon, following Alexander's death 'he placed the cities under the authority of his friends and installed garrison commanders and set in place those judges and *dioikētai* that he desired, as Perdikkas did not involve himself at all in these matters' (τὰς μὲν πόλεις τοῖς ἑαυτοῦ φίλοις παρέδωκε, καὶ φρουράρχους ἐγκατέστησε καὶ δικαστὰς ἀπέλιπε καὶ διοικητὰς οὓς ἐβούλετο, τοῦ Περδίκκου μηδὲ ἐν τούτοις πολυπραγμονοῦντος).

There are three groups of officials involved, if one excludes the judges: the friends administering the cities, who represent the civil administration, the *dioikētai* for the financial administration (section 5 below) and the garrison commanders.

Kappadokia was newly conquered then and it was, presumably, to be administered exactly like other satrapies in Alexander's empire. The μέν in the text seems to distinguish the city appointments from the rest, which are then linked to the mention of Perdikkas and the fact that he did not involve himself in this selection, suggesting that he would have been expected to do so.[10] If one accepts that the appointment of garrison commanders and financial administrators in satrapies, and their direct control, had been Alexander's prerogative, Perdikkas would simply have been following in his footsteps as his *de facto* successor. In other words, the satrap was not expected to appoint or control the garrison commanders or financial officials of his satrapy, but Kappadokia became an exception, since Perdikkas had other worries at that moment and could apparently count upon the loyalty of Eumenes, as subsequent events showed.

With Alexander's death and that of Perdikkas, there was no longer any central authority strong enough to impose this system and the Successors soon concentrated all the powers of their respective satrapies in their own persons.[11] Seleukos himself, as satrap of Babylonia, was required by Antigonos Monophthalmos to present his accounts (Diod. 19.55.3), but, if Antigonos, acting as the representative of the kings, controlled the financial administration of the satrapy, he would presumably not have needed to make such a demand.

Nevertheless, the system of separate financial administration in the provinces directly under the central authority had been tested and was awaiting the right conditions to reappear in the Seleukid empire, as the

---

[10] Also Griffith 1964: 28–9.   [11] Corsaro 1980: 1173–84.

new monarchy consolidated and the centrifugal tendencies after the death of Alexander became centripetal.[12]

4. SELEUKID FINANCIAL ADMINISTRATORS

A number of officials who were connected with financial administration appear in Seleukid documentary sources, for example διοικητής (*dioikētēs*), οἰκονόμος (*oikonomos*), ὁ ἐπὶ τῶν προσόδων (*ho epi tōn prosodōn*), ὁ οἰκονομῶν τὰ τοῦ ... (*ho oikonomōn ta tou* ...), ἐκλογιστής (*eklogistēs*), λογευτής (*logeutēs*), and it will be necessary to examine the function of each separately, in the context of the relevant texts, so as to build up a picture of the Seleukid system of financial administration.

There are significant differences in how various scholars have viewed these officials, as will become apparent when each is discussed in turn. This is, of course, reflected in quite different views of the administrative organization of the Seleukid empire.

Some of the officials are also known from the Ptolemaic kingdom and it would be interesting to know whether their functions there were similar.[13] Certainly this would not be unexpected, since both Seleukids and Ptolemies undoubtedly inherited some elements of administrative practice from the Achaemenids. Perhaps the major difference between the two might lie in the fact that, whereas Egypt had been only a single satrapy in the Achaemenid empire, the Seleukid empire represented a collection of several satrapies.

5. THE *DIOIKĒTĒS*, THE *OIKONOMOS* AND THE *EPI TŌN PROSODŌN*

a. The Ptolemaios dossier (Document 4)

Dating to the 190s BC, the Ptolemaios or Skythopolis dossier comes from Palestine just after it had been taken by the Seleukids from the Ptolemies.

---

[12] Corsaro 1980: 1184.

[13] It is not possible in this book to present details of Ptolemaic financial administration and compare them with what will be derived for the Seleukid empire. There is too much that is unclear, and a comprehensive study is certainly required by someone more knowledgeable in this area than myself. Préaux 1939 is still useful for the Egyptian royal economy overall, but does not deal at much length with the roles of the officials involved. Peremans 1978 provides a long list of titles used in the civil and financial administration, many of which are to be found in the Seleukid system as well, but there is no analysis of functions, hierarchy or administrative procedure. At the level of a village, the Tebtunis papyri give an interesting picture of the workings of the Ptolemaic economy (for example, D. J. Crawford 1971 and Verhoogt 1998), but there is no Seleukid source detailed enough so as to be able to draw comparisons. This applies also to the Zenon papyri (for example, Orrieux 1983). For the overall picture of the Ptolemaic administration and economy, Rupprecht 1994 provides a useful summary and references.

Antiochos III wrote to a number of officials ordering them to carry out
certain personal requests made to him by his governor of the newly conquered satrapy of 'Syria and Phoenicia', Ptolemaios. Ptolemaios' concerns,
as I read them in the inscription, were to regulate matters of judicial jurisdiction and to obtain *anepistathmeia*, freedom from billeting of troops, for
certain villages which had belonged to him before and others given him by
Antiochos more recently.

In the first memorandum (text D, lines 12–14), Ptolemaios requested
'that his own officials be allowed to handle disputes arising amongst the
peasants (*laoi*) of his own villages' (ὅσα μ[ὲ]ν ἂν ἦι ἐν ταῖς κώμαις [μου
το]ῖς λαοῖς [πρὸς α]ὐτοὺς ἐ[ξ]ῆι διεξά[γεσθαι] ἐπὶ τῶν παρ᾽ἐμοῦ), while
'those involving the inhabitants of other villages should be dealt with by the
oikonomos and the official in charge of the *topos*' (ὅσα δ᾽ ἂν ἦι πρὸς τοὺ[ς
τῶν] ἄλλων κωμῶ[ν ὅ] τε οἰκονό[μος καὶ ὁ τοῦ τόπ]ου πρ[ο]εστηκὼς
ἐπι[σκο]πῶσιν).

In the case of homicide, or matters of greater importance, the satrap
(Ptolemaios himself) should be involved. Furthermore, 'the garrison commanders and the officials in charge of *topoi* should under no circumstances
withhold their assistance from those who asked for it' (τοὺς δὲ φρουράρχους [καὶ τοὺς ἐ]πὶ τῶν τόπων τεταγμένους μὴ περι[ιδεῖν] κατὰ μηθένα
τρόπον τοὺς παρα[καλοῦντας]).

Topos in the above context is likely to be an administrative district, in
which case *ho tou topou proestēkōs* is 'the official in charge of the district',
the civil district commander.[14] This official may well have been a toparch –
and we do have references to toparchies in Seleukid Judaea,[15] as well as to

---

[14] The precise meaning of *topos* here is the subject of disagreement. Bertrand considers that it refers to
Ptolemaios' estate and has no official administrative sense. Thus *ho tou topou proestēkōs* ('the person
in charge of the *topos*') would be Ptolemaios' own official, his *régisseur sur place* or bailiff (1982: 171).
But if so, why change the wording and not use *tōn par' emou* ('my own officials') as before? The
implication would also be that the *oikonomos* was capable of settling all matters, whether of a civil
or financial nature, which is not the picture we have of a Seleukid *oikonomos* (see below). True,
topos in some instances simply denotes a particular geographical location, a village for instance,
or the best place for displaying an official inscription, e.g. *en tois epiphanestatois topois* ('in the
most visible locations'). In this inscription, however, *tous epi tōn topōn tetagmenous* ('the officials in
charge of districts') would make no sense unless these were officials responsible for specific districts.
Furthermore, they were distinct from the *phrourarchoi* ('garrison commanders'), whose jurisdiction
may or may not have coincided with districts.

[15] In 1 Macc. 11.34–5 Demetrios II conceded to the Jewish high priest, Jonathan, the revenue of three
nomoi of Samaria which were to be added to that of Judaea. Josephus refers to the same agreement
and *tōn triōn toparchiōn Samareias* ('concerning the three toparchies of Samaria') (*AJ* 13.125) while
specifying their names as *nomoi* elsewhere (*AJ* 13.126), obviously reflecting the Ptolemaic terminology
of pre-Seleukid Palestine. It is clear that taxation was assessed at the level of a toparchy. See also
Bikerman 1938: 198.

regional commands, meridarchies,[16] into which the satrapy of 'Syria and Phoenicia' had been subdivided. There is no mention in Seleukid Palestine of the hyparchy, the basic administrative subdivision of a Seleukid satrapy attested elsewhere, but there is such a mention in Ptolemaic Palestine.[17] The Ptolemaic hyparchies may have been too large as administrative units, when compared with the small hyparchies of, say, Asia Minor (see below), and, furthermore, the new satrapy was made up of quite disparate regions. It may have made sense, therefore, to introduce the intermediate subdivision of the meridarchy and apply a different term to the smaller units to avoid confusion.

Note that the garrison commanders (*phrourarchoi*) are distinguished in Ptolemaios' request from the administrators of the districts (*hoi epi tōn topōn tetagmenoi*). One can see that the former were not under his orders as satrap, since why else would the king need to become involved? As for the latter, this could be a catch-all term for every other official in a district, civil and financial. Some, such as the civil district commander, would have reported to Ptolemaios anyway, while others might have been under the king's direct control, the *oikonomoi*, for instance (see below).

As will be noted in other inscriptions later, a pair of officials was frequently associated in implementing decisions of the Seleukid administration in the same geographical area, the one with greater responsibility for civil and military matters, the other more involved with financial ones.[18] Where the dividing line in responsibility was would not always be clear, so sometimes both officials needed to act together.

In his first memorandum Ptolemaios was apparently claiming exemption from administrative interference in his own villages, as long as it was an internal matter. This memorandum was forwarded by the king to two *dioikētai*, Kleon and Heliodoros, with orders that Ptolemaios' request be implemented (text B). The officials concerned received identical letters suggesting that each was in charge of financial matters in a region or province within the satrapy in which some of Ptolemaios' villages happened to be located, so probably in a meridarchy.[19] They were to issue instructions to

---

[16] *Meridarchai* ('officers in charge of meridarchies') in Jos. *AJ* 12.201 and 1 Macc. 10.65. Bikerman also considers that the satrapy of Koile Syria was subdivided into *merides*, and these into *toparchiai* (*nomoi*) (1988: 123). Mørkholm's view is the same and he suggests examples of *merides*: Samaria (including Judaea) and Idumaia (including Jamnia) (1966: 108–9).

[17] Bagnall 1976: 14, 18–19.   [18] Also Corsaro 1985: 93.

[19] Gauthier considers the *dioikētai* administrators of royal domains (1989: 44). Corsaro suggests that those mentioned here may have been from the central administration, but allows for the possibility of two *dioikētai* in a satrapy or its subdivisions (1980: 1195).

the relevant *oikonomoi*, while Ptolemaios would presumably inform his own subordinates, the *epi tōn topōn proestēkotes*, the toparchs.

Clearly there was not just one *topos* involved but more, since Ptolemaios possessed villages in two administrative regions (meridarchies), whose *dioikētai* were called upon to intervene. So reference to *the* 'official in charge of the *topos*' is probably to *each* relevant toparch. In the same context, reference to *the oikonomos* may be to *each oikonomos*, suggesting that there was one for each administrative district within a region headed by a *dioikētēs*. One notes that in Ptolemaic Palestine each hyparchy had its *oikonomos*.[20]

The second part of the dossier deals with the problem of freedom from billeting for his villages requested by Ptolemaios and granted by the king, who gave the orders to four officials, with a tenfold financial penalty for damages caused in Ptolemaios' villages if the orders were violated. Copies of each of the four letters went to four other officials, one of whom has the same name as Heliodoros, one of the two *dioikētai* mentioned previously.

There have been a number of suggestions as to the precise functions performed by these eight individuals.[21] My own view is that, since the problem concerned damage caused by troops who were not under Ptolemaios' control, otherwise he could have taken action himself, the first four must have been military commanders of troops and garrisons in four regions (meridarchies) of the satrapy, while the second four were the corresponding financial officers of these regions, the *dioikētai*. The first group bore primary responsibility to ensure that the king's orders were carried out by their men and the second would take care of any damages to Ptolemaios should this become necessary. The idea that the second group consisted of *oikonomoi* is unlikely. Why would the king have communicated with them directly and not with their superiors, the *dioikētai*, as he had done earlier? The question may, of course, be asked, why were four *dioikētai* involved with Ptolemaios' problems when his villages were apparently located in the regions of only two? Presumably this is because troops moved around and there is no reason why those heading for one garrison commander might not pass through one of Ptolemaios' villages and cause trouble. The king was probably taking no chances. It is relevant that one *dioikētēs* of the judicial memoranda, Heliodoros, is common to the billeting memoranda, while the other, Kleon, is not, but this is not a problem, as the dates are different and officials may change positions. Finally, Strabo refers to four

---

[20] *C. Ord. Ptol.* 22.1.5; Bagnall 1976: 18–19.
[21] Corsaro considers these lower-ranking officials (1980: 1195), while Sartre accepts that perhaps some may have been *dioikētai* (1989: 124).

'satrapies' into which Koile Syria was divided, which may well be a reference to earlier meridarchies (16.2.1).[22]

Here again there appears to be a dual organization, this time at the regional level: a military commander associated with a financial officer, the *dioikētēs*. One would have expected a civil administrator to be paired with the *dioikētēs*, but this was a newly conquered province and it is possible that a meridarch combined both civil and military functions and reported to the king. At the district level, their respective subordinates would have been the toparch and the *oikonomos*.

What is interesting in the Ptolemaios dossier is that the king communicated directly with the *dioikētai* of regions after he had been asked to do so by the governor of the satrapy. It leads to the conclusion that the satrap had no direct authority over the financial officials, *dioikētai* and *oikonomoi*, operating within his satrapy. It may be argued, however, that this system of financial administration was applicable only to this newly conquered Ptolemaic territory and not general throughout the Seleukid empire, but an examination of other sources will show whether this was indeed the case.

b. *The case of Eumenes*

The appointment by Eumenes of *dioikētai* in Kappadokia has already been discussed (section 3 above). It is possible that the use of the plural here by Plutarch is a mistake and that he is simply referring to the financial officials of the satrapy in general, irrespective of rank. However, an *archidioikētēs* is mentioned in Kappadokia of the second or first century BC.[23] This does not specifically apply to a province, but to the Kappadokian kingdom as a whole and it is possible that there may have been regional *dioikētai* in Kappadokia.

c. *The Boulagoras inscription (SEG 1.366)*

This text refers to the efforts of Boulagoras to secure from Antiochos II the return of confiscated lands on the mainland of Asia Minor opposite Samos (lines 15–18): 'and on these matters he carried letters from Antiochos to our city and to the garrison commander reporting to him in Anaia and to the *dioikētēs*, according to which those who had had their property confiscated came into possession of it' (καὶ περὶ τούτων ἐκόμισεν ἐπιστολὰς

---

[22] Le Rider notes the division of Koile Syria into two satrapies after 162 BC (1995: 392).
[23] L. Robert 1963: 474.

[π]αρ' Ἀντιόχου πρός τε τὴν πόλιν ἡμῶν καὶ πρὸς τὸν ἐν Ἀναίοις ὑπ'
αὐτὸ[ν] τεταγμένον φρούραρχον καὶ πρὸς τὸν διοικητήν, δι' ὧν οἱ τότε
ἀφαι[ρ]εθέντες ἐγκρατεῖς ἐγένοντο τῶν ἰδίων).

In command of the region of Anaia was the phrourarch, as military commander of a newly reconquered territory and, apparently, the *dioikētēs*, as
financial administrator. The king had been followed by Boulagoras from
Ephesos to Sardeis (lines 10–11). So when he wrote, the *dioikētēs* was obviously not at the capital of the Lydian satrapy, but Boulagoras caught up with
him somewhere in the region of Anaia, Ionia. Although not certain from
the wording of the text, this *dioikētēs* may have had regional jurisdiction
only in Ionia, or else satrapal over Lydia, and just happened to be visiting
the region.

d. The Laodike letter to Iasos (Document 6)

Here is the relevant portion of the letter sent by Laodike, the wife of Antiochos III, to the city of Iasos (lines 15–18): 'I have written to Strouthion
the *dioikētēs* to deliver to the representatives of the *dēmos* each year, for
ten years, 1,000 Attic *medimnoi* of wheat, carrying it along with him
to the city' (γεγράφεικα Στρουθίωνι τῶι διοικητῆι ἐφ' ἔτη δέκα κατ'
ἐνιαυτὸν πυρῶν χιλίους μεδίμνους Ἀττικοὺς εἰς τὴν πόλιν παρακομίζοντα παραδιδόναι τοῖς παρὰ τοῦ δήμου)·

Strouthion was instructed to personally deliver the wheat to the city,
presumably from nearby royal storehouses, suggesting that he was not likely
to have been stationed very far away, as the verb παρακομίζω is translated
in LSJ: 'to carry along with one, escort, convoy'. Either a satrapal or a
regional financial jurisdiction within a satrapy is possible for Strouthion.[24]

e. The Apollonia-Salbake decree (Document 7)

The hipparch in command of the soldiers based in the area of Apollonia
proved to be of great help to the city: 'when envoys were sent to Ktesikles
the . . . and Menandros the *dioikētēs* on matters concerning the interests
of the *dēmos*' (πρεσβευτῶν δὲ πεμφθέντων περὶ τῶν συμφερόντων τῶι
δήμωι πρός τε Κτησικλῆν τὸν [– c. 14 –] καὶ Μένανδρον τὸν διοικητήν).

How one assesses the level of jurisdiction of Menandros the *dioikētēs* is
really determined by the missing function of Ktesikles, which is confusing.

---

[24] Corsaro considers possible a *dioikētēs* here for Ionia, a subdivision of a satrapy (1980: 1192), but
Gauthier does not regard a *dioikētēs* as an official of the central administration (1989: 44).

That Ktesikles was then a military/civil administrator, appearing alongside a financial administrator, is likely and στρατηγὸν Καρίας ('general in command of Karia') would fit the *lacuna*.[25] Ktesikles also appears, however, in connection with the earlier grant of timber by Antiochos III to Sardeis already referred to (Document 9), concerning which the king wrote to both his governor-general, Zeuxis, and to Ktesikles. There Ktesikles' function is likely to have been financial, since royal property was involved and Zeuxis represented the civil/military authority. I suggest that both inscriptions hold to the norm of paired civil and financial authority and that Ktesikles simply changed jobs in the course of his career, from *dioikētēs* of Lydia *c.* 213 BC to *stratēgos* of Karia later. However, what both inscriptions imply is the position of *dioikētēs* at the satrapal level and not the regional one within a satrapy. The pattern of multiple *dioikētai* in the satrapy of Koile Syria cannot be seen to have held in Asia Minor, just as the regional meridarchy did not appear there either.

f. Other references to dioikētai

Direct communication of the king with a *dioikētēs* can be seen also in Antiochos III's letters to Nysa[26] and Herakleia-Latmos (Document 10), where the king was confirming financial assistance to the city promised by his governor-general of western Asia Minor, Zeuxis. But note that, although Zeuxis was so highly placed, it was still the king who sent instructions to the *dioikētēs* on these matters.

The pairing of financial and civil/military officials that has been observed in the inscriptions discussed above may also be found in the Amyzon decree honouring Menestratos, whose good deeds consisted of writing several times to Zeuxis, Nikomedes and Chionis, 'the official in charge of Alinda' (τὸν ἐπ' Ἀλίνδων τεταγμένον).[27]

The inscription deals with the return of confiscated property and the synoikism of the Artemision, both matters necessarily involving both a civil and a financial administrator. Chionis may have been the *epistatēs* ('supervisor') of the city, while Nikomedes is likely to have been a *dioikētēs* and was himself honoured later.[28]

---

[25] J. and L. Robert could not fix Ktesikles' position, but suggested *epi tōn prosodōn* ('official in charge of revenue'), which would also fit. All they could say was that Ktesikles resided in the same place as Menandros (1954: 292). Gauthier considered Ktesikles of high rank, but refused to speculate further, though noting J. and L. Robert's solution as possible (1989: 42).

[26] *RC* 43; Ma 1997; 1999: no. 43.   [27] Robert and Robert 1983: no. 15; Ma 1997; 1999: no. 10.

[28] Robert and Robert 1983: no. 16; Ma 1997; 1999: no. 11. See Bagnall for possible joint jurisdiction in Ptolemaic Karia also (1976: 93, 101–2).

In their petition to Antiochos IV concerning their sufferings as a result of the Maccabean revolt, the Samaritans asked the king to issue instructions to two officials, Apollonios and Nikanor (Jos. *AJ* 12.261). The first was the meridarch of the region of Samaria, while the second is associated with the financial calculation that captured Jews could bring in the 2,000 talents required by the royal treasury (2 Macc. 8.9) and may have been the *dioikētēs* of the meridarchy, a similar situation to that in the Ptolemaios texts (above).

g. The epi tōn prosodōn

It has been suggested that the official entitled *epi tōn prosodōn* ('in charge of revenue') was the chief financial officer of the Seleukid empire[29] and the evidence usually called upon is Appian, *Syr.* 45, which refers to Antiochos IV, who 'ruled Syria and the surrounding nations, with Timarchos as satrap in Babylon and Herakleides in charge of revenue' (Συρίας καὶ τῶν περὶ αὐτὴν ἐθνῶν ἦρχε, σατράπην μὲν ἔχων ἐν Βαβυλῶνι Τίμαρχον, ἐπὶ δὲ ταῖς προσόδοις Ἡρακλείδην).

The μέν and δέ clearly relate the two officials in the text to a particular satrapy, Babylonia, where Timarchos was in charge of civil administration and Herakleides of financial administration, again a pairing of the two functions. But one would have expected Herakleides' title to be that of *dioikētēs*. True, but here it is a function that is being described, that of being responsible for revenues, which is not necessarily a title, just as *epi tōn pragmatōn* ('in charge of matters') is frequently used for someone acting for the king, who may be a Zeuxis, governor-general of western Asia Minor, or simply a Heliodoros on a mission to Jerusalem in the king's name investigating alleged misuse of Temple funds (2 Macc. 3.7), or even a Nikanor, *ta basilika prattōn* ('handling royal affairs') as the king's agent (Jos. *AJ* 12.261).

There is one other reference to an *epi tōn prosodōn* which should settle the issue: in *OGIS* 238, a Menandros with this title was honoured by the *phulakitai* ('guardsmen') of the hyparchy of Eriza. But, as noted earlier, when discussing the Apollonia-Salbake inscription of the same period, a Menandros was the satrapal *dioikētēs* and so, in all probability, the same person.

---

[29] Bikerman 1938: 128–9; Mørkholm 1966: 103. Again, there are widely differing views. Ma regards the post as a very high one, at the same level as the governor-general, Zeuxis (1997: 109). Corsaro considers that this official headed a separate branch of financial administration in a province, distinct from that of the *dioikētēs* (1980: 1196–7). Bengtson takes this as a title which replaced that of *oikonomos* at the head of each satrapy at the time of Antiochos III (1944: 127–9).

There is a problem, however, in that an *epi tōn prosodōn* at Antioch-Pyramos suggests a rather low-level official[30] and similarly one making a dedication at Susa to a *stratēgos*.[31] An *oikonomos* is better indicated in these cases.

So *epi tōn prosodōn* may not have been a title, but simply the description of the most important function of a financial administrator, that of the collection of revenue.[32]

h. The oikonomos *in the Laodike dossier (Document 3)*

This important inscription, involving an *oikonomos*, Nikomachos, in connection with a sale of royal land for which a survey was required, will be discussed in more detail later (section 9a below).

i. The Sardeis land conveyance (Document 11)

A transfer of royal land seems to be taking place in another inscription, where a Seleukid queen appears giving instructions concerning certain villages and fields (?) that some individual would receive in the *peri Sardeis oikonomia* ('the *oikonomia* of the district around Sardeis'). Note that the terminology here matches that of the *peri Erizan hyparchia* ('the hyparchy of the district around Eriza') in *OGIS* 238, that is, the district adjacent to a city, but possibly outside the city *chōra* and so tributary land administered directly by royal officials.[33] In my view it is probable that a hyparchy and an *oikonomia* describe one and the same district, depending upon the function of the official concerned, civil or financial, which would fit well with the pattern of dual responsibility at regional and district levels that has been observed several times already.

j. The stele of the Apollon Pleurenos temple

This inscription[34] probably dates to 188 BC, immediately after the takeover of Seleukid cities in Asia Minor by the Attalids, and concerns a request by Kadoas, the priest of Apollo, to his superior, the high priest Euthudemos.

---

[30] Carsana 1996: 49.   [31] Cumont 1931: 288–9.

[32] Some more quite different views expressed for the function of an *epi tōn prosodōn* are those of Kreissig: responsible for taxes from cities (1978: 60), Rapin: an official reporting to a *dioikētēs* (1996: 461) and Corsaro: the title *oikonomoi* took in the reign of Antiochos III (1980: 1191).

[33] Gauthier regards the district of the *oikonomos* in this case as relatively restricted, probably just the royal domains around Sardeis (1989: 132–4).

[34] Malay and Nalbantoğlu 1996.

The request had been made previously to Nikanor, the Seleukid high priest of all Asia Minor, but to no avail, presumably because of the change in the political situation. Kadoas had asked for something quite straightforward, that the high priest, his superior, write to Asklepiades, the *oikonomos*, so that he might grant permission for a stele to be erected with the names of initiates. Euthudemos did so, but directed his letter, addressed to Asklepiades, to a certain Diotimos, who then passed it on to another official, Attinas, who was presumably Asklepiades' superior. This would place the *oikonomos*, Asklepiades, on a rather low rung of the hierarchical ladder, responsible for a relatively insignificant local matter.

k. Economic texts from second-century BC Aï Khanoum

Although from the Graeco-Baktrian successor-state of the Seleukids, inscriptions found on jar fragments in the treasury of Aï Khanoum may indicate procedures followed in the Seleukid empire as well.

A typical text[35] reads: 'From Zenon. 500 drachms were counted by Oxeboakes and Oxubazos. Oxeboakes sealed [this container]' (παρὰ Ζήνωνος ἠρίθμηνται διὰ Ὀξηβοάκου καὶ Ὀξυβάζου δρχ φ· ἐσφράγισται Ὀξηβοάκης).

Similar texts mention other senders: Timodemos (4b), Philiskos (4c, 6), Straton (8d) and Nikeratos (12c), while Oxeboakes appears again in his role. The interpretation given is that Oxeboakes and his colleagues carried taxes from the *oikonomoi* of districts to the central treasury at Aï Khanoum, the use of jars being a normal way of transporting money in the ancient world.[36]

For comparison, one may note that the 'accountants' of the *Persepolis Fortification Texts* transported the commodity surpluses of storehouses and the animals and *šaumaraš* (silver?) collected from exchange to Persepolis (ch. 9.1a). A certain category of texts, the so-called 'labels',[37] record the contents of containers, presumably those that had been brought to Persepolis and stored. Many such 'labels' are to be found on tablets with a conical shape, which suggests that these tablets may have served as 'pot-stoppers'.

l. The Mnesimachos inscription (Document 5)

This important text, used several times already, gives us some idea of financial administration in the early Hellenistic period.

---

[35] Rapin 1983: 326, no. 4a.   [36] Rapin 1983: 351–4.   [37] Hallock 1969: 53–5.

Mnesimachos listed his villages and *klēroi* and the tax chiliarchies in which they had been assessed: 'tribute of the villages in the chiliarchy of Pytheus . . . in the chiliarchy of – agarios . . . in the chiliarchy of Sagarios, son of Koreis' (φόρος τῶν κωμῶν εἰς τὴν Πυθέου [. . . . . . χ]ιλιαρχίαν . . . εἰς τὴν [. . . . . .]αρίου χιλιαρχίαν . . . εἰς τὴν Σαγαρίου Κόρειδος χιλιαρχίαν).

It is possible that these tax chiliarchies were derived from the military organization of Alexander.[38] However, one may recall that the officials in charge of tax regions in the *Persepolis Fortification Texts* were likely to have had the rank of chiliarch (section 1 above) and the Greeks would most probably have termed their areas of jurisdiction 'chiliarchies'. There is no evidence that Alexander or the Successors made any drastic changes in administrative regions or districts – certainly the Achaemenid satrapies were retained. It is, therefore, quite possible that the chiliarch and chiliarchy were simply translations of the corresponding Persian terms initially. Later, however, there was a change in terminology, perhaps so as to avoid confusion with the military chiliarch of the Macedonian army, and there are two possibilities.

The first possibility is that the Achaemenid chiliarch became a Greek *dioikētēs*, which would fit well with the *Fortification Texts*, where the chiliarch was responsible for a region and had under him district officers (now *oikonomoi*), each responsible for a number of villages and storehouses. In favour of this is the fact that the Mnesimachos text locates a village first in a district and then in a chiliarchy. Against it is the fact that this would result in several *dioikētai* within a satrapy, which one has tended to exclude, except in the special circumstances of Koile Syria.

The second possibility is that the Achaemenid chiliarch became a Greek *oikonomos* and that the *chiliarchiai* later became *oikonomiai*. This is more likely, as *oikonomiai* are attested and probably corresponded to hyparchies, the name of the administrative division simply depending upon one's point of view: financial or civil (see above). However, one then lacks the Seleukid administrative organization reporting to the *oikonomos*, but, if the *Fortification Texts* are any guide, more junior officials probably supervised groups of villages. In the Persepolis organization at the time of the *Fortification Texts*, the next level up from the regional financial administrator was the satrapal one, occupied by Ziššawiš, the deputy of the 'satrap'. I suggest that his was the post later given to a *dioikētēs*, when financial administration was placed directly under the king.

---

[38] Corsaro 1980: 1204.

m. The functions of the dioikētēs and oikonomos

It is likely that Seleukid satrapies were subdivided into administrative districts referred to as hyparchies in Asia Minor and *pahatu* in Babylonia (section 7g below), which were probably quite small and often centred on a city. A parallel financial organization existed, answerable to the king and not the satrap. The epigraphic evidence called upon earlier suggests that this organization was in place at least from the time of Antiochos II, if not earlier.[39] The *dioikētēs* was the financial counterpart of the *stratēgos*/satrap in each satrapy and the *oikonomoi* of the hyparchs,[40] while the terms *huparchia* and *oikonomia* refer to the same geographical district, but from different points of view.

The responsibilities of the *dioikētēs* seem to have included matters of land and labour, the royal storehouses, revenue and expense. Certain decisions had apparently to be taken jointly with the satrap. It is quite likely that the *dioikētēs* also supervised the mints of a satrapy, since revenue and expense were to be handled mainly in coin and the purpose of a satrapal mint was to 'top up' any shortfall of coinage locally (ch. 11.4). The title *epi tōn prosodōn* was sometimes used for the *dioikētēs*, perhaps because revenue collection was his main responsibility.

The *oikonomos* reported to a *dioikētēs* and worked hand-in-hand with the hyparch, with whom he sometimes took decisions jointly, and also collaborated with the religious authorities in his district. His main functions seem to have been to manage royal land, look after local taxation receipts and settle small-scale expenses of the administration.[41]

---

[39] Those who recognize the existence of a separate financial branch tend to place the change in the reign of Antiochos III, e.g. Bengtson 1944: 127–8 and Bagnall 1976: 248, but Corsaro considers that it took place with the first Seleukids (1980: 1190). An interesting possibility is raised by the trilingual inscription from Xanthos of the very end of the Persian period. The dating formula in the inscription refers to Pixodaros as the satrap and to two archons of Lykia plus an *epimelētēs* ('supervisor') of Xanthos (Metzger 1979: 32). The possibility that one archon was a civil/military hyparch and the other a financial administrator should not be excluded.

[40] The same view is taken by Ma (1997: 110) and Musti, who suggested a central *dioikētēs* in addition (1984: 186), as did Bengtson (1944:113). Grainger considers, incorrectly I believe, that Seleukos I eliminated satrapies in some areas and made hyparchies the top administrative units, e.g. in Syria and Mesopotamia (1990b: 134–8).

[41] There are widely diverging views on the role of the *oikonomos*. For example, Rapin considers that an *oikonomos* sometimes corresponded to an *epi tōn prosodōn* and sometimes to a *gazophulax*, who managed a royal treasury (1996: 46). Musti believes that the *epi tōn prosodōn* replaced the *oikonomos* in later Seleukid history (1984: 186). Bagnall regards *oikonomoi* as managers of royal estates, not part of the administration (1976: 247). Rostovtzeff considers that royal land and peasants (*laoi*) were entrusted to the financial officials (1941: 465), while Ma attributes this function specifically to the *oikonomoi* (1997: 110). Corsaro views the *oikonomos* as the financial director of a satrapy, except in Koile Syria, where he considers him a low-ranking official placed directly under the satrap/*stratēgos*,

In one satrapy only is there likely to have been a slightly different organization, Koile Syria, where intermediate geographical subdivisions had been introduced, the meridarchies, for whose financial matters *dioikētai* may have become responsible. There was thus seemingly no *dioikētēs* at the satrapal level, but this did not change the authority of the *dioikētai* in any way or their direct control by the king.

6. THE *EKLOGISTĒS* AND THE *LOGEUTĒS*

a. The Achaios decree (Document 8)

This text, found in western Asia Minor and dating to 267 BC, refers to honours granted by the villagers of Neoteichos and Kiddioukome to two functionaries of the elder Achaios, to whom these villages apparently belonged. These functionaries were Banabelos, *ho ta tou Achaiou oikonomōn* ('the person in charge of the financial matters of Achaios') and Lachares, *ho eklogistēs tōn Achaiou* ('the accountant/assessor of the property of Achaios'), both receiving exactly the same yearly sacrifice, of one ram each, as compared to a bull for Achaios. The officials are twice mentioned, the second time with the order reversed, which suggests that they must have been of equal rank, that is, independent of one another hierarchically.

We may take *ho oikonomōn ta tou* – to be the same as an *oikonomos*, but for an individual and not the king.[42] Thus Banabelos would essentially have been managing the property of Achaios, for which there is a parallel in the Laodike land sale (Document 3), where the land being sold to the ex-queen was transferred on her behalf to Arrhidaios, *ho oikonomōn ta tēs Laodikēs*.

In LSJ, *eklogistēs* is rendered as 'accountant', 'reckoner'.[43] That Lachares was a financial official seems clear from this, but how did his function differ from that of Banabelos? The term suggests that calculation was involved and an assessor of taxes and rents for the villagers of Achaios would not be an unreasonable supposition. Since Achaios was a member of the royal family, one may suppose that his estate was a rather large one, a royal land grant, whose management was modelled closely on that of a financial district. The

---

with special responsibility for royal land in the initial Seleukid period (1980: 1191). Haussoullier concludes that the *oikonomos* saw to rents and taxes from the satrapy, with the *epi tōn prosodōn* as his superior (1901: 29).

[42] Also Ma 1997: 122; 1999: 149.

[43] Haussoullier notes that the *eklogistai* of the Didyma temple checked the construction accounts (1926: 125–7). Musti takes an *eklogistēs* to be an accountant (1984: 186).

Fortification Texts provide us with a clue from the Achaemenid period. The accounts of every storehouse were 'signed' by the district commander (or storekeeper) and the tax-inspector (*ullira*), who was apparently responsible not only for assessment of commodity tax but also for its collection. The *eklogistēs* of Achaios may well have fulfilled precisely this role.

b. The Apollonia-Salbake decree (Document 7)

This text, used earlier, makes mention of an *eklogistēs* in the royal administration, a certain Demetrios, who had intercepted the Apollonian ambassadors on their visit to Ktesikles and Menandros the *dioikētēs* and brought up the business of two sacred villages, after a complaint had been lodged by another Demetrios, the official in charge of sanctuaries.

One does not know what the problem was, but one may speculate that it was a question of whether the sacred villages belonged to Apollonia, and so were expected to pay taxes to the city, or whether the royal administration was entitled to tax them itself. So the function of Demetrios the *eklogistēs* may well have been that of a tax-assessor or inspector, matching that of Lachares in the Achaios decree. Since Demetrios was not approached in the first place by the Apollonian embassy, he is unlikely to have been at the level of Ktesikles, the satrap(?), or Menandros, the *dioikētēs*, whom the embassy came to see. So Demetrios may well have been a subordinate of the *dioikētēs*, at the same hierarchical level as an *oikonomos*, which matches what I have deduced from the Achaios decree.[44]

My conclusion, then, is that there were at least two branches of the financial administration under a satrapal *dioikētēs*, the first comprising the *oikonomoi* of districts, responsible for the land and peasants (*laoi*) and the handling of revenue and expenses, the second including one or more *eklogistai*, responsible for tax assessment and, probably, collection.

c. The Baktrian parchment

This interesting text[45] refers to one of the Graeco-Baktrian kingdoms and a city, Asangorna, probably in western Baktria, and is dated to *c.* 170 BC. The part that interests us reads: 'received by Menodotos the *logeutēs*, in the

---

[44] The tax function of the *eklogistēs* is also noted by J. and L. Robert (1954: 292–3), Corsaro, who regards this official as the assistant of the *dioikētēs* responsible for calculation, sharing out and control of taxes (1980: 1193–4) and Ma, who views him as a tax-collector or financial controller (1997: 109).

[45] Rapin 1996; cf. Bernard and Rapin 1994; Rea, Senior and Hollis 1994.

presence of -eos, who was sent with him by Demonax, the e-, and Simos, who was sent [?] by Diodoros, the official in charge of the revenues, . . . from S-os, son of Dataes, for the tax on sacrificial animals [?], the sum owed of 20 staters' (ἔχει Μηνόδοτος λογευτὴς συμπαρόντων [-]εου τοῦ συναπεσταλμένου ὑπὸ Δημώνακτος [[]] τοῦ γενομένο[υ] ἐ[—]εως καὶ Σίμου τοῦ διὰ Διοδώρου τοῦ ἐπὶ τῶν προσόδων [. . . . .] ε[.] ἀπὸ Σ [. . .]ου τοῦ Δατάου ἐξ ἱερείων τρα[?] [. . .]ωι ν[. .] στατήρων κ' τὰ καθήκοντα).

Though this is not, strictly speaking, a Seleukid document, it is likely that the Graeco-Baktrian kingdom continued administrative practices with which it had been familiar as a Seleukid satrapy, that is, until 246 BC at the latest.

Menodotos the *logeutēs* is probably a tax-collector – one of many, since he is not referred to with 'the' – receiving some payment from a tax payer, S-os, son of Dataes (ἔχει . . . ἀπό) in the presence of two other officials. The first of these, -eos, was the representative of a department of the administration headed by Demonax, to which Menodotos apparently also belonged, because -eos 'had been sent together with him' (συναπεσταλμένου). This could logically have been the tax assessment/collection department and one might just read ἐκλογέως (*eklogeōs*) in the inscription from ἐκλογεύειν (*eklogeuein*), as an alternative to ἐκλογιστοῦ (*eklogistou*) from ἐκλογίζειν (*eklogizein*) for the position of Demonax. The second official, Simos, was employed by the collector of revenues, Diodoros, who must have been either a *dioikētēs*, or, more probably, the *oikonomos* of the district centred on Asangorna (an *oikonomia*?). The picture of two departments involved in the collection of tax resembles that of the Achaemenid storehouses and also that observed at Seleukid Apollonia-Salbake (section 5e above).[46]

One question that arises is whether revenue was collected by officials of the Seleukid administration or by tax-contractors. The *logeutēs* in the Baktrian parchment may well have been a tax-collector on his rounds, as in Achaemenid Persis earlier (section 1 above). There is no specific mention in the sources of the use of Seleukid tax-contractors, other than the high priests of Judaea, but one cannot discount the possibility, certainly for the revenue of cities.

---

[46] Bernard and Rapin agree with the view that Menodotos was a tax-collector, but suggest that those present were witnesses to a sale of sacrificial victims on behalf of the state treasury. They take the *epi tōn prosodōn* as reporting to a *dioikētēs*, sometimes as an *oikonomos* and sometimes as a *gazophulax*, the official guarding a royal treasury (1994: 269–70).

7. OTHER FINANCIAL OFFICIALS

a. Mint officials

On Seleukid coinage, a symbol is frequently used to identify the mint where a particular issue was struck. Control marks are usually also present. Sometimes, a primary mark is quite long-lasting and associated with a range of secondary marks, each used over a number of coinage issues at the mint. These control marks can frequently be identified as consisting of letters from some person's name, but no study has as yet been undertaken of them.[47] I have suggested (section 5m above) that the *dioikētēs* may have been responsible for the mint(s) in his satrapy. It would be interesting to investigate whether primary control marks can be associated with the names of known *dioikētai*. If so, secondary control marks may identify mint-masters or coinage issues.

b. The epistatēs

The *epistatēs* ('supervisor'), mentioned in the sources as the Seleukid representative for subject cities[48] or temples, may have played a financial role as well, for example in supervising the collection of tax or the erection of stelae.[49] Amyzon honoured Menestratos, the *epistatēs* of the Artemision, for helping with the return of confiscated goods and the synoikism of the Artemision, both good deeds certainly involving a financial element.[50] Furthermore, this *epistatēs* corresponded directly on these matters with Nikomedes, whom I considered earlier to have been a *dioikētēs*, and Chionis *ton ep' Alindōn tetagmenon* ('the official in charge of Alinda'), who may have been his counterpart at Alinda. An *oikonomos* might have been expected to handle such matters, but one does not appear in the inscription, so perhaps the *epistatēs* fulfilled his role for a city.

c. The gazophulax

This is clearly the title of the commander of a treasury, but the guarding of precious-metal and commodity stocks was not necessarily a function

---

[47] The Houghton and Lorber 2002 catalogue provides details of all control marks used at Seleukid mints and will facilitate such an analysis.

[48] Robert and Robert 1983: 188 and L. Robert 1949: 22 for *epistatai* at Laodikeia-Nehavend, Seleukeia-Pieria and Laodikeia in Syria. See Allen for Attalid *epistatai* (1983: 105–6).

[49] Apollodoros at Laodikeia-Nehavend (Robert 1949: 7, 22).

[50] Robert and Robert 1983: no. 15; Ma 1997; 1999: no. 10.

of financial officials and sometimes seems to have been that of garrison commanders. Since both these and financial officers reported to the king and not to the satrap, royal control could still be exercised effectively. It is possible that the *eklogistēs* and the *oikonomos* saw to the collection and disbursal of funds and the *gazophulax* was only responsible for their safekeeping, although he may have been assigned the duties of the *oikonomos* in some cases.[51]

d. *The* agoranomos

The market supervisor, or *agoranomos*, is a classic feature of any Greek city. But could he also have been the king's representative for the collection of taxes in the marketplace? One has the example of Simon, the Seleukid *prostatēs tou hierou* ('official in charge of the sanctuary') in Jerusalem, who had wished to exercise the *agoranomos* function in place of Onias, the high priest, probably as tax-contractor for market dues (2 Macc. 3.4).

If this is accepted, a different reading of Antigonos' letter to Teos (Document 1) becomes possible. In §11 Antigonos gave instructions, couched as suggestions, that all movements of grain in and out of the city be declared in the *agora* and that those living outside the city should register the quantities of crops they wished to move out of their farms, but not to the city, so that they might pay the appropriate dues to the *agoranomos*. This official is not really seen here supervising the workings of the market, but actually collecting tolls and sales taxes. Since these were important sources of income for Seleukid kings from many cities, one wonders whether the *agoranomos* also functioned there as a royal tax-collector.

Some further evidence is provided by an inscription from Tyriaion of Phrygia Paroreios of the time of Eumenes II,[52] which shows the king associated with the function of the *agoranomos*: 'and we grant to you, for the present, the revenue accruing from the office of the *agoranomos* for the [purchase of] oil for the gymnasium' (καὶ δίδομεν ὑμῖ[ν ε]ἰς τὸ ἄλειμμα κατὰ τὸ παρὸν τὴν ἀπὸ τῆς ἀγορανομ[ί]ας πρόσοδον). This city had probably become subject to the Attalids only after Magnesia.

e. *The* bibliophulax

A *bibliophulax* is referred to in the Laodike dossier (Document 3), where this official, Timoxenos, is mentioned as having been sent instructions to record the sale to Laodike, along with the land survey, in the royal registry

---

[51] Rapin 1996: 461.   [52] Jonnes and Ricl 1997: 3–5, 24.

at Sardeis. It will be suggested in section 9a below that this official, in charge of a registry, may have been the direct subordinate of a satrapal *dioikētēs*.

One clay medallion from Uruk is stamped with a *bibliophulakikos* ('belonging to the *bibliophulax*') seal, perhaps signifying some sort of purchase or grant of royal land.[53] A royal land registry at Uruk is a possibility, but it is more likely that this office was located at a major capital, Seleukeia-Tigris, just as a transaction in Hellespontine Phrygia (above) had to be recorded at Sardeis. Local land registries may also have existed, with their appropriate officials.[54]

f. The chreophulax

In chapter 8.3a–b the *chreophulax* appeared with his seal on some *bullae* of Uruk (χρεοφυλακικὸς Ὄρχων or χρεοφυλακικὸς ἐν Ὄρχεις) and Seleukeia-Tigris (χρεωφυλάκων). The *chreophulakion*, or registry office, of the Greek world was used to register and store both public and private documents.[55] It is possible that at Uruk or Seleukeia certain transactions had to be registered at the *chreophulakion* so that tax could be collected, but it is difficult to prove this and the evidence would suggest that the *chreophulax* was not linked to the tax operation. For example, no *bulla* from Uruk, with a stamp for the salt tax (*halikēs*) or port dues (*limenos*) also has a *chreophulakikos* stamp and only some *bullae* with a stamp for the sales tax (*eponiou*) or slave tax (*andrapodikou*) do and not others. The *chreophulakōn* stamp at Seleukeia is not associated with any tax stamp other than the *katagraphēs*, which may not have been a tax, but simply an official registration, possibly of slaves.

Rather than viewing the *chreophulax* as an official of the administration, one should probably consider him a municipal officer, whose primary role was the safe-keeping of documents, whether of an official or private nature. In a smaller centre, such as Uruk, it is possible that he performed a dual function and co-operated in some way with the fiscal authorities.[56]

g. Officials in Babylonia

The titles and exact functions of Seleukid administrative officials in Babylonia are somewhat confusing.[57] The *paqdu* may have been the king's

---

[53] Rostovtzeff 1932: 71.   [54] Westermann 1921: 16.
[55] Rostovtzeff 1932: 57–63; McDowell 1935: 131–7.
[56] Also McDowell 1935: 136. Rostovtzeff, however, views the *chreophulax* only as an official of the administration (1932: 63).
[57] See Doty 1977: 44; Sherwin-White 1983a: 268–9; Spek 1985: 545; 1987: 63–4, McEwan 1988: 416–18; Kuhrt 1996: 52.

representative in the temples of Babylon and Uruk, but the king also communicated directly with the chief administrators of the temples, the *šatammu* at Babylon or the *rab-ša-reš-ali* at Uruk. The *pahat* of Babylon and the *šaknu* of Uruk were likely to have been royal appointees and may have corresponded to *epistatai* for these cities or hyparchs for their respective districts (*pahatu*). An *episkopos* ('overseer', *e-pi-is-ku-pu-su* in Akkadian) is also noted for Seleukid Nippur.[58]

A *dioikētēs* appears in a cuneiform inscription from Uruk relating to the sale of ration rights, with the note that 'afterwards these rations were fully entered in the communication of the *dioikētēs* (*di-i-qe-te-e-su*) of the house of the king (*bit šarri*)'.[59] There is a strong suggestion here of tax levied on the transaction.

'Royal assessors' (*emidu ša šarri*) are also noted,[60] whose title suggests that they may have corresponded to *eklogistai*.

h. Financial administrators of temples

Standing somewhat apart from royal, tributary and city land, that provided most of the rents, tribute and taxation and were possibly administered in the manner described above, the temples were also sources of revenue and destinations of expenditure for the kings.

Simon, the *prostatēs tou hierou* ('the official in charge of the sanctuary'), was the king's representative for the Temple of Jerusalem, probably keeping an eye on its finances and responsible for collection of tax,[61] since his report to the king of mismanagement of temple funds led to the 'raid' of Heliodoros (2 Macc. 3.4). *Prostatēs* can also be translated as 'protector', which may simply be a euphemism for *epistatēs* in the context of a religious sanctuary.[62] A similar use of this title (*pu-ru-su-tat-te-su* in Akkadian) appears in a temple record from Babylonia of the Parthian period.[63] The *paqdu* of the Babylonian temples (above) probably played a similar role.

---

[58] Spek 1992.
[59] McEwan considers *bit šarri* ('the house of the king') to be probably the administrative office of the crown in Uruk (1981a: 149–50). The same term was used in the document already noted from Babylonia concerning the 50 per cent rent to be paid by the Šamaš temple at Sippar or Larsa to the royal treasury, represented by a certain Iltalimatu, the *pahatu* (Spek 1995: 238–41). Given that a *pahat* seems to be a district centred on a city, equivalent to a hyparchy/*oikonomia*, might not Iltalimatu have corresponded to an *oikonomos*?
[60] Stolper 1994: 333.   [61] Schäfer 1995: 34.
[62] Note also the reference to a *prostatēs* at Amyzon in the period of the Successors (Robert and Robert 1983: 97).
[63] McEwan 1981b: 131; Spek 1985: 553–4.

Under Antiochos III, Nikanor was appointed high priest for Asia Minor, with authority for financial matters:[64] 'that he be responsible both for the sanctuaries and their revenues' (εἶναι αὐτὸν καὶ ἐπὶ τῶν ἱερῶν καὶ τὰς προσόδους τούτων). However, the high priest may actually have possessed limited authority, since Euthydemos, who must have succeeded Nikanor under the Attalids, was obliged to write to the *oikonomos* Asklepiades via the latter's superiors so that the priest of the temple of Apollon Pleurenos could obtain permission for a quite simple matter, the setting up of a stele with the names of initiates.[65]

At Apollonia-Salbake, in the reign of Antiochos III (Document 7), Demetrios the official in charge of the sanctuaries had complained to the *eklogistēs* Demetrios about some matter in connection with sacred villages, very possibly whether they were to pay tax to the city or to the royal treasury.[66] Note that Demetrios did not complain first to a superior, an *archiereus* ('high priest') of Asia Minor, and it is possible that this position was created later in the reign of Antiochos III.[67] The dossier of inscriptions regulating Nikanor's appointment to the post (see above) gives no indication that Nikanor was to replace someone else. Indeed, the king went to a lot of trouble to spell out to his governor-general, Zeuxis, what was involved, as when the post had been held by a certain Dion at the time of his grandfather, Antiochos II. So the high-priesthood of Asia Minor had probably fallen into abeyance when the Seleukids had lost much of the region in the intervening period.

At the same time, high-priesthoods were apparently created in Koile Syria, where Ptolemaios, the *stratēgos* of the satrapy, is noted as the *archiereus* (Document 4), and also at Daphne, the suburb of Antioch.[68]

i. Financial administrators of the armed forces

A separate financial administration for the armed forces is also likely, since a military accounts office is noted at Apameia (Strabo 16.2.10: τὸ λογιστήριον τὸ στρατιωτικόν). Clearly pay and supplies for the standing army and navy would have been the responsibility of some department of the administration, probably reporting directly to the king in view of

---

[64] Malay 1987; Ma 1997; 1999: no. 4, *SEG* 37.1010; Gauthier, *BE* 1989, 276.
[65] Malay and Nalbantoğlu 1996.   [66] Also Ma 1997: 110; 1999: 136.
[67] Debord sees evidence of a global policy for sanctuaries by Antiochos III, with possibly a separate fiscal organization (1982: 270).
[68] *RC* 44; Austin 1981: no. 175.

the importance of military expenditure (ch. 10.1), but more than this, one cannot say.

A chief secretary of the armed forces (ἀρχιγραμματεὺς τῶν δυνάμεων) appears in a late second-century BC inscription from Palestine[69] and also in Polybios (5.54.12), concerning the appointment, by Antiochos III, of such an official, Tychon, as *stratēgos* of the satrapy of the Erythraean Sea. It is quite possible that this position entailed financial responsibilities.

8. COMPARISON WITH ACHAEMENID PRACTICE

The structures of the Achaemenid and Seleukid systems of financial administration were derived from separate bodies of evidence, the former from the *Persepolis Fortification Texts*, the latter from Greek documents. They show considerable similarity, if one ignores the accounting function, for which one has no Seleukid information, and the Achaemenid 'apportioner' function, for which there was no Seleukid counterpart, as is to be expected, since a mainly monetary economy was now in place.

Financial administration seems to have been exercised in both empires at regional level (regional officer versus *dioikētēs*), with district subdivisions, where two functions were distinguished: revenue generation by tax-inspector and tax-collectors ('delivery man'/'deliverers', identified with *eklogistēs*/*logeutai*) and revenue safe-keeping and expenditure (district officer, identified with *oikonomos*). Certainly a pointer to this organization is the manner in which villages are defined in Greek texts by district and region.[70] In the Achaemenid system, we know that the administrative area of Persis, at least, was subdivided into regions (section 1 above), which was also the case in Seleukid Koile Syria, but, elsewhere, each Seleukid satrapy may have constituted just one financial region. What the Achaemenid situation was, we do not know.

On one point only was there a significant difference. The Achaemenid satrap was probably responsible for financial administration in his satrapy,

---

[69] Landau 1961.

[70] For example, in northern Syria, the Baitokaike inscription (*RC* 70) gives: 'the village of Baitokaike ... in [the district of] Tourgona of the Apameia satrapy' (κώμην τὴν Βαιτοκαι[κη]νὴν ... ἐν Τουργωνα τῆς περὶ Ἀπάμιαν σατραπίας), which was originally a hyparchy; in Parthian Kurdistan (Minns 1915: 28–9) we have: 'in the hyparchy of Baseira, in the area of the Baithabasta station, in the village of Kopana' (ἐν ὑπαρχείῃ Βασείροις πρὸς σταθμοῦ Βαιθαβαρτοις ἐν κώμη Κωπανει); in the Mnesimachos inscription (Document 5) one reads: 'the village of Perasasostra in [the district of] Morstou Udati, in the chiliarchy of -arios' (κώμη Περασασωστρα ἐν Μόρστου Ὕδατι ... εἰς τὴν [_____]αρίου χιλιαρχίαν). Certainly the last of these examples was associated with an area of fiscal control, since tax was to be paid to the chiliarch. Might not the others also indicate levels and areas of jurisdiction of the financial administration?

whereas the Seleukid king had withdrawn this function from his own satraps.

9. A NEED TO REINTERPRET SOME TEXTS

It has been argued that financial administration in satrapies was conducted by the *dioikētai* and their subordinates, *oikonomoi* and *eklogistai*, who received their orders directly from the king. In some matters, joint decisions had to be reached with the civil and military authorities: satraps, hyparchs, phrourarchs, *epistatai*, and suchlike. In this light, some well-known inscriptions may have to be rethought in terms of the roles of the officials appearing in them.

a. The Laodike dossier (Document 3)

This has already been discussed twice (chs. 6.3c; 8.1d). Metrophanes was informed by the king of the conditions of the sale to Laodike and instructed to (a) transfer the land to Laodike's bailiff, (b) see to the recording of the sale in the registry office at Sardeis and (c) prepare five stelae publishing the act (no. 18). Instructions were issued from an unnamed official to a subordinate to prepare two stelae and pay the necessary expense (no. 19). The hyparch of the district where the land was located received instructions from the *oikonomos*, Nikomachos, to conduct a land survey (no. 20).

Metrophanes is usually considered the satrap of Hellespontine Phrygia and the unnamed official of no. 19, issuing orders to Nikomachos.[71] Thus a chain of command is apparently established: satrap to *oikonomos* to hyparch. However, there are arguments against this:[72]

(1) In the second letter (no. 19), the orders issued by its author to the recipient were that two stelae be erected at Ephesos and Didyma detailing the sale and survey, while the information was provided that the *bibliophulax* at Sardeis had also been instructed to register these. Though any actions by the recipient of the letter were to be restricted to Ionia, the author seems to have had jurisdiction over all Lydia, while the actual land was situated in Hellespontine Phrygia, a different satrapy.

---

[71] For example, Ma 1997: 113; 1999: 141; Musti 1965: 156–7. Haussoullier is categorical that the king only communicated with the highest functionary in the satrapy, the *stratēgos* (1901: 22).

[72] Lockhart accepts the chain of command, but considers that the second letter (no. 19) was addressed to an official in another city for the erection of the two stelae there (1961: 188–92), a view shared by Musti 1957: 267–77.

(2) Only two stelae are noted in these orders, those of Ionia. But there was to be one more erected in the satrapy of Lydia, that at Sardeis, one at Ilion in Hellespontine Phrygia and one outside Seleukid territory, in Samothrake.

(3) The hyparch, who is normally considered a civil/military administrator, a subordinate of the satrap, is here seen taking orders from a financial official and not receiving them directly from his superior.

An interpretation of the texts, which would fit all the details they contain, is as follows:

(1) Metrophanes was the *dioikētēs* of Hellespontine Phrygia and the king communicated with him directly about a financial matter, this time concerning royal land, as he habitually did with his *dioikētai*.[73]

(2) Metrophanes instructed his *oikonomos* of the district, Nikomachos, for a survey to be carried out (not extant).

(3) Nikomachos requested a survey from his colleague, the civil administrator of the district, the hyparch -krates (note the equivalence of hyparchy and *oikonomia*), who had the specialized (military) personnel for the task. The hyparch obliged with his report (no. 20) which was forwarded by Nikomachos to Metrophanes.

(4) Metrophanes next saw to the recording of the sale and survey. He forwarded the king's instructions and the hyparch's survey to his colleague, the *dioikētēs* of Lydia (not extant).

(5) He, in turn, instructed his *oikonomos* in Ionia to erect two stelae, informing him at the same time that he had ordered the *bibliophulax* at Sardeis, who probably reported directly to him, to register the transaction in the royal registry (no. 19).

(6) The *bibliophulax* received his orders and recorded the sale (not extant).

(7) At the same time, the *dioikētēs* of Lydia issued orders to the *oikonomos* responsible for Sardeis (see above for its *oikonomia*) to erect a stele there too (not extant).

(8) Meanwhile, Metrophanes had already issued orders to his *oikonomos* responsible for the Troad to erect a stele at Ilion (not extant).

(9) One final act of Metrophanes would have been to communicate with the king's representative in Samothrake regarding the erection of the fifth stele or, perhaps, one of his *oikonomoi* may have been required to manufacture and ship it there (not extant).

What has finally survived is only what affected the Didymeion sanctuary, where the inscription was found, namely the king's instructions, the

[73] Also Bikerman 1938: 129.

survey and the communication of the financial officials responsible for that particular area.

b. Other texts

Here is how certain texts have been interpreted, in my view incorrectly: 'In the Aristodikides land grant (Document 2), the king wrote to Meleagros, who is normally considered to have been the *stratēgos* (satrap) of Hellespontine Phrygia. His task was to arrange for transfers of royal land to Aristodikides.'

Three inscriptions record instructions sent out by Antiochos III regarding the appointment of a high priestess in each satrapy for the cult of his wife, Laodike. In all cases the king wrote the same letter to a senior official, with instructions that 'copies of the letter, having been recorded on stelae, be displayed in the most prominent locations' (τὰ ἀντίγραφα τῶν ἐπιστολῶν ἀναγραφέντα εἰς στήλας ἀνατεθήτω ἐν τοῖς ἐπιφανεστά-τοις τόποις). The primary recipients sent a copy of the king's letter to subordinates with orders to do just that, Anaximbrotos to Dionytas for his district in Karia or Phrygia, Menedemos to Apollodoros and the city of Laodikeia-Nehavend and again to Thoas for his district somewhere in Media. Presumably, other subordinates received the same orders. The primary recipients have been considered satraps, their subordinates hyparchs or, in the case of Apollodoros, the royal *epistatēs* of the city.[74]

A similar procedure was used in the instructions sent by the king via Zeuxis, his governor-general in the West, to Philotas and then on to Bithys regarding the appointment of Nikanor as high priest in Asia Minor and its announcement on a stele,[75] while other subordinates of Philotas presumably received the same orders. Philotas has been considered a satrap, Bithys a hyparch.

In the Failaka inscription, Ikadion, considered a satrap, wrote to his subordinate, Anaxarchos, about matters which the king wished dealt with concerning sanctuaries on the island of Ikaros – land grants, tax exemptions, and suchlike – and also with instructions that the king's orders be displayed on a stele. Anaxarchos passed on Ikadion's letter to the inhabitants of Ikaros and his own order that it be displayed on a stele as soon as possible.[76]

---

[74] Clairmont 1948; L. Robert 1949: 5–29; 1967: 289–92.   [75] Malay 1987: 7–9.

[76] Roueché and Sherwin-White take the two officials as the governor of the satrapy and his subordinate, but they accept the possibility that the *dioikētēs* and the *oikonomos* might have been independent of the governor (1985: 30). See also Altheim and Stiehl 1965; Sherwin-White and Kuhrt 1993: 174–8.

I suggest that in *all* the cases listed above, the primary recipient is likely to have been the *dioikētēs* of the relevant satrapy and not the satrap/*stratēgos*, and that he then passed on the king's orders to an *oikonomos* in each district or an *epistatēs* in the case of a city. The matters were clearly of a financial nature – transfer of royal land, erection of stelae and the expense involved – which fell within the jurisdiction of financial officials. Furthermore, the king is known to have communicated directly with his *dioikētai* on these matters (section 5 above). The anomaly in the Laodike land sale, where the hyparch apparently received orders from the *oikonomos*, can be explained by the fact that both were jointly responsible for the district (hyparchy equivalent to *oikonomia*). The *oikonomos* transmitted the king's instructions to his colleague, because the latter had the personnel capable of carrying out the survey. Whether satrap or *dioikētēs*, the above inscriptions need rethinking.

10. ANTIOCHOS I AS FINANCIAL ADMINISTRATOR

Although much in Seleukid financial administration was a continuation of Achaemenid practice, several changes were initiated by Seleukos I in pursuance of his goal of transforming the economy into a money-based one. Had it not been, however, for his son and successor, Antiochos (I), the empire might have foundered early on. Antiochos should be given equal credit for placing it on a sound footing, as the real organizer.[77]

We have already caught glimpses of some of his measures. The establishment of the first new cities was his father's work, but Antiochos continued this project with intensity in the East from the time he was appointed viceroy there *c.* 291/0 BC (ch. 6.2a). In this connection, the policy of granting land with the right of attachment to a city may also have been his idea and for the reasons outlined in chapter 6.3h. The earliest inscription that mentions this is the Aristodikides land grant from his reign (Document 2).

The creation of mints in the Upper Satrapies, apart from Ekbatana, is Antiochos' work (ch. 11.1) and probably linked to his efforts to urbanize the region and expand the monetary economy. The change from small silver to a token bronze coinage may also be attributed to him and its introduction at Babylon can be dated by the *Astronomical Diary* of 274 BC (ch. 11.3d).

Changes in the form and contents of administrative and legal cuneiform texts are noted at about this time in Babylonia, which have been linked to fiscal and administrative measures of Antiochos I.[78] A new formulary seems

---

[77] Also Oelsner 1977: 79. [78] Doty 1977: 311–35; cf. Oelsner 1981: 41; Sherwin-White 1987: 27.

to be utilized at Uruk in contracts for urban land after 279 BC, while slave sale contracts appear only to 274 BC and those for arable land to 273 BC.[79] This is not to say that there were no such sales, but simply that Aramaic or Greek on parchment or papyrus may have been used in preference to Akkadian and cuneiform tablets. The suggestion, however, that registration and taxation of slaves were introduced at this time by Antiochos will not hold, as this was certainly also an Achaemenid practice,[80] unless it had fallen into abeyance and was reintroduced by the Seleukid king.[81]

The proliferation of taxes in the Seleukid empire (ch. 8.1–6) is not to be found in any document dating to the reign of Seleukos I, which does not prove that Antiochos was the initiator of a more complex and comprehensive tax system than his father's, but, added to the other evidence, might suggest it. Certainly the *galatikon* ('relating to the Galatians') tax imposed on Greek cities, ostensibly to pursue the war against the Galatians, was Antiochos' invention. Also, the earliest *bulla* from Seleukeia-Tigris with a salt-tax stamp dates to 287/6 BC (ch. 8.2c), when Antiochos was co-ruler, responsible for the East.

Finally, the direct involvement of the Seleukid king with financial administration in the provinces, his close link with *dioikētai*, is certainly attested in the reign of Antiochos II (section 5c above, the Boulagoras inscription) and, in my view, in the reign of Antiochos I, with the interpretation that may be given to the Aristodikides inscription (section 9b).

It was argued in chapter 7.3, mainly because of the reference to stratagems of men 'long since dead' and the reappearance once more of a 'whole' empire following Seleukos' conquest of Asia Minor, that the *Oikonomika* describes the situation in the Seleukid empire after 280 BC, which administrators-to-be would be interested in learning about. Linking this to what has been discussed above, it is possible to accept a reorganization of finances and financial administration of the empire by Antiochos I in about 275 BC.

II. CONCLUSIONS ON FINANCIAL ADMINISTRATION

Evidence from different regions and periods suggests that the Seleukid system of financial administration must have been quite uniform,[82] particularly after the changes introduced by Antiochos I in about 275 BC.

---

[79] But Spek notes a text (1995: no. 1) of 194 BC from Borsippa using the old (Neo-Babylonian) formulary, which probably indicates that the new formulary was not mandated by the administration.

[80] Stolper 1989.

[81] Spek views this as possibly due to the increased need of funds for the first Syrian War (2000a: 305–7).

[82] Also Rostovtzeff 1941: 517.

A parallel organization to the satrapal, independent of the satrap and local military commanders, dealt directly with the king. The *diokētai* were his financial representatives in the satrapies, and in subdivisions of at least Koile Syria, and were responsible for royal land, revenue and expenditure in their respective areas of jurisdiction. They may also have supervised royal mints and registry offices. In matters of joint jurisdiction, they co-operated with satraps and garrison commanders.

Under the *dioikētai*, the *eklogistai* were mainly responsible for setting the level of taxation and perhaps seeing to its collection by *logeutai*. The *oikonomoi* managed the royal land and any revenue, once it had been received, and also controlled expenditure in their financial districts. They co-operated with civil/military hyparchs, whose areas of jurisdiction probably coincided with their own. A separate group of officials (*hoi epi tōn hierōn*) supervised temples and their revenue, and there may have been a department of the administration dedicated to managing the expenses of the regular army.

In certain areas, the Seleukid supervisor (*epistatēs, prostatēs, episkopos, paqdu*) of a city or temple possibly filled the role of both hyparch and *oikonomos*, reporting to the *dioikētēs* of the satrapy on financial matters. In military districts (*phulakai*), or those with fortified treasuries, garrison commanders might sometimes take on the task of collecting tribute and taxation and safeguarding it (*gazophulakes*).

The overall impression is of an efficient financial organization, which must have been of some considerable help to the king in meeting his financial objectives.

General conclusions

I. THE SOLVING OF A PROBLEM

Although the source material concerning the Seleukid empire is quite
sparse, it proves sufficient, particularly when different genres of evidence
are combined, to enable one to form at least an outline picture of the
royal economy and its relationship to the underlying economy. In previous
chapters conclusions have been presented on the policies of the Seleukid
kings and their implementation with regard to land, revenue, surpluses,
expenditure and coinage and on their system of financial administration,
none of which will be repeated here.

What will be considered instead is whether the problem posed in
chapter 3 was indeed solved. It was stated there, as a hypothesis, that
Seleukos I had need of silver, with which to face the predominantly monetary expenses of a Hellenistic king. His task was to transform the mainly
commodity-based economy of his empire into a monetary one, from which
to extract as much silver revenue as possible. In order to achieve this, he
apparently took certain measures, which are nowhere stated explicitly in
some royal decree, but can be surmised from their effects.

City-building on an unprecedented scale and the strengthening of existing urban centres created the markets where it was possible for rural communities to sell their produce and afterwards pay their taxes in coin. The
royal administration thus had the means to settle its expenses with silver,
which it increasingly did, particularly for the armed forces, rather than with
commodities, which had been the norm under the Achaemenids. Indeed,
the lesser need for commodity revenue led to a freer disposal of royal land,
in the form of grants to individuals, attachment to cities or temples or even
outright sale, when this might better serve the kings' financial policy.

An adequate supply of coinage was created by locating mints in most
regions to serve local needs, but new Seleukid issues were only intended to
cover supply shortages in the administrative-payments–tax-collection cycle.

Foreign issues were allowed to circulate freely, and indeed constituted the majority of all coins in use, for most of the time, as long as they helped to promote local economic activity and so ultimately benefit the royal treasury.

Royal revenue was systematically maximized to the limit that could be afforded by subject communities and in a variety of ways, using whichever suited a particular situation best, but, more often than not, with the objective of increasing silver inflows. When a lessening of the taxation burden was granted, there was normally a short-term political gain envisaged by the king or a long-term economic benefit.

The personal interest of the Seleukids in the financial matters of their realm is reflected in the close control they kept of their provincial financial administrators, who were apparently independent of the satrapal governors.

The evidence suggests that the measures the Seleukids took were successful. This was a state that endured for nearly two centuries as an empire (to 129 BC), suffering territorial losses in this time, but able to recover from them. When the empire eventually succumbed, it was not so much due to internal structural problems, but because it was unfortunate enough to encounter, at the same time, two rising powers, Rome in the west and Parthia in the east, which, in the end, proved too strong for it.

2. THE NATURE OF THE SELEUKID ROYAL ECONOMY

How can one view the Seleukid royal economy in the context of the ongoing debate on the nature of the ancient economy?

The starting point is, naturally, M. I. Finley and his characteristically blunt statement in *The Ancient Economy*:

The ancients in fact lacked the concept of an *economy*, and, *a fortiori*, they lacked the conceptual elements which together constitute what we call *the economy*. Of course they farmed, traded, manufactured, mined, taxed, coined, deposited and loaned money, made profits or failed in their enterprises. And they discussed these activities in their talk and their writing. What they did not do, however, was to combine these particular activities conceptually into a unit.

Finley did, however, acknowledge that there was 'one Greek attempt at a general statement in the opening of the second book of pseudo-Aristotle's *Oikonomika*', and then went on to dismiss the half a dozen paragraphs as being noteworthy only for their 'crashing banality', while pointing out their 'isolation in the whole of surviving ancient writing' (page 21).

The *Oikonomika* has been central to my analysis of the Seleukid royal economy. The 'half a dozen paragraphs of crashing banality', contemptuously dismissed by Finley, have been treated extensively in chapters 7–11, with all the evidence that could be brought to bear for the Seleukid period. It was suggested that the *Oikonomika* may actually represent the conditions of the Seleukid empire, probably at the time of Antiochos I, and that the treatise is likely to have been intended as an instruction manual for would-be administrators of satrapies and cities. This becomes more likely from §7, where, after the previous listing of the different types of 'economies', the 'royal' and 'household' are no longer of interest: 'So, having discussed the divisions (of financial administration), we must next consider whether the satrapy, with which we may be dealing, or the city, is able to support all (the revenues) we have just detailed or most of them and, if so, to make use of them.'

And the text goes on to produce the *cardinal tenet* of financial management of a satrapy or city: 'And after this (we must consider) which of the revenues that are not present at all can be made to exist, or that are now small can be increased, or which of the expenses that are now incurred should be cut and by how much, without damaging the whole (administration).'

There is a clear **statement of policy** here: 'increase income and cut expenditure', which is not at all the same as saying that receipts should be greater than payments, for in the latter case both might well be on the increase or decrease simultaneously. In other words, the emphasis in the *Oikonomika* is not on the balancing of a budget, but on the maximization of *net* revenue, which, in modern terminology, one could also call *profit*, as it applies to a business enterprise. In this context, the satrapy or the city is regarded, from the point of view of the would-be administrator, as a business, whose profit is to be maximized. Taking this one step further, the Seleukid empire, composed of satrapies and semi-autonomous Greek *poleis* (and their equivalent in economic terms: native cities and temples), might justifiably be considered as the king's own business.

But, there is a proviso, that 'the whole' should not be damaged. Clearly, there was a realization that unduly high taxation sometimes had the opposite of the desired effect of increasing revenue, certainly beyond the short term. The numerous tax concessions granted by Seleukid kings (ch. 8.1–7; ch. 10.4c), often for a few years only, are clear indications of a ps.-Aristotelian economic policy. That Sardeis or Jerusalem, for example, should not pay taxes for a while and should receive subsidies for material purchases obviously served the purpose of helping these cities find their feet after a period of troubles. It has been suggested by me that this was not so much a gesture of philanthropy on the part of the king, as a straightforward economic calculation of how soon these cities could start generating revenue again for the royal treasury, although there were naturally political and social considerations to be taken into account as well.

One possesses less information about expenditure and clearly there is always the possibility that a reduction noted in the sources was one compelled by the circumstances and not by an act of policy. Nevertheless, it seems to me that the granting of land in usufruct (ch. 6.3a) is an example of a *policy* of reducing direct state expenditure and, at the same time, passing on the risk of exploitation of land to someone else. The supply of seed to settlers for a limited period, for example to the Babylonian Jews sent to Lydia and Phrygia (ch. 10.4b), also seems to have been part of a policy of limiting expenditure to what was absolutely necessary. Although we do not possess concrete information on the score, it is likely that the method of founding cities and awarding *klēroi* to settlers may have followed the same principle. The minting of coins only when the need arose to make payments, that is, when there was a shortage in the demand that could not be met from the supply, a 'topping up' essentially of the level in circulation, is yet another example of a *policy* of controlling expenses. A general re-striking of existing coins of other states ('Alexanders', 'Lysimachi', Athenian 'owls', etc.) might have been good for prestige purposes, but would have increased minting costs unduly and, since the coinage standard remained the same, without generating the profit that a change of standard could produce, as in Ptolemaic Egypt.

What this boils down to, then, is that, far from being a revenue-motivated state, the Seleukid seems to have been, to a certain extent, **profit-motivated**. In this sense, it was closer to a modern capitalist economy than Finley would have been willing to admit.

One may argue, of course, that today's business enterprise is indeed profit-motivated, but that a modern state is not. Some years ago this may have been true of many European and other countries, which sought to improve social services to their citizens beyond their means to pay for them from annual income, at the expense of an ever increasing public debt. But this is no longer the case. The prevailing idea today, in Europe certainly, is one of a balanced budget. Even more so, for those states burdened by a heavy public debt, which constitute the majority, a positive budget balance is desirable, so that the debt may be gradually reduced. To achieve this, the modern state has to resort to the same ps.-Aristotelian philosophy, of increasing revenue and reducing costs, as did the Seleukid state.

Finley points out that one major difference between the ancient and the modern economy is that there was no such thing in antiquity as public debt. This is true, but, if one considers a situation where there is a policy of continuously reducing public debt, using a budget surplus each year, as is the case in many countries today, there is no real difference between the two economies when viewed from the perspective of the government. In both cases it is an annual surplus that is desired.

Just as ps.-Aristotle recommended that this surplus – or, more accurately, the increase in revenue and the reduction in cost – should not be unduly large so as to damage the whole economy producing it, so too the government of a modern state has to play very carefully with its different sources of revenue and destinations of expenditure in order to balance economic growth, inflation, the external balance of payments, employment, security, and so on. Needless to say, the modern is a much more complex system to manage, but not a radically different one.

Let us consider one important task of a modern government: that of **managing the money supply**, that is, of ensuring that the right amount of money is available in order to maintain economic activity at a desired level. This is virtually the same phrase as I have used for the Seleukid state, but with a slightly different content for two of the terms employed: 'money' and 'economic activity at the desired level'.

'Money', in the modern sense, is almost entirely fiduciary, whereas in the Seleukid world it consisted mainly of coinage in precious metal (ch. 11.3). There was, of course, also the element of commodity exchange, which I consider to have been gradually reduced as part of a conscious policy of monetization. Today the bulk of money is 'paper' in one form or another, such as banknotes, cheques, savings accounts, overdrafts, and government bonds, and coins generally have a nominal value greater than the true value of their metal content. One may ignore the use of 'paper' in antiquity as insignificant, although not unknown, but there certainly was a considerable token element to Seleukid bronze coinage and a conscious effort to replace small silver, circulating at more or less its true value, with token-value bronze (ch. 11.3d). In essence, a bronze coin is representative of a certain value of money, as is a banknote or other medium of payment. So the difference between the use of token money in the Seleukid economy and a modern one is really just a question of scale.

'Economic activity at the desired level': in a modern capitalist state, the bulk of economic activity is generated by business enterprises and private individuals, who work, earn, save, invest and consume. The 'desired level' of money in circulation is set primarily by their needs and not by those of the state. By contrast, in the Seleukid empire, the 'desired level' of money/coinage was determined by the need to fuel the administrative-payments–tax-collection cycle (ch. 11.4–5). The interests of private individuals and their enterprises were secondary to this primary objective. Note that 'tax-collection' is being used here in a broad sense, namely all the income accruing to the Seleukid king from all sources. In this sense, the Seleukid 'royal' economy is closer to that of a former communist state with regard to the money supply, in that it is the 'public' sector which makes the greatest use of money and sets the 'desired level' for its own needs.

Another key activity of a modern state is to manage its **balance of payments**. Had I interpreted ps.-Aristotle's *exagōgima* and *eisagōgima* as 'exports' and 'imports', as many scholars do, there would have been no need to discuss the matter further. Clearly the 'royal' economy would then have been responsible for the management of the 'balance of payments' of the Seleukid state vis-à-vis the external world. But this is not how I have taken the meaning in chapters 7.1b and 9. Rather, I support the idea of the movement of money and commodities between the 'royal' economy on the one hand and the 'satrapal' and 'city' economies on the other, for example surpluses of taxation from the satrapies that were sent to the king, excess production from royal land sold to the cities. In modern terms the closest one can get to this is a system of federal government or one of central government and semi-autonomous regions, as in the case of Spain, where the satrapies and cities are represented by states or regions. The federal (or central) government receives some taxes from the state (or region), while others are used by the state for its own needs. Similarly, the federal government undertakes certain expenses for the state or possesses assets in its territory which, when the need arises, can be provided for the state's own use, such as the land or services of a military establishment. In this sense there is movement of money, goods and services between the federal or central government and the state or region, not unlike that between the 'royal' economy and the 'satrapal' or 'city' economies.

One other important activity of a modern state is that of **developing infrastructure**. This is an area which has been considerably downplayed with regard to ancient states, whose structures have generally been considered to be consumption-oriented for a ruling elite rather than investment-oriented. While this may be true generally, one cannot help but wonder at the size of investment made by the Seleukid kings when their many city foundations are considered, if it is accepted, as I have tried to argue, that the motivation was mainly economic. The king was disposing of productive land, thereby losing immediate revenue, and at the same time incurring the cost of supplying the settlers with their initial requirements in order that new cities might be established or old ones improved and expanded.

But this was an investment which, in the longer term, could be expected to yield greater income for the king through increased economic activity in the area and resulting higher taxation revenue.

When a land grant was made to a city, temple or individual (ch. 6.3–4), I have maintained that economic considerations were frequently uppermost in the king's mind. Land may have become unprofitable for him, since he no longer required so much commodity produce to pay his expenses, but silver instead. The king might also eliminate a cost that he had incurred previously, for example an official's salary, by replacing it with a land grant. This is not unlike the contemporary situation in Egypt, where the Ptolemies allocated *klēroi* to military settlers in at least partial compensation for their services, because of their need to save on silver. The Seleukid king apparently preferred to see himself more as a *rentier*, receiving rent and tax in silver with relatively little effort, rather than in the role of gentleman-farmer, responsible for producing and selling his crops, with all the uncertainties this entailed. The disposal of land to his subjects was, in a sense, a form of **privatization**. Modern states today increasingly sell off their assets when they consider that private enterprise can run them more efficiently and produce a greater net return for the state in terms of increased (taxation) revenue and reduced costs.

To summarize then, there do not seem to be essential differences in the economic priorities of the Seleukid state compared to those of many modern ones. In that sense, with regard to the primitivist–modernist debate, I firmly classify myself as a modernist, *but only in so far as the behaviour of the Seleukid state is concerned.* Since I have only been concerned incidentally with the wider economy of the Seleukid empire, the 'underlying economy' as I have termed it, it is not appropriate that I should take up a position on its nature here.

Coin hoards lists

I. LARGE SILVER

Pub	Hoard	Name	Province	Stat	Date	Qty	%Sel	%Ale	%Lys	%Oth
		MESOPOTAMIA								
o	1756	Mosul 1862–3?	Mesopotamia		c. 305	88	0	100	0	0
8	256	Failaka 1984	Arabia & Gulf		c. 285	27	30	70	0	0
o	1761	Babylonia c. 1900?	Mesopotamia		c. 280	102	31	67	0	2
4	33	Mashtal, Irak 1972/3	Mesopotamia	Pot	c. 260	69	28	70	0	2
o	1763	Tell Halaf 1913	Mesopotamia		246–240	128	30	44	20	6
1	68	Bahrain 1969/70	Arabia & Gulf	Exc	245–215	292	0	100	0	0
o	1765	Bahrain 1970	Arabia & Gulf	Pot	240–230	192	0	60	0	40
o	1764	Mesopotamia <1920	Mesopotamia		c. 230	60	50	33	5	12
o	1768	Mosul <1917	Mesopotamia		c. 200	24	0	8	92	0
o	1769	Mesopotamia 1914–18	Mesopotamia		195–190	90	42	6	43	9
o	1772	Urfa 1924	Mesopotamia		185–160	164	45	26	18	11
o	1771	Zivnik 1962	Mesopotamia	Pot	c. 175	26	96	0	4	0
o	1773	Tell Kotchek 1952	Mesopotamia		170–155	604	0	100	0	0
o	1774	Babylonia 1900	Mesopotamia	Exc	155–150	100	16	43	11	30
o	1808	Susa 1934–9	Susiane	Exc	150–100	41	66	32	2	0
o	1804	Susa 1933–4	Susiane	Pot	c. 140	83	67	20	5	8
o	1805	Susiana 1958–9	Susiane		c. 138	124	88	8	0	4
o	1806	Susiana 1965?	Susiane		c. 138	282	82	6	0	12
o	1778	Baghdad 1954	Mesopotamia		c. 136	141	100	0	0	0
o	1780	Tell Ahmar 1929	Mesopotamia	Pot	110–105	70	83	0	0	17
o	1812	Susa 1947–8	Susiane	Pot	c. 90	51	0	98	0	2
o	1782	Midyat <1950	Mesopotamia		c. 80	40	43	0	0	57
o	1784	Mardin c. 1953	Mesopotamia		60–55	31	6	0	0	94
o	1786	Basra c. 1955	Mesopotamia		c. 45	532	14	30	0	56
		UPPER SATRAPIES								
o	1734	Diyarbekir <1938	Armenia		290 280	100	100	0	0	0
o	1794	Pasargadai 1963	Persis		c. 280	34	24	76	0	0
o	1796	Kaswin 1964	Media		c. 275	86	53	47	0	0
1	58	Qazvin 1964	Media		c. 275	86	84	16	0	0
o	1798	Atrek c. 1965	Hyrkania		c. 209	1536	0	40	0	60
o	1735	Diyarbekir 1955	Armenia		c. 205	35	40	17	31	12
o	1822	Oxus River 1887	Sogdiane		180–170	167	17	60	1	22

(cont.)

Pub	Hoard	Name	Province	Stat	Date	Qty	%Sel	%Ale	%Lys	%Oth
		UPPER SATRAPIES (*cont.*)								
3	53	Aï Khanoum 1973	Baktria		*c.* 160	62	10	11	0	79
2	88	Balkh 1974?	Baktria		*c.* 150	191	7	1	2	91
0	1826	Khisht Tepe 1946	Baktria		*c.* 100	607	1	0	0	99
0	1813	Tehran 1922 (+9/554)	Media		90–85	418	71	5	0	24
0	1814	Gombad *c.* 1955	Hyrkania		*c.* 53	508	44	0	0	56
0	1744	Diyarbekir 1955	Armenia		*c.* 30	150	7	0	0	93
0	1746	Sarnakunk 1945	Armenia		30–25	70	19	0	0	81
		N. SYRIA AND KILIKIA								
0	1516	Aleppo 1893	N. Syria		*c.* 305	912	0	100	0	0
0	1522	Syria? *c.* 1964	N. Syria		305–280	40	100	0	0	0
0	1524	Aleppo 1933	N. Syria		290–280	92	18	80	0	2
0	1424	Mersin *c.* 1963	Kilikia		*c.* 280	31	10	48	39	3
0	1423	Armenak 1927 (+8/595)	Kilikia		275–270	685	1	41	58	0
8	3081	Meydancikkale A 1980	Kilikia	Pot	240–235	1704	7	40	4	49
8	3082	Meydancikkale B 1980	Kilikia	Pot	240–235	1742	5	12	3	80
8	3083	Meydancikkale C 1980	Kilikia	Pot	240–235	526	11	88	1	0
0	1529	Homs 1927	N. Syria		*c.* 230	50	18	0	78	4
0	1532	Homs 1934	N. Syria	Pot	*c.* 210	60	28	2	57	13
0	1535	Syria 1959	N. Syria		210–200	34	47	24	12	17
3	51	Midyat Mardin <1976	Kilikia		200–175	26	100	0	0	0
9	501	Oylum Hoyugu 1989	N. Syria		200–195	60	45	22	25	8
0	1536	Latakia 1946	N. Syria		*c.* 198	34	24	50	0	26
0	1537	Kosseir 1949	N. Syria		*c.* 190	40	10	53	13	24
0	1538	Dniye 1952	N. Phoenicia		*c.* 190	38	11	39	5	45
2	81	Syria 1971	N. Syria		*c.* 190	90	19	44	0	37
0	1547	Khan Cheikhoun 1940	N. Syria		170–160	103	0	79	0	21
1	77	Syria <1960	N. Syria		170–160	142	0	100	0	0
0	1544	Latakia 1759	N. Syria		*c.* 169	80	28	56	4	12
0	1546	Aleppo 1931	N. Syria		*c.* 164	35	17	49	0	34
6	37	Syria 1979	N. Syria		*c.* 160	156	51	26	13	10
8	434	Syria 1990	N. Syria		*c.* 160	65	75	2	11	12
0	1553	Antakya 1959	N. Syria		*c.* 150	28	100	0	0	0
0	1559	Akkar 1956	N. Syria		*c.* 150	69	1	57	0	42
0	1560	Ghonsle 1955?	N. Syria		*c.* 150	9	7	0	0	93
0	1433	Osmaniye 1968	Kilikia		*c.* 145	289	68	7	0	25
0	1555	Syria 1971	N. Syria		*c.* 145	150	100	0	0	0
0	1556	Syria 1906	N. Syria		145–140	38	8	16	0	76
8	360	Afamya 1986	N. Syria	Pot	145–125	1160	100	0	0	0
8	456	Syria 1984	N. Syria		*c.* 145	39	100	0	0	0
0	1557	Teffaha 1954	N. Phoenicia		*c.* 140	27	7	59	0	34
1	87	Cilicia 1972 (+2/90)	Kilikia		*c.* 140	595	2	1	0	97
8	471	Tartous 1987	N. Phoenicia		*c.* 120	140	24	67	0	9
0	1435	Cilicia 1848	Kilikia		*c.* 115	138	100	0	0	0
0	1568	Kessab 1952	N. Syria		*c.* 110	388	86	0	0	14

(*cont.*)

Pub	Hoard	Name	Province	Stat	Date	Qty	%Sel	%Ale	%Lys	%Oth
		ASIA MINOR								
0	1443	Asia Minor 1965	Und. A. Minor		*c.* 310	29	0	100	0	0
8	221	Turkey? 1987	Und. A. Minor		305–281	107	0	7	93	0
0	1398	Karaman 1969	Lykia		*c.* 300	49	0	100	0	0
0	1422	Asia Minor *c.* 1960	South A. Minor		*c.* 300	160	0	100	0	0
0	1399	Ankara *c.* 1913	Galatia		290–285	179	16	84	0	0
1	55	Asia Minor 1970	Und. A. Minor		290–280	294	4	96	0	0
0	1292	Mugla 1945	Karia		*c.* 280	31	0	0	13	87
0	1293	Manissa 1971	Lydia		*c.* 280	24	4	88	8	0
3	33	Karalar Usak 1960–9	Und. A. Minor		*c.* 280	52	0	83	17	0
1	56	Turkey 1973/4	Und. A. Minor		*c.* 275	94	2	97	1	0
0	1368	Asia Minor *c.* 1970	North A. Minor		*c.* 265	35	6	94	0	0
0	1403	Gordium 1959	Phrygia	Pot	*c.* 250	42	5	93	2	0
0	1447	Asia Minor? 1950	Und. A. Minor		*c.* 240	47	17	11	45	27
8	305	Turkey 1984	North A. Minor		*c.* 240	89	0	6	0	94
9	499	Sardes 1911 (0–1299)	Lydia	Pot	*c.* 240	47	30	43	21	6
0	1425	Pamphylia? 1964	Pamphylia		*c.* 230	31	10	48	39	3
0	1370	Asia Minor 1929	North A. Minor		*c.* 225	58	17	24	9	50
8	317	S.W. Asia Minor 1991	West A. Minor		*c.* 225	198	81	8	0	11
0	1369	Kirazli 1939 (+8/324)	Pontos		*c.* 220	190	17	71	9	3
0	1426	Asia Minor 1963	South A. Minor		210–200	34	3	47	24	26
0	1405	Gordium 1961	Phrygia	Pot	*c.* 205	100	39	37	15	9
0	1406	Gordium 1951	Phrygia	Pot	205–200	113	32	45	16	7
0	1303	Pergamum 1960	Mysia	Pot	*c.* 201	22	23	41	9	27
1	73	Asia Minor 1972	Und. A. Minor		*c.* 200	70	24	9	31	36
1	74	Asia Minor/N.S. 1970	Und. A. Minor		*c.* 200	148	71	2	10	17
8	370	Asia Minor 1989	Und. A. Minor		*c.* 195	463	14	21	65	0
0	1318	Sardes 1911	Lydia	Pot	*c.* 190	60	23	50	0	27
0	1410	Mektepini 1956	Phrygia		*c.* 190	752	13	65	15	7
0	1411	Asia Minor 1963	Cent. A. Minor		*c.* 190	81	35	40	2	23
0	1413	Ayaz-In *c.* 1953	Cent. A. Minor		190–188	170	21	55	0	24
0	1450	Asia Minor 1949	Und. A. Minor		*c.* 190	251	41	7	41	11
8	376	Turkey	Und. A. Minor		*c.* 190	21	0	100	0	0
5	43	Pamphylia 1977+V134	Pamphylia		*c.* 180	247	22	76	1	1
8	428	Turkey 1990	Und. A. Minor		*c.* 170	24	0	100	0	0
7	105	Konya 1981	Cent. A. Minor		160–140	84	0	99	0	1
0	1432	Asia Minor 1964	South A. Minor		*c.* 150	22	0	27	14	59
0	1453	Asia Minor *c.* 1962	Und. A Minor		150–140	86	9	0	0	91
8	445	Ninica 1987	Und. A. Minor		*c.* 150	536	6	94	0	0
0	1454	Asia Minor *c.* 1959	Und. A. Minor		*c.* 125	119	13	0	0	87
		KOILE SYRIA								
0	1514	Tel Tsippor 1960	Palestine		*c.* 311	59	0	100	0	0
2	54	Byblus 1971	Phoenicia		*c.* 310	22	0	100	0	0

(*cont.*)

Pub	Hoard	Name	Province	Stat	Date	Qty	%Sel	%Ale	%Lys	%Oth
		KOILE SYRIA (*cont.*)								
0	1515	Byblus 1931	Phoenicia	Pot	309–308	140	0	98	0	2
0	1519	Beirut 1964	Phoenicia		*c.* 300	27	4	96	0	0
0	1520	Galilee 1964	Palestine		*c.* 300	35	0	100	0	0
8	433	Maaret en-Numan 1980	Phoenicia		*c.* 162	536	32	49	4	15
0	1591	Tyre 1954	Phoenicia		*c.* 145	20	15	0	0	85
8	458	Galilee?	Palestine		*c.* 145	64	100	0	0	0
1	86	Cheikh Miskin 1967	Phoenicia		143–142	167	100	0	0	0
0	1593	Ras-Baalbek 1957	S. Syria		*c.* 140	43	26	0	0	74
0	1594	Saida 1862–3	Phoenicia		*c.* 140	70	100	0	0	0
7	109	Hebron 1979	Palestine		*c.* 140	44	39	0	0	61
9	529	Dura 1975	Palestine		*c.* 140	87	31	0	0	69
0	1597	Khan el-Abde 1938	Phoenicia		*c.* 138	118	31	0	0	69
8	464	Ramallah 1992	Palestine		*c.* 135	29	100	0	0	0
3	61	Hebron 1976	Palestine		*c.* 131	124	100	0	0	0
9	533	Tyre 1987	Phoenicia		129–128	109	100	0	0	0
0	1599	Phoenicia *c.* 1966	Phoenicia		126–125	30	100	0	0	0
0	1601	Nablus 1891?	Palestine		*c.* 125	36	83	0	0	17
0	1602	Capernaum 1957	Palestine		*c.* 125	78	100	0	0	0
0	1603	Bethlehem 1971	Palestine		*c.* 125	51	100	0	0	0
8	469	Jerusalem 1991	Palestine		*c.* 125	83	100	0	0	0
0	1604	Thalalaia 1953	S. Syria		*c.* 120	24	58	0	0	42
8	472	Waqqas 1982	Palestine		*c.* 120	90	100	0	0	0
3	63	Haifa 1969	Palestine		113–112	36	100	0	0	0
8	477	Haifa 1969	Palestine		113–112	21	100	0	0	0
0	1605	Haifa 1969	Palestine		*c.* 112	24	100	0	0	0
9	544	Marisa 1989	Palestine		*c.* 112	25	100	0	0	0
8	479	Baalbek? 1979	S. Syria		*c.* 110	76	86	0	0	14
0	1607	Jericho 1965–6	Palestine		*c.* 100	109	95	0	0	5
0	1619	Tripolis 1884–5	Phoenicia		100–50	110	57	0	0	43
9	550	Rafah 1968	Palestine		100–75	52	54	0	0	6
0	1609	Gaza 1969	Palestine		*c.* 95	51	96	0	0	4
0	1610	Palestine <1941	Palestine		*c.* 86	34	6	0	0	94
8	511	Lebanon 1987	Phoenicia		*c.* 85	26	35	0	0	65

2. SMALL SILVER

Pub	Hoard	Name	Province	Stat	Date	Qty	%Sel	%Ale	%Lys	%Oth
		MESOPOTAMIA								
0	1763	Tell Halaf 1913	Mesopotamia		246–240	224	0	98	2	0
0	1764	Mesopotamia <1920	Mesopotamia		*c.* 230	34	26	68	6	0
0	1799	Susa 1948–9	Susiane	Exc	210–200	20	0	95	5	0
0	1768	Mosul <1917	Mesopotamia		*c.* 200	37	0	95	5	0
0	1806	Susiana 1965?	Susiane		*c.* 138	42	100	0	0	0
		UPPER SATRAPIES								
0	1822	Oxus River 1887	Sogdiane		180–170	137	20	73	0	7
0	1803	Kuh i-Tuftan	Gedrosia		*c.* 140	25	76	0	0	24
0	1813	Teheran 1922 (+9/554)	Media		90–85	843	1	0	0	99
9	556	Artaxata 1972	Armenia	Exc	80–70	21	5	5	0	90

(*cont.*)

Pub	Hoard	Name	Province	Stat	Date	Qty	%Sel	%Ale	%Lys	%Oth
		N. SYRIA AND KILIKIA								
o	1516	Aleppo 1893	N. Syria		*c.* 305	37	o	100	o	o
o	1423	Armenak 1927 (+8/595)	Kilikia		275–270	1216	o	96	3	1
o	1534	Bab 1944	N. Syria		250–200	212	1	88	8	3
8	3081	Medancikkale A 1980	Kilikia	Pot	240–235	694	1	97	2	o
8	3082	Medancikkale B 1980	Kilikia	Pot	240–235	44	o	91	2	7
8	3083	Medancikkale C 1980	Kilikia	Pot	240–235	605	1	97	2	o
9	501	Oylum Hoyugu 1989	N. Syria		200–195	74	o	89	7	4
6	37	Syria 1979	N. Syria		*c.* 160	80	38	o	o	62
o	1552	Arab el Mulk 1940	N. Syria		*c.* 150	28	4	o	o	96
3	60	S. E. Turkey (+4/64)	Kilikia		*c.* 142	750	100	o	o	o
		ASIA MINOR								
o	1444	Asia Minor 1961	Und. A. Minor		*c.* 300	205	o	99	o	1
o	1445	Asia Minor <1951	Und. A. Minor		*c.* 300	40	o	100	o	o
2	60	Asia Minor 1970's	Und. A. Minor		*c.* 300	22	o	100	o	o
3	30	Afyon? Turkey <1976	Cent. A. Minor		*c.* 300	75	o	100	o	o
7	61	Denizli 1963	Und. A. Minor		*c.* 300	129	o	98	2	o
8	238	Asia Minor 1993	Und. A. Minor		*c.* 300	27	o	100	o	o
9	472	Cullugore 1989	West. A. Minor		300–275	25	o	100	o	o
9	474	Dandiri 1942	West. A. Minor		300–275	73	o	99	1	o
o	1292	Mugla 1945	Karia		*c.* 280	21	o	71	5	24
o	1401	Gordium 1959	Phrygia	Pot	*c.* 280	50	o	94	6	o
o	1446	Asia Minor *c.* 1967	Und. A. Minor		*c.* 280	45	o	82	18	o
8	267	Denizli 1982	Und. A. Minor		*c.* 280	35	o	100	o	o
9	487	Unknown 1995	Und. A. Minor		260–250	80	o	99	1	o
9	488	Unknown <1985	Und. A. Minor		260–230	31	o	100	o	o
o	1369	Kirazli 1939 (+8/324)	Pontos		*c.* 220	612	1	96	2	1
8	445	Ninica 1987	Und. A. Minor		*c.* 150	70	o	97	3	o

3. GOLD

Pub	Hoard	Name	Province	Stat	Date	Qty	%Sel	%Ale	%Lys	%Oth
		MESOPOTAMIA								
o	1806	Susiana 1965?	Susiane		*c.* 138	2	100	o	o	o
		UPPER SATRAPIES								
7	78	Tarik Darreh 1974	Media		226–225	100	100	o	o	o

(cont.)

Pub	Hoard	Name	Province	Stat	Date	Qty	%Sel	%Ale	%Lys	%Oth
		UPPER SATRAPIES (*cont.*)					·			
8	312	Tarik Darreh 1974	Media		226–225	55	55	40	0	5
0	1822	Oxus River 1887	Sogdiane		180–170	31	31	0	0	69
		N. SYRIA AND KILIKIA								
0	1553	Antakya 1959	N. Syria		*c.* 150	4	100	0	0	0
		ASIA MINOR								
0	1442	Asia Minor *c.* 1950	Und. A. Minor		*c.* 310	24	0	100	0	0
0	1294	Maeander Valley 1895	Karia		300–250	13	0	100	0	0
0	1404	Gordium 1963	Phrygia	Pot	*c.* 223	5	40	60	0	0
0	1369	Kirazli 1939 (+8/324)	Pontos		*c.* 220	13	15	46	38	1

Documents and translations

The version of each text used is that of the first reference given in each case, unless otherwise stated. Only relevant parts of the texts have been provided, with my own translation. Interpolations in round brackets are simply intended to make the translation more readable.

DOCUMENT I. ANTIGONOS' LETTER TO TEOS REGARDING THE SYNOIKISM WITH LEBEDOS

RC 3.

Summary §1–9
Antigonos Monophthalmos settled the details of the synoikism between Teos and Lebedos.

Summary §10, lines 72–80

The Lebedians wished to be allowed to set up a fund to import grain in order to create a reserve, which the Teians seconded and even asked for more money. Antigonos was not pleased with the idea.

(80)   ἡμεῖς δὲ πρότερον μὲν οὐ[κ ἐβουλόμεθα μηδεμιᾶι πό-]
λει δίδοσθαι τὰ σιτηγήσια μηδὲ σίτου γίνεσθαι παράθε[σιν, οὐ θέλοντες τὰς]
[π]όλεις εἰς ταῦτα ἀναλίσκειν χρήματα συχνὰ οὐκ ἀναγκαῖα [ὄντα, ἐβουλόμεθα δὲ]
[ο]ὐδὲ νῦν ποιεῖν τοῦτο, πλησίον οὔσης τῆς φορολογουμέ[νης χώρας ὥστε ἐὰν χρεία]
[γ]ίνηται σίτου, εὐχερῶς οἰόμεθα εἶναι μεταπέμπεσθαι ἐκ [ταύτης ὁπόσ-]
(85) [ο]ν ἄν τις βούληται·

In the past we did not desire to give any city the right of importing grain or of creating a reserve store of grain, because we did not wish the cities to spend money on these things which were often not necessary. And neither did we desire to do this now, as the taxed land is close by, so that, if there were need for grain, we believe that as much as necessary could easily be requested to be brought from it.

Summary §10, lines 85–94

The king explained that he did not normally allow cities to import grain because he did not wish them to fall into debt, but in this case he would make an exception. He then introduced a new subject:

§11.   τῶν δὲ σίτων]
(95) καὶ εἰσαγωγὴν καὶ ἐξαγωγὴν πάντων ἀποδειχθῆνα[ι ἐν τῆι στοᾶι τῆς ἀγο-]
ρᾶς, ὅπως ἐάν τισι μὴ λυσιτελῆι κατάγουσιν εἰς τὴν ἀ[γορὰν ἀπὸ ταύτης ποιεῖσ-]
θαι τὴν ἐξαγωγήν, ἐξουσία ἦι θεῖσιν τὰ τέλη ἐπὶ τῶν [ἐν τῆι ἀγορᾶι ἀποδει-]
χθέντων ἐξάγειν· ὅσαι δ᾽ ἂν κῶμαι ἢ ἐπαύλια ὦσιν ἔξ[ω τῆς πόλεως]
[ὑμ]ῶν, νομίζομεν δεῖν προσαφορισθῆναι ἑκάστωι ἐγγ[ράψαι μὲν ὁπόσους ἂν καρ-]
(100) [πο]ὺς ἐξάγειν βούληται ἀπὸ τῆς ἀγροικίας, ἐπαγγείλαν[τα δὲ τῶι]
ἀγορανόμωι καὶ τὰ]
[τ]έλη διορθωσάμενον ἐξάγειν.

§11. The movements in and out (of the city)[1] of all grain should be declared in the portico of the agora so that, if it is not profitable for someone to bring (his produce) to the agora in order to send it out from there, he should have the right to send it out, having paid the dues on what was declared in the agora. And with regard to those villages and farms that are outside your city, we think that it would be a good idea to

---

[1] The use of the terms 'imports' and 'exports' has been avoided in the translation, in keeping with the policy noted in chapter 1.3 of leaving the meaning as general as possible until the text can be further analysed. In the case of this inscription, it is not only the grain imports and exports of the city as political unit that are liable to sales taxes and tolls, but also the transfers between the city and its own *chōra* or even within the *chōra*, in short all movements of grain. The key to understanding the text is the distinction made between the city (as urban centre) and the villages and farms outside it, which were presumably part of the city's *chōra*, otherwise of what interest would they have been to the market commissioner?

require each person to register the amount of produce he wished to send out of his farm, so that he might send it out, having informed the market commissioner and paid the dues.

Summary §12

Finally, three men each from Teos and Lebedos would be nominated to see to any details concerning the synoikism that might have been omitted.

DOCUMENT 2. THE ARISTODIKIDES DOSSIER

RC 10–13.

No. 10 First land grant to Aristodikides

Βασιλεὺς Ἀντίοχος Μελεά-
γρωι χαίρειν· δεδώκαμεν Ἀριστοδικίδει τῶι Ἀσσίωι
γῆς ἐργασίμου πλέθρα δισχίλια προσενέγκασθαι
πρὸς τὴν Ἰλιέων πόλιν ἢ Σκηψίων· σὺ οὖν σύνταξον
(5) παραδεῖξαι Ἀριστοδικίδει ἀπὸ τῆς ὁμορούσης τῆι
Γεργιθίαι ἢ τῆι Σκηψίαι, οὗ ἂν δοκιμάζηις, τὰ δισχίλια
πλέθρα τῆς γῆς, καὶ προσορίσαι εἰς τὴν Ἰλιέων ἢ τὴν
Σκηψίων. Ἔρρωσο.

King Antiochos to Meleagros, greetings. We have given Aristodikides of Assos 2,000 plethra of cultivable land to be attached to the city of Ilion or that of Skepsis. So issue orders that from the land bordering on that of Gergis or Skepsis, whichever you think best, 2,000 plethra of land be conveyed to Aristodikides and attached to that of Ilion or Skepsis. Be in good health.

No. 11 Second land grant

Βασιλεὺς Ἀντίοχος Μελε-
άγρωι χαίρειν· ἐνέτυχεν ἡμῖν Ἀριστοδικίδης ὁ
Ἄσσιος, ἀξιῶν δοῦναι αὐτῶι ἡμᾶς ἐν τῆι ἐφ᾽ Ἑλλησ-
πόντου σατραπείαι τὴν Πέτραν, ἣμ πρότερον
(5) εἶχεν Μελέαγρος, καὶ τῆς χώρας τῆς Πετρί[δ]ος
ἐργασίμου π[λ]έθρα χίλια πεντακόσια, καὶ ἄλλα
γῆς πλέθρα δισχίλια ἐργασίμου ἀπὸ τῆς ὁμορούσης τῆι πρότερον δοθείσηι αὐτῶι μερίδι·
καὶ ἡμεῖς τήν τε Πέτραν δεδώκαμεν αὐτῶι, εἰ
(10) μὴ δέδοται ἄλλωι πρότερον, καὶ τὴν χώραν τὴν
πρὸς τῆι Πέτραι καὶ ἄλλα γῆς πλέθρα δισχίλια
ἐργασίμου, διὰ τὸ φίλον ὄντα ἡμέτερον παρεσ-
χῆσθαι ἡμῖν τὰς καθ᾽ αὐτὸν χρείας μετὰ πάσης
εὐνοίας [κ]αὶ προθυμίας· σὺ οὖν ἐπισκεψάμενος,
(15) εἰ μὴ δέδ[ο]ται ἄλλωι πρότερον αὕτη ἡ Πέτρα, πα-

ράδειξον αὐτὴν καὶ τὴν πρὸς αὐτῆι χώραν Ἀριστοδικίδηι, καὶ ἀπὸ τῆς βασιλικῆς χώρας τῆς ὁμ[ο-]
ρούσης τῆι πρότερον δεδομένηι χώραι Ἀριστοδ[ι-]
κίδηι σύνταξον καταμετρῆσαι καὶ παραδεῖξαι
(20) αὐτῶι πλέθρα δισχίλια, καὶ ἐᾶσαι αὐτὸν προσενέγκασθαι πρὸς ἣμ ἂμ βούληται πόλιν τῶν ἐν τῆι χώρα[ι]
τε καὶ συμμαχίαι· οἱ δὲ βασιλικοὶ λαοὶ οἱ ἐκ τοῦ τό-
που ἐν ὧι ἐστιν ἡ Πέτρα ἐὰμ βούλωνται οἰκεῖν ἐν τῆ[ι]
Πέτραι ἀσφαλείας ἕνεκε, συντετάχαμεν Ἀριστο-
(25) {το}δικίδηι ἐᾶν αὐτοὺς οἰκεῖν· ἔρρωσο.

King Antiochos to Meleagros, greetings. Aristodikides of Assos came to us and requested that we give him (the village of) Petra in the Hellespontine satrapy, which Meleagros formerly held, and 1,500 plethra of Petra's cultivable land and another 2,000 plethra of cultivable land from that bordering on the first lot given to him. And we gave him Petra, as long as it had not been given to someone else previously, and the land of Petra and 2,000 more plethra of cultivable land, because he has provided services to us as our friend with goodwill and eagerness. So, after having investigated whether Petra had not been given to someone else previously, transfer it and its surrounding land to Aristodikides, and, from the royal land that is adjacent to that given earlier to Aristodikides, order the measurement and transfer to him of 2,000 plethra, and allow him to attach it to whichever city he wishes of those in (our) country and alliance. (Regarding) the royal laoi of the district in which Petra lies, if they wish to reside in Petra for reasons of security, we have ordered Aristodikides to allow them to live (there). Be in good health.

No. 12 Revision of the second land grant

Βασιλεὺς Ἀντίοχος Μελεάγρωι χαίρειν· ἐνέτυχεν ἡ-
μῖν Ἀριστοδικίδης, φάμενος Πέτραν τὸ χωρίον καὶ τὴν
χώραν τὴν συγκυροῦσαν, περὶ ἧς πρότερον ἐγράψαμεν
διδόντες αὐτῶι, οὐδ᾽ ἔτι καὶ νῦν παρειληφθῆναι διὰ τὸ Ἀθη-
(5) ναίωι τῶι ἐπὶ τοῦ ναυστάθμου ἐπικεχωρῆσθαι, καὶ ἠξί-
ωσεν ἀντὶ μὲν τῆς Πετρίτιδος χώρας παραδειχθῆνα[ι]
αὐτῶι τὰ ἴσα πλέθρα, συγχωρηθῆναι δὲ καὶ ἄλλα πλέθρα δισχίλια, προσενέγκασθαι πρὸς ἣν ἂμ βούληται
τῶμ πόλεων τῶν ἐν τῆι ἡμετέραι συμμαχίαι, καθά-
(10) περ καὶ πρότερον ἐγράψαμεν· ὁρῶντες οὖν αὐτὸν
εὔνουν ὄντα καὶ πρόθυμον εἰς τὰ ἡμέτερα πράγμ[α-]
τα βουλόμεθα πολυωρεῖν τἀνθρώπου, καὶ περὶ
τούτων συγκεχωρήκαμεν· φησὶν δὲ εἶναι τῆς
Πετρίτιδος χώρας τὰ συγχωρηθέντα αὐτῶι
(15) πλέθρα χίλια πεντακόσια· σύνταξον οὖν καταμετρῆσαι Ἀριστοδικίδηι καὶ παραδεῖξαι γῆς
ἐργασίμου τά τε δισχίλια καὶ πεντακόσια πλέθρα καὶ ἀντὶ τῶν περὶ τὴν Πέτραν ἄλλα ἐργα-

σίμου χ[ί]λια πεντακόσια ἀπὸ τῆς βασιλικῆς χώ-
(20) ρας τῆς συνοριζούσης τῆι ἐν ἀρχῆι δοθείσηι
αὐτῶι παρ' ἡμῶν· ἐᾶσαι δὲ καὶ προσενέγκασθα[ι]
τὴγ χώραν Ἀριστοδικίδην πρὸς ἢν ἂν βούλητα[ι]
πόλιν τῶν ἐν τῆι ἡμετέραι συμμαχίαι, καθάπερ καὶ ἐν τῆι πρότερον ἐπιστολῆι ἐγράψαμε[ν·]
(25)   ἔρρωσο.

King Antiochos to Meleagros, greetings. Aristodikides has come to us saying that the place Petra and the land belonging to it, about which we had previously written giving them to him, has not as yet been received, because it had been assigned to Athenaios the commander of the naval base, and he requested that there be conveyed to him, instead of the land of Petra, the same number of plethra, *and that there be given to him another 2,000 plethra to be attached to whichever city he wishes of those in our alliance, as we wrote earlier. Seeing therefore that he is well disposed and eager with regard to our affairs, we wish to favour the man greatly and have conceded this. He says that the land of Petra conceded to him was 1,500* plethra. *So order that there be measured and conveyed to Aristodikides both the 2,500* plethra *of cultivable land and, in place of that around Petra, another 1,500* plethra *of cultivable land from the royal land bordering on that given to him by us initially. And also allow Aristodikides to attach the land to whichever city he wishes of those in our alliance, just as we wrote in the previous letter. Be in good health.*

No. 13   *Covering letter of Meleagros*

Μελέαγρος Ἰλιέων τῆι βουλῆι καὶ τῶι δήμω χαί-
ρειν· ἀπέδωκεν ἡμῖν Ἀριστοδικίδης ὁ Ἄσσιος ἐπιστολὰς παρὰ τοῦ βασιλέως Ἀντιόχου, ὧν τἀντίγρα-
φα ὑμῖν ὑπογεγράφαμεν· ἐνέτυχεν δ' ἡμῖν καὶ αὐ-
(5) τὸς φάμενος, πολλῶν αὐτῶι καὶ ἑτέρων διαλεγομένων καὶ στέφανον διδόντων, ὥσπερ καὶ ἡ-
μεῖς παρακολουθοῦμεν διὰ τὸ καὶ πρεσβεῦσαι ἀ-
πὸ τῶν πόλεών τινας πρὸς ἡμᾶς, βούλεσθαι τὴν
χώραν τὴν δεδομένην αὐτῶι ὑπὸ τοῦ βασιλέως Ἀν-
(10) τιόχου καὶ διὰ τὸ ἱερὸν καὶ διὰ τὴν πρὸς ἡμᾶς εὔνοι-
αν προσενέγκασθαι πρὸς τὴν ὑμετέραν πόλιν· ἃ
μὲν οὖν ἀξιοῖ γενέσθαι αὐτῶι παρὰ τῆς πόλεως, αὐτὸς ὑμῖν δηλώσει· καλῶς δ' ἂν ποήσαιτε ψηφισάμε-
νοί τε πάντα τὰ φιλάνθρωπα αὐτῶι καὶ καθ' ὅτι ἂν
(15) συγχωρήσηι τὴν ἀναγραφὴν ποησάμενοι καὶ στη-
λώσαντες καὶ θέντες εἰς τὸ ἱερόν, ἵνα μένηι ὑμῖν
βεβαίως εἰς πάντα τὸγ χρόνον τὰ συγχωρηθέντα·
ἔρρωσθε.

Meleagros to the Council and Assembly of the Ilians. Aristodikides of Assos has given me letters from the king, of which I have prepared copies for you. He also visited me himself saying that, although many others had spoken to him and presented him with crowns – something which I also observe as some of the cities have sent embassies to me too – he wishes to attach the land that is given to him by King Antiochos to your city, both because of the sanctuary and of his goodwill towards you. So those things which he requires that the city should do for him, he will inform you of himself. You would do well to vote the full range of privileges for him and whatever he may agree to and record these on a stele and set it up in the sanctuary, so that everything agreed to may be secured for you for all time. Be in good health.

DOCUMENT 3. THE LAODIKE DOSSIER

RC 18–20.

No. 18 Land sale to Laodike

Βασιλεὺς Ἀντίοχος Μητροφάνει χαίρειν. Πεπ[ρά-]
καμεν Λαοδίκηι Πάννου κώμην καὶ τὴμ βᾶριν καὶ τὴν προσοῦσαν χώραν τῆι κώμηι, ὅρος τῆι τε Ζελείτιδι χώραι καὶ τῆι Κυζικ-
ηνῆι καὶ τῆι ὁδῶι τῆι ἀρχαίαι, ἣ ἦμ μὲν ἐπάνω Πάννου κώμης, σ[υ-]
(5) [ν]ηροτρια[σμένη δὲ ὑπὸ τῶ]ν γεωργούντων πλησίον ἕνεκεν τοῦ ἀ-
ποτεμέσθαι τὸ χωρίον – τὴμ μὲν Πάν[νου κώμην ὑπα]ρχούσαν συμβαίνει ὕστερον γεγενῆσθαι – καὶ εἴ τινες <ε>ἰς τὴν χ[ώ]ραν ταύτην ἐμ[πί-]
πτουσιν τόποι καὶ τοὺς ὑπάρχοντας αὐτο[ῖς λ]αοὺ[ς πα-]
νοικίους σὺν τοῖς ὑπάρχουσιν πᾶσιν καὶ σὺν ταῖς [τοῦ ἑ-]
(10) νάτου καὶ πεντηκοστοῦ ἔτους προσόδοις, ἀρ[γυ-]
ρίου ταλάντων τριάκοντα – ὁμοίως δὲ καὶ εἴ τινες ἐ-
[κ] τῆς κώμης ταύτης ὄντες λαοὶ μετεληλύθασιν εἰς ἄλλου-
ς τόπους – ἐφ᾽ ὧι οὐθὲν ἀποτελεῖ εἰς τὸ βασιλικὸν καὶ κυρία ἔ[σ-]
ται προσφερομένη πρὸς πόλιν ἣν ἂν βούληται· κατὰ ταῦτα δ[ὲ]
(15) καὶ οἱ παρ᾽ αὐτῆς πριάμενοι ἢ λαβόντες αὐτοί τε ἕξουσιν κυρίως καὶ πρὸς πόλιν προσοίσονται ἣν ἂμ βούλω[ν]ται,
ἐάμπερ μὴ Λαοδίκη τυγχάνει πρότερον προσενηνεγμένη πρὸς πόλιν, οὕτω δὲ κεκτήσονται οὗ ἂν ἡ χώρα ἦι προσωρισμένη ὑπὸ Λαοδίκης· τὴν δὲ τιμὴν συντετάχα-
(20) μεν ἀνενεγκεῖν εἰς τὸ κατὰ ΣΤΡΑΤΕΙΑΝ γαζοφυλάκ[ι-]
ον ἐν τρισὶν ἀναφοραῖς, ποιουμένου<ς> τὴμ μὲν μίαν ἐν τῶι Αὐ-
δναίωι μηνὶ τῶι ἐν τῶι ἑξηκοστῶι ἔτει, τὴν δὲ ἑτέραν ἐ[ν]
τῶι Ξανδικῶι, τὴν δὲ τρίτην ἐν τῶι ἐχομένωι τριμήνωι·
σύνταξον παραδεῖξαι Ἀρριδαίωι τῶι οἰκονομοῦντι τὰ Λαοδί-
(25) κης τήν τε κώμην καὶ τὴν βᾶριν καὶ τὴν προσοῦσαν χώραν
καὶ τοὺς λαοὺς πανοικίους σὺν τοῖς ὑπάρχουσιν αὐτοῖς
πᾶσιν, καὶ τὴν ὠνὴν ἀναγράψαι εἰς τὰς βασιλικὰς γραφὰς
τὰς ἐν Σάρδεσιν καὶ εἰς στήλας λιθίνας πέντε· τούτων τὴμ μὲν μίαν θεῖναι ἐν Ἰλίωι ἐν τῶι ἱερῶι τῆς Ἀθηνᾶς,
(30) τὴν δὲ ἑτέραν ἐν τῶι ἱερῶι τῶι ἐν Σαμοθράικηι, τὴν δὲ ἑτέραν ἐν Ἐφέσωι ἐν τῶι ἱερῶι τῆς Ἀρτέμιδος, τὴν δὲ τε-

τάρτην ἐν Διδύμοις ἐν τῶι ἱερῶι τοῦ Ἀπόλλωνος, τὴν
δὲ πέμπτην ἐν Σάρδεσιν ἐν τῶι ἱερῶι τῆς Ἀρτέμιδος· εὐ-
θέως δὲ καὶ περιορίσαι καὶ στηλῶσαι τὴν χώραν καὶ [προσ-]
(35) [ἀναγρά]ψαι τὸν περιορισμὸν εἰς τὰς στήλας τὰ[ς προ-]
[ειρημένας· ἔρρωσο. νθ'] Δίου ε̅.

King Antiochos to Metrophanes, greetings. We have sold to Laodike the village of Pannos
and the mansion and the land belonging to the village, bounded by the land of Zeleia
and by that of Kyzikos and by the ancient road that lies above the village of Pannos,
which has been ploughed by the neighbouring farmers, so that they may take the place
for themselves – it happens that the present village of Pannos was established later – and
(have transferred) any settlements that may be included in this land and the laoi *that*
live in them, with all their households and all their belongings and with the income
of the fifty-ninth year, for 30 talents of silver – and it will be the same if some people
from this village had moved to other places – on the terms that she will owe nothing
to the royal treasury and will have the right to offer (to attach the land) to whichever
city she chooses. In the same way, those buying or receiving from her will also have the
right to attach (the land) to the city of their choice, unless Laodike has made an earlier
attachment to a city, in which case they will own the land as part of the city attached
to by Laodike. We have ordered that the price be paid at the Strateia treasury in three
instalments, the first being made in the month of Audnaios of the sixtieth year, the other
in (the month of) Xandikos and the third in the following quarter. Issue orders that
the village and the mansion and the surrounding land be conveyed to Arrhidaios, the
bailiff of Laodike, along with the laoi *with all their households and all their belongings,*
and record the sale in the royal registry at Sardeis and on five stone stelae. Of these one
is to be set up at Ilion in the temple of Athena, another in the temple (of the Gods) in
Samothrake, another at Ephesos in the temple of Artemis, the fourth at Didyma in the
temple of Apollo and the fifth at Sardeis in the temple of Artemis. Survey the boundaries
of the land and mark them with boundary stones immediately and record the survey
on the above-mentioned stelae. Be in good health. Year 59, the 5th of Dios . . .

No. 19   *Covering letter of Metrophanes*

[   ] Α? [τὸ ἀντίγραφον τοῦ]
[προστάγματος τοῦ γραφέ]ντος ὑφ' αὑτο[ῦ   ]
[   ] τοῖς δὲ ἄλλοις [   ]
[θεῖν]αι τὰς στήλας ἐν τ[αῖς δεδηλωμέ-]
(5) [ναις πόλεσιν· σὺ] ο[ὖ]γ ἐπακολουθήσας τῆι παρὰ τ[οῦ βα-]
[σιλέω]ς ἐπιυ τολῆι ἀπέγδοσιν ποίησαι καὶ σύντα[ξον]
[ἀ]ναγράψαι τήν τε πρᾶσιν καὶ τὸν περιορισμὸν εἰς [στ-]
ήλας λιθίνας δύο, καὶ τούτων θεῖναι τὴμ μὲν μ[ίαν]
ἐν Ἐφέσωι ἐν τῶι ἱερῶι τῆς Ἀρτέμιδος, τὴν δὲ ἑτέραν
(10) ἐν Διδύμοις ἐν τῶι ἱερῶι τοῦ Ἀπόλλωνος, τὸ δὲ ἀνά[λω-]
μα τὸ ἐσόμενον εἰς ταῦτα δοῦναι ἐκ τοῦ βασιλικο[ῦ·]
ἵνα δὲ στηλωθῆι τὴν ταχίστην ἐπιμελές σοι γεν[έ-]

σθω, καὶ ὡς ἂν συντελεσθῆι γράψον καὶ ἡμῖν· ἐπεστά[λ-]
καμεν δὲ καὶ Τιμοξένωι τῶι βυβλιοφύλακι καταχω[ρί-]
(15) σαι τὴν ὠνὴν καὶ τὸν περιορισμὸν εἰς τὰς βασιλικὰς γραφὰς τὰς ἐν Σάρδεσιν, καθάπερ ὁ βασιλεὺς γέγραφ[εν. νθ´]
Δαισίου.

*the copy of the order written by him . . . and to the others . . . to set up the stelae
in the designated cities. So, in accordance with the king's letter, issue the contract and
order that both the sale and survey be recorded on two stone stelae, and that, of these,
one be set up at Ephesos in the temple of Artemis, the other at Didyma in the temple
of Apollo, the payment required for this being made from the royal treasury. Make it
your duty to see that the setting up of the stelae is done as quickly as possible and, when
it is completed, inform me in writing. I have sent instructions also to Timoxenos the*
bibliophulax *to record the sale and the survey in the royal registry at Sardeis, as the
king wrote. Year 59, Daisios . . .*

No. 20   Report of the Hyparch

το[ῦ περιορισμοῦ]
[τὸ ἀντίγραφον· - - - -] Πάννο[υ κώμη καὶ ἡ βᾶρις]
[καὶ ἡ προσοῦσα χώρα καὶ οἱ ὑπάρχοντε]ς λαο[ί, παρεδείχ-]
[θη] δὲ Ἀρριδαίωι τῶι οἰκονομοῦντι τὰ Λαοδίκης [ὑπ]ὸ [- - - - - -]
(5) [κ]ράτους τοῦ ὑπάρχου ἥ τε κώμη καὶ ἡ βᾶρις καὶ ἡ προσοῦσ[α χώ-]
[ρα] κατὰ τὸ παρὰ Νικομάχου τοῦ οἰκονόμου πρόσταγμα [ὧι]
[ὑ]πεγέγραπτο καὶ τὸ παρὰ Μητροφάνους καὶ τὸ παρὰ τοῦ β[α-]
[σι]λέως γραφὲν πρὸς αὐτόν, καθ᾽ ἃ ἔδει περιορισθῆναι· ἀπὸ
[μ]ὲν ἡλίου ἀνατολῶν ἀπὸ τῆς Ζελειτίδος χώρας τῆς μὲν
(10) [π]ρὸς τὴν Κυζικηνὴν ὁδὸς βασιλικὴ ἡ ἀρχαία ἡ ἄγουσα ἐπ[ὶ]
Πάννου κώμης ἐπάνω τῆς κώμης καὶ τῆς βάρεως, ἡ συ[ν-]
[δ]ειχθεῖσα ὑπό τε Μενεκράτου Βακχίου Πυθοκωμίτου
[κ]αὶ Δάου Ἀζαρέτου καὶ Μηδείου Μητροδώρου Παννοκωμ[ι-]
τῶν, καταρηρομένη δὲ ὑπὸ τῶν γειτνιώντων τῶι τόπωι· ἀπὸ
(15) δὲ ταύτης παρὰ τὸν τοῦ Διὸς βωμὸν τὸν ὄντα ἐπάνω τῆς
βάρεως καὶ ὡς ὁ τάφος ἐν δεξιᾷ τῆς ὁδοῦ· ἀπὸ δὲ τοῦ
[τ]άφου αὐτὴ ἡ ὁδὸς ἡ βασιλικὴ ἡ ἄγουσα διὰ τῆς Εὔπαν-
[ν]ήσης ἕως ποταμοῦ τοῦ Αἰσήπου· ἐστηλώθη δὲ καὶ
[ἡ χώ]ρα κατὰ τὰ ὅρια τὰ παραδειχθέντα.

*The copy of the survey . . . the village of Pannos and the mansion and the surrounding
land and the existing* laoi, *was conveyed to Arrhidaios, the bailiff of Laodike, by
-krates the hyparch, the village and the mansion and the surrounding land, according
to the written order of Nikomachos the* oikonomos, *to which were attached that
of Metrophanes and that which the king wrote to him, according to which it was
necessary to make a survey. Starting from the east, from the land of Zeleia, which is
towards Kyzikos, along the ancient royal road leading to the village of Pannos above*

the village and the mansion – that shown by Menekrates, the son of Bakchios, from the village of Pythos, and Daos, the son of Azaretos, and Medeios, the son of Metrodoros, from the village of Pannos – which is ploughed by those neighbouring the land (of the village of Pannos). From this (road), and from the altar of Zeus that lies above the mansion, to the tomb to the right of the road. From this tomb, along the royal road leading through the Eupannese, to the Aisepos river. Markers were also set up along the boundaries that were pointed out.

DOCUMENT 4. THE PTOLEMAIOS DOSSIER

Fischer 1979, with Bertrand 1982: 11–17; cf. Landau 1966; *BE* 1970, 627; *BE* 1971, 73.

Text A

(1) [Βα]σιλεὺς Ἀν[τί]οχος Πτ[ο]λεμαίωι χαίρειν· [–

[ἡμ?]ᾶς σύνταξ[ον ἀνα]γράψαν[τας] ἐν στήλαις λιθ[ίναις –

[τὰ]ς ἐπισ[τ]ολὰ[ς ἀνα]θεῖναι ἐν [ταῖ]ς ὑπάρχουσαις [σοι κώμαις· γεγράψαμε]

δὲ

περὶ το[ύτων Κλέωνι καὶ Ἡ]λι[ο]δώρωι τοῖς δ[ιο]ικηταῖς ἵν[α ἐπακολουθῶσιν.]

ζιρ, Ὑπερβερε[ταίου, - -.]

King Antiochos to Ptolemaios, greetings . . . order that the letters be inscribed on stone stelae and set up in the villages belonging to you. We have written to Kleon and Heliodoros, the dioikētai, to follow up these matters. Year 117(?), month of Hyperberetaios . . .

Text B

(5) [Βα]σιλεὺ[ς Ἀντίο]χος [Κλέ]ων[ι] χαίρ[ει]ν· τὰ καταγ[εγραμμένα παρ’

ἡμῶν?] τῶι στρατηγῶι

[-]ΠΙΥΝ [- - - - - - -] καὶ ἀπι[-]ΜΗΑΙΕΣ [-]ΕΝ[- -]ΤΗ[- - - - - - -]ω αὐτῶι κατὰ τὸ

[-]δοθὲν διὰ [- - - -]ΝΤΩ [- - -]ΔΟΜΗ[- - - - - - - - -]ενηι χώ[ραι.]

τὴν [α]ὐ[τὴ]ν [Ἡλιοδώρωι.]

King Antiochos to Kleon, greetings. What we have written concerning the general . . . And the same (letter) to Heliodoros.

Text C

[Βα]σιλεὺ[ς Ἀντίοχος Κλέωνι] χαίρειν· τοῦ ὑπομνή[ματος οὗ ἔδωκ]ε[ν ἡ]μῖν Πτ[ολεμαῖος]

[ὁ στ]ρατηγ[ὸς καὶ ἀρχιερεὺς ὑπο]τέτακται τὸ ἀντίγ[ραφον· γεν]έσθω [οὗ]ν ὥσπερ

ἀξιοῖ. δ [ιρ, -, -.]

King Antiochos to Kleon, greetings. A copy of the memorandum given to us by Ptolemaios the general and high priest is attached. Do as he requests. Year 114(?) . . .

Text D (Bertrand)

(11) [Βασ]ιλεῖ Ἀν[τιόχωι ὑπ]όμνημα παρὰ Πτολεμ[αίου] στρατηγοῦ καὶ ἀρχιερ[έως περὶ τῶν]
[γινομ]ένων [ἐγκλη]μάτων· ἀξιῶ γραφῆναι [ὅπως] ὅσα μ[ὲ]ν ἂν ἦι ἐν ταῖς κώμαις [μου]
[το]ῖς λαοῖς [πρὸς α]ὐτοὺς ἐ[ξ]ῆι διεξά[γεσθαι] ἐπὶ τῶν παρ' ἐμοῦ ὅσα δ' ἂν ἦι πρὸς τού[ς
[τῶν] ἄλλων κωμῶ[ν ὅ] τε οἰκονό[μος καὶ ὁ τοῦ τόπ]ου πρ[ο]εστηκὼς ἐπι[σκο]πῶσιν· ἐάν δὲ
[περὶ] φό[νου] ἦι ἢ καὶ μείζονα δοκῆ[ι εἶναι ἀνα]πέμπηται ἐπὶ τὸν ἐν Σ[υρ]ίαι κ[αὶ] Φ[ο]ινίκηι
[σ]τρατηγόν· τοὺς δὲ φρουράρχους [καὶ τοὺς ἐ]πὶ τῶν τόπων τεταγμένους μὴ περι[ιδεῖν
κατὰ μηθένα τρόπον τοὺς παρα[καλοῦντας·] τὴν [α]ὐτὴν ['Η]λιοδώρωι.

Memorandum to King Antiochos from Ptolemaios the general and high priest concerning disputes that arise. I request that written instructions be issued to the effect that my own people handle those (disputes) that arise between the laoi *of my own villages, while those that involve the inhabitants of other villages be examined by the* oikonomos *and the official in charge of the district. If it is a matter of homicide or is considered of greater importance, it should be sent on to the general of Syria and Phoinike. The garrison commanders and the officials in charge of districts should not ignore in any way those who appeal to them (for assistance). And the same (memorandum) to Heliodoros.*

Text E

(18) [Βα]σιλεὺς Ἀντίοχος Κ[λέω]νι χαίρειν· [τοῦ ὑπ]ομνήματος οὗ ἔδω[κεν ἡμῖν]
[Πτ]ολεμαῖος ὁ στρατηγὸς καὶ ἀρχιερεὺς ὑποτ[έτακτα]ι τὸ ἀντίγραφον·
[γεν]έσθω οὖν καθάπερ ἀξιοῖ.   διρ', Αὐδναίου, δ.

King Antiochos to Kleon, greetings. Attached is the copy of the memorandum which Ptolemaios, the general and high priest, gave us. Do as he requests. Year 114 (?), fourth (day) of (the month of) Audaios.

Text F

(21) [Βασ]ιλεῖ μεγάλω[ι] Ἀντιόχωι ὑπόμνημα [παρὰ Πτολ]εμ[αίου] στρατηγοῦ
[καὶ] ἀρχιερέως· ἀξιῶ, ἐάν σοι φαίνηται, [β]ασιλεῦ, [γραφῆναι –] πρός τε
[Κλέ]ωνα καὶ Ἡλιόδω[ρο]ν [τοὺ]ς διοικητὰς εἰς τὰς ὑπ[αρχ]ούσας μοι κώ[μ]ας
[ἐγ]γτήσει καὶ εἰς [τ]ὸ πα[τ]ρικὸν καὶ εἰς [ἃ]ς σὺ προ[σ]έταξας καταγράψ[αι]
[μη]θενὶ ἐξουσίαν εἶναι ἐπισταθ[μ]εύειν κατὰ μ[ηδε]μίαν [π]αρεύρεσιν
[μ]ηδ' ἑτέρους ἐπα<γά>γειν μηδ' ἐπιβολὴν ποιήσασ[θ]αι ἐπὶ τ[ὰ] κτήματα
μ[η]δὲ λαοὺς ἐξάγειν· τὴν αὐτ[ὴ]ν Ἡλιοδώρωι.

Memorandum to Great King Antiochos from Ptolemaios the general and high priest. I request, if it appears so to you, o king, that you send written instructions to Kleon and Heliodoros, the dioikētai, *so that no one should have the authority, under any pretext, to billet in the villages that I own with right of inheritance and in those that you ordered be transferred to me, nor bring others there, nor requisition any possessions, nor carry off the* laoi. *And the same (memorandum) to Heliodoros.*

Text G

(28) Β [α]σιλεὺς Ἀντίοχος Μαρσύαι χαίρειν· ἐν[ε]φ[ά]νισεν ἡμῖν
[Π]τολεμαῖ[ος ὁ] στρατηγὸς καὶ ἀρχιερεὺ[ς] πλείο[νας] τῶν διοδε[υ]ομένων
καταλύειν τε μετὰ βίας ἐν ταῖς κώμα[ις] αὐτοῦ [καὶ] ἄλλα ἀδικήματα
οὐκ ὀλίγα συντελεῖσθαι μὴ προσέχοντας τ[οῖς παρ'] ἡμ[ῶ]ν ἐπιστα[λεῖσι]
περὶ τούτων· [ἐ]πιμέλεια οὖν ποιο[ῖ]<ς>, ὅπως μὴ μόν[ον] κ[ω]λύο[ν]τα[ι - -,
ἀλλὰ καὶ ζη[μιῶ]νται δεκαπλαῖς αἷς ἂν ποιῶνται βλάβα[ις· –
ἡ αὐτὴ [Λυσα]νίαι, Λέοντι, Διονίκωι.

King Antiochos to Marsyas, greetings. Ptolemaios the general and high priest has informed us that many of those passing through take quarters by force in his villages and commit not a few other crimes, paying no attention to the orders we have sent about these matters. So make it your duty not only to prevent them, but also to fine them ten times the cost of the damage they do. The same (memorandum) to Lysanias, Leon and Dionikos.

Text H

(35) [Β]ασιλεὺς Ἀντίοχος Ἡλιοδ[ώ]ρωι χαίρειν· τῆς ἐπιστ[ολῆς ἧς]
[γ]εγράφαμεν πρὸς Μαρσ[ύ]αν ὑποτέτακται τὸ ἀντίγραφο[ν· σὺ δ' οὖν]
ἐπακολού[θει·]   ζιρ', Ξ[α]νδ[ίκου, -.]

King Antiochos to Heliodoros, greetings. Attached is a copy of the letter we have written to Marsyas. So follow this up.

Text I

(38) [Υ]πετάγ[η ἡ πρὸς Μαρ]σύαν· ἡ αὐτὴ Θεοδότωι τ[ῆ]s [πρ]ὸς Λυσανία[ν,]
Ἀπολλοφάνει τῆς π[ρὸς Λέοντα, Π]λουτογέν[ει] τῆς πρὸς Διόνικον.

Attached is the (memorandum) to Marsyas. The same (memorandum) to Lysanias for Theodotos, to Leon for Apollophanes, to Dionikos for Ploutogenes.

DOCUMENT 5. THE MNESIMACHOS INSCRIPTION

Buckler and Robinson 1912; Buckler and Robinson 1932; cf. Atkinson 1972; Billows 1995: 137–45.

Column I

[- - c. 36 - -] ἐπερωτήσαντος Χαιρέο[υ ὑπ]ὲ[ρ τούτ]ω[ν διαιρ]έσε[ως]
[γεγενημένη]ς καὶ ὕστερον ἐπέκρινέ μοι τὸν οἶκον Ἀντίγονος· ἐπειδὴ νῦν οἱ νεωποῖαι
τὸ χρυσίον τῆς

[παρακαταθή]κης τὸ τῆς Ἀρτέμιδος ἀπαιτοῦσιν παρ' ἐμοῦ, ἐγὼ δὲ οὐκ ἔχω πόθεν ἀποδώσω αὐτοῖς, ἔστι οὖν

[τὸ καθ' ἓν το]ῦ οἴκου κῶμαι αἵδε (αἳ) καλοῦνται Τοβαλμουρα κώμη ἐν Σαρδιανῶι πεδίωι ἐν Ἴλου ὄρει· προσκύρουσιν δὲ

(5) [πρὸς τὴν κώ]μην ταύτην καὶ ἄλλαι κῶμαι ἢ καλεῖται Τανδου καὶ Κομβδιλιπια, φόρος τῶν κωμῶν εἰς τὴν Πυθέου

- - - - χ]ιλιαρχίαν τοῦ ἐνιαυτοῦ χρυσοῖ πεντήκοντα· ἔστι δὲ καὶ κλῆρος ἐν Κιναροα πλησίον Τοβαλμουρα,

[φόρος το]ῦ ἐνιαυτοῦ χρυσοῖ τρεῖς· ἔστι δὲ καὶ ἄλλη κώμη Περιασασωστρα ἐν Μορστου ὕδατι, φόρος εἰς τὴν

[- - - - - -]αρίου χιλιαρχίαν τοῦ ἐνιαυτοῦ χρυσοῖ πεντήκοντα ἑπτά· ἔστι δὲ καὶ (ἐν) Μορστου ὕδατι κλῆρος

ἐν Να[γ]ριοα, φόρος εἰς τὴν Σαγαρίου Κόρειδος χιλιαρχίαν χρυσοῖ τρεῖς ὀβολοὶ χρυσίου τέσσαρες· ἔστι δὲ

(10) καὶ ἄλλη κώμη ἐν Αττουδδοις ἢ καλεῖται Ἴλου κώμη, φόρος τοῦ ἐνιαυτοῦ χρυσοῖ τρεῖς ὀβολοὶ χρυσίου τρεῖς·

ἐκ πασῶν οὖν τῶν κωμῶν καὶ ἐκ τῶν κλήρων καὶ τῶν οἰκοπέδων προσκυρόντων καὶ τῶν λαῶν πανοικίων

σὺν τοῖς ὑπάρχουσιν καὶ τῶν ἀγγείων τῶν οἰνηρῶν καὶ τοῦ φόρου τοῦ ἀργυρικοῦ καὶ τοῦ λητουργικοῦ καὶ τῶν

ἄλλων τῶν γινομένων ἐκ τῶν κωμῶν καὶ χωρὶς τούτων ἔτι πλέον, τῆς διαιρέσεως γενομένης,

ἐξαίρημα ἔλαβεν Πύθεος καὶ Ἄδραστος ἐν Τ(ο)βαλμουροις αὐλήν, καὶ ἔξω τῆς αὐλῆς εἰσὶν οἰκίαι τῶν

(15) λαῶν καὶ τῶν οἰκετῶν καὶ παράδεισοι δύο σπόρου ἀρταβῶν δεκαπέντε, καὶ ἐν Περιασασωστροις

οἰκόπεδα σπόρου ἀρταβῶν τριῶν καὶ παράδεισοι σπόρου ἀρτα(β)ῶν τριῶν καὶ οἰκέται οἱ κατοικοῦντες

ἐν τούτωι τῶι τόπωι, ἐν Τ(ο)βαλμουροις Ἔφεσος Ἀδράστου, Καδοας Ἀδράστου, Ἡρακλείδης Βελετρου,

Τυιος Μανεου Καΐκου, ἐν Περιασασωστροις οἱ κατοικοῦντες Καδοας Αρμανανδου, Ἄδραστος Μανεου.

Chaireas having inquired into these matters, a division was made and afterwards Antigonos confirmed the estate for me. Since the temple officials are now demanding from me the money of the loan of Artemis, and I do not have the means to pay them, named here are the villages comprising each part of my property:

Tobalmoura village, in the plain of Sardeis, in the district of Ilos. Belonging to this village are other villages named Tandos and Kombdilipi, the tax of the villages of 50 gold staters annually (being paid) in the chiliarchy of Pytheos . . .

There is also an allotment at Kinaroa, near Tobalmoura, (paying) a tax of 3 gold staters annually.

There is also another village, Periasasostra, in Morstos Waters (district), (paying) tax of 57 gold staters annually in the chiliarchy of . . . . arios.

There is also, in Morstos Waters (district), an allotment at Nagrioa, (paying) tax of 3 gold staters and 4 gold obols annually in the chiliarchy of Sagarios the son of Koreis.

There is also another village in the district of Attoudda called the village of Ilos, (paying) tax of 3 gold staters and 3 gold obols annually.

So from all the villages and allotments and the housing plots associated with these and the laoi *with all their households and possessions and the wine jars and the money tax and the labour tax and the other things which are produced from the villages, and apart from these even more, when the division was made, Pytheos and Adrastos received a portion set apart:*

In Tobalmoura, a country house and, outside the house, the dwellings of the laoi *and the slaves and two cultivable plots (of an area) requiring 15* artabai *of seed.*

In Periasasostra, housing plots (of an area) requiring 3 artabai *of seed and cultivable plots (of an area) requiring 3* artabai *of seed.*

And the slaves living on this land, in Tobalmoura: Ephesos of Adrastos, Kadoas of Adrastos, Herakleides of Beletros, Tyios of Maneas, the son of Kaikos, and those living in Periasasostra: Kadoas of Armanandos and Adrastos of Maneas.

Column II

[- - c. 16 - - μηθ]ὲ[ν ἐξέστω μή]τε ἐμοὶ μήτε [τοῖς ἐμοῖς ἐκγόνοις μήτ]ε [- - c. 10 - -]

μήτε ἄλ(λ)ωι μηθενὶ μηκέτι ἀπολύσασθαι· καὶ ἐάν τις ἐμποιῆται ὑπέρ τινος τῶν κωμῶν ἢ τῶν κλήρων

ἢ ὑπὲρ τῶν ἄλλων τῶν ὧδε γεγραμμένων ἐγὼ καὶ οἱ ἐμοὶ ἔκγονοι βεβαιώσομεν καὶ τὸν ἀντιποιούμενον

ἐξαλλάξ(ο)μεν, ἐὰν δὲ μὴ βεβαιώσομεν ἢ παρὰ τὴν συγγραφὴν παραβαίνωμεν τήνδε γεγραμμένην

(5) ἐπ[ὶ] τὰς κώμας καὶ τοὺς κλήρους καὶ τὰ χωρία καὶ τοὺς οἰκέτας ἅπαντας εἰς τὰ Ἀρτέμιδος ἐχέτωσαν,

καὶ οἱ νεωποιοὶ ὑπὲρ τούτων ἐκδικαιούσθωσαν καὶ κρινέσθωσαν πρὸς τοὺς ἀντιποιουμένους

ὡς ἂν βούλωνται, καὶ ἐγὼ Μνησίμαχος καὶ οἱ ἐμοὶ ἔκγονοι ἀποτείσομεν εἰς τ(ὰ) Ἀρτέμιδος

χρυσοῦς δισχιλίους ἑξακοσίους πεντήκοντα, καὶ ὑπὲρ τῶν γενημάτων καὶ τῶν καρπῶν

ἐὰν μὴ καρπεύσωνται ἐν ἐκείνωι τῶι ἔτει εἰς τὰ Ἀρτέμιδος ὁπόσου οὖν χρυσίου ἄξια ἦι καὶ ταῦτα

(10) ἀποδώσομεν, καὶ τῶν οἰκοδομη(μά)των καὶ φυτευμάτων τῶν τῆς Ἀρτέμιδος ἢ ἄλλο τι ὅ τι ἂν ποιήσωσιν

ὅσου χρυσίου ἄξια ἦι τὴν ἀξίαν ἀποδώσομεν, μέχρι δὲ ὅσου μὴ ἀποδῶμεν ἔστω ἡμῖν ἐν παρακαταθήκηι

τέως ἂν ἅπαν ἀποδῶμεν· ἐὰν δὲ τὰς κώμας ἢ τοὺς κλήρους ἢ τῶν ἄλλων τι τῶν ὑποκειμένων

ἐὰν ὁ βασιλεὺς ἀφέληται τῆι Ἀρτέμιδι διὰ Μνησίμαχον, τὸ χρυσίον οὖν τὸ ἀρχαῖον τὴν παρακαταθήκην

τοὺς χιλίους τριακοσίους εἰκοσιπέντε χρυσοῦς αὐτοὶ παραχρῆμα ἀποδώσομεν εἰς τὰ Ἀρτέμιδος

(15) ἐγὼ Μνησίμαχος καὶ οἱ ἐμοὶ ἔκγονοι, καὶ τῶν οἰκοδομημάτων καὶ φυτευμάτων τῆς Ἀρτέμιδος
ὅσου ἂν ἄξια ἦι τὴν ἀξίαν ἀποδώσομεν παραχρῆμα, καὶ ὑπὲρ τῶν γενημάτων καὶ τῶν καρπῶν
ἐὰν μὴ καρπεύσωνται ἐν ἐκείνωι τῶι ἔτει εἰς τὰ Ἀρτέμιδος ὁπόσου ἂν χρυσίου ἄξια ἦι καὶ ταῦτα
ἀποδώσομεν, μέχρι δὲ ὅσου μὴ ἀποδῶμεν ἔστω ἂν ἐμοὶ ἐν παρα(κα)ταθήκηι καὶ ἐν τοῖς ἐμοῖς ἐκγόνοις
ἕως ἂν ἅπαν ἀποδῶμεν εἰς τὰ Ἀρτέμιδος· καὶ ἡ πρᾶξις τέως ἂν ἐξ ἡμῶν μήπω γένηται ἐξεῖναι.

it shall not be permitted either to me or to my descendants or to . . . or to anyone else to be released any longer from (this agreement).

And if someone makes a claim concerning one of the villages or the allotments or concerning the other things that have been written here, I and my descendants will act as guarantors and turn away the contenders, and if we do not act as guarantors or (if we) violate the written agreement concerning the villages and the allotments and the plots of land and the slaves, let all belong to Artemis, and let the temple officials take the contenders to court and be judged in whatever manner they wish. And I, Mnesimachos, and my descendants will pay Artemis 2,650 gold staters. And for the (grain) produce and (fruit) crop, if they have not been harvested that year for Artemis, as much money as they are valued at, and we shall pay this. And for the buildings and plantings of Artemis and for any additions they make, we shall pay whatever sum they are valued at. And as long as we have not paid something, let this be considered a loan until we have paid everything.

And if the king takes away from Artemis, because of Mnesimachos, the villages or the allotments or any of the other things, I, Mnesimachos, and my descendants will immediately pay back to Artemis the original loan, the 1,325 gold staters. And, concerning the buildings and plantings of Artemis, whatever the value is that amount we will pay immediately. And, concerning the (grain) produce and (fruit) crop, if they have not been harvested that year for Artemis, we will pay whatever sum they are valued at. And, as long as we have not paid something, let this be considered a loan to me and to my descendants until we have paid everything to Artemis. And let action (of recovery) of debts) be permitted (against us) as long as we do not do so.

DOCUMENT 6. THE LAODIKE LETTER TO IASOS

Pugliese Carratelli 1969.

　　　　προαιρουμένη δὴ καὶ ἐγὼ ἀκόλου-
θα πράσ<σ>ειν τῆ<ι> σπουδῆ<ι> αὐτοῦ καὶ ἐκτενείαι καὶ διὰ
τοῦτο καταθέσθαι τινα εὐεργεσίαμ μὲν εἰς τοὺς
ἀσθενοῦντας τῶν πολιτῶν, εὐχρηστίαν δὲ κοι-
(15) νὴν τῶι σύμπαντι δήμωι, γεγράφεικα Στρουθίωνι τῶι διοικητῆι ἐφ᾽ ἔτη δέκα κατ᾽ ἐνιαυτὸν πυρῶν χιλίους μεδίμνους Ἀττικοὺς εἰς τὴν πόλιν παρακομί-

ζοντα παραδιδόναι τοῖς παρὰ τοῦ δήμου· εὖ οὖν ποή-
σετε συντάξαντες τοῖς μὲν ταμίαις παραλαμβά-
(20) νοντας τακτοῦ πλήθους ἐγδιοικεῖν, τοῖς δὲ προστά-
ταις καὶ οἷς ἂν ἄλλοις κρίνητε προνοεῖν ὅπως τὸ γινόμενον διάφορον ἐκ τούτων κατατιθῶνται εἰς προίκας
ταῖς τῶν ἀσθενούντων πολιτῶν θυγατράσιν, διδόντες μὴ πλέον Ἀντιοχέων δραχμῶν τριακοσίων ἑκάσ-
(25) τηι τῶν συνοικιζομένων·

*and because I am also inclined to act in accordance with his (i.e. the king's) interest
and consideration, and because of this to perform some benefaction for citizens in need
and a good deed for the city as a whole, I have written to Strouthion the* dioikētēs *to
bring to the city and deliver to the representatives of the city each year for ten years 1,000
Attic* medimnoi *of wheat. So you will do well to order the financial officials, upon
receiving it, to sell a regular amount and to (order) the* prostatai, *and whomever else
you decide, to arrange that the resulting income be set aside as dowries for the daughters
of poor citizens, giving not more than 300 drachms of Antiochos to each of those due to
be married.*

DOCUMENT 7. THE APOLLONIA-SALBAKE DECREE

Robert and Robert 1954.

(4) [. . . πρεσβευ-]
[τῶν δ]ὲ πεμφθέντων περὶ τῶν [συμφερόντων]
[τῶι δ]ήμωι πρός τε Κτησικλῆν τὸν [- - c. 9 - -]
[- - - - -] καὶ Μένανδρον τὸν διοικητὴ[ν ἐκτενῶς]
(8) [ἑαυτὸ]ν ἐπιδούς, ὅτε οἱ πρεσβευταὶ ἀπ[ῆλθον, καὶ]
[συνε]ισπορευόμενος αὐτοῖς ἔσπευδεν εἰ[ς τὸ πάν-]
[τα πορι]σθῆναι πε[ρὶ] ὧν ἠξιοῦμεν· ἔτι δὲ καὶ Δ[ημη-]
[τρίου] τοῦ ἐγλογιστοῦ εἰσκαλεσαμένου τοὺς
(12) [πρεσ]βευτὰς ὑπὲρ ὧν ἐμπεφανίκει αὐτῶι Δημή-
[τριος] ὁ τεταγμένος ἐπὶ τῶν ἱερῶν, καὶ διαμ[φι]σβη[τή-]
[σαντο]ς πρὸς αὐτοὺς ὑπὲρ τῶν ἱερῶν κωμῶν [Σ]αλε[ι-]
[ων τε] τῶν ὀρεινῶν καὶ Σαλειων τῶν πεδεινῶ[ν]
(16) [- - - - -]μενος παρεκάλει Δημήτριον μηθὲν τῶν
[προυπα]ρχόντων τῶι δήμωι κινεῖν ἐπὶ τῆς αὐτο[ῦ] πρα-
[- - - - - -]ίας, ἀλλὰ ἐᾶν διαμένειν καθάπερ [ἕ]ως
[τοῦ νῦν] . . .

When ambassadors were sent to Ktesikles the – and Menandros the dioikētēs *on matters
concerning the interests of the city, he gave freely of his time when the ambassadors
left and, accompanying them, sought eagerly to bring about everything that we were
requesting.*
    And also, when Demetrios the eklogistēs *summoned the ambassadors on the matter
which had been brought before him by Demetrios, the official in charge of sanctuaries,*

and entered into a dispute with them (the ambassadors) regarding the sacred villages of the Saleioi of the mountains and the Saleioi of the plains, interceding (?) he asked Demetrios not to include within his jurisdiction (?) anything that had previously belonged to the city, but to allow it to remain as before.

DOCUMENT 8. THE ACHAIOS DECREE

Wörrle 1975.

Βασιλευόντων Ἀντιόχου καὶ [Σ-]
ελεύκου πέμπτου καὶ τεσσαρακο-
στοῦ ἔτους μηνὸς Περιτίου ἑ-
(4) π' Ἑλένου ἐπιμελητοῦ <τοῦ> τό[πο]υ ἐκκλησί-
ας γενομένης ἔδοξε Νεοτειχείταις
καὶ Κι<δ>διοκωμίταις· ἐπειδὴ Βανά-
βηλος ὁ τὰ τοῦ Ἀχαιοῦ οἰκονομῶν καὶ Λα-
(8) χάρης Πάπου ἐγλογιστὴς τῶν
Ἀχαιοῦ εὐεργέται αὐτῶν γεγένηντ-
αι κατὰ πάντα καὶ κοινῆι καὶ ἰδίαι ἕκασ-
του ἀντειλημμένοι εἰσὶν κατὰ τ[ὸ-]
(12) μ πόλεμον τὸν Γαλατικὸν καὶ πολλῶν αὐτῶν γενομένων αἰχ[μ]α-
λώτων ὑπὸ τῶν Γαλατῶν ἐμφα-
νίσαντες Ἀχαιῶ[ι] ἐ[λυτ]ρώ[σα]ντο,
(16) ἐπαινέσαι τε αὐτοὺς καὶ ἀ<να>γράψαι
τὴν εὐεργασίαν αὐτῶν εἰς στή-
λην λιθίνην καὶ στῆσαι ἐν τῶι
τοῦ Διὸς ἱ<ε>ρῶι ἐμ Βαβα κώμηι καὶ
(20) ἐν τῶι τοῦ Ἀπόλωνος ἐν Κιδδίου
<κώμηι>, δεδόσθαι δὲ αὐτοῖς καὶ ἐγγόνοις
εἰς πάντα τὸν χρόνον προεδρίαν
ἐν ταῖς δημοτελέσιν ἑορταῖς,
(24) θύειν δὲ καὶ Ἀχαιῶι κυρίωι τοῦ τό-
που καὶ σωτῆρι κατ' ἐνιαυτὸν
ἐμ μὲν τῶι τοῦ Διὸς ἱερῶι βοῦν,
Λαχάρηι καὶ Βαγαβήλωι εὐεργέται[ς]
(28) κριοὺς δύο ἐν τῶι τ[οῦ Ἀ]πόλλωνος
ἱερῶι τῶι ἐγ Κιδδίου κώμηι, ἱερεῖα τρία
ὅπως εἰδ[ῶ]σι καὶ οἱ ἄλλοι ὅτι Νεοτ[ει-]
χεῖται καὶ Κι[δ]διοκωμῖται ὑφ' ὧ[ν]
(32) ἄν τι πάθωσι ἀγαθ[ὸ]ν ἐπίσταν-
ται τιμὰς ἀντιδιδόναι.

When Antiochos and Seleukos were kings, in the forty-fifth year, in the month of Peritios, when Helenos was epimelētēs *of the district, an assembly having taken place, the following was decided by the Neoteichitai and Kiddiokomitai:*

Since Banabelos, the oikonomos *of Achaios, and Lachares, son of Papos, the* eklogistēs *of Achaios, have become their benefactors in all things, and and (since) both the communities and each person individually received help from them during the Galatian War, when many were taken prisoners by the Galatians, (whom) they ransomed acting on behalf of Achaios,*

(1) *that they be praised and their benefaction recorded on a stone stele and that (this) be set up in the sanctuary of Zeus in the village of Baba and in that of Apollo in the village of Kiddion,*

(2) *that the privilege of a front seat at public festivals be given to them and their descendants,*

(3) *that an annual sacrifice be offered for Achaios, as lord of the place and saviour, of an ox in the temple of Zeus and for Lachares and Banabelos, as benefactors, two rams in the sanctuary of Apollo at Kiddion village, a total of three sacrificial animals, so that others should learn that the Neoteichitai and the Kiddiokomitai know how to return honours to those who do them some good.*

DOCUMENT 9. THE LETTER OF ANTIOCHOS III TO THE SARDIANS

Ma 1997; 1999: no. 1; cf. Gauthier 1989: no. 13, Inv. 63.118.

-ΑΤΑΛ - - - ΚΕΙΑΝΤ-Ι - - *c.* 22–24 – Ω
διορθώσεσθε ἐν ἔτεσιν τρισίν, ε[ὐ]θέ[ω]ς δὲ καὶ ξυλὴν
εἰς τὸν συνοικισμὸν τῆς πόλεως κόψαι καὶ ἐξαγαγέσθαι
(4) ἐκ τῶν ἐν Ταρανζοις ὑλῶν καθ' ἂν συγκρίνη Ζεῦξις· *vac.*
παραλύομεν δὲ καὶ τῆς προσεπιβληθείσης εἰκοστῆς
ἐπὶ τὴν πολιτικὴν καὶ τὸ γυμνάσιον ὧι πρότερον ἐχρῆσθε
συντετάχαμεν ἀποκαταστῆσαι ὑμῖν καὶ γεγράφαμεν
(8) περὶ πάντων πρὸς Ζεῦξιν καὶ Κτησικλῆν· ὑπὲρ αὐτῶν δὲ
τούτων ἀπαγγελοῦ[[ο]]σιν ὑμῖν καὶ οἱ περὶ Μητρόδωρον. *vac.*
    Ἔρρωσθε.   θϞ Ξανδίκου έ.

should be dealt with within three years; and immediately to cut the (necessary) wood for the reconstruction of the city and to take it from the forests of Taranza, as Zeuxis may decide. We also exempt you from the one-twentieth (tax) that had been added to the city tax and have ordered that the gymnasium you used previously be restored for you. On all these matters we have written to Zeuxis and Ktesikles. Metrodoros and his colleagues will inform you about these things. Be in good health. (Year) 99, the fifth (day) of (the month of) Xandikos.

DOCUMENT 10. THE LETTERS OF ANTIOCHOS AND ZEUXIS TO HERAKLEIA-LATMOS

Wörrle 1988; cf. Ma 1997; 1999: no. 29; Sahin 1987.

A. Letter of Antiochos

N I

(8)   - - Θέλοντες δὲ καὶ κατὰ τὰ λοιπὰ πο-
[λυ]ωρεῖν ὑμῶν τά τε ὑπὸ Ζεύξιδος συγχωρηθέντα ὑμῖν κυροῦμεν
[καὶ] πρὸς τῶι ὑποκειμένωι πλήθει εἰς ἐλαιοχρίστιον τοῖς νέοις ἀπο-
[τάσσομεν κα]τ᾽ ἐνιαυτὸν καὶ ἄλλους μετρητὰς τριάκοντα. Τό τε
(12) [ἐσόμενον ἀ]νήλωμα εἰς τὴν ἐπισκευὴν τοῦ ὑδραγωγίου οἰόμε-
[θα δεῖν δίδο]σθαι ἐκ βασιλικοῦ ἐφ᾽ ἔτη τρία, καὶ περὶ τούτων γεγράφαμεν
[- - c. 8/9 - - τ]ῶι διοικητῆι.

And because we also wished to look after your welfare in the future, we have both confirmed the concessions made to you by Zeuxis and have assigned for the anointing of the youth another 30 metrētai *of oil a year in addition to that already allocated. And as for the funds that will be required for the repair of the aqueduct, we think it right that these should be paid from the royal treasury for three years, and on these matters we have written to . . . the* dioikētēs.

B. Letter of Zeuxis

Ambassadors of the Herakleians had appeared requesting concessions by the king, which Zeuxis repeated in his preamble:

N II

                     – καὶ παρακαλέσοντας τά τε ὑπὸ τῶν βασιλέων συγκεχωρημένα
[συνδιατηρηθῆν]αι ὅπως ὑπάρχη καὶ μετὰ ταῦτα ἥ τε ἀνεπισταθμεία καὶ τὰ
(16) [– c. 16/17 – κ]αὶ τὰ τέλη καὶ ἔγγαια καὶ τὰ εἰσαγώγια καὶ ἐξαγώγ[ια]
–

and asking that both the concessions already granted by the kings be maintained as they are (today) and also that, after this, freedom from billeting and . . . and sales taxes and dues having to do with land, as well as import and export custom duties . . .

N III

[πρ]ᾶσις, δίδωται δὲ καὶ ἐκ βασ[ιλικοῦ εἰς χρῆ]σιν τῆς πόλεως μάλιστα {μὲν}
μὲν πλέον εἰ δὲ μή γε τάλαντα [- - c. 5 - - ὡ]ς πρότερον καὶ τὸ ἐλαιοχρίστιον δ[ι-]
αμένηι τὸ ἀποτεταγμένον τοῖς ν[έοις, ὃ] ἐπεκηρύσσετο τῆι ὠνῆι τοῦ λιμέ-
(4) νος, ἀξιώσαντες δὲ καὶ ἀτέλειαν συγχωρῆσαι τῶν τε ἐκ τῆς γῆς καρπῶν πάντων καὶ τοῦ ἐννομίου τῶν τε κτηνῶν καὶ τῶν σμηνῶν ἐφ᾽ ἔτη ὅσ᾽ ἂν φαίνηται καὶ ζεύγη τοῖς πολίταις, μνησθησομένους δὲ καὶ ὅπως σῖτος δοθῆι τῆι πό-
[λ]ει δωρεὰν καὶ ἀτέλεια{ν} τοῦ τε εἰσαγομένου εἰς τὴν πόλιν καὶ τοῦ πωλουμέ-
(8) νου καὶ ἵνα οἱ ἐξάγοντες ἐκ τῆς τοῦ βασιλέως εἰς τὴν πόλιν ἐπί τε τὰς
ἰδίας χρείας καὶ εἰς πρᾶσιν ἀτελεῖς ὦσιν –

sale, and shall be given from the royal treasury for the use of the city as before, preferably more, but at least — talents; and that the supply of oil that was designated for the anointing of the youth, which was purchased from the (proceeds of the) public auction of port dues, remain (as before); and requesting that tax exemption be granted to the citizens on all agricultural produce and on pasturage rights for animals and beehives for as many years and yokes as judged appropriate; and that they (the ambassadors) be mindful (to request) that free grain be supplied to the city and tax exemption on that imported into the city and that sold there, and that those who brought (grain) from royal land to the city both for their own use and for sale be tax-exempt . . .

This was followed by Zeuxis' answer, with a reference to imports: εἰ]σαγωγη[, and . . .

N IV

(6)   – ἐπιχωροῦμεν δὲ ὑμῖν καὶ τὴν πανήγυριν ἀτελῆ συντελεῖν ο[ὔ- -] [τως ὥσπερ] καὶ πρότερον εἰώθειτε ἄγειν - -

and we permit you to conduct the religious festival tax-free in the same manner that you used to earlier . . .

DOCUMENT 11. THE SARDEIS LAND CONVEYANCE

Ma 1997; 1999: no. 41; cf. Gauthier 1989: no. 7, Inv. 64.6.

- - [ἡ] βασίλισσα γέγρα[φεν] - -
- - ΕΝΕΙ τῶν περὶ ΗΜΑΣΕΙ - -
- - ἐν τῆι περὶ Σάρδεις οἰκον[ο]μία[ι] - -
(4) – Πορσουδδα κώμην καὶ ΣΑΝΝ.ΦΕ –
- - ΤΑΙΣ κατὰ τοὺς προυπάρχοντ[ας περιορισμούς?] - -
– ΣΙΝ ἐν ταῖς κώμ[αι]ς καὶ τοῖ[ς] ἀγ[ροῖς?] - -
– ΤΑΙ αὐτός τε καὶ οἱ ἔγγονοι αὐτοῦ –
(8) — Υ – ΠΛΗ.ΩΝΤΟ –

(Laodike) the queen has written to . . . -enes of our . . . in the oikonomia of the district around Sardeis . . . the village of Porsoudda and . . . according to the pre-existing (surveys?) . . . in the villages and fields(?) . . . he and his descendants . . .

DOCUMENT 12. ANTIOCHOS III'S LETTER CONCERNING JERUSALEM

Jos. *AJ* 12.138–44.

Βασιλεὺς Ἀντίοχος Πτολεμαίῳ χαίρειν· τῶν Ἰουδαίων καὶ παραυτίκα μέν, ἡνίκα τῆς χώρας ἐπέβημεν αὐτῶν, ἐπιδειξαμένων τὸ πρὸς ἡμᾶς φιλότιμον, καὶ παραγενομένους δ' εἰς τὴν πόλιν λαμπρῶς ἐκδεξαμένων καὶ μετὰ τῆς γερουσίας ἀπαντησάντων, ἄφθονον δὲ τὴν χορηγίαν τοῖς στρατιώταις καὶ τοῖς ἐλέφασι παρεσχημένων, συνεξελόντων δὲ καὶ τοὺς ἐν τῇ ἄκρα φρουροὺς τῶν Αἰγυπτίων, ἠξιώσαμεν καὶ αὐτοὶ τούτων αὐτοὺς ἀμείψασθαι καὶ τὴν πόλιν αὐτῶν ἀναλαβεῖν κατεφθαρμένην ὑπὸ τῶν

περὶ τοὺς πολέμους συμπεσόντων καὶ συνοικίσαι τῶν διεσπαρμένων εἰς αὐτὴν πάλιν
συνελθόντων· πρῶτον δὲ αὐτοῖς ἐκρίναμεν διὰ τὴν εὐσέβειαν παρασχεῖν τὴν εἰς τὰς
θυσίας σύνταξιν κτηνῶν τε θυσίμων καὶ οἴνου καὶ ἐλαίου καὶ λιβάνου, ἀργυρίου
μυριάδας δύο καὶ σεμιγδάλεως ἀρτάβας ἱερὰς κατὰ τὸν ἐπιχώριον νόμον, πυρῶν
μεδίμνους χιλίους τετρακοσίους ἑξήκοντα, καὶ ἁλῶν μεδίμνους τριακοσίους
ἑβδομήκοντα πέντε· τελεῖσθαι δ᾽ αὐτοῖς ταῦτα βούλομαι καθὼς ἐπέσταλκα, καὶ τὸ
περὶ τὸ ἱερὸν ἀπαρτισθῆναι ἔργον τάς τε στοὰς καὶ εἴ τι ἕτερον οἰκοδομῆσαι δέοι· ἡ δὲ
τῶν ξύλων ὕλη κατακομιζέσθω ἐξ αὐτῆς τε τῆς Ἰουδαίας καὶ ἐκ τῶν ἄλλων ἐθνῶν καὶ
ἐκ τοῦ Λιβάνου μηδενὸς πρασσομένου τέλους· ὁμοίως δὲ καὶ τοῖς ἄλλοις ἐν οἷς ἂν
ἐπιφανεστέραν γίγνεσθαι τὴν τοῦ ἱεροῦ ἐπισκευὴν δέῃ· πολιτευέσθωσαν δὲ πάντες οἱ
ἐκ τοῦ ἔθνους κατὰ τοὺς πατρίους νόμους, ἀπολυέσθω δ᾽ ἡ γερουσία καὶ οἱ ἱερεῖς καὶ οἱ
γραμματεῖς τοῦ ἱεροῦ καὶ οἱ ἱεροψάλται ὧν ὑπὲρ τῆς κεφαλῆς τελοῦσι καὶ τοῦ
στεφανιτικοῦ φόρου καὶ τοῦ περὶ τῶν ἁλῶν· ἵνα δὲ θᾶττον ἡ πόλις κατοικισθῇ δίδωμι
τοῖς τε νῦν κατοικοῦσιν καὶ κατελευσομένοις ἕως τοῦ Ὑπερβερεταίου μηνὸς ἀτελέσιν
εἶναι μέχρι τριῶν ἐτῶν· ἀπολύομεν δὲ καὶ εἰς τὸ λοιπὸν αὐτοὺς τοῦ τρίτου μέρους τῶν
φόρων ὥστε αὐτῶν ἐπανορθωθῆναι τὴν βλάβην· καὶ ὅσοι ἐκ τῆς πόλεως ἁρπαγέντες
δουλεύουσιν, αὐτούς τε τούτους καὶ τοὺς ὑπ᾽ αὐτῶν γεννηθέντας ἐλευθέρους ἀφίεμεν,
καὶ τὰς οὐσίας αὐτοῖς ἀποδίδοσθαι κελεύομεν.

*King Antiochus to Ptolemaios, greetings. Inasmuch as the Jews, from the very moment
when we entered their country, showed their eagerness to serve us and, when we came
to their city, gave us a splendid reception and met us with their senate and furnished
an abundance of provisions to our soldiers and elephants, and also helped us to expel
the Egyptian garrison in the citadel, we have seen fit on our part to reward them for
these acts and to restore their city which has been destroyed by the hazards of war, and
to re-people it by bringing back to it those who have been dispersed abroad. In the first
place we have decided, on account of their piety, to furnish them for their sacrifices
an allowance of sacrificial animals, wine, oil and frankincense to the value of 20,000
pieces of silver, and sacred artabai of fine flour in accordance with their native law
and 1,460 medimnoi of wheat and 375 medimnoi of salt. And it is my will that these
things be made over to them as I have ordered, and that the work on the temple be
completed, including the porticoes and any other part that it may be necessary to build.
The timber, moreover, shall be brought from Judaea itself and from other nations and
Lebanon without the imposition of a toll charge. The like shall be done with the other
materials needed for making the restoration of the temple more splendid. And all the
people of the nation shall have a form of government in accordance with the laws of their
ancestors, and the senate, the priests, the scribes of the temple and the temple-singers
shall be relieved from the head taxes which they pay and the crown tax and the salt
tax. And, in order that the city may the more quickly be re-peopled, I grant both to the
present inhabitants and to those who may return before the month of Hyperberetaios
exemption from taxes for three years. We also relieve them for all time from the third
part of the tribute, so that their losses may be made good. And as for those who were
carried off from the city and are slaves, we herewith set them free, both them and the
children born to them, and order that their property be restored to them.*

DOCUMENT 13. DEMETRIOS I'S LETTER TO JONATHAN

Jos. *AJ* 13.49–53.

. . . τοὺς γὰρ πλείστους ὑμῶν ἀνήσω τῶν φόρων καὶ τῶν συντάξεων ἃς ἐτελεῖτε τοῖς πρὸ ἐμοῦ βασιλεῦσιν καὶ ἐμοί, νῦν τε ὑμῖν ἀφίημι τοὺς φόρους οὓς ἀεὶ παρείχετε· πρὸς τούτοις καὶ τὴν τιμὴν ὑμῖν χαρίζομαι τῶν ἁλῶν καὶ τῶν στεφάνων, οὓς προσεφέρετε ἡμῖν, καὶ ἀντὶ τῶν τρίτων τοῦ καρποῦ καὶ τοῦ ἡμίσους τοῦ ξυλίνου καρποῦ τὸ γινόμενον ἐμοὶ μέρος ὑμῖν ἀφίημι ἀπὸ τῆς σήμερον ἡμέρας· καὶ ὑπὲρ κεφαλῆς ἑκάστης ὃ ἔδει μοι δίδοσθαι τῶν ἐν τῇ Ἰουδαίᾳ κατοικούντων καὶ τῶν τριῶν τοπαρχιῶν τῶν τῇ Ἰουδαίᾳ προσκειμένων Σαμαρείας καὶ Γαλιλαίας καὶ Περαίας τούτου παραχωρῶ ὑμῖν ἀπὸ τοῦ νῦν εἰς τὸν ἅπαντα χρόνον· καὶ τῶν Ἱεροσολυμιτῶν πόλιν ἱερὰν καὶ ἄσυλον εἶναι βούλομαι καὶ ἐλευθέραν ἕως τῶν ὅρων αὐτῆς ἀπὸ τῆς δεκάτης καὶ τῶν τελῶν· τὴν δὲ ἄκραν ἐπιτρέπω τῷ ἀρχιερεῖ ὑμῶν Ἰωνάθῃ, οὓς δ' ἂν αὐτὸς δοκιμάσῃ πιστοὺς καὶ φίλους, τούτους ἐν αὐτῇ φρουροὺς καταστῆσαι, ἵνα φυλάσσωσιν ἡμῖν αὐτὴν· καὶ Ἰουδαίων δὲ τοὺς αἰχμαλωτισθέντας καὶ δουλεύοντας ἐν τῇ ἡμετέρᾳ ἀφίημι ἐλευθέρους· κελεύω δὲ μηδὲ ἀγγαρεύεσθαι τὰ Ἰουδαίων ὑποζύγια· τὰ δὲ σάββατα καὶ ἑορτὴν ἅπασαν καὶ τρεῖς πρὸ τῆς ἑορτῆς ἡμέρας ἔστωσαν ἀτελεῖς· τὸν αὐτὸν τρόπον καὶ τοὺς ἐν τῇ ἐμῇ κατοικοῦντας Ἰουδαίους ἐλευθέρους καὶ ἀνεπηρεάστους ἀφίημι.

For I will free you from most of the tribute and taxes that you paid to the kings before me and to me personally. And now I free you from the tribute you always paid. In addition, I exempt you from the salt tax and the crown tax that you offered me, and I exempt you from this day on of the value of the third part of the grain crop and the half of the fruit crop which was my due. And I grant to you from now and for all time that which was given to me as head taxes by those living in Judaea and the three toparchies of Samaria adjoining it and Galilee and Peraia. And let Jerusalem be sacred and inviolate and exempt up to her boundaries from tolls and taxes. I cede control of the citadel to Jonathan, your high priest, that he may place those whom he judges faithful and friends in it as guards, so that they may guard it for us. And every Jew who has been taken prisoner or enslaved in my kingdom, I set free. And I order that the animals of Jews not be requisitioned. And let the Sabbaths and every feast-day and three days before a feast-day be tax-free. And in the same manner I will let the Jews living in my kingdom be free and undisturbed.

DOCUMENT 14. DEMETRIOS II'S LETTER TO JONATHAN

1 Maccabees 11.34–5.

ἑστάκαμεν αὐτοῖς τά τε ὅρια τῆς Ἰουδαίας καὶ τοὺς τρῖς νομοὺς Ἀφεραίμα καὶ Λίδδα καὶ Ῥαμαθαὶμ προσετέθησαν τῇ Ἰουδαίᾳ ἀπὸ τῆς Σαμαρίτιδος καὶ πάντα τὰ συγκυροῦντα αὐτοῖς πᾶσι τοῖς θυσιάζουσιν εἰς Ἱεροσόλυμα ἀντὶ τῶν βασιλικῶν, ὧν ἐλάμβανεν ὁ βασιλεὺς παρ' αὐτῶν τὸ πρότερον κατ' ἐνιαυτὸν ἀπὸ τῶν γενημάτων τῆς γῆς καὶ τῶν ἀκροδρύων· καὶ τὰ ἄλλα τὰ ἀνήκοντα ἡμῖν ἀπὸ τοῦ νῦν τῶν δεκατῶν καὶ τῶν τελῶν τῶν ἀνηκόντων ἡμῖν καὶ τὰς τοῦ ἁλὸς λίμνας καὶ τοὺς ἀνήκοντας ἡμῖν στεφάνους, πάντα ἐπαρκέσομεν αὐτοῖς.

and we have confirmed to them (the Jews) the boundaries of Judaea. And the three districts of Apheraima, Lydda and Ramathaim have been added to Judaea from Samaria, with everything belonging to them, in favour of those who sacrifice at Jerusalem instead of paying royal taxes, which the king received from them earlier each year from the crops and fruit trees. And the other things that belong to us of the tolls and taxes and the salt tax and the crowns due to us, all these from today we relieve them of.

DOCUMENT 15. THE BAITOKAIKE GRANT

RC 70; cf. Jalabert and Mouterde 1970.

Lines 1–3. Order of a king Antiochos to Euphemos to execute the following instructions:

Προσενεχθέντος μοι περὶ τῆς ἐνεργ[ε]ίας θεοῦ Διὸς Βαιτοκαίκης
(5) ἐκρίθη συνχωρηθῆναι αὐτῷ εἰς ἅπαντα τὸν χρόνον ὅθεν καὶ ἡ δύναμις τοῦ
θεοῦ κατέρχεται κώμην τὴν Βαιτοκαι[κη]νήν, ἣν πρότερον ἔσχεν Δημήτριος
Δημητρίου τοῦ Μνασαίου ἐν Τουργωνα τῆς περὶ Ἀπάμιαν σατραπείας, σὺν τοῖς
συνκύρουσι καὶ καθήκουσι πᾶσι κατὰ τοὺς προϋπάρχοντας περιορισμοὺς
καὶ σὺν τοῖς τοῦ ἐνεστῶτος ἔτους γεν[ν]ήμασιν, ὅπως ἡ ἀπὸ ταύτης πρόσοδος
(10) ἀναλίσκηται εἰς τὰς κατὰ μῆνα{ς} συντελουμένας θυσίας καὶ τἄλλα τὰ πρὸς
αὔξη-
σιν τοῦ ἱεροῦ συντείνοντα ὑπὸ τοῦ καθεσταμένου ὑπὸ τοῦ θεοῦ ἱερέως, ὡς εἴ-
θιστα, ἄγωντι δὲ κατὰ μῆνα πανηγύρεις ἀτελεῖς τῇ πεντεκαιδεκάτῃ καὶ
τριακάδι, καὶ εἶναι τὸ μὲν ἱερὸν ἄσυλον τὴν δὲ κώμην ἀνεπίς<τ>α(θ)μον, μηδεμιᾶς
ἀπορρήσεως προσενεχθείσης·

Having been informed of the power of the god Zeus of Baitokaike, I have decided to grant to him for all time that from which the power of the god is derived, namely the village of Baitokaike, which Demetrios, the son of Demetrios, the son of Mnasaios, formerly possessed in Tourgona (district) in the satrapy of Apameia, along with everything that goes with it and belongs to it within the existing boundaries, and also the harvests of the current year, so that the revenue from these be expended on the monthly sacrifices and the other things which contribute to the prosperity of the sanctuary by the priest of the sanctuary, as is habitual. And let festivals that are exempt from taxation be held each month on the 15th and the 30th days. And let the sanctuary be inviolable and the village free from billeting, since no objection has been made to this.

References

Abbreviations of journal titles correspond to those in *L'Année Philologique*

Abel, F.-M. (1949) *Les livres des Maccabées*. Paris.

Adams, D. G. (1958) *Iraq's People and Resources*. Berkeley.

Adams, R. McC. (1965) *Land behind Baghdad. A History of Settlement in the Diyala Plains*. Chicago and London.

(1981) *Heartland of Cities*. Chicago.

Adams, R. McC. and H. J. Nissen (1972) *The Uruk Countryside – the Natural Setting of Urban Societies*. Chicago.

Adamson, P. B. (1985) 'Problems of storing food in the ancient Near East', *WO* 16: 5–15.

Alcock, S. E. (1993) 'Surveying the peripheries of the Hellenistic world', in Bilde *et al.* (1993): 162–75.

(1994) 'Breaking up the Hellenistic world: survey and society', in *Classical Greece – Ancient Histories and Modern Archaeologies*, ed. I. Morris. Cambridge: 171–90.

Algaze, G. *et al.* (1991) 'The Tigris–Euphrates archaeological reconnaissance project: a preliminary report of the 1989–1990 seasons', *Anatolica* 17: 175–240.

Allen, R. E. (1983) *The Attalid Kingdom*. Oxford.

Altheim, F. and R. Stiehl (1965) 'Die Seleukideninschrift aus Failaka', *Klio* 46: 273–81.

Andreades, A. M. (1929) 'Antimène de Rhodes et Cléomène de Naucratis', *BCH* 53: 1–18.

(1933) *A History of Greek Public Finance*, vol. 1. Cambridge, Mass.

Andreau, J., P. Briant and R. Descat (eds.) (1994) *Economie antique. Les échanges dans l'antiquité: le rôle de l'état*. Saint-Bertrand-de-Comminges.

(eds.) (1997) *Economie antique. Prix et formation des prix dans les économies antiques. Entretiens d'archéologie et d'histoire*. Saint-Bertrand-de-Comminges.

(eds.) (2000) *Economie antique. La guerre dans les économies antiques. Entretiens d'archéologie et d'histoire*. Saint-Bertrand-de-Comminges.

Aperghis, G. G. (1996) 'Travel routes and travel stations from Persepolis'. M.A. dissertation. University College London.

(1997a) 'Alexander's hipparchies', *AncW* 28/2: 133–48.

(1997b) 'Surplus, exchange and price in the Persepolis Fortification Texts', in Andreau, Briant and Descat (1997): 277–90.

(1998) 'The Persepolis Fortification Tablets – another look', in *Achaemenid History XI. Studies in Persian History: Essays in Memory of David M. Lewis*, ed. M. Brosius and A. Kuhrt. Leiden: 35–62.

(1999) 'Storehouses and systems at Persepolis – evidence from the Persepolis Fortification Tablets', *JESHO* 42: 152–93.

(2000) 'War captives and economic exploitation', in Andreau, Briant and Descat (2000): 127–44.

(2001) 'Population – production – taxation – coinage: a model for the Seleukid economy', in *Hellenistic Economies*, ed. Z. H. Archibald *et al.* London and New York: 69–102.

(forthcoming) 'City building and the Seleukid royal economy' in *Hellenistic Economies II*, ed. Z. Archibald *et al.* London and New York.

Applebaum, S. (1986) 'The settlement of Western Samaria from Hellenistic to Byzantine times: a historical commentary', in S. Dar (1986): 257–69.

Arav, R. (1986) 'Settlement patterns and city planning in Palestine during the Hellenistic period 322–37 BCE'. Ph.D. dissertation. New York.

Ashton, R. H. J. (1994) 'The Attalid poll-tax', *ZPE* 104: 57–60.

Atkinson, K. M. T. (1968) 'The Seleucids and the Greek cities of western Asia Minor', *Antichthon* 2: 32–57.

(1972) 'A Hellenistic land conveyance', *Historia* 22: 45–74.

Austin, M. M. (1981) *The Hellenistic World from Alexander to the Roman Conquest.* Cambridge.

(1986) 'Hellenistic kings, war and the economy', *CQ* 36: 450–67.

Avi-Yonah, M. (1978) *Hellenism and the East.* Jerusalem.

Aymard, A. (1938) 'Une ville de la Babylonie séleucide', *REA* 40: 5–42.

Badian, E. (1965) 'The administration of the empire', *G&R²* 12: 166–82.

Bagnall, R. S. (1976) *The Administration of the Ptolemaic Possessions outside Egypt.* Leiden.

Bagnall, R. S. and B. W. Frier (1994) *The Demography of Roman Egypt.* Cambridge.

Balty, J. C. (2000) 'Claudia Apamea. Données nouvelles sur la topographie et l'histoire d'Apamée', *CRAI*: 459–81.

Bandinelli, R. B. (ed.) (1977) *Storia e civiltà dei Greci*, vol. VIII: *La società ellenistica. Economia, diritto, religione.* Milan.

Bar-Kochva, B. (1977) 'Manpower, economics and internal strife in the Hasmonean state', in *Armées et fiscalité dans le monde antique, Colloque Paris 14–16 Oct 1976*, ed. H. van Effenterre. Edition CNRS 936. Paris: 167–96.

(1979) *The Seleucid Army.* Cambridge.

Beaulieu, P. A. (1989) 'Textes administratifs inédits d'époque hellénistique provenant des archives du *Bit Reš*', *RA* 83: 53–87.

Beaumont, P., G. H. Blake and J. M. Wagstaff (1976) *The Middle East – a Geographical Study.* London.

Behrend, D. (1973) 'Rechtshistorische Betrachtungen zu den Rechtdokumenten aus Mylasa und Olymos', in *VI Kongress für griechische und lateinische Epigraphie (1972)*. Munich: 145–68.

Bellinger, A. R. (1963) *Essays on the Coinage of Alexander the Great*. ANSNS 11. New York.

Beloch, J. (1886) *Die Bevölkerung des griechisch-römischen Welt*. Leipzig.

Bengtson, H. (1944) *Die Strategie in der hellenistischen Zeit: ein Beitrag zum antiken Staatsrecht*, vol. 11. Munich.

Berlin, A. M. (1977) 'From monarchy to markets: the Phoenicians in Hellenistic Palestine', *BASOR* 306: 75–88.

    (1997) 'Between large forces. Palestine in the Hellenistic period', *Biblical Archaeologist* 60: 3–51.

Bernard, P. (1973) *Fouilles d'Aï Khanoum*, vol. 1: *(Campagnes 1965, 1966, 1967, 1968)*. Mémoires DAFA 21. Paris.

    (1985) *Fouilles d'Aï Khanoum*, vol. IV: *Les monnaies hors trésors. Questions d'histoire gréco-bactrienne*. Mémoires DAFA 28. Paris.

    (1994) 'L'Asie Centrale et l'empire séleucide', *Topoi* 4: 473–511.

    (1995) '1. Une légende de fondation hellénistique: Apamée sur l'Oronte d'après les cynégétiques du pseudo-Oppien. 11. Paysages et toponymies dans le Proche-Orient hellénisé', *Topoi* 5: 353–408.

Bernard, P. and C. Rapin (1994) 'Un parchemin gréco-bactrien d'une collection privée', *CRAI*: 261–94.

Bertrand, J. M. (1982) 'Sur l'inscription d'Hefzibah', *ZPE* 46: 167–74.

Berve, H. (1988 [reprint of 1926 edition]) *Das Alexanderreich auf prosopographischer Grundlage*. Salem, N.H.

Bikerman, E. (1935) 'La charte séleucide de Jérusalem', *REJ*: 4–35.

    (1938) *Institutions des Séleucides*. Paris.

    (1988) *The Jews in the Greek Age*. Cambridge, Mass.

Bilde, P. *et al.* (eds.) (1993) *Centre and Periphery in the Hellenistic World*. Aarhus.

Billows, R. A. (1995) *Kings and Colonists*. Leiden.

Boffo, L. (1985) *I re ellenistici e i centri religiosi dell'Asia Minore*. Florence.

Bogaert, R. (1977) 'Il commercio internazionale e le banche', in Bandinelli (1977): 375–99.

Boiy, T. (2000) 'Dating methods during the early Hellenistic period', *JCS* 52: 115–21.

Bopearachchi, O. (1991) *Monnaies gréco-bactriennes et indo-grecques*. Paris.

    (1994) 'L'indépendence de la Bactriane', *Topoi* 4: 515–19.

Börker, C. (1974) 'Griechische Amphorenstempel vom Tell Halaf bis zum persischen Golf', *Baghdader Mitteilungen* 7: 31–49.

Boucharlat, R. (1985) 'Suse, marché agricole ou relais de grande commerce. Suse et la Susiane à l'époque des grands empires', *Paléorient* 11/2: 71–82.

Braun, T. (1995) 'Barley cakes and emmer bread', in *Food in Antiquity*, ed. J. Wilkins *et al.* Exeter: 25–37.

Breckwoldt, T. (1995/6) 'Management of grain storage in Old Babylonian Larsa', *AOF* 42/3: 64–88.

Briant, P. (1973) 'Remarques sur les *laoi* et esclaves ruraux en Asie Mineure hellénistique', in *Actes du colloque 1971 sur l'esclavage*. Paris: 93–133, reprinted in Briant (1982b): 95–135.

(1978) 'Colonisation hellénistique et populations indigènes. La phase d'installation', *Klio* 60: 57–92, reprinted in Briant (1982b): 227–62.

(1979) 'Des Achéménides aux rois hellénistiques: continuités et ruptures', *ASNP³* 9: 1375–414, reprinted in Briant (1982b): 291–330.

(1980) 'Communautés rurales, forces productives et mode de production tributaire en Asie achéménide', *Zaman* 2: 75–100, reprinted in Briant (1982b): 405–30.

(1982a) *Etats et pasteurs au Moyen-Orient ancien*. Cambridge.

(1982b) *Rois, tributs et paysans*. Paris.

(1982c) 'Colonisation hellénistique et populations indigènes II', *Klio* 64: 83–98, reprinted in Briant (1982b): 263–79.

(1985) 'Dons de terres et de villes: l'Asie Mineure dans le contexte achéménide', *REA* 87: 53–71.

(1986) 'Guerre, tribut et forces productives dans l'empire achéménide', *DHA* 12: 33–48.

(1990) 'The Seleucid kingdom, the Achaemenid empire and the history of the Near East in the first millennium BC', in *Religion and Religious Practice in the Seleucid Kingdom*, ed. P. Bilde *et al.* Aarhus: 40–65.

(1994a) 'De Samarkhand à Sardes et de la ville de Suse au pays des Hanéens', *Topoi* 4: 455–67.

(1994b) 'Prélèvements tributaires et échanges en Asie Mineure achéménide et hellénistique', in Andreau, Briant and Descat (1994): 69–81.

(ed.) (1995) *Dans les pas des Dix-Mille, Pallas* 43.

(1996) *Histoire de l'empire perse*. Paris.

(ed.) (2001)*Irrigation et drainage dans l'antiquité, qanats et canalisations souterraines en Iran, en Egypte et en Grèce*. Paris.

Briant, P. and R. Descat (1998) 'Un registre douanier de la satrapie d'Egypte de l'époque achéménide', *Le commerce en Egypte ancienne*, ed. N. Grimal and B. Menu. Cairo: 59–104.

Bringmann, K. and H. von Steuben (1995) *Schenkungen hellenistischer Herrscher an griechische Städte und Heiligtümer*, vol. I. Berlin.

Brinkman, J. A. (1984) 'Settlement surveys and documentary evidence: regional variation and secular trend in Mesopotamian demography', *JNES* 43: 169–80.

Broshi, M. (1979) 'The population of western Palestine in the Roman-Byzantine period', *BASOR* 236: 1–10.

Broughton, T. R. S. (1951) 'New evidence on temple-estates in Asia Minor', in *Studies in Roman Economic and Social History in Honour of Allan Chester Johnson*, ed. P. R. Coleman-Norton. Princeton, N.J.

Buck, C. and W. Petersen (1944) *A Reverse Index of Greek Nouns and Adjectives*. Chicago.

Buckler, W. H. and D. M. Robinson (1912) 'Greek inscriptions from Sardes', *AJA* 16: 11–82.

(1932) *Sardis*, vol. vii.i: *Greek and Latin Inscriptions*. Leiden.

Bunge, J. G. (1976) 'Die Feiern Antiochos IV Epiphanes in Daphne im Herbst 166 v. Chr.', *Chiron* 6: 53–71.

Burford, A. (1993) *Land and Labor in the Greek World*. Baltimore and London.

Burn, A. R. (1984) *Persia and the Greeks*. London.

Buttrey, S. E. and T. V. Buttrey (1997) 'Calculating coin production, again', *AJN*² 9: 113–35.

Buttrey, T. V. (1993) 'Calculating ancient coin production: facts and fantasies', *NC* 153: 335–52.

(1994) 'Calculating ancient coin production ii: why it cannot be done', *NC* 154: 341–52.

Cadell, H. and G. Le Rider (1997) *Prix du blé et numéraire dans l'Egypte lagide de 305 à 173*. Brussels.

Callataÿ, F. de (1995) 'Calculating ancient coin production: seeking a balance', *NC* 155: 289–311.

(1997) *L'histoire des guerres mithridatiques vue par les monnaies*. Louvain-la-Neuve.

Callataÿ, F. de, G. Depeyrot and L. Villaronga (1993) *L'argent monnayé d'Alexandre le Grand à Auguste*. Brussels.

Cameron, G. G. (1948) *Persepolis Treasury Tablets*. Chicago.

Carsana, C. (1996) *Le dirigenze cittadine nello stato seleucidico*. Como.

Carter, G. F. (1983) 'A simplified method for calculating the original number of dies from die link statistics', *American Numismatic Society Museum Notes* 28: 195–206.

Casson, L. (1984) *Ancient Trade and Society*. Detroit.

Cavaignac, E. (1923) *Population et capital dans le monde méditerranéen antique*. Oxford.

(1951) *L'économie grecque*. Paris.

Charles, M. P. (1984) 'Introductory remarks on the cereals', *BullSumAgric* 1: 17–31.

(1985) 'An introduction to the legumes and oil plants of Mesopotamia', *BullSumAgric* 2: 39–62.

(1987) 'Onions, cucumbers and the date palm', *BullSumAgric* 3: 1–21.

(1988) 'Irrigation in lowland Mesopotamia', *BullSumAgric* 4: 1–39.

(1990) 'Traditional crop husbandry in southern Iraq', *BullSumAgric* 5: 47–64.

Chaumont, M. L. (1982) 'Recherches sur quelques villes helléniques de l'Iran occidental', *IA* 17: 147–73.

Cherry, J. F. (1983) 'Frogs around the pond: perspectives on current archaeological survey projects in the Mediterranean region', in *Archaeological Survey in the Mediterranean Area*, ed. D. R. Keller and D. W. Rupp. BAR International Series 155. London: 375–416.

Clairmont, C. (1948) 'Ein Edikt Antiochos' III', *M.H.* 5: 218–26.

Clark, C. and M. Haswell (1970) *The Economics of Subsistence Agriculture*, 4th edn. London.

Cocquerillat, D. (1968) *Palmeraies et cultures de l'Eanna d'Uruk (559–520)*. Berlin.

Cohen, G. M. (1978) *The Seleucid Colonies*. Historia Einzelschriften 30. Wiesbaden.

(1983) 'Colonization and population transfer in the Hellenistic world', in *Egypt and the Hellenistic world*, ed. E. van't Dack *et al.* Louvain: 63–74.

Cohen, G. M. (1991) 'Κατοικίαι, κάτοικοι and Macedonians in Asia Minor', *AncSoc* 22: 41–50.

(1995) *The Hellenistic Settlements in Europe, the Islands and Asia Minor.* Berkeley.

Coin Hoards, vol. I (1975). The Royal Numismatic Society. London.

Coin Hoards, vol. II (1976). The Royal Numismatic Society. London.

Coin Hoards, vol. III (1977). The Royal Numismatic Society. London.

Coin Hoards, vol. IV (1978). The Royal Numismatic Society. London.

Coin Hoards, vol. V (1979). The Royal Numismatic Society. London.

Coin Hoards, vol. VI (1981). The Royal Numismatic Society. London.

Coin Hoards, vol. VII (1985). The Royal Numismatic Society. London.

Coin Hoards, vol. VIII (1994), ed. U. Wartenberg, M. J. Price and K. A. McGregor. The Royal Numismatic Society. London.

Coin Hoards, vol. IX (2002), ed. A. R. Meadows and U. Wartenberg. The Royal Numismatic Society. London.

Cook, J. M. (1973) *The Troad.* Oxford.

Corsaro, M. (1980) '*Oikonomia* del re e *oikonomia* del satrapo', *ASNP*[3] 10: 1163–219.

(1985) 'Tassazione regia e tassazione cittadina dagli Achemenidi ai re ellenistici: alcune osservazioni', *REA* 87: 73–95.

Crampa, J. (1969) *The Greek Inscriptions*, in *Labraunda*, vol. III/1. Lund.

Crawford, D. J. (1971) *Kerkeosiris – an Egyptian Village in the Ptolemaic Period.* Cambridge.

Crawford, M. H. (1970) 'Money and exchange in the Roman world', *JRS* 60: 40–8.

(1974) *Roman Republican Coinage.* Cambridge.

(1987) 'Tableware for Trimalchio', in *Art and Production in the World of the Caesars*, ed. T. J. Cornell, M. H. Crawford and J. A. North. Milan: 37–44.

Cumont, F. (1926) *Fouilles de Doura-Europos.* Paris.

(1931) 'Inscriptions grecques de Suse', *CRAI*: 233–50, 278–92.

Dar, S. (ed.) (1986) *Landscape and Pattern: an Archaeological Survey of Samaria: 800 BCE – 636 CE.* BAR International Series 308. Oxford.

Daux, G. (1934) 'Χειροτέχνιον', *RPh*[3] 8: 361–6.

Davesne, A. and G. Le Rider (1989) *Gülnar*, vol. II: *Le trésor de Meydancikkale (Cilicie Trachée 1980).* Paris.

Davesne, A. and V. Yenisoganci (1992) 'Les Ptolémées en Séleucide: le trésor d'Hüseyinli', *RN*[6] 34: 23–36.

Davies, J. K. (1984) 'Cultural, social and economic features of the Hellenistic world', in *Cambridge Ancient History*, vol. VII, part, 1: *The Hellenistic World*, ed. F. W. Walbank *et al.* 2nd edn. Cambridge: 257–320.

(1998) 'Ancient economies: models and muddles', in *Trade, Traders and the City*, ed. H. Perkis and C. Smith. London and New York: 225–56.

Debord, P. (1982) *Aspects sociaux et économiques de la vie religieuse dans l'Anatolie gréco-romaine.* Leiden.

Del Monte, G. F. (1997) *Testi dalla Babilonia Ellenistica*, vol. I: *Testi cronografici.* Studi Ellenistici IX. Pisa and Rome.

Descat, R. (1985) 'Mnésimachos, Hérodote et le système tributaire achéménide', *REA* 87: 97–112.

(1989) 'Notes sur la politique tributaire de Darius Ier', in *Le tribut dans l'empire perse*, ed. P. Briant and C. Herrenschmidt. Louvain and Paris: 77–92.

(1997) 'Le tribut et l'économie tributaire dans l'empire achéménide', *Topoi* Suppl. 1: 253–62.

Doty, L. T. (1977) 'Cuneiform archives from Hellenistic Uruk'. Ph.D. dissertation. Yale.

(1978) 'The archive of the Nana-iddin family from Uruk', *JCS* 30: 65–90.

(1979) 'An official seal of the Seleucid period', *JNES* 38: 195–7.

Downey, G. (1961) *A History of Antioch in Syria*. Princeton, N.J.

Doxiades, C. A. and J. G. Papaioannou (1974) *Ecumenopolis*. Athens.

Driver, G. R. ([1957]1965) *Aramaic Documents of the Fifth Century* BC. Abridged and revised edn. Oxford.

Duncan-Jones, R. P. (1994) *Money and Government in the Roman Empire*. Cambridge.

(1997) 'Numerical distortion in Roman writers', in Andreau, Briant and Descat (1997): 147–59.

Esty, W. W. (1986) 'Estimation of the size of a coinage: a survey and comparison of methods', *NC* 146: 185–215.

Finley, M. I. (1985) *The Ancient Economy*, 2nd edn. Berkeley and Los Angeles.

Fischer, T. (1979) 'Zur Seleukideninschrift von Hefzibah', *ZPE* 33: 131–8.

Flacelière, R. (1935) 'Inscriptions de Delphes du IIIe siècle av. J.-C.', *BCH* 59: 7–35.

Foraboschii, D. (2000) 'The Hellenistic economy: indirect intervention by the State', in *Production and Public Powers in Classical Antiquity*, ed. E. Lo Cascio and D. W. Rathbone. Cambridge Philological Society, Suppl. 26. Cambridge: 37–43.

Forbes, R. J. (1950) *Metallurgy in Antiquity*. Leiden.

Foulon, E. (1996) '*Hypaspistes, peltastes, chrysaspides, argyraspides, chalkaspides*', *REA* 98: 53–63.

Foxhall, L. and H. A. Forbes (1982) 'Σιτομετρεία: the role of grain as a staple food in classical antiquity', *Chiron* 12: 41–90.

Fraser, P. M. (1972) *Ptolemaic Alexandria*, vol. I text and vol. II notes. Oxford.

(1996) *Cities of Alexander the Great*. Oxford.

Freyne, S. (1980) *Galilee from Alexander the Great to Hadrian 323 BCE to 135 CE: a Study of Second Temple Judaism*. Wilmington, Del.

Frézouls, E. (ed.) (1987) *Sociétés urbaines, sociétés rurales dans l'Asie Mineure et la Syrie hellénistiques et romaines. Actes du colloque organisé à Strasbourg, Nov. 1985*. Strasbourg.

Funck, B. (1978) 'Zu den Landschenkungen hellenistischer Könige', *Klio* 60: 45–55.

Gallant, T. W. (1985) 'The agronomy, production and utilization of sesame and linseed in the Graeco-Roman world', *BullSumAgric* 2: 153–8.

(1991) *Risk and Survival in Ancient Greece*. Padstow.

Gardin, J.-C. and B. Lyonnet (1978–9) 'La prospection archéologique de la Bactriane orientale (1974–1978): premiers résultats', *Mesopotamia* 13–14: 99–154.

Garnsey, P. (1988) *Famine and Food Supply in the Graeco-Roman World*. Cambridge.

(1992) 'Yield of the land', in *Agriculture in Ancient Greece. Proceedings of the 7th International Symposium at the Swedish Institute at Athens, 16–17 May 1990*, ed. B. Wells. Stockholm: 147–53.

(1998) 'Mass diet and nutrition in the city of Rome', in *Cities, Peasants and Food in Classical Antiquity. Essays in Social and Economic History*, ed. P. Garnsey. Cambridge: 229–42.

Gauthier, Ph. (1989) *Nouvelles inscriptions de Sardes*, vol. II. Geneva.

(1991) ''Ατέλεια τοῦ σώματος', *Chiron* 21: 51–68.

Gibson, M. (1992) 'Patterns of occupation at Nippur', in *Nippur at the Centennial. Papers read at the 35e Rencontre Assyriologique Internationale, Philadelphia 1988*, ed. M. de Jong-Ellis. Philadelphia: 33–54.

Goldstein, J. A. (1976) *I Maccabees*. Anchor Bible 41. New York.

(1983) *II Maccabees*. Anchor Bible 41a. New York.

Golenko, V. K. (1993) 'Notes on the coinage and currency of the early Seleucid state – I: the reign of Seleucus I', *Mesopotamia* 28: 71–167.

(1995) 'Notes on the coinage and currency of the early Seleucid state – II–IV: the reigns of Antiochus I to Antiochus III', *Mesopotamia* 30: 51–203.

Golubcova, E. S. (1972) 'Sklaverei und Abhängigkeit im hellenistischen Kleinasien', in *Die Sklaverei in hellenistischen Staaten im 3.-1. Jh. v. Chr.*, ed. T. V. Blavatskaja, E. S. Golubcova and A. I. Pavlovskaja. Wiesbaden: 107–70.

Grainger, J. D. (1990a) *The Cities of Seleukid Syria*. Oxford.

(1990b) *Seleukos Nikator – Constructing a Hellenistic Kingdom*. London.

(1991) *Hellenistic Phoenicia*. Oxford.

(1996) 'Antiochos III in Thrace', *Historia* 45: 329–43.

(1999) 'Prices in Hellenistic Babylonia', *JESHO* 42: 303–25.

Grant, M. (1982) *From Alexander to Cleopatra: the Hellenistic World*. London.

Grayson, A. K. (1975) *Assyrian and Babylonian Chronicles*. Locust Valley, N.Y.

Green, P. (1990) *Alexander to Actium*. Berkeley.

Griffith, G. T. (1935) *The Mercenaries of the Hellenistic World*. Cambridge.

(1964) 'Alexander the Great and an experiment in government', *PCPhS* 190: 23–39.

Groningen, B. A. van (1933) *Aristote. Le second livre de l'Economique*. Leiden.

Groningen, B. A. van and A. Wartelle (1968) *Aristote économique*. Paris.

Grote, K. (1913) *Die griechische Söldnerwesen der hellenistischen Zeit*. Jena.

Gruen, E. S. (1984) *The Hellenistic World and the Coming of Rome*, 2 vols. Berkeley.

Hahn, I. (1978) 'Königsland und königliche Besteurung im hellenistischen Osten', *Klio* 60: 11–34.

Hallock, R. T. (1960) 'A new look at the Persepolis Treasury Tablets', *JNES* 19: 90–100.

(1969) *Persepolis Fortification Tablets*. Chicago.

(1978) 'Selected Fortification texts', *Cahiers de la DAFI* 8: 109–36.

Halstead, P. (1995) 'Plough and power: the economic and social significance of cultivation with the ox-drawn ard in the Mediterranean', *BullSumAgric* 8: 11–22.

Hammond, N. G. L. (1992) *The Macedonian State*. Oxford.

(1995) 'Philip's innovations in Macedonian economy', *SO* 70: 22–9.

(2000) 'The continuity of Macedonian institutions and the Macedonian king-doms of the Hellenistic era', *Historia* 49/2: 141–60.

Hammond, N. G. L. and G. T. Griffith (1997) *A History of Macedonia*, vol. II. Amsterdam.

Hannestad, L. (1984) 'The pottery from the Hellenistic settlements of Failaka', in *Arabie orientale, Mésopotamie et Iran méridional*, ed. R. Boucharlat and J.-F. Salles. Paris: 67–83.

Hatzopoulos, M. B. (1988) *Une donation du roi Lysimaque*. Athens.

(1996) *Macedonian Institutions under the Kings*, 2 vols. *Meletemata* 22. Athens.

Haussoullier, B. (1901) 'Les Séleucides et le temple d'Apollon Didyméen', *RPh*² 25: 6–42.

(1926) 'Inscriptions de Didymes. Comptes de la construction du Didymeion IV', *RPh*² 50: 125–52.

Heichelheim, F. (1930) *Wirtschaftliche Schwankungen der Zeit von Alexander bis Augustus*. Jena.

Hengel, M. (1981) *Judaism and Hellenism*. London.

Hennig, D. (1995) 'Staatliche Ansprüche an privaten Immobilienbesitz', *Chiron* 25: 235–82.

Hepper, F. N. (1987) 'Trees and shrubs yielding gums and resins in the ancient Near East', *BullSumAgric* 3: 107–14.

Herrmann, G. *et al.* (1993) 'The International Merv Project, preliminary report on the first season (1992)', *Iran* 31: 39–62.

Herrmann, P. (1965) 'Antiochos der Grosse und Teos', *Anatolia* 9: 29–160.

Hodkinson, S. (1988) 'Animal husbandry in the Greek *polis*', in *Pastoral Economies in Classical Antiquity*, ed. C. R. Whittaker. Cambridge Philological Society Suppl. 14. Cambridge: 35–74.

Holt, F. L. (1993) *Alexander the Great and Bactria*. Leiden.

(1999) *Thundering Zeus. The making of Hellenistic Bactria*. Berkeley.

Hopkins, K. (1978) *Conquerors and Slaves*. Cambridge.

(1980) 'Taxes and trade in the Roman empire (200 BC – AD 400)', *JRS* 70: 101–25.

Hornblower, S. (1994) 'Persia', in *Cambridge Ancient History*, vol. VI: *The Fourth Century BC*, ed. D. M. Lewis *et al.* 2nd edn. Cambridge: 45–96.

Horowitz, W. (1991) 'Antiochus I, Esagil and a celebration of the ritual for renovation of temples', *RA* 85: 75–7.

Houghton, A. (1980) 'Notes on the early Seleucid victory coinage of "Persepolis"', *SNR* 59: 5–14.

(1989a) 'The royal Seleucid mint of Seleucia on the Calycadnus', in *Kraay–Mørkholm Essays: Numismatic Studies in Honour of C. M. Kraay and O. Mørkholm*, ed. G. Le Rider *et al.* Louvain-la-Neuve: 77–98.

(1989b) 'The royal Seleucid mint of Soli', *NC* 149: 15–32.

Houghton, A. and K. Lorber (2002) *Seleucid Coins, a Comprehensive Catalogue*. New York.

Houghton, A. and W. Moore (1984) 'Some early northeastern Seleucid mints', *American Numismatic Society Museum Notes* 29: 1–9.

How, W. W. and J. Wells (1989) *A Commentary on Herodotus*, vol. I. Oxford.

Howgego, C. (1995) *Ancient History from Coins*. London.

Invernizzi, A. (1993) 'Seleucia on the Tigris: centre and periphery in Seleucid Asia', in Bilde *et al.* (1993): 230–50.

(1994) 'Babylonian motifs on the sealings from Seleucia-on-the-Tigris', in Sancisi-Weerdenburg, Kuhrt and Root (1994): 353–64.

Jähne, A. (1978) 'Zwei Tendenzen gesellschaftlicher Entwicklung im Hellenismus', *Klio* 60: 137–50.

Jalabert, L. and R. Mouterde (1970) *Inscriptions grecques et latines de la Syrie*, vol. VII. Paris.

Jesus, P. de (1978) 'Metal resources in ancient Anatolia', *AS* 28: 97–102.

Joannès, F. (1995) 'L'itinéraire des dix-mille en Mésopotamie et l'apport des sources cunéiformes', in Briant (1995): 173–200.

(1997) 'Prix et salaires en Babylonie du VIIe au IIIe siècle avant notre ère', in Andreau, Briant and Descat (1997): 313–33.

Jones, A. H. M. (1937) *The Cities of the Eastern Roman Provinces*. Oxford.

(1940) *The Greek City from Alexander to Justinian*. Oxford.

(1974) *The Roman Economy*, ed. P. A. Brunt. Oxford.

Jonnes, L. and M. Ricl (1997) 'A new royal inscription from Phrygia Paroreios: Eumenes II grants Tyriaion the status of a polis', *EA* 29: 1–30.

Kinns, P. (1983) 'The Amphictionic coinage reconsidered', *NC* 143: 1–22.

Koch, H. (1988) 'Herrscher in der Persis unter Seleukiden und Parthern', *WO* 19: 84–95.

(1990) *Verwaltung und Wirtschaft im persischen Kernland zur Zeit der Achämeniden*. Wiesbaden.

Kramer, C. (1982) *Village Ethnoarchaeology. Rural Iran in Archaeological Perspective*. New York.

Kreissig, H. (1976) 'L'esclavage dans les villes d'Orient pendant la période hellénistique', in *Actes du colloque 1973 sur l'esclavage (Besançon 2–3 mai, 1973)*. Paris: 237–55.

(1977a) 'Landed property in the "Hellenistic" Orient', *Eirene* 15: 5–26.

(1977b) 'Tempelland, Katoiken, Hierodulen in Seleukidenreich', *Klio* 59: 375–80.

(1978) *Wirtschaft und Gesellschaft in Seleukidenreich*. Berlin.

Kuhrt, A. (1990) 'Achaemenid Babylonia: sources and problems', in Sancisi-Weerdenburg and Kuhrt (1990): 177–94.

(1995a) *The Ancient Near East*, 2 vols. London.

(1995b) 'The Assyrian heartland in the Achaemenid period', in Briant (1995): 239–54.

(1996) 'The Seleucid kings and Babylonia: new perspectives on the Seleucid realm in the East', in *Aspects of Hellenistic Kingship*, ed. P. Bilde *et al.* Aarhus: 41–54.

Kuhrt, A. and S. Sherwin-White (eds.) (1987) *Hellenism in the East*. London.

(1991) 'Aspects of Seleucid royal ideology: the cylinder of Antiochus I from Borsippa', *JHS* 111: 71–86.

(1994a) 'General observations by the authors of *From Samarkhand to Sardis*', *Topoi* 4: 449–59.

(1994b) 'The transition from Achaemenid to Seleucid rule in Babylonia: Revolution or evolution?', in Sancisi-Weerdenburg, Kuhrt and Root (1994): 311–27.

Landau, Y. H. (1961) 'A Greek inscription from Acre', *IEJ* 11: 118–26.

(1966) 'A Greek inscription found near Hefzibah', *IEJ* 16: 54–70.

Launey, M. (1950) *Recherches sur les armées hellénistiques*, 2 vols. Paris.

Le Bas, P. and W. H. Waddington (1972 reprint) *Inscriptions grecques et latines recueilles en Asie Mineure*, vol. 1. Hildesheim and New York.

Leriche, P. (1987) 'Urbanisme défensif et occupation du territoire en Syrie hellénistique', in Frézouls (1987): 57–79.

(1994) 'L'Orient séleucide: les données archéologiques', *Topoi* 4: 531–40.

Le Rider, G. (1965) *Suse sous les Séleucides et les Parthes*. Paris.

(1989) 'La Golfe Persique à l'époque Séleucide: exploration archéologique et trouvailles monétaires' *RN*[6] 31: 248–52.

(1992) 'Les clauses financières des traités de 189 et 188', *BCH* 116: 267–77.

(1993) 'Les ressources financières de Séleucos IV (187–175) et le paiement de l'indemnité aux Romains', in *Essays in Honour of Robert Carson and Kenneth Jenkins*, ed. M. Price, A. Burnett and R. Bland. London: 49–67.

(1994a) 'Antiochos IV (175–164) et la monnayage de bronze séleucide', *BCH* 118: 17–34.

(1994b) 'Notes de numismatique', *Topoi* 4: 469–71.

(1995) 'La politique monétaire des Séleucides en Coelé Syrie et en Phénicie après 200', *BCH* 119: 391–404.

Lerner, J. D. (1995/6) 'Seleucid decline over the eastern Iranian plateau', *Berytus* 42: 103–12.

(1999) *The Impact of Seleucid Decline on the Eastern Iranian Plateau*. Historia Einzelschriften 123. Stuttgart.

Lewis, D. M. (1987) 'The King's dinner (Polyaenus IV 3.32)', in Sancisi-Weerdenburg and Kuhrt (1987): 79–87.

Lo Cascio, E. (1999) 'La popolazione dell' Egitto romano', in *La démographie historique antique*, eds. M. Bellancourt-Valdher and J.-N. Corvisier. Artois: 153–69.

Lockhart, P. N. (1961) 'The Laodice inscription from Didyma', *AJPh* 82: 188–92.

Lyonnet, B. (1990) 'Les rapports entre l'Asie Centrale et l'empire achéménide d'après les données de l'archéologie', in Sancisi-Weerdenburg and Kuhrt (1990): 77–92.

(1994) 'L'occupation séleucide en Bactriane orientale et en Syrie du N. E.', *Topoi* 4: 541–6.

Ma, J. (1997), 'Antiochos III and the cities of western Asia Minor'. Ph.D. dissertation, Oxford University.

(1999) *Antiochos III and the Cities of Western Asia Minor*. Oxford.

Magie, D. (1950) *Roman Rule in Asia Minor*. Princeton, N.J.

Malay, H. (1983) 'A royal document from Aigai in Aiolis', *GRBS* 24: 349–53.
  (1987) 'Letter of Antiochos III to Zeuxis with two covering letters (209 BC)', *EA* 10: 7–15.
Malay, H. and C. Nalbantoğlu (1996) 'The cult of Apollon Pleurenos in Lydia', *Türk Arkeoloji Dergisi* 4: 75–81.
Marchese, R. T. (1986) *The Lower Maeander Flood Plain*, vol. 1. BAR 292i. London.
Maresch, K. (1996) *Bronze und Silber*. Papyrologica Coloniensia xxv. Opladen.
Marfoe, L. *et al.* (1986) 'The Chicago Euphrates archaeological project 1980–1984: an interim report', *Anatolica* 13: 37–148.
Masson, V. M. (1982) *Das Land der tausend Städte*. Munich.
Matthers, J. *et al.* (1978) 'Tell Rifa'at 1977: preliminary report of an archaeological survey', *Iraq* 40: 119–62.
McCarthy, J. (1983) *Muslims and Minorities. The Population of Ottoman Anatolia and the End of the Empire*. New York.
  (1990) *The Population of Palestine*. New York.
McDowell, R. H. (1935) *Stamped and Inscribed Objects from Seleucia on the Tigris*. Ann Arbor, Mich.
McEwan, G. J. P. (1981a) *Priest and Temple in Hellenistic Babylonia*. Wiesbaden.
  (1981b) 'Arsacid temple records', *Iraq* 43: 131–43.
  (1982) 'An official Seleucid seal reconsidered', *JNES* 41: 51–3.
  (1988) 'Babylonia in the Hellenistic period', *Klio* 70: 412–21.
McGovern, W. E. (1980) 'Missing die probabilities, expected die production and the index figure', *American Numismatic Society Museum Notes* 25: 209–23.
Meriç, R. and J. Nollé (1985) 'Neue Inschriften aus der Umgebung von Philadelphia in Lydien: Badinca', *EA* 5: 20–6.
Merker, I. L. (1975) 'A Greek tariff inscription in Jerusalem', *IEJ* 25: 238–44.
Metzger, H. (1979) *Fouilles de Xanthos*, vol. vi: *La stèle trilingue du Létoon*. Paris.
Meyers, E. M., J. F. Strange and D. E. Groh (1976) 'The Meiron excavation project: archaeological survey in Galilee and Golan', *BASOR* 230: 1–24.
Mieroop, M. van de (1997) *The Ancient Mesopotamian City*. Oxford.
Millar, F. (1987) 'The problem of Hellenistic Syria', in Kuhrt and Sherwin-White (1987): 110–33.
  (1993) *The Roman Near East*. Cambridge, Mass.
Milns, R. D. (1987) 'Army pay and the military budget of Alexander the Great', in *Festschrift G. Wirth*, ed. W. Will. Amsterdam: 233–56.
Minns, E. H. (1915) 'Parchments of the Parthian period from Avroman in Kurdistan', *JHS* 35: 22–65.
Mollo, P. (1996) 'Il problema dell' ἁλική seleucide alla luce dei materiali degli archivi di Seleucia sul Tigri', in *Archives et sceaux du monde hellénistique, Turin, 13–16 January 1993*, ed. M.-F. Boussac and A. Invernizzi. BCH Suppl. 29. Paris: 145–56.
Momeni, D. (1970) 'The population of Iran: a dynamic analysis'. Ph.D. dissertation. University of Texas. Austin.
Moretti, L. (1977) 'L'economia ellenistica', in Bandinelli (1977): 319–25.
Mørkholm, O. (1963) *Studies in the Coinage of Antiochus IV of Syria*. Copenhagen.

(1966) *Antiochus IV of Syria*. Copenhagen.

(1967) 'The monetary system of the Seleucid kings until 129 BC', in *The Pattern of Monetary Development in Phoenicia and Palestine in Antiquity (International Numismatic Convention, Jerusalem 1963)*, ed. A. Kindler. Tel Aviv: 75–87.

(1970) 'The Seleucid mint at Antiochia on the Persian Gulf', *American Numismatic Society Museum Notes* 16: 31–44.

(1976) 'Hellenistic coin hoards from the Persian Gulf', in *Actes du 8ème Congrès International de Numismatique Sep. 1973*. Paris: 123–4.

(1979) 'Some reflections on the early cistophoric coinage', *American Numismatic Society Museum Notes* 24: 47–61.

(1982) 'Some reflections on the production and use of coinage in Ancient Greece', *Historia* 31: 290–305.

(1984) 'The monetary system in the Seleucid empire after 187 BC', in *Ancient Coins of the Graeco-Roman World*, ed. W. Heckel and R. Sullivan. Waterloo, Ontario: 93–114.

(1991) *Early Hellenistic Coinage*. Cambridge.

Murray, O. (1966) "Ο ἀρχαῖος δασμός', *Historia* 15: 142–56.

Musti, D. (1957) 'Osservazioni in margine a documenti della cancellaria ellenistica', *ASNP*² 26: 267–84.

(1965) 'Aspetti dell'organizzazione seleucidica in Asia Minore nel II sec. a. c.', *PP* 20: 153–60.

(1966) 'Lo stato dei Seleucidi', *SCO* 15: 61–197.

(1984) 'Syria and the East', in *Cambridge Ancient History*, vol. VII, part I: *The Hellenistic World*, ed. F. W. Walbant et al.. 2nd edn. Cambridge: 175–220.

(1987) *L'economia in Grecia*. Bari.

Newell, E. T. (1977) *The Coinage of the Western Seleucid Mints*. New York.

(1978) *The Coinage of the Eastern Seleucid Mints*. New York.

Oelsner, J. (1977) 'Zur Sklaverei in Babylonien in der chaldäischen, achämenidischen und hellenistischen Zeit', *AOF* 5: 71–80.

(1978) 'Kontinuität und Wandel in Gesellschaft und Kultur Babyloniens in hellenistischer Zeit', *Klio* 60: 101–16.

(1981) 'Gesellschaft und Wirtschaft des seleukidischen Babylonien', *Klio* 63: 39–44.

(1986) *Materialen zur Gesellschaft und Kultur in hellenistischer Zeit*. Budapest.

Orrieux, C. (1983) *Les papyrus de Zenon*. Paris.

Osborne, R. (1987) *Classical Landscape with Figures*. London.

Papazoglou, F. (1997) *Laoi et paroikoi. Recherches sur la structure de la société hellénistique*. Belgrade.

Pastor, J. (1997) *Land and Economy in Ancient Palestine*. London.

Peremans, W. (1978) 'Notes sur l'administration civile et financière de l'Egypte sous les Lagides', *AncSoc* 10: 139–49.

Piejko, F. (1988) 'Letter of Eumenes II to Tralles concerning inviolability and tax exemption for a temple. After 188 BC', *Chiron* 18: 55–69.

(1989) 'Two Attalid letters on the *asylia* and *ateleia* of Apollo Tarsenus 185 BC', *Historia* 38: 395–409.

Postgate, J. N. (1974) *Taxation and Conscription in the Assyrian Empire*. Rome.

(1992) *Early Mesopotamia: Society and Economy at the Dawn of History*. London and New York.

Potts, D. T. (1984) 'On salt and salt-gathering in ancient Mesopotamia', *JESHO* 27: 225–71.

(1990) *The Arabian Gulf in Antiquity*, vol. II. Oxford.

(1997) *Mesopotamian Civilization. The Material Foundations*. Ithaca, N.Y.

Powell, M. A. (1996) 'Money in Mesopotamia', *JESHO* 39: 224–42.

Poyck, A. P. G. (1962) *Farm Studies in Iraq*. Wageningen, Netherlands.

Préaux, C. (1939) *L'économie royale des Lagides*. Brussels.

(1969) 'Epoque hellénistique', in *Troisième conférence internationale d'histoire économique, Munich 1965*. Paris: 41–74.

(1978) *Le monde hellénistique*, 2 vols. Paris.

Price, M. J. (1968) 'Early Greek bronze coinage', in *Essays in Greek Coinage presented to Stanley Robinson*, ed. C. M. Kraay and G. K. Jenkins. Oxford: 90–104.

(1992) *The Coinage in the Name of Alexander the Great and Philip Arrhidaeus*. Zurich and London.

Pritchett, W. K. (1971) *The Greek State at War, Part I*. Berkeley.

Pugliese Caratelli, G. (1969) 'Supplemento epigrafico di Iasos', *ASAA* 45/6: 437–86.

Rapin, C. (1983) 'Les inscriptions économiques de la trésorie hellénistique d'Aï Khanoum (Afghanistan)', *BCH* 107: 315–72.

(1996) 'Nouvelles observations sur le parchemin gréco-bactrien d'Asangôrna', *Topoi* 6: 458–69.

Rapin, C. and M. Isamiddinov (1994) 'Fortifications héllenistiques de Samarcande (Samarkand-Afrasiab)', *Topoi* 4: 547–65.

Rappaport, U., J. Pastor and O. Rimon (1994) 'Land, society and culture in Judea in the 4th–2nd centuries BCE', *Transeuphratène* 7: 73–82.

Rathbone, D. W. (1990) 'Villages, land and population in Graeco-Roman Egypt', *PCPhS* 216 (n.s. 36): 103–42.

Rea, J. P., R. C. Senior and A. S. Hollis (1994) 'A tax receipt from Hellenistic Bactria', *ZPE* 104: 261–80.

Reger, G. (1994) *Regionalism and Change in the Economy of Independent Delos, 314–167 BC*. Berkeley.

Rehm, A. (1997) *Inschriften von Milet, Teil I (MILET VI I)*. Berlin and New York.

Robert, L. (1949) 'Inscriptions séleucides de Phrygie et d'Iran', in *Hellenica. Recueil d'épigraphie, de numismatique et d'antiquités grecques*, vol. VII, ed. L. Robert. Paris: 5–29.

(1963) *Noms indigènes dans l'Asie Mineure gréco-romaine*. Paris.

(1967) 'Encore une inscription grecque d'Iran', *CRAI*: 281–96.

Robert, J. and L. Robert (1954) *La Carie, histoire et géographie historique*, vol. II: *Le plateau de Tabai et ses environs*. Paris.

(1983) *Fouilles d'Amyzon en Carie*, vol. I: *Exploration, histoire, monnaies et inscriptions*. Paris.

Robinson, D. M. (1958) 'A new *logos* inscription', *Hesperia* 27: 74–8.

Rostovtzeff, M. (1910) *Studien zur Geschichte des römischen Kolonates*. Leipzig and Berlin.

(1932) 'Seleucid Babylonia. Bullae and seals of clay with Greek inscriptions', *YCLS* 3: 1–114.

(1941) *Social and Economic History of the Hellenistic World*, 3 vols. Oxford.

Roueché, C. and S. Sherwin-White (1985) 'Some aspects of the Seleucid empire: the Greek inscription from Failaka in the Arabian Gulf', *Chiron* 15: 1–39.

Rupprecht, H.-A. (1994) *Kleine Einführung in die Papyruskunde*. Darmstadt.

Sachs, A. and H. Hunger (1988) *Astronomical Diaries and Related Texts from Babylonia*, vol. I: *Diaries from 653 BC to 262 BC*. Vienna.

(1989) *Astronomical Diaries and Related Texts from Babylonia*, vol. II: *Diaries from 261 BC to 165 BC*. Vienna.

(1996) *Astronomical Diaries and Related Texts from Babylonia*, vol. III: *Diaries from 164 BC to 61 BC*. Vienna.

Sahin, S. (1987) 'Epigraphica Asiae Minoris neglecta et iacentia II – Dokumente aus Herakleia am Latmos', *EA* 9: 55–9.

Saliou, C. (1992) 'Les quatre fils de Polémocratès (*P.Dura* 19). Texte et archéologie', *Syria* 69: 65–100.

Salles, J.-F. (1987) 'The Arab-Persian Gulf under the Seleucids', in Kuhrt and Sherwin-White (1987): 75–109.

(1991) 'Du blé, de l'huile et du vin', in Sancisi-Weerdenburg and Kuhrt (1991): 207–36.

Sancisi-Weerdenburg, H. (1989) 'Gifts in the Persian empire', in *Le tribut dans l'empire perse*, ed. P. Briant and C. Herrenschmidt. Paris: 129–46.

Sancisi-Weerdenburg, H. and A. Kuhrt (eds.) (1987) *Achaemenid History*, vol. II: *The Greek Sources*. Leiden.

(eds.) (1990) *Achaemenid History*, vol. IV: *Centre and Periphery*. Leiden.

(eds.) (1991) *Achaemenid History*, vol. VI: *Asia Minor and Egypt: Old Cultures in a New Empire*. Leiden.

Sancisi-Weerdenburg, H., A. Kuhrt and M. C. Root (eds.) (1994) *Achaemenid History*, vol. VIII: *Continuity and Change*. Leiden.

Sarkisian, G. Kh. (1969) 'City land in Seleucid Babylonia', in *Ancient Mesopotamia*, ed. I. M. Diakonoff. Moscow: 312–31.

Sartre, M. (1989) 'Organisation du territoire et pouvoirs locaux dans la Syrie héllenistique et romaine', *Transeuphratène* 1: 119–28.

(1995) *L'Asie Mineure et l'Anatolie d'Alexandre à Dioclétien*. Paris.

Schäfer, P. (1995) *The History of the Jews in Antiquity*. Luxembourg.

Scheidel, W. (1999) 'Salute, agricolture e populazione in Egitto nell' età romana e nel XIX secolo', in *Demografia, sistemi agrari, regimi alimentari nel mondo antico. Atti del Convegno Internazionale di Studi, Parma, 17–19 ottobre 1997*, ed. D. Vera. Bari: 309–24.

Schönert-Geiss, E. (1978) 'Das Geld im Hellenismus', *Klio* 60: 131–6.

Schottky, M. (1989) *Media Atropatene und Gross-Armenien in hellenistischer Zeit*. Bonn.

Seton-Williams, M. V. (1954) 'Cilician Survey', *AS* 4: 121–74.

Seyrig, H. (1958) 'Antiquités syriennes – 67. Monnaies contremarquées en Syrie', *Syria* 35: 187–97.

(1970) 'Antiquités syriennes – 92. Séleucus I et la fondation de la monarchie', *Syria* 47: 290–311.

(1973) *Trésors monétaires séleucides.* Paris.

Sharma, R. (1988) *Kingship in India.* New Delhi.

Sherwin-White, S. (1982) 'A Greek *ostrakon* from Babylon of the early third century BC', *ZPE* 47: 51–70.

(1983a) 'Babylonian Chronicle fragments as a source for Seleucid history', *JNES* 42: 265–70.

(1983b) 'Ritual for a Seleucid king at Babylon?', *JHS* 103: 156–9.

(1985) 'Ancient archives: the edict of Alexander to Priene, a reappraisal', *JHS* 105: 69–89.

(1987) 'Seleucid Babylonia: a case study for the installation and development of Greek rule', in Kuhrt and Sherwin-White (1987): 1–31.

Sherwin-White, S. and A. Kuhrt (1993) *From Samarkhand to Sardis.* London.

Shipley, G. (1993) 'Distance, development, decline? World-systems analysis and the "Hellenistic" world', in Bilde *et al.* (1993): 271–83.

(2000) *The Greek World after Alexander 323–30 BC.* London.

Slotsky, A. L. (1992) 'The Bourse of Babylon: an analysis of the market quotations in the Astronomical Diaries of Babylonia'. Ph.D. dissertation. Yale.

(1997) *The Bourse of Babylon: Market Quotations in the Astronomical Diaries of Babylonia.* Bethesda, Md.

Smith, P. E. L. and T. Cuyler Young Jr (1972) 'The evolution of early agriculture and culture in Greater Mesopotamia: a trial model', in *Population Growth: Anthropological Implications*, ed. B. Spooner. Cambridge, Mass.: 1–59.

Spek, R. J. van der (1985) 'The Babylonian temple during the Macedonian and Parthian domination', *BO* 42: 541–62.

(1987) 'The Babylonian city', in Kuhrt and Sherwin-White (1987): 57–74.

(1992) 'Nippur, Sippar and Larsa in the Hellenistic period', in *Nippur at the Centennial*, ed. M. de Jong Ellis. Philadelphia: 235–60.

(1993a) 'The Astronomical Diaries as a source for Achaemenid and Seleucid history', *BO* 50: 91–101.

(1993b) 'New evidence on Seleucid land policy', in *De Agricultura*, ed. H. Sancisi-Weerdenburg *et al.* Amsterdam: 61–77.

(1994) '. . . en hun machthebbers worden weldoeners genoemd'. *Religieuze en economische politiek in het Seleucidische Rijk.* Amsterdam.

(1995) 'Land ownership in Babylonian cuneiform documents', in *Legal Documents of the Hellenistic World*, ed. M. J. Geller and H. Maehler. London: 173–245.

(1998a) 'Cuneiform documents in Parthian history: the Rahimesu archive. Materials for the standard of living', in *Das Partherreich und seine Zeugnisse*, ed. J. Wiesehöfer. Historia Einzelschriften 122. Stuttgart: 205–58.

(1998b) 'Land tenure in Hellenistic Anatolia and Mesopotamia', in *XXXIV. International Assyriology Congress, 6–10/VII/1987, Istanbul*, ed. V. Donbaz *et al.* Ankara: 137–47.

(2000a) 'The effect of war on the prices of barley and agricultural land in Hellenistic Babylonia', in Andreau, Briant and Descat (2000): 293–313.

(2000b) 'The Seleucid state and the economy', in *Production and Public Powers in Classical Antiquity*, ed. E. Lo Cascio and D. W. Rathbone. Cambridge Philological Society, Suppl. 26. Cambridge: 27–36.

Staviskij, B. Ja. (1986) *La Bactriane sous les Kushans*. Paris.

Stein, O. (1922) *Megasthenes und Kautilya*. Vienna.

Stolper, M. W. (1974) 'Management and politics in Later Achaemenid Babylonia: new texts from the Murašu Archives'. Ph.D. dissertation, Michigan.

(1985) *Entrepreneurs and Empire*. Leiden.

(1989) 'Registration and taxation of slave sales in Achaemenid Babylonia', *Zeitschrift für Assyriologie* 79: 80–101.

(1994) 'On some aspects of continuity between Achaemenid and Hellenistic Babylonian legal texts', in Sancisi-Weerdenburg, Kuhrt and Root (1994): 329–51.

Sumner, W. M. (1986) 'Achaemenid settlement in the Persepolis plain', *AJA* 90: 3–31.

Tarn, W. W. (1927) *Hellenistic Civilization*. London.

Temin, P. (2002) 'Price behaviour in ancient Babylon', *Explorations in Economic History* 39: 46–60.

Thompson, M., O. Mørkholm and C. M. Kraay (eds.) (1973) *An Inventory of Greek Coin Hoards*. New York.

Treister, M. Y. (1996) *The Role of Metals in Ancient Greek History*. Leiden.

Tscherikover, V. (1959) *Hellenistic Civilization and the Jews*. Philadelphia.

(1973) *Die hellenistischen Städtegründungen von Alexander dem Grössen bis auf die Römerzeit*. New York. Reprint of 1927 edn issued as *Philologus*, Suppl. XIX,1.

Tuplin, C. (1987a) 'The administration of the Achaemenid empire', in *Coinage and Administration in the Athenian and Persian Empires*, ed. I. Carradice. Oxford: 109–66.

(1987b) 'Xenophon and the garrisons of the Achaemenid empire', *Archäologische Mitteilungen aus Iran* 20: 167–245.

Valtz, E. (1993) 'Pottery and exchanges: imports and local production at Seleucia-Tigris', in *Arabia Antiqua. Hellenistic Cultures around Arabia*, ed. A. Invernizzi and J.-F. Salles. Rome: 167–82.

Vargyas, P. (1997) 'Les prix des denrées alimentaires de première nécessité en Babylonie à l'époque achéménide et hellénistique', in Andreau, Briant and Descat (1997): 335–54.

Verhoogt, A. M. F. W. (1998) *Menches, Kommogrammateus of Kerkeosiris*. Papyrologica Lugduno-Batava XXIX. Leiden.

Vogelsgang, W. (1985) 'Early historical Arachosia in South-East Afghanistan: meeting-place between East and West', *IA* 20: 55–99.

Walbank, F. W. (1981) *The Hellenistic World*. London.

Wallenfels, R. (1994) *Uruk: Hellenistic Seal Impressions in the Yale Babylonian Collection*, vol. I: *Cuneiform Tablets*. Mainz.

Welles, C. B. (1934) *Royal Correspondence in the Hellenistic Period: a Study in Greek Epigraphy*. New Haven, Conn.

Welles, C. B., R. O. Fink and J. F. Gilliam (1959) *The Excavations at Dura-Europus. Final Report*, vol. V,1: *The Parchments and Papyri*. New Haven, Conn.

Wenke, R. J. (1975/6) 'Imperial investments and agricultural developments in Parthian and Sassanian Khuzestan: 150 BC to AD 640', *Mesopotamia* 10–11: 31–217.

Westermann, W. L. (1921) 'Land registers of western Asia Minor under the Seleucids', *CPh* 16: 12–19, 391–2.

Wiesehöfer, J. (1994) *Die 'dunklen Jahrhunderte' der Persis*. Munich.

Wilkinson, T. J. and D. J. Tucker (1995) *Settlement Developments in the North Jazira, Iraq*. Warminster.

Will, E. (1979) *Histoire politique du monde hellénistique*, vol. I. Nancy.
    (1982) *Histoire politique du monde hellénistique*, vol. II. Nancy.
    (1988a) 'La capitale des Seleucides', in *Akten des XIII Internationalen Kongress für klassische Archäologie, Berlin 1988*. Berlin: 259–65.
    (1988b) 'La population de Doura-Europos: une évaluation', *Syria* 65: 315–21.
    (1994) 'Notes de lecture', *Topoi* 4: 433–47.

Willcox, G. H. (1987) 'List of trees and shrubs of economic importance in Iraq', *BullSumAgric* 3: 101–6.

Wolski, J. (1982) 'Le problème de la fondation de l'état gréco-bactrien', *IA* 17: 131–46.

Wörrle, M. (1975) 'Antiochos I, Achaios der Ältere und die Galaten', *Chiron* 5: 59–87.
    (1979) 'Epigraphische Forschungen zur Geschichte Lykiens III', *Chiron* 9: 83–111.
    (1988) 'Inschriften von Herakleia am Latmos I: Antiochos III, Zeuxis und Herakleia', *Chiron* 18: 421–76.

Zadok, R. (1978) 'The Nippur region during the Late Assyrian, Chaldaean and Achaemenian periods, chiefly according to written sources', *Israel Oriental Series* 8: 266–332.

Index

LaVergne, TN USA
31 March 2011
222463LV00002B/15/P